W9-DCJ-219

METHOD IN ETHICAL THEORY

*Essay and Monograph Series
of The Liberal Arts Press*

OSKAR PIEST, FOUNDER

METHOD
IN ETHICAL THEORY

ABRAHAM EDEL

Professor of Philosophy
The City College
of the City University of New York

THE **BOBBS-MERRILL** COMPANY, INC.
A SUBSIDIARY OF HOWARD W. SAMS & CO., INC.
Publishers • INDIANAPOLIS • NEW YORK

Library of Congress Catalog Card No. 62-11790
Copyright © 1963 by The Bobbs-Merrill Company, Inc.
Printed in the United States of America
First Edition

PREFACE

This methodological book occupies a central place in a long-term program of research in ethical theory on which I have been engaged. Several fruits of this research have already been published. *Ethical Judgment: The Use of Science in Ethics* [1] is a pilot study, focusing on the problem of ethical relativity and how the sciences might help in ethical judgment. *Anthropology and Ethics* [2] is a collaborative work with an anthropologist, exploring the relations of ethics to anthropology and attempting to establish coordinates for mapping moralities in their relation to social and cultural life. *Science and the Structure of Ethics* [3] explores the role that science—especially scientific results—plays in the actual structure of ethical theory. The present book attempts to work out a methodological approach for ethical theory that will be both critical and comprehensive, one that will do justice to the factual bases as well as the normative functions of ethics. It aims to point a way through what is increasingly spoken of in ethical writings as "the present impasse," "the deadlock in ethics," or "the conflict of schools." I hope to follow up these works with specific studies of the influence of different sciences in ethical theory as a whole, and with integrative analyses of major ethical concepts.

Several of my previously published papers have been incorporated into this volume, with some revisions and additions. I should like to acknowledge with gratitude permission granted by the following, for the use of these materials:

Philosophy and Phenomenological Research, for "Coordinates of Criticism in Ethical Theory" (Vol. VII, No. 4 [June, 1947], 543-77), reprinted in Chapter Two.

[1] Glencoe, Ill., 1955.

[2] May Edel and Abraham Edel, *Anthropology and Ethics* (Springfield, Ill., 1959).

[3] "International Encyclopedia of Unified Science," Vol. II, No. 3 (Chicago, 1961).

The University of Pennsylvania Press and the American Philosophical Association, for "Ethical Reasoning," from *Academic Freedom, Logic, and Religion,* edited by Morton White (Philadelphia, 1953), Vol. II, included in Chapter Six. A section on the naturalistic fallacy in the original paper has here been omitted and incorporated into Chapter Five.

Philosophy of Science, for "Concept of Values in Contemporary Philosophical Value Theory" (Vol. XX, No. 3 [July, 1953], 198-207), included in Chapter Eight.

The Fress Press of Glencoe, Illinois, for "Scarcity and Abundance in Ethical Theory," in *Freedom and Reason,* "Studies in Philosophy and Jewish Culture in Memory of Morris Raphael Cohen," Jewish Social Studies Publications, No. 4 (New York, 1951), reprinted in Chapter Twelve.

The Journal of Philosophy, for "The Evaluation of Ideals" (XLII [1945], 561-77), included in Chapter Fifteen as the section entitled "Criteria for the Evaluation of Specific Ideals."

Two of the chapters were originally written to be delivered as lectures on special occasions: Chapter Five to the New York Philosophical Circle, and Chapter Fourteen to the General Seminar of the Graduate Faculty, New School for Social Research, both in November, 1957.

The initial study of ethical frameworks out of which issued Chapters Two and Fifteen, on coordinates of criticism in ethical theory, and the theory of ideals, was done during my tenure as a Guggenheim Fellow in 1944-45. The systematic shaping of the methodological ideas embodied in the book took place during a year of intensive work on a grant from the Rockefeller Foundation in 1952-53, at which time some of the chapters were worked out. I should like to express my appreciation for this assistance.

I should like also to thank the Dartmouth College Library for its attentive hospitality during the many summers when I used its facilities in doing research.

The debt which I owe to colleagues in philosophy and in the psychological and social sciences, both in their writings and in critical discussion over the years, is too vast to admit of even selective enumeration.

A.E.

To Yervant H. Krikorian
In Friendship and Esteem

CONTENTS

METHOD IN ETHICAL THEORY

INTRODUCTION

Readers of traditional treatises on ethical theory sometimes find the writers looking upon their disagreements as a kind of intellectual game, on the assumption that men agree about what is right and wrong but disagree only on the reasons. On such a view, morality is secure, speculation on it more precarious. At times it has required the bravado of a Nietzsche to penetrate such smugness with the assertion that his aim was to *overthrow* traditional morality. The contemporary world, since 1914, or at latest since 1933, has known better. It has seen the widest range of conflicts. Some have been practical conflicts, some have been the battle of moral feeling against sheer cruelty and inhumanity. But many have been serious differences about the form that morality itself should take. There is no gainsaying the fact that much of traditional morality has been called into question, whether in outright disagreement, or in the more subtle form of questioning its significance or wondering about its credentials.

If the search for dependable answers on the moral level today increasingly seeks theoretical assistance on the philosophical level, we must not underestimate the difficulties in this fresh arena. There is, it is true, considerable production of works in theoretical ethics, but the reader is likely to be impressed by the extent of controversy and disagreement. He may even despair, thinking of the vast problems that so urgently need the kind of aid that systematic theory might give. But such despair is premature. The situation in morals is like that in medicine. You do not stop treating the sick just because there is controversy about basic concepts and underlying theories, even about individual diagnoses. You do your best and keep going. Sometimes you succeed without knowing quite why. Sometimes your experience helps illuminate the theoretical issues. You know that theory is concerned with the frontier, and if it has its own problems and controversies, the only remedy is to push on.

Such is the state in ethical theorizing today. It is pushing on. Certainly, it is giving much less assistance to morality than might have been hoped for. It seems to be in a methodological mood. It is questioning its own enterprise, asking what it can do and what it cannot do. Some thinkers regard this as a kind of disease and resort to the old quip that fields which cannot produce results talk about methods. But talk about methods is increasingly part of every advanced and fruitful field as well.

The hypothesis underlying this present book is that speeding up the process of securing maximal contributions from ethical theory for solving moral problems involves the fullest self-conscious focusing on method. Only so can we improve the quality of theorizing. It will not do instead to run away from theory. Systematic self-consciousness about method involves canvassing the different kinds of approaches in ethical theory today, attempting to determine their relationships, and entering into the technical controversies with which they have become involved. For one of the greatest difficulties today is a lack of communication among the different kinds of inquiries that are going on. This produces misunderstanding as well as duplication, and the outcome sometimes is the familiar battle of schools without clarification of the way in which the issues might be resolved. This in turn obscures genuine advances that are being made. Sometimes it blocks the channels to assistance that might come from other types of inquiry.

There seem to be four main ways of dealing with materials in ethical theory today. One is *analytic;* it deals with terms and concepts, and it thinks about clarifying relationships; it sharpens tools and refines methods. A second is *descriptive;* it is constantly on the alert for phenomena to be accurately described, classified, and interpreted—moral qualities, moral feelings, moral situations, moral relationships. A third is *causal-explanatory;* no sooner is there a phenomenon or even a suspicion of one, than it is raising questions about functional relations and causes, a knowledge of which it expects will deepen understanding. A fourth is *evaluative;* it approaches everything in a critical mood, and immediately asks for, sets up, or applies standards.

Alongside all of these we shall set up a *comparative* approach, which, we shall see, plays a great part in helping us put into focus both the problems and varieties of proposed solutions of the different methods.

No attempt will be made in advance to show the value of such a scheme of inquiry. It is to the exposition and results of the inquiry organized in this particular way that we must look for the value which I believe it has in advancing the systematic development of ethical theory.

Part One will deal with comparative method as the most general in type. The remaining parts will study the problems of each of the other four in turn.

No attempt will be made to advance to those theories that in such a science of inquiry. It is to the exposition and results of the inquiry organized in this particular way that we must look for the value which I believe it has in advancing the systematic development of ethical theory.

Part One will deal with comparative method as the most general in type. The remaining parts will study the problems of each of the other four in turn.

PART ONE

COMPARATIVE METHOD

CHAPTER ONE

THE COMPARATIVE STANDPOINT

It is surprising that self-conscious comparative method has played so small a part in ethical theory. In the study of other human fields it has an established place—witness comparative religion, comparative linguistics, or comparative jurisprudence. Under the influence of evolutionary ideas in the early part of the twentieth century, there was some attention to comparative morality, usually with the hope of setting up a ladder of moral ascent. In recent anthropological work, there is considerable attention given to cultural variability in human values, and some attempt to look for common elements. But in ethical theory, as distinct from moral codes, the very idea of comparative study might seem to be misplaced. If we are looking for a theory that is "true" or "correct," or at least "adequate," why bother collecting erroneous theories except to expose error or eliminate confusion? When the correct answer to a problem is arrived at, the wrong ones are discarded, unless you turn them over to the psychologist and historian to learn about the process of learning. Even if an intellectual theory is construed as an intellectual instrument, old theories are eventually replaced by better new ones. Comparative ethics might be at best a hobby, like collecting old cars.

Perhaps the best way to face this question is to see what gains have come from the comparative study of moralities, and then ask how far similar gains might be expected in ethical theorizing. The comparative study of morality has taught us a number of notable lessons. (1) It liberates us from a narrowing ethnocentrism in which we think of our moral rules as the fixed order of nature. (2) It helps us discover what common or invariant elements there may really be in human life under different conditions. (3) It reveals the different ways in which human beings have tried to do similar jobs, and prompts us to develop criteria for success in doing these jobs. (4) It gives us clues to the relation of morality to the cultural and socio-historical life of man. (5) It

9

widens our awareness of the forms of expression that the human spirit has taken and conveys a sense of its creative character.

These contributions involve use of all the methods with which we deal. Comparative morality leads in directions that are analytic, descriptive, causal-explanatory, and evaluative. If comparative method is to be helpful in ethical theorizing, it will have a general scope, useful in the many different tasks that ethical theory may undertake and the many different paths that it may follow.

If the nature of ethical theory were completely established or agreed upon, the extent to which comparative method might be employed would be easier to grasp. If ethical theories corresponded to physical theories in different stages of development over the history of mankind, it would be clear that the later supplants the earlier and incorporates what is useful in it. If ethical theories were like different species, flourishing in different environments, then it would certainly be worth sudying them comparatively and extending the search for specimens. In many respects, ethical theories are in the same predicament as religions. Some say certain religions are true and others are false; others say all religions are true but seek the same truth in different ways; still others say all religions are psychological expressions not to be judged as true or false. How shall we decide between such different conceptions of the very nature and tasks, in the case of ethical theory? At the very least, one has to compare the way in which different ethical theories conceive their task.

The fact is that ethical theory has to some extent engaged in comparisons in its reciprocal theoretical criticisms. But it stops short because it lacks the initial neutrality of the comparative spirit. To ask too soon who is correct and what is to be discarded is to run the risk of employing insufficiently analyzed notions of correctness. Criticism becomes impressionistic. The method of the Parthian shot—scoring a hit and dashing away—will not do for philosophy. Self-conscious criticism requires instead systematic criteria of the nature and tasks of criticism itself, and this is the road that leads inevitably to comparative studies.

There seems to be no reason why the benefits of comparative method listed above should not accrue to ethical theory. Little inspection is required to realize that there are provincialisms from which comparative study may release us. What is invariant and what is local, what universal tasks are attempted with what different theoretical configurations, what criteria have been and can be employed in estimating the worth of a theory itself, how far ethical theory is dependent in its source and in its evaluative criteria on different phases of the life of man, how far theory is revealing and how far creatively constructive—these are not questions to be settled in the confines of a single theoretical tradition or the introspections of a single consciousness.

One of the great difficulties in the comparative study of ethics is the paucity of primary materials; we do not even have a clear array of differing moral codes. How far could linguistic science in its study of morphology and syntax have gone without the vast comparative data of different languages and language families on the face of the globe? Ethical theory has so far only a limited base of operations—reflection within an overlapping set of moralities covering scarcely more than a couple of historical traditions. In a recent work dealing with morality, carried out in collaboration with Dr. May Edel,[1] we projected the concept of a *moral map of the globe in historical depth,* and tried to work out in a comparative way some of the dimensions that would be employed in such mapping. But even there we did not make the map. It is premature even to suggest the outlines of such a map for ethical theories. But it is not premature to elaborate the idea of a systematic comparative ethics, and to try to see what questions of research and inquiry would be raised in dealing with almost any of the familiar topics of ethical theory. It can be employed in surveying the modes of analysis that have been used in ethics, in collecting the descriptive criteria that have been suggested for delineating the moral field, in listing the alternative causal hypotheses that are often silent partners in ethical theories, and in rendering explicit the various modes of evaluation that are conveyed in different ethical theories.

Underlying this whole method is a marked shift in the way we look at ethical theory. The growth of an ethical theory is a truly impressive phenomenon. A human being, grappling with problems, using categories that have come down through the ages, joining the knowledge of his time to the purposes of his day, seeks to develop ideas on the most serious of issues for men—

[1] May Edel and Abraham Edel, *Anthropology and Ethics* (Springfield, Ill., 1959).

how they may guide the policies of their lives. Ethical theories have accumulated. They deserve at least the attention that a work of art or a novel receives in criticism and analysis. And they need this in historical perspective, for historical and cultural contexts enter more deeply into philosophizing than is customarily thought, and not simply as an outside causal influence. This will be explored in greater detail in Part Four.

It need scarcely be added—but it is safer to avoid confusions—that comparative method as such does not *solve* questions of ethical theory by itself. It can reveal new problems and point to fresh ways of going on. It is ground-breaking in character. It can also show what degree of convergence and divergence there has been. But perhaps its strongest contribution in its sorting and sifting is the way in which it helps inquiry to reformulate the very terms of its questions. And so it may spare us the greatest of philosophical pains—that of discovering that we were trying to answer questions that should have been asked in a different way!

I shall start here by presenting two sample studies in comparative method. Of these two studies in Part One, the first begins as a comparison of criticisms of pleasure-theory in ethics and develops into a search for coordinates of criticism in general, as a way of mapping the structure of an ethical theory. The second is designed as a self-conscious application of comparative method in dealing with a single central problem—the point at which prescriptiveness is located in an ethical theory. It uses this to attempt a clarification of the kinds of controversies that have raged in contemporary ethics about cognitivist versus practicalist approaches to ethical terms and methods.[2]

---

[2] Another application of comparative method to a single ethical problem of considerable dispute will be found in my *Ethical Judgment: The Use of Science in Ethics* (Glencoe, Ill., The Free Press, 1955). There the issue of ethical relativism versus ethical absolutism was construed as one of the extent of unavoidable ethical indeterminacy; ethical indeterminacy itself referred to the theoretical obstacles in getting determinate answers to moral questions. Comparative method was used to trace the different roots and different residence of ethical indeterminacy in different theories (see especially pp. 30-36), and so to find out how far it was involved in certain linguistic-logical assumptions, in certain factual assumptions, and so on.

Comparative method was also used in *Anthropology and Ethics*, at various points, in dealing with ethical theories and structural properties of moralities. See especially Chapters Eleven and Fourteen.

CHAPTER TWO

COORDINATES OF CRITICISM
IN ETHICAL THEORY

The evaluation of ethical theories has become almost a traditional part of the task of constructing an ethical theory. In most books on ethics it is a standard way of warming up to the task, clearing the ground, and preparing one's building materials. Not infrequently, if there were no tearing down there would be little with which to rebuild.

That creators of systems have so often felt themselves to be making a fresh start is not surprising. The complexity of the subject matter, the clash of social interests, and especially social changes over the centuries explain sufficiently the slowness of a common development. While the lack of an accumulated body of ethical propositions may be lamented by those who look enviously at the progress of the sciences and call for a scientific ethics, there is a widespread tendency to accept this situation as necessary. More disturbing, however, from the point of view of the history of ideas, is the failure to develop principles of criticism of ethical theories. One expects on this level to find consolidation of wisdom even though many factors perpetuate difference of results. And even if the field of criteria of criticism is itself a battleground of differing ethical theories one expects a more definite sense of the type of inquiry on which the critics are engaged. As it is, one may read different criticisms of the same theory and hardly recognize that the critics are talking about the same thing.

My attention was first drawn sharply to this phenomenon in the case of pleasure-theory. Bradley attacks hedonism as unrealizable, unworkable, immoral. Kant's objection to the identification of good with pleasure seems ultimately to be that it does not yield necessary moral laws. G. E. Moore finds the logic of hedonism to be riddled with contradictions. Marx traces the development of pleasure as a category from its meaning in the hands of a luxury-loving aristocracy to its universalization by the middle classes. Dewey is chiefly concerned with its falsity as a theory of human nature, and Freud tests it as a basic account of motivation. Carlyle condemns utilitarianism as a "universal syllabus of sentimental twaddle." And Hartmann says with a sense of finality, "To criticize utilitarianism philosophically is an easy game. All its preposterous consequences have their root in the banal confusion of the good and the useful." [1] These are but a few specimens of the diversity of critical perspecitves to be found in ethical treatises and texts, in psychological and economic studies, and in more general presentation in various forms of literature.

It would indeed be an interesting undertaking to look at pleasure-theory [2] through the eyes of its critics and study the doctrine by such a method of philosophic refraction. The multiplication of perspectives will at least reveal how many-sided an ethical theory can be. While Peter's idea of Paul may give me a better idea of Peter than it does of Paul, to see Paul through many eyes renders it less likely that I will miss his special features. Perhaps in some cases I can correct for refraction by assessing Peter's biases and special interests. Even in direct acquaintance I ought not to forget that I too constitute a refracting medium.

Such an inquiry could have different possible objectives. It might be directed to a study of refracting media and thus reveal the values of the critics. It might be an attempt to probe more deeply into the original by multiplying hypotheses concerning its allegedly true or real meaning. Or it might be directed to the very process of critical evaluation itself in order to exhibit its phases, dimensions, or types.

It was with the third of these objectives that I originally surveyed the criticisms of pleasure-theory presented in various treatises and texts on ethics. As might have been anticipated, the process of criticism stood out as a multiple enterprise, and the object of criticism—an ethical theory—was brought thereby into sharper focus. The divergences of critics were seen to stem from concentration on different parts of the theory as well as from

---

[1] *Ethics*, tr. Stanton Cóit (New York, 1932), I, 140.

[2] This term is used in the general sense of the identification of the good with pleasure, and not confined to one historical form (e.g., utilitarianism), simply because critics have not so limited it in their criticism.

conflicting theories concerning these parts. But the juxtaposition of the criticisms seemed to me to accomplish what no single one of them did—nor even the original itself. It secured a prismatic effect revealing the range of constituents in a unified ethical theory. And it offered thereby a set of starting points for considering the nature of ethical systems. It provided coordinates for locating an ethical theory whether for criticism or construction.

The purpose of this present study is not to report on the experiment I have described but to proceed to the more systematic discussion of these main lines or coordinates of criticism. Illustration at most points will, however, be taken from the critiques of pleasure-theory.

LOGICAL COORDINATES OF CRITICISM

Any theory in any field may, of course, be criticized from a logical point of view. It may be estimated for its consistency, for its choice of fundamental terms in the light of possible applications, for its definitions and procedures, and for the validity of its inferences. Logical techniques enable the structure of the theory to be extracted for special study. For example, in the language of every ethical treatise one may discern a sublanguage which may be designated as a specifically ethical language. Criticisms of an ethical theory may sometimes turn out on analysis to be objections to the special selection of terms and rules of the ethical language, or to specific interpretation given some of these terms. It will, therefore, prove profitable to establish logico-linguistic coordinates and set such criticisms within that framework. Under logical coordinates we include: selection of terms, definitory relation of terms, rules for construction of statements, coordinating definitions regarded as conventions, and so forth. Clearly we have here not merely syntactic elements, but also some semantic and even pragmatic elements. Seven types of such elements are here examined.

(1) There are, in the first place, certain specifically ethical terms, such as 'good,' 'bad,' 'right,' 'wrong,' 'virtue,' 'vice.' Most of these occur in most ethical languages; there is therefore little basis for differential criticism on this point. Sometimes, however, some

theories make central use of terms which others do not, e.g., 'highest good' (*summum bonum*), 'common good,' or 'general good.'

(2) There are often definitory statements relating ethical terms to one another. For example, in some ethical languages 'right' is defined as 'productive of the greatest good'; in others 'good' as an ethical term is narrowed to 'morally good' and defined as 'expressing a state of character which tends toward what is right'; in still others there may be no statements relating 'right' and 'good.' Often, this last position is expressed by saying that 'right' and 'good' are independent ethically undefined terms. In fact, much of the controversy concerning the relation of ethical terms has been cast as a question whether a given ethical term is defined or undefined. From a purely logical point of view, however, any definition of one term by means of another can be read in the reverse direction. Thus "*x* is right in situation *s*, if, and only if, *x* is productive of most good in situation *s*" provides a connection between both terms and implicitly defines each with reference to the other.

Criticisms of hedonism sometimes contain an implicit definition of 'good' which is used as a basis for rejecting the view that identifies pleasure with the good. For example, Plato's *Gorgias* (495ff.) suggests such a definition in the arguments Socrates uses to reject Callicles' equation of 'good' and 'pleasure.' Socrates points out that a man may have pleasure and pain in the same part at the same time (drinking while thirsty) but he cannot have good and evil. Again, the coward would be as good as the brave man since both may have equal joy at the enemy's departure. In these and subsequent arguments, one may extract a set of definitory assumptions: "A man cannot have good and evil at one time," "If a bad man and a good man share a given property, then that property is not identical with the good," "Order is good and disorder is evil," and so forth. Similarly, in Aristotle's *Nicomachean Ethics* (Book X) his argument that pleasure is not ruled out by its nature from being the good involves the assumption that "if *x* is the good, *x* is an activity complete in itself." In contrast, Kant in his *Critique of Practical Reason* [3] argues that to begin with the concept of good and derive obligation

[3] T. K. Abbott, *Kant's Theory of Ethics* (London, 1879), pp. 218ff.

from it commits one to some type of hedonism and should be rejected because we cannot thereby derive a moral law giving universal commands. This implies that however 'good' is to be used, the system is so to be constructed that the outcome will be statements of a certain universal form. Such criticisms of pleasure-theory are best clarified in the first instance by being seen as expressing different demands concerning the ethical language to be employed.

(3) There are usually some implicit rules about the combination of constituents in the formation of statements containing ethical terms. For example, if 'right' is a predicate, the subject must be a term designating an act by a human being or group of human beings. Where 'good' is a predicate, the selection of its subject-type is often an important part of an ethical theory. Thus in different theories the subject is sometimes limited to terms designating *states of consciousness, universals, things,* or *occurrences.* More drastic limitations are found in some ethical theories (e.g., Kant's), while others (e.g., Perry's) remove all limitations as to type of subject. Pleasure-theory by identifying 'intrinsic goodness' with 'pleasantness' is committed to the rule that only states of consciousness constitute the subject of an ethical proposition with 'good' as predicate.[4]

Some criticisms of hedonism may be regarded logically as simply rejections of this rule. Thus G. E. Moore's well-known argument in *Principia Ethica,* that the existence without consciousness of a beautiful world is better than the similar existence of an ugly, filthy world, is formulated in such expressions as ". . . *is it irrational to hold* that it is better that the beautiful world should exist, than the one which is ugly? *Would it not be well,* in any case, to do what we could to produce it rather than the other? Certainly *I cannot help thinking* that it would." [5] Appeal to rationality and inability to think otherwise obscures the nature of the criticism. It is better to separate it into the accept-

---

[4] Except where 'good' is used in the derivative sense of 'productive of pleasure.'

[5] *Principia Ethica* (Cambridge, England, 1903), pp. 83-84 (my italics). It is interesting to note that Moore later suggested translating 'good' into 'worth having for its own sake,' which meant limiting the subject to experiences ("Is Goodness a Quality?" in *Aristotelian Society, Supplementary Volume XI* [1932], 122-24).

ance or rejection of a certain rule of language and the statement of reasons for the choice among alternatives.

(4) Sometimes there are statements relating specific ethical terms to the terms of a special science, often psychology; for example, "Good is the object of desire," "Bad conduct is what you feel remorse about." These provide interpretations for the ethical terms. Where the scientific terms presumably designate some type of natural event, the ethical terms thus acquire procedures for application; psychological descriptions of desire and remorse would enable one accepting the above statements to identify in experience that which is good and conduct which is bad. Statements of the form described are thus conventions similar in type to "coordinating definitions" or "operational interpretations." [6]

Pleasure-theory usually involves such definitions at some point or other. Sometimes 'good' is thus correlated with the feeling of pleasure. More often, however, 'good' is correlated with the psychological term 'what a man aims at' or something similar; the assertion that pleasure is identical with good thus becomes an empirical statement.[7]

Considerable controversy about whether such coordinating definitions are permissible in ethics is found in some treatises. G. E. Moore calls any attempt to equate the term 'good' with any phase of existence or reality the naturalistic fallacy. In short, he rejects this type of statement for ethics. Others, in similar fashion, but with the purpose of preserving pleasure-theory, resort to fundamental intuitions of the identity of 'good' and 'happiness.' [8]

(5) There are usually also in an ethical language implicit rules about the general statement forms that will be permitted. Every ethical language allows singular statements; if it did not, the theory would be inapplicable to action. Usually singular ethical statements are regarded as empirical. Of nonsingular types, some ethical languages permit only empirical probability statements, others empirical laws, while still others insist on nonempirical

[6] These are to be distinguished from *nominal definitions* which may also contain non-ethical terms, e.g., "Courage is virtue in matters involving fear and confidence."

[7] Cf. J. S. Mill, *Utilitarianism* (London, 1863), Ch. IV.

[8] For a sophisticated form of such an appeal, see Sidgwick's *Methods of Ethics* (6th ed.; London, 1901), Bk. III, Ch. XIV ("Ultimate Good").

laws. As was pointed out above, the insistence that a theory of ethics be so formulated as to yield absolute laws is the controlling influence in Kant's ethics and the basis of his repeated rejection of hedonistic elements.[9] Some positivist approaches have insisted that fundamental ethical assertions are most correctly stated in the imperative form or in the optative form.[10]

(6) Ethical languages will, of course, allow for analytically true and analytically false statements. "Courage is productive of good" is analytically true in a system in which 'courage' is defined in terms of 'virtue,' 'virtue' in terms of 'right,' and 'right' in terms of 'good.' Similarly, "courage is evil" would be analytically false. In the development of a theory, consistency will be expected among the theorems.

Criticisms of ethical theories sometimes aim at revealing inconsistencies, that is, at showing that certain statements within the theory can be shown to be both analytically true and analytically false. Where established, such criticism of course calls for revision of the theory. But great care should be exercised lest the source of the contradiction be a tacit definition or assumption imported by the critic. For in that case his accusation of inconsistency means merely that his own assumptions are inconsistent with the theory he is criticizing. For example, G. E. Moore accuses egoistic hedonism of asserting that each man's happiness is the sole good—"that a number of different things are *each* of them the only good thing there is—an absolute contradiction!" [11] But this rests on Moore's refusal to allow the form of expression 'my own good,' whereas egoism gives it a primary place in its theory. Hence the contradiction is not internal to egoistic hedon-

9 See, for example, *Critique of Practical Reason*, Abbott tr., *op. cit.*, pp. 157-58: hedonism gives only subjectively necessary laws, such as "who would like to eat bread should contrive a mill." Even if there were thorough agreement of all finite rational beings on the objects of pleasure and pain, this unanimity would be only contingent. Thus there would be no a priori practical laws. Cf. pp. 174-75: Even if universal happiness were made the object of the will the result would be only general rules, not universal rules "which must hold good always and necessarily."

10 For the imperative, see, for example, A. J. Ayer, *Language, Truth and Logic* (London, 1936), Ch. VI. For the optative, see, for example, Bertrand Russell, *Religion and Science* (New York, 1935), p. 235.

11 *Principia Ethica*, p. 99.

ism, but indicates a difference in the formation-rules of egoistic theory and Moore's theory.

(7) Sometimes there is an implicit reference in an ethical theory to an addressee. This is not usually recognized because it is assumed that ethical statements are addressed to any individual. Even where the description of circumstances limits the reference to a person finding himself in such circumstances, one may begin with the universal quantifier "For any x, if x finds himself in such-and-such circumstances, then. . . ." But the general form may obscure differences, just as "To whom it may concern" at the head of a letter means sometimes "To a prospective employer," at others "To the admissions committee of any professional school to which Mr. X may apply." Confusion results from taking the letter to be indiscriminately applicable.

Such a confusion appears to underlie the criticism that utilitarianism makes an unwarranted transition from each man pursuing his own happiness to each man pursuing the greatest happiness of the greatest number. Mill's formulation in Chapter Four of his *Utilitarianism* is, no doubt, obscure, but he does distinguish the reference when he says "each person's happiness is a good *to that person,* and the general happiness, therefore, a good *to the aggregate of all persons.*" [12] Bentham even more explicitly separated the cases of individual and public good. His ditty on criteria of measurement, after listing six, adds "Such pleasures seek if private be thy end; If it be public, let them wide extend." [13] Now on Bentham's view the calculation is made by an individual in relation to a collection of individuals in two types of situations. One is in the field of private morality when he comes to realize that virtue in its various forms pays him well as an investment. The other is in the field of social control where the individual calculating is a legislator. It is the legislator's task to produce an artificial identification of interests by a system of punishments and rewards. But the legislator is also an individual pursuing his own pleasure. He is driven to use the criterion of the greatest pleasure of the greatest number by techniques of

12 My italics.
13 *Principles of Morals and Legislation,* Ch. IV. Cf. *Theory of Legislation* (Ogden ed.; New York, 1931), p. 31: "When the calculation is to be made in relation to a collection of individuals, yet another element is necessary."

representative government such as short terms of parliament, so that he has to stand for re-election. Each of the electorate is concerned with his own interests, but the legislator's personal interest will become identical with that of the majority. Similarly, the educator will find himself driven to develop such motives and pleasures in the younger generation as conform to the utilitarian principle. Mill recognizes that people can thereby find their pleasures in conduct guided by the greatest happiness principle. A whole theory of law, government, and education is therefore telescoped in Mill's transition from personal to general happiness. Whether he is correct or not, we are saved from dismissing his argument as a logical fallacy by recognizing the distinction in the addressee.

So long as we remain strictly within the domain of logical criticism, the function of criticism is limited to the exhibition of differences between the structures of theories. Judgment may be passed in terms of such criteria as simplicity, clarity, facilitation of inference, but beyond this, logical criticism provides no basis for the preference of one as against another structure. Such preference would need reference to the empirical materials to which the structure is applied. The separation of logical from other coordinates, however, achieves clarity by enabling the critic to focus on the point of difference. We can ask of Kant why there is this tremendous insistence on a priori laws as the form of ethical statements. We can look for what is at issue in the conflict of theories when they express the crux of their disagreement in the opposition between defining 'right' in terms of 'good' or 'good' in terms of 'right.' In this sense, logical criticism is preparatory to the tasks of scientific, historical, and valuational criticism.

SCIENTIFIC COORDINATES OF CRITICISM

Many criticisms of ethical theories turn out on analysis to be questioning their factual assumptions. To establish scientific coordinates for criticism involves, therefore, selecting the typical scientific questions at the base of assumptions in ethical theories.

Now every ethical theory, so far as I can see, has some implicit conception of the *stage* and the *dramatis personae* of the ethical process. What it takes to be the ethical phase of existence and

life and human relations can be construed by a careful and lit-
eral-minded scrutiny. This concept of the ethical stage is not here
offered merely as broad metaphor, but as a technique of scientific criticism. That the result in the case of some traditional
theories may appear strange is a commentary on those theories
and the effectiveness of a mode of analysis that reveals their
crudeness. For the kind of stage employed in a theory represents
pretty clearly its assumptions about human nature and its picture of man and society.[14]

The dramatis personae have varied considerably in western ethical theories. In most cases there is the central figure of the individual who is in the act of decision; sometimes there is a
whole group surrounding the individual; sometimes, the individual is himself lost in the group. At times, the individual acts as
a body with a full complement of passions; at other times he
appears as a self, governing the body. Occasionally there is a
divine voice at the upper boundary of the field, or an overarch-
ing reason sending messages to the self. In some naturalistic
theories the stage is very bare. There are no divine and satanic
beings wrestling for the individual soul; only a body appears and
the dramatis personae are hosts of impulses and appetites, desires
and feelings. Other human beings are recognized as existing off-
stage, but they cannot appear on it; at best they are represented
by feelings about them, of which they may be causes.

The fundamental type of ethical action is likewise limited
by the furnishings of the stage. In the theory of egoistic hedonism, for example, there is only one person and equipment for
weighing and measuring. Pleasures and pains enter at the side
and are weighed and measured. Some are accepted, some rejected;
pains are never accepted alone, only small pains with large plea-

14 I was tempted to this metaphor of the ethical stage as a kind of field or
space by A. F. Bentley's procedure in *Behavior, Knowledge, Fact* (Blooming-
ton, Indiana, 1935). Bentley uses as a laboratory the writings of psychologists
and inquires whether they take as the space of their objects of study that
inside the body, or include also the place on the surface where stimuli impinge on the body, or add a few feet beyond the body as room for action,
or go even further. I have developed the concept of the ethical stage as a
systematic technique for extracting the factual assumptions of ethical theories
in my *Science and the Structure of Ethics,* "International Encyclopedia of
Unified Science," Vol. II, No. 3 (Chicago, 1961), Ch. II.

sures to which they are chained and cannot be dislodged. In utilitarianism, there are many persons, but for the most part each goes on by himself in the same way. Some, especially legislators, keep an eye on others and manipulate their acceptance and rejection of pleasures and pains.

Scientific criticism may center either on the selection of the cast of characters or on their mode of action. Since we are dealing with a real process, not a fictitious drama, the identity of the characters may be called into question. Are there really such beings? Do they actually look like that? Furthermore, their style of acting and the whole plot may be questioned. Here the criticism may proceed from scientific knowledge that such characters do not act in such-and-such a way.[15] In the ethical process the dramatis personae according to a given theory are introduced by what we described above as the coordinating or operational interpretations of ethical terms.[16] The plot is mediated by a psychological theory of human motivation and action. Scientific criticism thereby is directed at the field delimited by the interpretation of the ethical terms and at the underlying psychology of the theory.

In the case of pleasure-theory there are various estimates of the selection of pleasure as the focus of ethics. These center on analysis of the meaning of pleasure and its properties. There are in the first place controversies on whether it can be regarded as feeling separate from activity, whether it admits only of quantitative differences or also of qualitative ones (Bentham vs. J. S. Mill), whether it is identical with preferring or separate but correlated with it. It is interesting to note that Bentham thought of the identification of good with pleasure as providing an objective basis for morals and as overthrowing the various forms of caprice which he summarized as the "principle of sympathy and

15 It may also be valuational, e.g., "Although this is one way in which such characters act, I do not approve of your choice of plot." This type of criticism will be considered below in connection with valuational coordinates.

16 Where the legitimacy of any such interpretations—naturalistic or metaphysical—is denied, the effect is often to set a stage without furnishings and to reduce action to a single person looking up at the stars off-stage. For such an estimate of G. E. Moore's ethical theory, see the writer's "The Logical Structure of G. E. Moore's Ethical Theory," in *The Philosophy of G. E. Moore*, ed. P. A. Schilpp (Evanston and Chicago, 1942), pp. 170ff.

antipathy." Bradley, in contrast, criticizes the fundamental operations in the application of the concept of pleasure: "What is the
sum of pleasures, and how many go to the sum? All of how many
is it, and when are we at the end? After death or in life?" [17]
Dewey objects to the utilitarian choice: "They make light of the
steady and controllable factor, the factor of disposition, and
fasten upon just the things which are most subject to incalculable accident—pleasures and pains—and embark upon the hopeless enterprise of judging an act apart from character on the
basis of definite results." [18] And Hartmann suggests both that
the psychology of pleasure and pain is too complex to rest an
ethics on it and that in fact when it is effectively used, as by
Epicurus, happiness ceases to be an emotional value subjectively
felt and becomes "only the outer vehicle of a complete scale of
tacitly recognized values of a higher order." [19]

Such criticisms are scientific in precisely the same sense that
questions about the selection of standards for length in physics
are scientific. Pleasure as a psychological entity may be estimated
against desire or impulse or ideals in building up an ethical
theory just as platinum iridium may be estimated against other
metals for its use as a standard of length or platinum or mass,
and the operations in computing pleasures and pains may be
compared to the operations in the formulation of units and computing physical measurements. In both cases, of course, there are
certain goals implied—in physics building up a stable science,
and in ethics developing a theory capable of guiding conduct.[20]

Critiques of psychological processes assumed in pleasure-theory
are frequent. Some charge it with confusing the object of desire
with other elements that may be present in consciousness in the
process of choice and achievement. Thus T. H. Green says: "It is
the consciousness that self-satisfaction is thus sought in all en-

[17] *Ethical Studies* (2nd ed., rev.; Oxford, 1927), p. 97.

[18] *Human Nature and Conduct* (New York, 1930), p. 50.

[19] *Ethics*, I, 132.

[20] Value elements implicit in such estimation will be considered below in
connection with valuational coordinates. For a defense of hedonism against
the type of objections listed above, see Felix Cohen, *Ethical Systems and
Legal Ideals* (Falcon Press, 1933), pp. 185ff. His treatment, however, stresses
analyses of mathematical operations rather than precise psychological interpretations.

acted desire, in all desire that amounts to will, combined with the consciousness that in all self-satisfaction, if attained, there is pleasure, which leads to the false notion that pleasure is always the object of desire." [21] More common is the criticism that hedonism confuses the object of desire with the cause of desire; whereas a present feeling of pleasure in anticipation of achievement may be part cause of one's having the desire, pleasure is not always what desire is directed toward.[22] James compared the idea that pleasure is the end of desire to the view that because no steamer can go to sea without consuming coal, therefore going to sea has no other motive than coal consumption.

Other critiques transcend the level of introspective psychology and estimate the hedonistic account of man in terms of a wider theory of human processes and development. Thus Dewey at many points in his writings makes scientific incorrectness a central feature in his criticisms of hedonism. For example, in *Human Nature and Conduct* he says: "The essentials of this false psychology consist in two traits. The first, that knowledge originates from sensations (instead of from habits and impulses), and the second, that judgment about good and evil in action consists in calculation of agreeable and disagreeable consequences, of profit and loss." [23]

In contrast, Freud seems to start by taking the pleasure-principle for granted as one way of viewing human processes: "Any given process originates in an unpleasant state of tension and thereupon determines for itself such a path that its ultimate issue coincides with a relaxation of this tension, i.e., with avoidance of pain (*unlust*) or with production of pleasure. When we consider the psychic processes under observation in reference to

---

[21] *Prolegomena to Ethics* (Oxford, 1883), § 158. William James, in similar fashion, says: "Thus it happens that round all our impulses merely as such, there twine, as it were, secondary possibilities of pleasant and painful feeling, involved in the manner in which the act is allowed to occur." The confusion thereby caused is that of pursued pleasure with mere pleasure of achievement (*Psychology* [New York, 1890], II, 556).

[22] This objection is well formulated by G. E. Moore, *Principia Ethica,* pp. 69-70.

[23] Modern Library ed., p. 189. Cf. p. 199: "The baby does not move to the mother's breast because of calculation of the advantages of warmth and food over against the pains of effort."

such a sequence we are introducing into our work the *economic* point of view." [24] Freud finds, however, that the pleasure-principle is not supreme, although it represents a strong tendency in the psyche. It is first checked by the reality-principle under the influence of the instinct of the ego for self-preservation. Thus circuitous routes to pleasure are adopted and pain endured to achieve the goal. The processes of repression also bring it about that certain impulses which otherwise might have brought pleasure are experienced in their gratification as pain. Beyond these Freud finds certain phenomena—especially a compulsion to repeat traumatic experiences and the fact that in analysis there is repetition of experience rather than memory, in spite of pain —which seem incapable of explanation by the pleasure-principle. On such grounds he posits a death instinct, a tendency in living organic matter towards the reinstatement of an earlier condition, the peace of the inorganic world. He even speculates whether "The pleasure-principle is then a tendency which subserves a certain function—namely, that of rendering the psychic apparatus as a whole free from any excitation, or to keep the amount of excitation constant or as low as possible." [25]

These brief illustrations show the way in which criticism, in each case proceeding from a special theory of psychology, estimates the characters and type of plot or action embodied in a given ethical theory. It is important to add that not all such scientific criticism rests on the science of psychology. Much of it does, since the individual man has been a central figure on most ethical stages, and in the case of pleasure-theory the individualistic emphasis is part of the essence. But other ethical theories often set the stage so that scientific criticism will be predominantly biological (as in group-survival ethical analyses), or socio-historical (as in class theories). [26]

---

[24] *Beyond the Pleasure Principle*, tr. C. J. M. Hubback (Boni and Liveright), p. 1.

[25] *Ibid.*, p. 81.

[26] Sometimes the whole picture of the universe becomes relevant as part of the ethical stage—it is usually an implicit background—so that criticism will be scientific, cosmological, or theological, depending upon the type of method accepted in the philosophy at the basis of the criticism. See, for example, Ignatius W. Cox, *Liberty, Its Use and Abuse* (New York, 1939), pp.

HISTORICAL COORDINATES OF CRITICISM

The development of each of the two preceding types of criticism was hindered by a special obstacle. In the case of logical coordinates, the intuitive theory that the concept and the proposition are meanings directly grasped by the mind in understanding the symbols long stood in the way of efforts to extricate problems of linguistic rules from problems of interpretation and reference. In the case of scientific coordinates, there was the frequent failure to distinguish between the assertion that a particular description of human motivation is incorrect and the claim that it leads to undesirable results in character and action.[27] Similarly, the attempt to establish historical coordinates has been seriously hampered by an undue separation, inherited from a dualistic philosophy, between the *content* of a theory and its *context*.

This distinction has been a controlling one in the normative disciplines, such as logic, ethics, and esthetics. To know the physical, social, and historical *context* of the formulation of a proposition, of the development of a moral outlook, of the creation of a work of art, has been regarded as irrelevant to the criticism of its *content*. The former is causal explanation, a scientifically legitimate but normatively irrelevant enterprise. The latter is governed by utterly different categories—truth, goodness, beauty. Any attempt to criticize content on historical grounds has therefore been labelled a genetic fallacy.[28]

The sharp separation of content and context is understandable in the dualistic tradition, where the one belongs to the domain of the mental, often the timeless, and the other to the physical and temporal. Its survival in criticism guided by a naturalistic philosophy is, however, anomalous. It embodies a confusion be-

---

51-52: utilitarianism is criticized because it makes man an end in himself, whereas "the absolutely ultimate extrinsic end of man's volitional activity is God's glory."

27 These valuational elements in psychological criticism will be considered below. They were omitted above even where they occurred in the same contexts as the examples cited.

28 Chapter Ten below discusses in detail the relation of causal inquiry and content of ideas; Chapter Eleven considers the genetic fallacy.

tween enterprise and subject-matter. There is no doubt that the enterprise of explaining and that of criticizing are distinct—one is scientific, the other evaluative. And there must, of course, be some initial delineation of content to provide something to be explained scientifically. But it does not follow that there is a separate subject-matter or content for each enterprise; nor need the initial delineation of content be final. The scientific discovery of context may extend the domain of content for the process of evaluation. Whether it does so or not in any particular case cannot be judged a priori. It must be determined by a careful comparison of the features of the context with those of the initial content to see whether they fit together forming an extended pattern.

Suppose, for example, that a philosophic manuscript on ethics contains a chapter on jealousy. Suppose further that it provides merely a broad outline, as ethical treatises are prone to do. Defining jealousy as a passion and the jealous man as a type, it then goes on to trace the effects of the feeling, the coloring it gives to human relations, the degree to which it is frustrating or motivating to action. Although the treatise passes ethical judgment on the passion, suppose we are never told its objects. Is it then irrelevant whether the writer is thinking of jealousy concerning sex, property, or prestige, whether he lived in Victorian England or among the Eskimo? The social and historical context of his work might tell what he was really talking about, and even his personal history might not merely explain but also extend the content of his exposition. Of course it is possible that there is an "essence" to jealousy common to all its objects and therefore capable of being treated independently, but this discovery would be the outcome of comparison of specific contents and could not be postulated in advance.

Many concepts in ethical writings are in the same position as jealousy in our hypothetical illustration. Certainly harmony, liberty, justice, become the barest abstractions without reference to cultural and institutional context which a given writer has in mind. If he has written also on law, politics, or education, we may usually gather from these writings what is the specific content of his ethical ideas. If he has limited himself to "pure" ethics, the study of his social context is our only resort to amplify the content of his theory. It is obvious that such a search may also reveal much about the causes of his holding the theory, what influences shaped his views, even what motives attended his elaboration of them. But this use of the material is to be distinguished from the discovery of content.

The meaning of 'pleasure' in criticisms of pleasure-theory is itself one of the best illustrations of the need for historical coordinates of criticism. We noted above that it has been the center of considerable psychological controversy. Does such psychological investigation best reveal, however, what Bentham was bent upon as the meaning of his doctrine? Dewey takes the hedonistic psychology in Bentham's theory to be "in the broad sense, an historic accident." [29] Others take this element to be central, as indeed Bentham himself did, since he used it as a framework. An attempt to resolve such differences as to the major content of his theory must therefore rest not on what difficulties introspection may reveal about the meaning of pleasure, but on what social, cultural, and historical content the concept bears in the context of Bentham's whole philosophic outlook and application, and in the milieu of his life and activity.

Estimates of Bentham from such a point of view give body to his abstract reckonings of pleasure. Wesley Mitchell, for example, offers an interpretation of the felicific calculus in which pleasure is equated with profit, pain with loss, the unit of sensation is taken as the dollar, the hedonic calculus as accounting, and the maximizing of net pleasure as the maximizing of net profits.[30] Mitchell regards this parallelism as no accident. He was led to his interpretation by the observation that while pecuniary concepts played a large part in economic life, they were ignored in classical economics in favor of discussion in terms of marginal utility. The fact was that the essence of pecuniary rationality had already entered into the tacit assumptions of hedonic psychology. The treatment of hedonism as a universal law of human nature represented all mankind as ruled by the psychological parallel of pecuniary logic. Fundamentally what we have here, Mitchell

29 Dewey and Tufts, *Ethics* (rev. ed.; New York, 1932), p. 263.

30 "The Rationality of Economic Activity," *Journal of Political Economy*, March, 1910, p. 213. See also Part I of this article, February, 1910, pp. 97-113, and "Bentham's Felicific Calculus," *Political Science Quarterly*, June, 1918.

says, is "a system of ideas inculcated in a recalcitrant human nature by the development of pecuniary institutions." [31]

Now while such an interpretation of Bentham throws light on the social influences that molded his thought, it does more than that. *It actually explicates the social content of his theory.* If we line up the various meanings of 'pleasure' as we see them in the critics of Bentham—a feeling to be observed by introspection, an act of preference to be observed in a man's directional conduct, money as it existed in the economic transactions of Bentham's day—it is perfectly clear that the last of these has the properties which Bentham ascribed to pleasure, and the others do not. It follows that money is either what Bentham is really talking about, or else that he is modelling his account of feeling or preference on the properties of money. In his article on "Bentham's Felicific Calculus," Mitchell quotes a fragment from Bentham in which this is almost explicitly stated: "Money is the instrument for measuring the quantity of pain or pleasure. Those who are not satisfied with the accuracy of this instrument must find some other that shall be more accurate, or bid adieu to Politics and Morals." [32] Bentham does recognize the inadequacy of the measuring instrument, and especially that the increase of wealth and happiness are not directly proportional for large sums. But the important point is that the properties of pleasure on his theory are the properties of money, so that the effective standard in his determination of desirable conduct and satisfactory social forms in the application of his criteria remains the pecuniary one.

The clearest recognition that even abstract ethical concepts have historical and institutional content is found in Karl Marx, and most specifically in his treatment of pleasure-theory.[33] "The philosophy of pleasure was never anything else but the clever language of certain pleasure-privileged social classes." [34] Marx traces the development of the concept as it passed from the no-

---

[31] *Ibid.,* p. 214.

[32] Given in the Appendix to Vol. I of Halevy's *Radicalisme Philosophique.* For a discussion of these fragments see Laird, *The Idea of Value* (Cambridge, 1929), pp. 326-30.

[33] See the section from his *The German Ideology* on Bentham and Utilitarianism, translated by Sidney Hook in his *From Hegel to Marx* (New York, n.d. [c. 1936]), pp. 315-22.

[34] *Ibid.,* p. 316.

bility to the bourgeoisie. Among the extravagant court nobility pleasure-theory was a naïve philosophy of life, expressing their mode of life. The bourgeoisie generalized it, applying it to all individuals in abstraction from their condition of life. It became the official economic category of luxury, and with the economic growth of the bourgeoisie was given the content of typical economic activity. "The apparent absurdity which dissolves all the manifold relations of human beings to each other into the *one* relation of utility—this apparent metaphysical abstraction proceeds from the fact that within modern bourgeois society all relations are subsumed under the one abstract money and business relation." [35]

Marx comments on the way in which Holbach analyzed such individual activities as speaking and loving as relationships of utility and use, thrusting aside their own characteristic significance and interpreting them as expressions of the artificially introduced relation of utility.[36] He notes that the utility relation here has the quite definite meaning of exploitation, and that the utility derived out of a relationship is foreign to it. These properties fit precisely the activity of the bourgeoisie: "Only *one* relation is intrinsically valid for him—the relation of exploitation; all other relations are valid only insofar as they can be subsumed under this relation. And even when relations appear which cannot be directly classified as one of exploitation, he at the very least does so in his illusions. The material expression of this utility is money, the measure of value of all things, human beings and social relations." [37] Benthamism represents the culmination of this philosophical development, and ethical theory is presented as "the private-exploitation of the given world by the particular individual." [38]

Marx's treatment of the concept of pleasure shows clearly

---

[35] *Ibid.*, p. 317. Cf. Marx's *Critique of Political Economy*, tr. Stone (Chicago, 1904), p. 73: "all bourgeois relations, being gilt or silver plated, have the appearance of money relations."

[36] Marx's analysis here is quite parallel to his analysis of use-value and exchange-value in the early part of *Capital* (Vol. I) and his *Critique of Political Economy*. Articles of diverse and characteristic use-value acquire as commodities the character of exchange-value. Specific character sinks into the background and the bare fact of some use-value is of significance only because it is a necessary condition of exchange-value.

[37] *Ibid.*, p. 318.   [38] *Ibid.*, p. 321.

what may be meant by a historical dimension of ethical criticism. Pleasure-theory or hedonism is regarded in this light not as a name for a fixed ethical theory but as a developing sequence of theoretical expressions of human life. Thus no single theory is, so to speak, plotted unless it is set in a reference to place and time. The social content of that theory is to be found in the historical, institutional, or cultural materials of that place and time. It is quite probable that the historical content of a given abstract concept will vary from one period to the next.

We need not here enter into the view that ethical theories "express" or "reflect" social and historical conditions. This is a complex conception requiring independent analysis, and covering under one idea questions of both content and causation. Our concern here is with the former, not the latter. And the position we are suggesting is that no element in an ethical theory is exempt from an inquiry into its historical content. This holds as well for the elements examined in our treatment of logical and scientific coordinates. For example, the demand for ethical "laws" noted above, although the abstract meaning may be the same, has a different social meaning at different times, depending upon whether the concept is cast, for example, in terms of divine commands or regularities in nature's machine. Even beyond that, the meaning of nature's machine shifts as mechanism begins to play a different social role. Similarly, the insistence on the separation of the 'right' and the 'good' may have in one context the historical content of the conflict of religious duty and secular interest; in another it may pit the will of a dominant class operating through the state against the claims for fundamental social reform.

What types of social and historical factors constitute the usual historical content of ethical ideas is a still further question. Answers vary in terms of different theories of history, and their correctness will be a function of the scientific truth of those theories.

VALUATIONAL COORDINATES OF CRITICISM

Valuational elements permeate the whole field of ethical criticism. In some sense the acceptance or rejection of any logical, scientific, or historical element is guided by values. Even where the question at issue is purely factual, the implicit guiding principle is the value of truth, embedded in the original designation of the question as purely factual. The same is true in logical questions where the values are those of systematic order. Our main concern, however, is not with such standardized evaluations, but with the more special ones that enter into ethical criticism. Some of these are external to the theory before the critic; they appear as his criteria when he registers approval or disapproval of the various features in the theory. Others, more subtle, are elicited by him from the material he is examining. They are carried, as it were, in the parts of the theory in one or another fashion.

It is to be noted that in seeking valuational coordinates of criticism, the term 'value' is being used in a broad sense. It covers anything from specific interests with a definite content in terms of desires, aims, strivings, to the most general shade of approval or disapproval. The critic of a given theory who points out the values that it carries with it need not necessarily mean by 'value' what the theory intends by it. He may, of course, use it in the same sense; thus he may be pleased by pleasure-theory or displeased by it. Or it may not be necessary to explore the connection between his sense of 'value' and the theory's. Thus if the critic shows that holding to a given theory imparts to a man specific attitudes in the conduct of his life, we may say that he has shown some of the values it carries with it without asking whether these attitudes are to be analyzed as indirect expectancies of maximum pleasure.

External criticism of pleasure-theory is often straightforward, even blunt. It is rejected as a "pig's philosophy." Bentham himself recognized the ascetic principle as opposed to the utility principle and argued that philosophers subscribing to the former were animated by a desire for applause or the pleasures of reputation, while ascetic devotees mistakenly hoped to increase their pleasure in another life.

Values carried along by the theory can be discovered only by careful examination of the structure and functioning of the theory itself. For these reasons, we may best consider this problem by reviewing each of the elements already discussed and seeing in each case what types of values or value-quality are conveyed by its use.

Logical elements. To what extent is the selection of one or another alternative, in each of the seven points considered, expressive of specific values?

(1) The mere selection of specific ethical terms does not at first sight appear to carry values with it. As noted above, most of these terms occur in most of the theories. There are, however, occasional striking differences between the terms of different theories which may prove significant. For example, it is a commonplace observation that ancient ethics pursued the *summum bonum,* whereas modern ethics cast its inquiry as concerned primarily with the rules of duty or right action. Sidgwick, who accepts this distinction, attributes the transition "chiefly to the influence of Christianity, but partly also to that of Roman jurisprudence." [39] It is, of course, to be expected in the light of our discussion of historical coordinates above, that even abstract formulations such as these will have historical content. And it is an hypothesis to be explored historically that there is a residual value-quality carried along by them as a correlate of the different types of problems to which each formulation was a response. But even apart from such detailed historical inquiry it is clear that a theory in which there is a highest good, especially if it is regarded as more or less attainable by a man, has a different value-quality in the attitude that it represents and imparts, from one in which, let us say, there is no highest good, only an ever-receding good inviting endless struggle. Similarly there is a different value-quality in theories in which the 'general good' appears, and those in which such a concept is elaborately composed out of the good of individuals. [40]

(2) Definitory statements relating ethical terms to one another often express definite values. For example, in the light of the controversies that have centered on the relation of the 'right' and the 'good,' we cannot regard alternative rules as purely linguistic conventions capable perhaps of translation into one another in the fully expanded theories in which they are used. For reducing 'right' to 'good' often carries the view that the rules of right are merely generalized methods of achieving the

[39] *Outlines of the History of Ethics* (5th ed.; London, 1906), p. 7.

[40] Marx and Engels suggest that the "general good" is "the illusory form of communal life" (*The German Ideology* [International Publishers], p. 23).

good in an unstable world. Reducing 'good' to 'right' may mean directing men's energies away from the apparent goods of unsophisticated men toward an eternal set of objects of striving. To treat the concepts as irreducible may point the way to conceiving man as living in two worlds—the phenomenal world of desire and the rational world of duty.

The mere choice of terms, as in (1), and their posited relation, as in (2), does not of itself determine the type of content. Some reference is required to the meaning or interpretation of the terms. This is clear from extreme cases. The Stoics, in their use of the concept of the *summum bonum,* treat 'good' as fundamental, but the content of the good turns out to be obeying the rules that others call rules of right (virtue is the greatest good).[41] On the other hand, the theological utilitarians find room for hedonistic content in a theological framework. Paley, for example, holds that God "wills and wishes the happiness of his creatures," and that the way to learn the will of God concerning any action is "to inquire into the tendency of that action to promote or diminish the general happiness." [42] Kant, it will be recalled, in spite of his opposition to pleasure-theory, seems ready to allow the pursuit of happiness as a matter of duty.

There is thus no specific valuational content adhering to the mere inclusion of a certain term in an ethical language or in regarding it as fundamental in relation to others. The values are conveyed, however, in the meaning assigned to it, and are a function of that interpretation rather than of logical convention. It follows that the selection of one as against another set of definitions should not be regarded by the critic as purely a logical act. The virtue of the initial logical abstraction lies in the preparatory articulation of structure. It does not eliminate the problem of the social and historical bases and function of ethical terminology.

41 Sidgwick, as a matter of fact, treats Stoicism as representing the transition in part from the ancient to the modern formulation described above (*op. cit.,* p. 97).

42 William Paley, *The Principles of Moral and Political Philosophy* (10th Amer. ed.; Boston, 1821), Bk. II, Ch. 5. Cf. Bk. I, Ch. 7: "Virtue is the doing good to mankind, in obedience to the will of God, and for the sake of everlasting happiness."

(3) Rules about the way in which constituents may be combined in ethical statements appear to some extent to define the scope or interest of a particular ethical theory. Kant's ascription of the predicate 'good without qualification' solely to 'will' as subject [43] tends to narrow the scope of ethics to problems of the nature of volition as against desire. Of course, the restriction does not follow from the mere choice of subject, but from this combined with his interpretation of will. The value-quality of his rule is further evident, when combined with the tacit assumption that the purpose of ethics is the guidance of conduct, in his account of moral motivation.[44] In contrast, Perry's readiness to allow any type of subject for 'good' expresses an initial tolerance of human desires which appears explicitly in his principle of Universal Love. Love is "an interested support of another's pre-existing and independently existing interest," and "It does not prescribe the object of the loved interest, but desires that that interest shall have its object, *whatever* that object." [45] In pleasure-theory the same tolerance appears not as an implicit rule of formation of sentences in which 'good' is predicate, but in Bentham's refusal to distinguish qualities of pleasure.

(4) This last illustration shows that what is accomplished by formation-rules about the permissible subject-type can equally well be accomplished by coordinating definitions. The two are closely related since the prescribed subject-type serves merely to limit the sort of coordinating definitions that will be acceptable. It is not surprising, therefore, that coordinating definitions are of central importance in designating the particular subject-matter of ethics. As a result, they are often the vehicle for some implicit conception of the task of ethics. Among the various conceptions of the business of ethics are that it is to guide conduct, to be a method of resolving doubt in choice, to establish order, to justify a certain set of moral practices, to provide a vision of the ideal, to intensify feeling in human consciousness. These starting points embody different values or shades of value;

[43] In the first sentence of the first section of his *Fundamental Principles of the Metaphysic of Morals*.

[44] Cf. his remarks on education in the Second Part of the *Critique of Pure Practical Reason* (Abbott tr.), *op. cit.*, pp. 359ff.

[45] *General Theory of Value* (New York, 1926), pp. 677-78.

hence, implicit selection of one or another objective for ethics, guided though it may be by more general philosophic conceptions, exhibits value-quality.

This valuational role of the identification of 'good' with pleasure stands out clearly in many of the critiques of that identification. When Rashdall says that "We cannot therefore reconcile Hedonism with the moral standard which Mill practically recognizes by adopting his distinction between higher and lower pleasure," [46] he means more than that Mill is inconsistent. For he implies that hedonism and not the moral standard is to be abandoned. Seth implies a similarly agreed upon role of ethics when he argues that while hedonism does well to emphasize the claims of sensibility in human life, its history "is itself a demonstration of the impossibility of an ethic of pure sensibility." [47] T. H. Green decides that the hedonistic theory of motives makes the utilitarian theory of ultimate good "intrinsically unavailable for supplying motive or guidance to a man who wishes to make his life better," thereby furnishing "a practical reason for seeking a substitute in another theory of ultimate good." [48] Kropotkin, although he praises Bentham's general spirit and lofty aim, and accepts pleasure or personal gratification as a framework, criticizes even the greatest happiness of society as the basis of morality: "this conception, taken by itself, is too abstract, too remote, and would not be able to create moral habits and a moral mode of thought. That is why, from the most remote antiquity, thinkers have always sought a more stable basis of morality." [49]

Value-assumptions concerning the general task of ethics often appear as assumptions about particular accomplishments expected of the ethical enterprise. For example, it may be taken for granted that the results should be uniform rather than productive of individual variability, or that the moral life must be

46 Hastings Rashdall, *Ethics* (London, n.d.), p. 27. In quoting this and other criticisms we are not, of course, concerned with the correctness of the criticism but with its implied values.

47 James Seth, *A Study of Ethical Principles* (5th ed.; New York, 1900), p. 146.

48 *Prolegomena to Ethics*, § 356.

49 *Ethics, Origin and Development,* tr. Friedland and Piroshnikoff (New York, 1924), p. 335.

continuous rather than discrete. Thus Bradley objects that "what brings pleasure to one brings none to another; and so with pain. You can speak generally beforehand, but it may not apply to this or that man. And the consequence is that the Almanack and its moral rules are no authority. It is right to act according to them. It is right to act diametrically against them." [50] And Dewey complains that "the moral life is left a series of shreds and patches, where each act is torn off, as to its moral value, from every other. Each act is right or wrong, according as *it* gives pleasure or pain, and independently of any whole of life." [51] Such properties assigned to the moral life are more clearly seen as values which it is expected that any successful ethical theory will achieve, and which thereby guide acceptance or rejection of any proposed interpretation of ethical terms.

It should be noted that the values do not inhere merely in the fact that a certain kind of coordinating definition is used. The specific material properties of the entities concerned contribute to the result. Thus while Bradley criticizes the selection of pleasure as the good because it makes ethics subjective and variable, Bentham, it is worth recalling, thought that the use of pleasure as the good would make ethics objective and measurable rather than arbitrary and capricious. Clearly, they cannot mean the same thing by pleasure.[52]

(5) No sharp line can be drawn between expecting the ethical enterprise to yield certain types of results, and the general demand that only certain general statement-forms be permitted. It follows that such linguistic rules may carry with them certain value-expectations. Thus Kant's insistence on absolute laws is definitely imparting certain values to ethical construction and thereby to conduct. Broadly speaking, they may be epitomized as the values of rigor or uniformity or nondeviation. If we look to their more specific content, the values may be esthetic; this is suggested by his coupling of "the starry heavens above and the moral law within" as objects of admiration and awe.[53] Or they may represent a mistrust of nature and the estimate of proba-

---

50 *Ethical Studies*, p. 93.

51 *Outlines of A Critical Theory of Ethics* (Ann Arbor, 1891), p. 36.

52 See the discussion of historical coordinates above.

53 In the Conclusion of the *Critique of Practical Reason*.

bilities, as expressed in his scornful rejection of the "serpentine windings" of utilitarianism. Or they may express the needs of stability and reliance in an increasingly commercial world. The emphasis on truth and promises in Kant's work suggests this possible atmosphere of his fundamental values in ethics; his very stress on the absolute character of law in science at times seems almost to be the assurance that nature keeps her promises strictly.

In the utilitarian ethical structure, the form of generalization is not the absolute rule. In spite of Bentham's frequent rationalism in asserting premises almost as axioms for ethical calculation in specific fields, the logical status of generalizations is that of lessons of experience. They partake of probability, not necessity. They convey the value-tone of a world in which experience counts as wisdom, in which careful reckoning has enabled man to make safe investments, although there is, of course, some risk in any investment.

(6) That ethical languages allow for analytically true and analytically false statements, that deduction is possible and consistency expected, carries with it no special values other than those of systematic order. Nevertheless, there are two ways in which the demand for consistency can be seen in ethical theory to acquire a value-content beyond its purely logical meaning. One way is by contrasting it with ethical theories that make a virtue out of some form of irrationality, that stress feeling or impulse in a way which makes it essentially nonrational or even opposed to reason. The second is by noting that specific values enter in applying the concept of consistency to values and acts of valuing. Thus the ethical disparagement of ambivalence is more than the recognition of logical contradiction, since a man can have two opposing desires concerning the same thing at the same time. It is therefore rather a positive valuation of activity and a negative valuation of what hinders or thwarts action or generates frustration. Similarly, to speak of a man's having opposing valuations at different times is not strictly to charge him with inconsistency, but to imply that such rapidity of change is a negative value.[54] Judgments of consistency thus may

54 For a fuller examination of the meaning of 'consistency' and 'contradiction' in the case of values and valuing, see my "Naturalism and

act as vehicle for values concerning the area in which conflict is to be avoided, whether it be the same man at the same time, the same man over a life-span, or a society of men. The second of these is the area implied in most hedonisms, since it is to the maximum pleasure over his lifetime that a man's calculations would refer.

(7) The phenomenon of the addressee in an ethical theory by its very nature expresses some purpose, therefore carries some values. Ethical statements are not intended as monologues but as discourse to others, whether they be construed as descriptive, imperative, hortative, or optative. Whole ethical disputes may be addressed only to a particular class of men. For example, in Aristotle's *Eudemian Ethics* it is pointed out that the controversy whether the best life is that of the intellect, of political ambition, or of pleasure, does not concern those who spend their lives in menial pursuits, and it is utterly irrelevant to slaves. Similarly, a book about the ethical obligations of the courtier is not addressed to the mass of the people, except in a fluid society in which anyone may win his way to the court. The ethics of a caste society will be addressed to everybody only insofar as it attempts a justification of the caste system and urges upon people the appropriate obedience or deference. But large parts of the ethical system may concern one or another of the castes alone.

That by and large ethics in the western tradition has come to be addressed to everyone—whether in the strict form of Kantian rules or in the implication that anyone might find himself in the situation discussed—thus carries the value-tone of a common humanity and a common ethic. That this is clearly a value-element may be seen by contrast with the Nazi "ethics," if we may stretch the term in such usage, which is addressed only to a single mythical blood group. In addition to common humanity, it is possible that the values of abstract individualism are carried along in the implicit mode of address in our ethical system.[55]

Ethical Theory," in *Naturalism and the Human Spirit*, ed. Y. H. Krikorian (New York, 1944), pp. 85-89; also p. 84, on the attempt to build up a whole good for a whole man, as in Sidgwick's theory.

[55] This is seen enlarged, as it were, in our legal system, in which such categories as contract are systematized most generally in terms of the wills of allegedly equal persons, rather than specifically in terms of the kind of

We may conclude that the selection, in most of the logical elements considered above, between one or another type of structure, constitutes usually a specific valuational act and not merely a preference in terms of the criteria of logical fruitfulness or systematic order. It is important, however, to raise the question whether the value clings to the abstract logical form or to the way in which it is interpreted, and, more generally, to distinguish the several points at which the value may be carried. Clearly, there is no single answer for all the elements, and the difficulties are multiplied if we look for the values in constellations of elements as against individual elements.[56] But three possible loci of value may be distinguished.

(a) The first is the bare logical form. Now it seems hardly likely that specific values will cling simply to the choice of a term regarded purely as a symbol but without its semantic reference, or to the use of a set of sentential functions without indicating the meaning of the class to which the values of the variable refer, or even to formation-rules without importing more than a logical meaning to their terms. And considerable analysis is yet required to see whether such formal elements can carry any value-quality at all. But there does seem to me to be some sense in which it is not impossible that they should carry values. And this is in the sense of drastically limiting the possibilities of ethical construction.

Consider, for example, what an ethical theory would be like in which a fundamental relation, in all other respects serving the purposes of our ordinary term 'better,' were by postulate fixed as nontransitive. It would follow that such an ethical system could not infer that A is better than C because A is better than B and B is better than C. The system would be limited to statements of comparative value only—if they were permitted

---

subject matter and typical situations. For a comparative discussion of the extent of the group in moralities, see *Anthropology and Ethics*, Ch. IX.

[56] It is, as a matter of fact, more probable that values are carried in constellations rather than in unitary elements. We have noted at a number of points above the manner in which the same value-effect may be secured in different ways. We have not, however, attempted any description of constellations, since the present study aims to discover whether and how value-components enter, not to map their typical content in the western ethical tradition.

at all—through some procedure of direct comparison. Value-measurement would thereby be for the most part eliminated. Again, suppose that a theory imposed a rule that ethical statements should be singular in form. This would yield an ethical "nominalism," denying the possibility of a specific system of ethics. It need not entail a metaphysical nominalism since there may be other than singular statements in nonethical domains. The kind of ethics resulting may be naturalistic or non-naturalistic. It may hold to intuitive singular statements immediately grasped or it may treat the singular ethical assertion as a rough estimation of so many factors entering into a unique combination that no generalizations are possible.[57]

Now to prescribe nonmeasurement or nonsystem to an ethical field may not by itself seem to carry a value. But once the ethical language that embodies these prescriptions is put to use, the way in which it may limit possibilities will rule against some values and allow ready entry to others. In this way, the abstract logical form may act as a selective vehicle or conductor for values, even though by itself it may show no value-content. Only careful comparative analysis could determine which logical elements are selective value-conductors, which never are, whether there are any whose value-content in use· is invariant for all constellations they may enter, or for all interpretations or historical conditions (which seems unlikely).

(b) The second locus of value carried by logical elements of an ethical theory is the *general* meaning of the element, which it acquires on a broad psychological or historical interpretation. Suppose, for example, that 'good' is given a *subjective* interpretation. Prior to specification of the subjective mode intended—feeling, desire, opinion, or some other type—does the resort to a subjective interpretation carry a value with it? It would seem at least to bring the flavor of variability and relativity. Thus Köhler suggests concerning objectivity that certain theorists who

---

[57] Compare the similar view of some "legal realists" in the domain of law, according to whom law is just a name for a heap of cases and legal rules are just fictions; e.g., Jerome Frank, *Law and the Modern Mind* (New York, 1935). Predictability in law is not, however, ruled out thereby on nonlegal (e.g., psychological or economic) grounds, although there are no specifically legal rules.

desire a system of strictly valid rules "would prefer an objectiv-
istic interpretation of value, since 'objective' means 'outside of
us,' 'independent' and 'valid' all at the same time. What is objective phenomenally exhibits, indeed, more steadiness on the
average than does the everchanging stream of our subjective
life." [58]

Now it is quite possible that the value-quality of subjectivity
stems from the contrast between the more orderly natural world
and the less orderly stream of consciousness. If this is so, its
value-quality may be invariant. (Even here, however, whether it
is regarded as a positive or a negative value—whether the variability in the nature of values is welcomed or deprecated—is a
question of external criticism.) In contrast, it is conceivable that
in some cultural tradition distinct from our western civilization
subjectivity might convey fixity as against the physical flux.
Certainly mental habits and prejudice sometimes show greater
constancy than nature viewed through Heracleitean spectacles.
If this is theoretically conceivable, perhaps the value-quality of
subjectivity has a greater cultural and historical component, and
is a function of specific theories and attitudes in the development
of western religions, philosophies, and institutions.

(c) The third locus of values carried by logical elements of an
ethical theory may be the more specific psychological or historical meaning of the element, not simply its abstract logical form
or its general interpretation. We noted such issues above, in discussing the relation of 'right' and 'good,' the meaning of 'law,'
and just above, the possible cultural basis of value-quality in subjectivity. It is especially clear in such concepts as 'law.' Thus the
discovery of law in one age is evidence of design, hence God's
existence. At a later age religion is deemed strengthened by
breaking the reign of law in favor of indeterminism. Similarly,
an interpretation of the good as order carries a different value
according to the psychological or social meaning of the concept.
Compare, for example, William James's disparagement of the
tender-minded, whose search for a well-ordered universe seems a
kind of personal weakness, with the political appeal to law and
order. The latter, too, varies when used predominantly against

[58] Wolfgang Köhler, *The Place of Value in a World of Facts* (New York,
1938), p. 76. Cf. p. 40.

a lynch mob and when used for a fascistic suppression of liberty.[59]

Such specific values that logical elements in an ethical theory convey in a particular psychological constitution or socio-historical setting tend to cling not merely to isolated elements, but to the general logical structure. It is an interesting problem for comparative criticism of ethical theories to discover the way in which the clustering of elements in a constellation may act as a vehicle of value in a specific context. Thus the choice of fundamental terms may combine with that of formation-rules, of co-ordinating definitions, of implicit addressee, to produce a pattern that more readily conveys order or variability, authority or democracy, within the given context.

Scientific elements. In what way, if any, does the conception of human nature in an ethical theory—the use of a particular stage and dramatis personae or insistence upon a particular kind of plot—convey general or specific values?

It has often been noted that the theory of human nature bears a special relation to the theory of politics or social action. This stands out clearly in the political philosophers. Plato's scheme of three classes with the philosopher-kings on top is justified by an analysis of the soul in which reason has the task of coercing inherently disorderly desires or passions. Hobbes rests his case for absolute sovereignty on the natural war of each against all. The anarchist opposition to the state is coupled with a natural principle of mutual aid among mankind, running up through the animal world. Social conservatism often looks for a theory of fixed instincts, whereas social reform calls for the plasticity of the human material.

We need not enter here into the precise character of such relations. A priori, the political theory may be a deduction resting on the psychological theory as partial evidence. Or, conversely, the psychological theory may be an expression or reflection of an already assumed political position, and may serve as an instrument to justify it. In any case, it follows that the theory of human nature conveys some value-attitude. On the one hand,

[59] A labor spokesman's description of terroristic strikebreaking by company police and special gangs deputized by a hostile sheriff once began with the statement: "Then law and order broke loose."

it is important to stress that this "vehicle function" characterizes a true as well as a false theory. On the other hand, false theories useful as vehicles for political values may hinder a true theory's acceptance if its values would oppose those embedded in the false theories.

The value-carrier qualities of a psychological theory of human nature stand out most clearly if the theory is seen as a guide to an individual. It tells him how to analyze himself and his aims, how to set himself to judge himself and his directions. To that extent the theory not merely describes (truly or falsely), but sets the stage, provides certain tools or methods, and encourages or recommends certain attitudes or character traits.

These various value-phases of a theory of human nature stand out clearly in hedonism and the criticisms of it. The stage it provides narrows the field of ethical consideration, as compared, for example, with a theory that endows human beings with social sympathies from the outset. Thus Dewey complains, in his early book, *Outlines of a Critical Theory of Ethics,* that since pleasure is purely individual and exclusive, a state of feeling that can be enjoyed only while felt and only by the one feeling it, "to set it up for the ideal of conduct is to turn life into an exclusive and excluding struggle for the possession of the means of personal enjoyment; it is to erect into a principle the idea of the war of all against all. No end more thoroughly disintegrating than individual agreeable sensation could well be imagined." [60]

The methods furnished by the theory to a man who asks how he is to judge, likewise impart a definite value-quality. In broad outline, he is to be an empiricist, not to act on intuition, impulse, or on grounds of some inherent rationality in the cosmos. But his empiricism is given a definite character in two ways. In the first place, his ultimate data are specified as pleasures; what this entails has been considered in the diverse interpretations of pleasure above. In the second place, the special form of his activity is that of the accountant.

The net result of setting the stage in this way and furnishing such methods is to urge upon the individual habits developing a special kind of character. If the hedonistic theory were psychologically true, these character-values would have some status

[60] Ann Arbor, 1891, p. 52.

of unavoidability. Critics who regard the theory as false can therefore see it more clearly as hortatory. Thus Dewey, in *Human Nature and Conduct,* intersperses among criticisms of its truth, criticisms to the effect that it tends toward a type of character that is undesirable. "If such a theory has any practical influence, it is to advise a person to concentrate upon his own most subjective and private feelings. It gives him no choice except between a sickly introspection and an intricate calculus of remote, inaccessible, and indeterminate results." [61] It is interesting to note, however, that instead of considering this a normative criticism, Dewey concludes the paragraph: "The first objection therefore to deliberation as a calculation of future feelings is that, if it is consistently adhered to, it makes an abnormal case the standard one." Similarly, in a later chapter, he criticizes the utilitarians for retaining "the notion that the good is future, and hence outside the meaning of present activity," [62] as if it were a misunderstanding of the nature of activity. It is equally intelligible, however, as an attempt to develop a character that will find its center of gravity in its propulsive effort, that will fear to pause in the moment lest it takes it eyes off the future, a character geared to progressive accumulation rather than to possession. In an earlier context, Dewey does recognize that utilitarianism's "commendation of an elaborate and impossible calculus was in reality part of a movement to develop a type of character. . . ." [63]

It may be recalled, finally, that criticism concerning the values conveyed by the scientific element in an ethical theory may take two forms. One is an exhibition of the values actually conveyed. This is the major task, since they are not usually clear at first glance, and emerge only when the theory is considered in its operation. The second form is external criticism, which would give the critic's own estimate of these values. This may take the simple form, in the present case, of disapproving of the calculative character, or the more complex form of estimating the role of such a character in the period in which it was im-

[61] P. 201.   [62] *Ibid.,* p. 290.

[63] *Ibid.,* p. 205. In this context, however, Dewey takes the character to include wide social outlook and sympathy. This is consonant with his view that the hedonistic framework in utilitarianism was an historical accident.

plicitly advanced by the theory. Such criticism passes over from the scientific element to the historical element.

Historical elements. To what extent does the historical content of an ethical theory—the content that emerges when we locate the theory in its own socio-historical context—convey general or specific values?

In the simplest and most superficial sense, this question calls for an evaluative estimate of the ethical theory in its own time. What effect, if any, did it have on men, on groups, on movements? T. H. Green pays tribute to the influence of utilitarianism: "No other theory has been available for the social or political reformer, combining so much truth with such ready applicability. No other has offered so commanding a point of view from which to criticize the precepts and institutions presented as authoritative." [64] And in spite of his disagreements, Green concludes that on the whole it "has tended to improve human conduct and character." [65] Such an estimate may be supplemented by historical study of the influence of the utilitarians in the nineteenth century. Similar inquiries can be carried out for Democritus and Epicurus, for Helvetius and Holbach. In such historical analyses, we would find on the one hand the hypothesis of beneficent influence, on the other the hypothesis of hedonism in its various forms as a mode of corruption and thisworldliness.

In a more profound sense, the search for values carried by the historical content of a theory goes far beyond the question of its influence. It calls for relating the theory and its various elements to the values of men in the period. And any attempt to do so reveals that the historical content of an ethical theory often not merely *carries* values but *consists of* values, that is, social interests and attitudes of groups of men.

Thus, for example, if we revert to Wesley Mitchell's interpretation of Bentham's hedonism in terms of pecuniary rationality, the historical content of the ethical theory becomes the strengthening of pecuniary institutions and the stabilization in the conduct of life of attitudes that support such institutions. Hence, the historical content of the theory becomes the content of the

[64] *Prolegomena to Ethics,* § 329.

[65] *Ibid.,* § 331.

typical economic activity developed by the bourgeoisie at the period under consideration. As such the ethical theory may be seen in its historical perspective as part of the movement of a group or class with definite aims, inviting allegiance or rejection. In this sense the discovery of socio-historical content already involves the exhibition of valuational elements.

The further criticism of the values thus revealed is, of course, a case of external criticism. The critic may identify himself with the movement by accepting its aims. Or he may set it off as Nietzsche implied when he remarked that man did not seek happiness, only the Englishman. Or similarly as Marx did when he said that it became eventually a pure apologia for existing conditions. Such external criticism rests on the prior exhibition of the historical values, at least to some degree. Its fullest exhibition lies in showing the relations of groups of men with their varying or common aims. Its minimum exhibition is the presentation of a general tone to the ethical theory, broadly inclining its adherents in a certain historical direction.

SOME THEORETICAL IMPLICATIONS

A number of important theoretical conclusions emerge from the establishment of coordinates of criticism, and more especially from the observed role of valuational coordinates. These conclusions go beyond the functions of criticism and touch the underlying problem of the nature of ethical theory itself.

The value-base of ethical theories. We found values present in almost every part of an ethical theory. They were carried along in the logical structure, imparted by the scientific basis, and constituted the very content of the historical aspect. Nor were these values merely implements of criticism; we distinguished the values brought by the critic to external criticism from those he revealed as conveyed by the theory. Especially in considering the logical structures we saw that the very definition of ethics in terms of its interest, scope, and assigned task involved value-elements or value-quality in the broad sense of the term. Thus criticism discovers, and similarly construction implies, a value-base on which an ethical theory is set up, and without which there would be no ethics.

There would appear to be no a priori characterization of this base, no initial limitation to its possible specificity. The base might consist simply of the most general aim of guiding life or resolving problems by action (as against vision or understanding alone), or it might be as detailed as the aims of victory in war, where, as in Spartan society, the armed camp is deemed the natural state. Thus we might speak of guidance-ethics, vision-ethics, war-ethics, peace-ethics, scarcity-ethics, abundance-ethics, and so forth, if in fact there were value-bases that bore in the values or aims that composed them the particular stamp in question.

That *moralities* or *specific* systems of rules and values have such a character has long been recognized not merely from the historical relativity of forms, but from the analysis of moral philosophers. Hartmann, for example, calls attention to the moralities of the community and the individual, of power, of justice, of love, of labor, of moderation, of struggle, of peace, of repression, of revolt, of authority and acceptance, of the remote, of action, of enjoyment.[66] In another context, introducing the problem of the supreme value, he says:

> Every current morality is acquainted only with certain values, or even only with one, which it then emphasizes, in order to relate everything else to it. Every current morality, therefore, has a substance of truth in it, however one-sided it may be. For a fragment of true valuational knowledge is in every one of them, however much each seems to contradict the others.
>
> It becomes a task for ethics to resolve such contradictions— so far as they may be resolved.[67]

In posing this ethical problem, Hartmann clearly distinguishes possibilities:

> For ultimately the question is whether the desired unity of values must after all be a value, whether it could not consist of a highest principle which was not a valuational principle. Even this question cannot be decided beforehand. Just as the principle of motion need not itself be a motion, of life not itself life, just as the principles of knowledge are evidently far from being knowledge, so the universally ruling principle of the domain of value could very well be something else than a value.[68]

[66] *Ethics*, I, 77-78.   [67] *Ibid.*, II, 65.
[68] *Ibid.*, p. 70.

Hartmann's formulation distinguishes three elements—the particular moralities stressing different values, the role of ethics as systematic unifier of values, and the question whether ethical principles are themselves values. Our analysis in the present study enables us to suggest an answer to the question. But in order to do so certain distinctions have to be carefully drawn.

Moralities, ethical theories, and ethical frameworks. Although 'morals' and 'ethics' are derived respectively from Latin and Greek words both meaning customs, ordinary philosophic usage has developed a clear distinction between them. A moral system is a set of rules of conduct, preferred qualities of character, typical approved goals, within a given community. There have obviously been many moral systems. An ethical theory is a system of justification for a morality. As such it provides a set of concepts and principles by means of which the morality is upheld as reasonable and guidance is provided for moot points or clashes in applying the morality. The relation of an ethical theory to a morality is very much like that of the prevalent conception of justice in a country to the system of positive law of that country. There have been several different ethical theories, sometimes in connection with roughly the same morality. For example, similar moral codes have been justified as divine commandment within a theological ethics and as tending to the greatest happiness of the greatest number in a utilitarian ethics. Where two different ethical theories justify the same set of moral rules, it is probable that they point to different results in moot cases or would differ on the points at which changes in moral rules would be legitimate.[69]

A further distinction I should like to introduce is that between an ethical theory and an ethical framework. Much of the discussion and criticism of ethical theories is really concerned only with their fundamental ideas. This is true also of the present study. The kinds of elements in an ethical theory located along

[69] Compare the similar relation between a political philosophy and a political institution. For example, the absolute monarchy was justified both by the divine right of kings theory and by the Hobbesian theory of its necessity to avert the war of every man against all others. But the acceptance of the second ground made the justification empirical and contingent upon there being no better way to achieve the end of peace.

the lines of the coordinates developed above constitute what I shall call an *ethical framework*. The framework includes at least the basic logical ideas, methods, scientific approaches, and assumptions with which the theory operates. Beyond the framework but definitely part of the theory is the host of theoretical deductions, empirical laws, and special methods that constitute the bulk of the ethics. One has only to turn the pages of Bentham's writings on ethics and jurisprudence to see how wide is the content of the theory beyond the framework, both in the scope of its analytical development and in the array of empirically established materials. Thus there are analyses of types of pleasure and pain, of sensibility, of will and act, motives, dispositions, sanctions. There are rules developed as a basis of politics and law, such as that every man is to count as one, or that quantity being equal, the pain of loss is to be reckoned greater than the pleasure of gain.[70] There is the elaboration and justification of virtues and vices. There are deductions concerning the fundamental aims of social control, and specifically of law. It does not matter that many of the assertions may be called propositions of psychology, and that some of the results coincide with propositions of morality. It simply underlines the fact that part of the theory of ethics, that is a system justifying morality and providing guidance for its application, is psychological, and that the end products of ethical theory (as in the outline of virtues) shade imperceptibly into the morality whose justification is sought.

The value-character of ethical frameworks. In the light of these distinctions, it is clear that the unity of a moral system is expressed in and sometimes hammered out by its ethical theory. Similarly, the attempt to unify the values found in different moral systems, as Hartmann proposes, is to be found in the development of a unified ethical theory. But we have seen that every ethical theory is constructed on a framework, and that a value-base appears to underlie every aspect of the framework and guide its character. If that is so, Hartmann's question whether ethical principles are themselves values must be answered in the affirmative; at least they often convey values and

---

[70] Whether the status of such rules is that of special values or deductions from fundamental assumptions, or empirical generalizations, is itself a question for the ethical theory to determine.

have a value-quality. In that case, however, the diversity of morals is reproduced on the higher level of ethics, and presumably the search for unity—at least by those who value unity—begins again. Is there then an over-all ethics? Or, in terms of our analysis, can there be at least an over-all ethical framework?

One such alternative would be the ideal of a neutral framework in which all value-differences were expressed as part of the explicit value-content. This alternative is encouraged by the scientific possibility of transparent rather than opaque symbols. That there are difficulties in its way is clear from our analysis of values in the logical elements. That these elements, and the scientific elements, could be made neutral and discard all value-quality seems highly unlikely.

The other alternative is the development of a universal base consisting of standardized values. This is suggested by analogy with the growth of the physical sciences. Here, after many centuries, the values inherent in the process have become explicit and adopted, even constitutive of the method, in spite of some conflicting analyses of scientific method. Thus the ideal of "saving the phenomena" enunciated in Greek science becomes a condition of a logically adequate hypothesis. However, there still appear to be some value-elements in some controversies, such as those about "mechanism." The development of an over-all framework in this direction is not theoretically impossible. It would not abandon a value-quality, but would embody explicitly and express a set of values. In its logical and scientific elements these values would be the ones inherent in the method of science. Such a tendency is aided by the growth of the psychological and social sciences and the stabilization of an account of human nature. In its historical elements, however, the development of a standardized ethical framework is dependent upon the more specific character of the value-base. It is possible that no standardized base would be accepted until the unification of the globe with the emergence of crucial common human problems has forged a minimum common morality adequate to support a minimum common ethic.

Exactly the opposite may, however, be the case. The rates of change of ethical framework, morality, and value-base are certainly quite distinct. The strain on a given ethical framework may become much greater because of the shift in the value base, and the framework may crack while the morality still appears untouched. In that case the reconstruction of the framework may play a part in the reconstruction of the morality. This is not an uncommon social phenomenon. People may be asked to change the reasons for their practice long before they are asked to change their practice. This is indicative of contradictions arising but not yet matured within their practice itself.[71]

Whether the system of morality or the ethical framework is "nearer" to the value-base is a socio-historical rather than a logical problem. At present, for example, the utter destructiveness of war makes the need for international peace and security a central element in the value-base; any ethical outlook that expects serious consideration must face this problem. This points to a shift in ethical frameworks to a formulation of the good in global rather than in individual terms. The specific changes required in our morality to yield cooperative attitudes are, however, by no means equally clear.

In any case, the concept of the value-base plays a central role in this analysis. This base, closely tied to the problems of life and practice, appears to have almost a constitutive role in ethical theory. We have not in this study examined it directly, but discovered its existence and general character by finding valuational elements in the various parts of the ethical framework. Its fuller examination could proceed along two lines. One is the comparative study of implicit value-bases in traditional ethical theories. The second is the study of bases in life and practice as revealed by the psychological, social, and historical sciences, for these sciences study the existential matrix out of which ethical theories and moralities alike emerge.[72]

71 Cf. the example, given above, of Hobbes' empirical justification for absolute monarchy proposed instead of the divine right of kings, but rejected by those in power. Similarly, the philosophic attempts in America to reject a Spencerian theory of absolute private property were offering a social instead of an individual basis for the same property rights; the immediate changes they implied in practice were minimal compared to those in theory. Yet in due course such conceptions became the basis of New Deal measures against "economic royalty."

72 For further discussion of this problem, see my *Ethical Judgment*, Ch. IX, in which a more specific concept of the value-base is developed.

We may, in conclusion, consider one possible objection, which, while apparently trifling, will illustrate that the method of our study of criticism can be applied to our own account. It may be asked why we speak of a 'value-base' and of 'value-quality' carried in the different parts of the framework. Why do we, in short, allow ourselves the broad use of the term mentioned above? [73] Is not the meaning and use of such a term determined by some ethical framework which we are implicitly employing? And what values does *it* convey?

This is in part a verbal question. Instead of valuational co-ordinates we could have spoken of need or aim or interest co-ordinates. All that was meant by value-quality was that the item in question involved some attitude to the conduct of life, some tone of approval or disapproval, some indication of interest, some direction of aim or wish, some for-or-against. It is also possible that the wider use of the term 'value' itself exhibits an attitude of initial tolerance to human inclination, whereas a narrower use exhibits a tendency to treat inclinations as prima facie ethically neutral until they prove their case in terms of a specific theory of values.[74]

All such points of difference can become explicit in the construction of an ethical framework. There is no level of criticism that is itself exempt from criticism. All criticism is either from within, attempting to refine the framework under scrutiny, or external, from the point of view of another framework. And just as criticism that is self-conscious makes clear its object as well as its basis, so the establishment of coordinates of criticism is at the same time the beginning of a systematic answer to the question, "What is an ethical theory?"

[73] At the beginning of the discussion of valuational coordinates.
[74] For the general value concept, see below, Ch. VIII.

CHAPTER THREE

THE LOCUS OF PRESCRIPTIVENESS

The purpose of this chapter is to propose a fresh approach in the way of handling prescriptiveness in ethical theory. It is an attempt to break through what is increasingly felt as a deadlock in the controversies of cognitivism and anti-cognitivism. The approach suggested here issues from an analytic comparison of the way in which different theories have handled this component; it may accordingly be seen as a lesson suggested by comparative method. I shall introduce the approach by a brief historical analogy, follow up with the comparative consideration of prescriptiveness in several contemporary ethical analyses, scrutinize the criteria for 'correctness' in this domain of analysis, and conclude with recommendations for the handling of prescriptiveness in the continuation of contemporary theoretical endeavor.

THE WOES OF A HOMELESS CATEGORY

Let us remind ourselves of the travels of *necessity* in the history of modern philosophy. Cast from its central eminence as pure necessary being, prior to and presupposed by any finite contingent existent, it wandered far afield in search of a home. David Hume, that arch-subverter of traditional categories, thrust it out of nature, into the narrow confines of subjectivity. Kant, assimilating necessity to universality, sought to give it a place in the a priori. Logicians suggested a place in the logical necessity of analyticity, and phenomenologists assured it that it could always remain in the demanding qualities of the field of direct awareness. And, while it wandered, the great debate went on, as to whether necessity belonged in nature, in some ultimate behind-the-scenes reality, in our minds, in phenomena, in logic, in psychological habit, and so on.

Perhaps we may learn from the history of necessity how to analyze the present predicament of prescriptiveness. It too was once firmly entrenched in a well-built mansion. The dominance of theological philosophy in the medieval world gave it a place in the will of God. Its imperative quality lay in the fact of God's command, and its magnetic quality was evidenced in the aspiration of the individual soul. Then came the breakup of the medieval world system. Where was prescriptiveness to go? It might be in the edicts of reason, but reason was soon reduced to the slave of the passions. It might be in the pressures of desire, but desire seemed too varying and competitive to provide a stable place—at best it would be a base (Hobbesian) hovel. It might be in the cool reflection of a sensitive onlooker, or in the structure of a Kantian conscience in which prescriptiveness, like necessity, was tied to the universal, or it might be divided in Bergsonian style between the weight of habit and the upward surge of aspiration. Prescriptiveness today is still being pulled from one spot to another, without a place to call its own.

A homeless category is a dreadful thing. It wanders here and there, sighing or demanding, like an ancient Greek shade, moving restlessly until it is decently buried. If it has no place to call its own, it may stumble into some perfectly peaceful philosophical area and overturn it until it is dislodged. Of course, there is always a chance that the errant category may be lost in the marshes of ordinary language. But one cannot count on its staying there. Toughened by its struggles, it may emerge as the center of a philosophical revolt. This is what is happening with prescriptiveness. If not given a proper place it will usurp the whole area. Ethics is in danger of becoming merely prescriptive or dominantly prescriptive, merely practical or dominantly practical—if the image cast in contemporary theory is to be trusted.

PROPOSED LOCATIONS FOR PRESCRIPTIVENESS

Let us now consider a number of the locations proposed for prescriptiveness in a variety of twentieth-century treatments.

In the phenomenal field. That one or another type of prescriptiveness is to be found directly in the phenomenal field is the theme of several converging approaches. It is implicit in the way G. E. Moore treated good as a non-natural quality to be directly apprehended as a property of a whole which was set off in imagination as a world by itself. It is explicit in Hartmann's phenomenological intuitionism with its interpretation of value as an ought-to-be, directly grasped by the sensitive observer; in the more classical type of intuitionism, such as W. D. Ross's treatment of obligation as a separate, directly intuitable property; or in A. C. Ewing's use of fittingness as a fundamental concept resting on intuitive apprehension.[1]

The most self-conscious development of this outlook about the location of prescriptiveness is to be found in contemporary Gestalt approaches. Köhler expounds the generic notion of requiredness as a property discernible within the phenomenal field.[2] Asch likewise draws the line sharply between the discerned property in the field and judgments of causality or underlying needs. He goes so far as to say that authority, however peremptory, is "as powerless to introduce into the human mind the distinction between a just and an unjust act as it is to establish a discrimination between red and green." [3] Mandelbaum, in what is up to this point the fullest treatment of the Gestalt approach in ethics, goes on to reject teleological analysis of requiredness as defining the meaning of ethical judgments. For him, the basic situation is one of direct moral judgment, and here we find "the phenomenon of a 'reflexive demand,' that is, of an 'objective' demand which is experienced as being directly leveled against the person apprehending it." [4] The vector points to the self, but the self is not in the picture. In fact, as you read the description, you may feel like dodging to get out of the way, so vivid is the account of the vectorial quality. But it is no use, the arrow turns where you go, and you are left facing its sharp point.

As a quality of a rule. The view that prescriptiveness adheres to law or rule, and that it is detectable in a man's feeling of re-

---

1 See G. E. Moore, *Principia Ethica*, pp. 83-85, 91. (Cf. my "The Logical Structure of G. E. Moore's Ethical Theory," in *The Philosophy of G. E. Moore*, pp. 156ff.); N. Hartman, *Ethics* (New York, 1932); W. D. Ross, *The Right and the Good* (Oxford, 1930), and *Foundations of Ethics* (Oxford, 1939); A. C. Ewing, *The Definition of Good* (New York, 1947).

2 Wolfgang Köhler, *The Place of Value in a World of Facts* (New York, 1938), Ch. III.

3 Solomon E. Asch, *Social Psychology* (Englewood Cliffs, N. J., 1952), p. 356.

4 Maurice Mandelbaum, *The Phenomenology of Moral Experience* (Glencoe, Ill., 1955), p. 51.

spect or awe in the presence of the moral law, has been thoroughly familiar since Kant. That moral law itself has a kind of binding quality is very often taken for granted. The question then becomes one of distinguishing moral from nonmoral laws. An interesting contemporary formulation along these lines is to be found in C. I. Lewis's "The Rational Imperatives." Casting his inquiry in terms of critiques or modes of criticism, Lewis distinguishes rules of the critique of consistency, of cogency, of prudence, and of justice. Since he believes these not avoidable for any human being, he regards them all—parting company here with Kant—as categorical in their imperativeness. And in these terms he goes on to offer a definition of the moral: "The moral critique is that whose rules take precedence, in case of conflict with any other rule of doing. That is the sense in which even moral egoists intend the term 'moral': they are egoists by believing that it is the rules of prudence which so take precedence." [5] Primary prescriptiveness thus finds its locus in the rules that function as or are apprehended as ultimately decisive.

In the means-end relation. It is comforting to reflect that however much philosophers may disagree about the locus of prescriptiveness, they will always allow it some place in the means-end relation. This is the familiar hypothetical necessity—do X if you want Y, because X is an indispensable means to the achievement of Y. Some philosophies, however, go as far as to say that this is ultimately the sole locus of prescriptiveness.

Some types find a single end *in fact* present for all men. Hence, since we can count on the goal pursued, the force of a moral judgment must rest with its designation of means. Traditional hedonism with its goal of pleasure and the avoidance of pain, and utilitarianism with its greatest happiness of the greatest number are familiar examples; although even here, we must remember, Sidgwick looked for the moral force also in an intuition that pleasure is good. In recent ethical theory, MacBeath, after examining the varying ways of life of primitive peoples, concludes that all people start with the same raw materials of the human

[5] C. I. Lewis, "The Rational Imperatives," in *Vision and Action*, "Essays in Honor of Horace M. Kallen on His Seventieth Birthday," ed. Sidney Ratner (New Brunswick, N. J., 1953), p. 165. For John Ladd's comparable use of criteria of legitimacy and superiority, see below, p. 178.

make-up, that they aim at the same formal or highly general end (whether construed as happiness or keeping the world going evenly, or harmony, and so forth), but that they are, as it were, experimenting with different operative ideals to give expression to that make-up and to achieve that end, and different institutions to actualize those ideals.[6] On such a view, it would follow that the prescriptiveness comes from a felt instrumental relation, either explicit or implicit, to an end that is either consciously felt as accepted or actually operative.

Other types do not require a single end. Variable goals will do, although those means which are necessary to all these varying goals will have a much greater prescriptive force. This is the role played in Hobbes by the unavoidable necessity for law and order. In contemporary ethics, Dewey [7] takes it to be a lesson of the sciences of man that all desire or striving occurs in a more or less structured problem situation. Hence, pursuit of a goal is a means to solving the problem, and no matter how end-like the goal seems in consciousness it is capable of being estimated for the success with which it will, in terms of the consequences of its pursuit, solve the problems which generated the situation. Hence, appraisal is fundamentally relevant everywhere, and the prescriptive element lies in the means-end relation broadly construed.

In the expression of attitude. How Stevenson, looking for a "vital" sense of good, and focusing on the "magnetism" of goodness, was led to develop a concept of emotive meaning in ethics, is a familiar chapter in twentieth-century ethical theory.[8] Prescriptiveness on this analysis is located in the expressive force in the functioning of language, or in the persuasive endeavor of the utterance. A primary model is one like this: "This is wrong" means the same as, "I disapprove of this; do so thou." Prescriptiveness is expressed in the imperative part.

In a practical endeavor. While emotivism stressed the element of feeling expressed or attitude conveyed, a whole host of im-

6 A. MacBeath, *Experiments in Living* (London, 1952).

7 See especially *Theory of Valuation* (Chicago, 1939).

8 Charles L. Stevenson, "The Emotive Meaning of Ethical Terms," *Mind*, XLVI (1937). See also his *Ethics and Language* (New Haven, 1944), and A. J. Ayer, *Language, Truth and Logic* (London, 1936), Ch. VI. For further consideration of emotivism, see below, pp. 143-44, 155ff.

mediately subsequent theorists underscored the more directly practical aspects of ethical judgment. Their practicalism went so far as to remove the cognitive in ethics from its traditional primary place: the so-called 'ethical judgment' or 'judgment of practical reason' was no longer to be construed as discernment of ethical fact, but as an active process of decision. Even reflection on a general principle was not primarily theoretical: "When I *subscribe* to the principle, I do not state a fact, but make a moral decision," said Hare,[9] implying that the ethical judgment was itself the decisional act or its expression, not a report of a separate subscription. We are told that "the typical moral problem is not a spectator's problem or a problem of classifying or describing conduct, but a problem of practical choice and decision." [10] Aristotle's treatment of the practical syllogism as issuing in action was invoked as the correct path of ethical theory in locating the prescriptive element.[11] Various areas of practice were ransacked to show the diverse practical functioning of language in ritual and ceremonial, legal judgment, performatory formulae, guiding, and so on, and these were presented as models for understanding the use of ethical terms. In a far different strain, but with the same effect, existentialist outlooks underscored the first-personal context of ethical decision where all knowledge is secondary and its recommendations reversible, and the awful lonely act of decision carries with it the total weight of absolute responsibility.[12]

This practicalism is the high point of the revolt of prescriptiveness against its dislocation. Whether it places prescriptiveness in the pragmatic functioning of language or in the living vital experience reflects other theoretical components.

In the syntax of language. There has been some tendency to stow prescriptiveness safely away in the syntax of ethical language and thus have it on constant display in the use of ethical sen-

[9] R. M. Hare, *The Language of Morals* (Oxford, 1952), p. 196.

[10] Stuart Hampshire, "Fallacies in Moral Philosophy," *Mind*, LVIII (1949), p. 468.

[11] John Ladd, "Reason and Practice," in *The Return to Reason: Essays in Realistic Philosophy*, ed. John Wild (Chicago, 1953).

[12] For this stress, see, for example, Jean-Paul Sartre, *Existentialism and Humanism* (London, 1948). For emphasis on the living personal situation as against treating either others or oneself as "It," see Martin Buber, *I and Thou* (Edinburgh, 1937).

tences. Interesting preliminary philosophical treatment of this possibility has been carried out by Hare and by Hall.[13] There is a difference, however, in their underlying approach. Hare is a practicalist who believes that the prescriptive element has to show clearly because it is irreducible in the commending function by which moral judgment guides. Hall, on the other hand, takes value in ethics to be a metaphysical category just as fact is in the field of knowledge; accordingly, he would like to have the structure of a normative sentence in an ideal language reveal what he takes to be the structure of value.

In the way terms function in the valuational act. Such an approach is proposed by Philip B. Rice in an attempt to do justice to the tension of the practicalist and the cognitivist emphases.[14] Focusing on "the central and indispensable jobs that ethical terms have to perform," he finds that the indispensable function of the 'ought' is a trigger function, expressing the fact that a choice has been made and serving as a signal to release the specific action. (Similarly, in the case of 'good' the cognitive element plays a comparable central role.) This trigger function he calls the *matrix meaning* of the term. But he resists the tendency to give it either an unqualifiedly primary place with the practicalist or an unqualifiedly secondary place with the cognitivist. Instead, a distinction of context is carefully drawn, for example, in facing the relation of 'ought' and 'good': "So far as the prescriptive element goes, the 'ought' is basic, and the 'good' as a conditional prescription is a function of the 'ought'; on the other hand, with respect to the descriptive element, the 'ought,' asserting that the act promotes the maximum organization of goods over evils, is a function of the 'good.' This is our suggested solution of the much disputed question whether the 'good' or the 'ought' is primary. Each is primary in one respect, and derivative in the other." [15]

In the content of the valuational act. This differs from Rice's view in that it is less concerned with the functioning of ethical terms as the locus of prescriptiveness. In fact, it is the traditional

---

13 R. M. Hare, *op. cit.;* Everett W. Hall, *What is Value?* (London, 1952). See below, p. 144, and the comment on deontic logics, pp. 144-45.

14 Philip Blair Rice, *On the Knowledge of Good and Evil* (New York, 1955), Ch. VI, esp. pp. 108ff.

15 *Ibid.,* pp. 232-33.

cognitivist view, whether naturalistic or non-naturalistic. Prescriptiveness is to be found in the actual phenomena of valuation. Ethical judgments are fundamentally analyzed reports of certain types of experience and their tensions and qualities. The having of the moral experience and the judgment about it are to be sharply distinguished, and it is in the former that prescriptiveness is to be sought.

There will of course be different candidates for the exact locus, depending on the types of analysis of the experience assumed to be correct. The phenomenological account of requiredness is one candidate. Or, if moral experience is a certain type of psychological tension, then prescriptiveness is to be found in the feeling of tension. If the phenomena involved are essentially some types of guilt experience, then prescriptiveness has to be analyzed as a certain qualitative dimension in that experience (e.g., that one part of the self is felt as authoritatively accusing another part), and so on. If the experience is one of reflective desire—for example, of something for its own sake, as in many traditional accounts— then the prescriptive element may lie in part in the quality of desire and in part in the reflective component of appraisal.[16] If the experience involves, on its reflective side, considering what the attitude of oneself would be under ideal conditions or what an ideal observer would approve of,[17] then the locus of the prescriptive element will be found by studying how ideals arise and function and how one identifies with ideal observers.

On such a view the attempt to regard prescriptiveness as in any way located in the judgment rather than in the experience and its context is to look in the wrong direction. Physical formulae about magnetism do not do the attracting, nor do equations about light themselves light up, except by special ingenious electrical arrangement. Even a trigger function may best be seen in terms of the material that is set off and its explosive properties.

[16] See, for an excellent analysis of goodness in desiderative terms, Charles A. Baylis, "Intrinsic Goodness," *Philosophy and Phenomenological Research*, XIII (Sept., 1952), 15-27.

[17] E.g., the type of position presented by Richard B. Brandt in "The Status of Empirical Assertion Theories in Ethics," *Mind* (Oct., 1952), or in the theoretical parts of his *Hopi Ethics* (Chicago, 1954).

Possibility of a multiple or movable location. The underlying assumption of most theories is that prescriptiveness is to have one location. But of course there may be several, and we may very well be dealing with a family of prescriptiveness rather than one type. Bergson, as we mentioned in the preliminary comparison with necessity, suggested two fundamentally distinct types of obligation.[18] Certainly, aspiration towards the good and obligation to perform one's duty jostle one another continually in the history of ethics.

Another possibility, even when there is only one type of prescriptiveness, is a movable location, which varies with where we stand. In evaluating proposed paths of conduct, we may look for authoritative judgment to our inner convictions or ideal aspirations. In judging our convictions or allegiances, we may look to consequences and relations in the outer world.[19] Or again, in a Deweyan vein, ends are justified in terms of the problem to which their pursuit would offer a solution, and taking on fresh problems is warranted by their being generated in the pursuit of those ends. In all such outlines of the moral process, the element of prescriptiveness shuttles from one side to the other.

Let the types of domiciles offered so far suffice to raise the problem. They have the advantage of corresponding, more or less, to specific ethical theories that have been advanced and are firmly maintained by different philosophers. No doubt a little ingenuity could fashion other proposed locations for prescriptiveness in a still more complex way—a type of speculative "non-Euclidean" activity not to be spurned in liberating the theoretical imagination in ethics. But for the present, the situation is complex enough as it stands.

HOW CAN WE DECIDE CORRECTNESS?

The question of resolution among these conflicting location theories is complicated by the fact that criteria of correctness are by no means clear or agreed upon in this domain. Where are we

18 Henri Bergson, *The Two Sources of Morality and Religion* (New York, 1935).

19 Royce portrays such a dialectic in his *Philosophy of Loyalty* (New York, 1911), Lecture I, pp. 24-38.

to appeal? Let us trace the implicit answers in some of the theories we have considered.

Ontological and epistemological certification. In plain language this means arguing that because one has structured ethical categories along the lines of a particular metaphysics or epistemology, one must be correct. This used to be a very respectable procedure before the suspicion arose (articulated by Kant for ontology, but ignored by him in epistemology) that the metaphysics itself may be geared to serve ethical needs. We may use what happened to Kant's moral law approach as a brief object lesson of the likely fate of such a priorism.

Kant coupled with his emphasis on moral law as the locus of prescriptiveness a partial account of the "feeling" of awe or respect in reflecting on which one discerns one's relation to the law. He insisted that this was no ordinary psychological reaction in the naturalistic sense, and distinguished it carefully from any calculation of self-love or fear of punishment. But as often happens when an object is put in the spotlight and a mode of cognition is left in the shade, human curiosity turns to the latter. Men began to ask whether respect is directed toward law after all. Durkheim took it to be directed to the group, as well as resulting from group pressures on the individual. Bovet saw it as the outcome of relations among individuals themselves and regarded respect as directed toward persons and not toward rules of law. Piaget, who reports this development,[20] seeks to discover the way in which rules mature both in behavior and consciousness, and where respect is directed, by looking to the child in the developing or creating process. Piaget finds a distinction between the unilateral respect and constraint which characterizes the child's relation to older people and the mutual respect of age-mates. In such analyses, as well as in the psychological accounts of psychoanalytical theory, the relation to law is ultimately traced to the relation to persons. Kant himself, as a matter of fact, points in this direction when he translates his categorical imperative into his human imperative that no man be used as a means alone; also when he regards moral law as expressing man's self-legislation as a rational being. Rational personality rather than

[20] Jean Piaget, *The Moral Judgment of the Child* (New York, 1932), p. 95.

the law in which it expresses itself would seem then to be the ultimate object of respect.

The lessons of such an outcome may be applied also to a view like C. I. Lewis's described above. We may ask why he locates prescriptiveness in the ultimate decisiveness of some type of law. Is it introspectively evident? Or is this an invariant outcome of phenomenological inspection? Or is it because morality arises in the context of a critique and a critique has no meaning without reference to principles, so that ultimately what he is doing is analyzing usage or appealing to a pragmatic justification? In any case, it is not ontological or epistemological certification.

Introspection. We might, of course, slip almost unnoticed into introspection, and say as Hall does in rejecting Moore's view that good is a unique simple quality, ". . . it would seem not. Speaking for myself, I do not so find it in my experience. Nor, apparently, do others, to go by what they say." [21] But can we so lightly sweep aside what some find just because others do not so find it? Experience may be fashioned within a wider range of differences than we ordinarily think, and why must we assume that it is a quality that is invariably observable? In any case, how can we rely on personal introspection for a general conclusion? That I find myself thinking in English proves nothing about the people of other countries. Cultural, subcultural, and temperamental differences may enter into sensitivity as well.

Phenomenal inspection. The appeal to the results of phenomenal inspection seems to suggest a greater objectivity, since it eschews genetic-psychological considerations and concentrates directly on the analysis of the field of awareness. It is well to aim at discovering the generic characteristics of all moral experience, relying on the central fact that men do make moral judgments.[22] But this does not guarantee the unity sought. It is at least theoretically possible that the prescriptiveness dealt with may be one only by family resemblance, in which *A* resembles *B* in one respect and *B* resembles *C* in another, and we see them as all one family because they are genetically related. The Gestalt approach seems to assume too readily the presence of uniform qualities in all fields, and similarly, not to have faced fully the

21 Everett Hall, *op. cit.*, p. 5.
22 Maurice Mandelbaum, *op. cit.*, pp. 36, 42.

problem of changes in the phenomenal field. The differences are sometimes dismissed as referring to content, not structure. But they arise even in the reports of sensitive inquirers within questions of structure. For example, on the familiar issue of prima facie obligations, Mandelbaum speaks as if all but the one that is accepted drop out in the discernment of what is fitting in the particular situation presented in the field.[23] This amounts to saying that the conflicting rules in a situation of moral decision appear as candidates *prior* to the decision, but that in the awareness of the field those that do not prevail simply have retired. The phenomenal field thus described by Mandelbaum has what I should term a *particularistic decisive* structure. It is particularistic because it is determined by the concrete detail of the situation and it is decisive because there is in the field no residual "tug" as it were, of the possibilities rejected, no remains of their conflict. Compare with this Hartmann's conception of unavoidable guilt, in which, for example, the stain of a lie told for a moral purpose hangs on,[24] in which therefore the element of moral conflict remains as the sense of unavoidable violation of value. Of course, this may be describing an earlier stage in the decision process, but since Hartmann insists that unavoidable guilt can only be borne and not disposed of, it is more likely that we have here an alternative structuring of the moral field. (It might, genetically, rest on temperamental differences or personality differences.) And, so far as I can see, the phenomenological approach has provided no criteria for deciding which of two such alternatives is correct.

Investigation of usage. The same problem arises if we appeal to the analysis of usage and then try to reject usage that differs from the one we favor as somehow incorrect. Because such procedures are common, it is worth looking even if only briefly at a particular case. Take, for example, Hare's insistence on the primacy of evaluative (practical, commending) meaning of ethical terms as against descriptive meaning. There is clear sailing as long as the usage examined is in accordance with the theory. But the other side begins to show up in a number of contexts. Because decisions cannot be taught but principles can, some parents "turn

[23] *Ibid.*, p. 74.

[24] N. Hartmann, *Ethics*, II, 281-85.

their children into good intuitionists, able to cling to the rails, but bad at steering around corners." [25] Yet if one is seeing how the terms are used, those children certainly take them in a descriptive sense. Again, although the evaluative meaning of 'good' is regarded as primary, there is some suggestion that the descriptive meaning is more prominent when standards are stable than when they are being created or changed.[26] Then later we are told that "the evaluative meaning might get lost, or at least wear thin." [27] But this is seen as stability hardening into ossification. In short, if we use the evaluative meaning of ethical terms as primary, we are sensible people. If we use the descriptive as primary, we have been misdirected by our parents or we are becoming ossified! Actually, Hare states his justification explicitly and it has little to do with usage. He gives two reasons.[28] One is that "we have knowledge of the evaluative meaning of 'good' from our earliest years, but we are constantly learning to use it in new descriptive meanings, as the classes of objects whose virtues we learn to distinguish grow more numerous." The second reason is "that we can use the evaluative force of the word in order to *change* the descriptive meaning for any class of objects." These reasons appear to be pragmatic or purposive. The first is a decision to define 'good' by some element that is constant throughout, rather than, say, by a succession of changing indices suitable to succeeding conditions. The second expresses the fear, no doubt warranted, of hardening or conservatism in evaluations. But that these objectives require the particular policies in the use of 'good' is not altogether clear. Elements of descriptive content may be constant from our earliest years (e.g., the pleasure element), and it may be better policy to assign primacy to some important content element that changes in a continuous way rather than to what is constant. Whether we can use the evaluative force of the word to change its descriptive meaning may depend on what sort of commending people are used to, and how much resistance it has set up! Our aim here is not to examine Hare's position in detail, but simply to point out that it has several presuppositions about what men are like and how they are influenced, and about what is desirable policy in the

25 R. M. Hare, *op. cit.*, p. 75.
27 *Ibid.*, p. 147.
26 *Ibid.*, pp. 116-26.
28 *Ibid.*, pp. 118-19.

use of terms, and that it is much clearer to render such criteria of preference explicit than to rest the case on usage or on some special concept of use.

These remarks apply also, of course, to decision about the correctness of the emotive theory's analysis. For here, too, we are faced with a variety of usage. Since language does have emotive functions, we can find some contexts in which, and some people for whom, the emotive aspect predominates to such an extent that in a purely descriptive analysis of usage it will have to be given parity or even predominance in the account of meaning. But in other contexts or in other people's usage, the role of the emotive may be so reduced as to justify speaking only of emotive accompaniments, not emotive meaning.

Appeal to empirical invariants. To what extent can an appeal to empirical invariants help determine the correct location of prescriptiveness? The discovery of empirical invariants is, of course, very important, but whether it helps seems to depend on the kind discovered. For example, suppose it were found that a necessary condition for a person feeling morally bound is that he has a certain chemical in the bloodstream. This would be very important—since it might open the way to intensifying or dulling the moral sense—but it would not establish that prescriptiveness lies in the bloodstream. Such hypothetical illustrations are often used to establish the irrelevance of empirical invariants to ethical inquiry. But this does not follow. Other types of invariants might prove relevant. For example, if MacBeath or Dewey are presenting an accurate picture of what we may call functional invariants [29] (omitting here consideration of the tremendous scope of evidence required), then they have shown the range of instrumental requiredness. But it is quite possible at the same time that this type of prescriptiveness does not coincide with what goes on in consciousness or is found in the phenomenological field. MacBeath thinks it does because he believes primitive peoples sense the social contribution of their moral rules; whereas Mandelbaum argues that the teleological relation is found in reflection on justification and does not constitute the content of requiredness in the phenomenological field. Letting go the question

[29] As briefly outlined above in considering the means-end location for prescriptiveness.

whether one is right or both are right but referring to differently structured fields, we must at least recognize that there are many functional relations between consciousness and underlying process, that may not be recognized in the experience. For example, how many people really feel pain as a warning signal rather than as simply an evil to be gotten rid of? Even if man, as it is often said, does turn nature's means into ends in consciousness, it is not clear that once he discovers this fact he ought, as Dewey often seems to, turn them back again into means. In any case, whatever be the alternative possibilities, no one follows automatically, and without reference to one or another set of purposes. It follows that even the discovery of important empirical invariants of the functional type does not *by itself* settle the question of the location of prescriptiveness. But it does contribute in posing the question more fully and in showing what is possible and what is unavoidable.

Empirical invariants of a special order are involved in Rice's attempt, noted previously, to work out a synthesis of the practicalist and cognitivist positions. Ultimately, he is relying on the lessons of experience about the use of ethical terms in the valuational act. It is worth exploring this briefly because it shows how close is the dependence of analyses of the way ethical language is employed upon primarily psychological assumptions. Thus, in speaking of the trigger-function of 'ought,' Rice is careful to point out that the gun may not go off just because the trigger is pulled, since some inhibiting factors may also be present. But he does treat 'ought' as expressive of choice having taken place. Yet questions might be raised about this. Does it happen in every use of 'ought' or only in its use by the normal man or the good man? May it not be that in their opposites, when they judge that something ought to be done, no choice has taken place but only a certain movement which is hindered and may not issue in choice, not to speak of subsequent action? Perhaps the matrix meaning of the 'ought' is really more minimal if it is to be universally applicable; it may consist only in determining that certain stores of energy are to be closed off for any other alternative than the specified act. (In the bad man these stores of energy may be very low.)

Such problems indicate that the location of prescriptiveness in the way ethical terms function in the valuational act or situation has to rest on a detailed psychology of valuation, not merely on its general contours. Rice does seem occasionally to recognize this ultimately secondary role of language in the investigation. For example, he asks in the context of goodness, "How does the normative term acquire its prescriptiveness except by transference from the tendency of the object to arouse conation?" [30] But if this is so, then perhaps more can be learned about the location of prescriptiveness in studying conation than in studying its linguistic shadow.

Pragmatic and purposive bases. In the various theories considered, there has been little appeal to the desirability of one location as compared with another. But the reference to pragmatic criteria of decision is implicit in some of the modes of determining correctness. Lewis regards the rule of prudence as categorical because it is unavoidable for a human being. One analysis of usage is sometimes preferred to another because it is more clarifying, makes more distinctions that are useful, and so on. Dewey's formulation seems to aim at advancing personal growth, liberation of impulse, and heightened consciousness, as well as to be revealing functional connections. The practicalist analysis of ethical terms seems to assume we should go on using them in the way and for the purposes we have been doing.

Stevenson's theory of persuasive definitions recognizes this purposive function of theoretical elements. In this respect, it is in the same tradition as Nietzsche's looking at a man's ethics to learn what the man was like, or Marx analyzing an ethical theory to see what class position it reflected.[31] But in the construction of his own models at the outset, he believes himself to be carrying on a neutral analysis which, we are told at a subsequent point, is limited to ". . . the evaluative considerations that directly concern and guide the process of inquiry itself." [32] In fact, I have always had the feeling that the initial models were subject to analysis as persuasive in precisely the same sense in

[30] Philip B. Rice, *op. cit.*, p. 211.

[31] For a detailed attempt to see how valuational elements may be carried in even abstract logical conceptions in ethics, see above, pp. 41ff.

[32] Charles L. Stevenson, *Ethics and Language* (New Haven, 1944), p. 161. Cf. pp. 1, 222.

which he later analyzes others' definitions as persuasive. For anyone casting his ethical judgments in terms of these models—that is, the fully self-conscious faithful emotivist—would unavoidably be fashioning his inner relations and his relations to others in a very particular way. This component, more directly valuational than simply pragmatic, is underscored in Margaret Mac-Donald's assessment when she says: "The emotive theory dissolves the hardness of moral judgments into the softness of a romantic preoccupation with a personal gospel and a private missionary society. It is a lucky accident that our gospels sometimes agree and that intercommunion occurs between the one-man sects. This seems an exaggerated moral protestantism." [33]

It would seem, then, that there can be no advance limitation of the kind of pragmatic and purposive criteria that can enter into the judgment of a correct location of prescriptiveness. But in each context they should be rendered as explicit as possible.

AN ALTERNATIVE HYPOTHESIS

Restructuring the problem. In the the light of the different criteria for correctness and their analysis, we can no longer ask the simple general question, What is the correct location of prescriptiveness? Instead, we must ask several questions.

We can ask where prescriptiveness is actually located, in given individuals, groups, subcultures, cultures, theories. This is a descriptive matter, involving some degree of analysis as well, and a given answer in a given context is either true or false.

We can also ask where it is desirable to locate the prescriptive element on the assumption that some choice is possible. From this point of inquiry, the various theories previously examined might be construed as invitations to build in prescriptiveness along different lines. The decision of which invitation to accept is then like a decision which of several domiciles to adopt. It is made in terms of explicit or implicit aims or purposes in the light of knowledge of man and his world and the consequence of the various alternatives. How comfortable are the quarters—how well integrated will prescriptiveness be in the general setting of life?

[33] Margaret MacDonald, "Ethics and the Ceremonial Use of Language," in *Philosophical Analysis,* ed. Max Black (Ithaca, N. Y., 1950), p. 220.

Who are the neighbors—will prescriptiveness be tied to the emotions or the rational faculties? Can business be carried on in the premises—will prescriptiveness play an active part in life or be relegated to some side channel? Is there a good view—will prescriptiveness have an over-all view of life or merely look up a blind alley? And so on.

There are, of course, further questions we can ask about either the described locations or the recommended ones. For example, is one more "natural" than another? Such a claim need not be question-begging; it may mean simply that harder cultural effort will have to be exerted to secure one location than to secure another, that some go against the grain and give rise to more frustrations, disturbances, etc. This kind of claim may hold against some—for example, against a pattern of prescriptiveness that involves turning a sparkling child into a passive obedient will-less subject. Or again, some patterns might be seen as fixations on an immature level—for example, one in which prescriptiveness remained a purely external command. Again, there is much in the current demand for the "authentic" or the "genuine" in human relations to suggest that a profounder satisfaction may come from a location of the prescriptive in a binding quality of human relations than in an inner isolated individual will or a transcendent all-embracing authority. Such claims raise serious analytic questions. They involve a fusion of the descriptive and the purposive in a complex pattern. For this reason we shall not take time to go into them here; we shall limit our consideration to the directly descriptive and the directly purposive, which in any case constitute the strands in these more elaborate patterns.

A guiding hypothesis. Underlying such a restructuring of the location problem are two basic assumptions—one concerning the unavoidability of prescriptiveness, the second concerning its possible variable forms.

The first and more obvious assumption, which we shall take for granted, is that every ethical theory embraces prescriptiveness somewhere or other, that it is not a question of noncognitivist theories monopolizing it and cognitivist theories rejecting it. Of course, to make such an assumption is already to embody a number of conclusions about human life, feeling, and society. For a world in which there was no prescriptiveness is not inconceivable. Kant conceived of a holy will which would find no tension in relation to the moral law, and a world of holy wills is not unimaginable. Even the ubiquity of prescriptiveness during one period in human history need not guarantee its perpetuation under all future conditions. Its phenomena might be vestigial or constitute the survival of a temporary scaffolding in the development of the individual. For example, Julian Huxley takes conscience to be an early mechanism operating in a rough all-or-none way, charging what passes through it with the quality of guilt-feeling, until reason grows strong enough to take over.[34] Nevertheless, in spite of conceivable opposites and probable lowly origins, prescriptiveness would seem to be firmly grounded, at least as a minimum, both in the problems and stresses of individual development and in the social necessities for regulation and control. Any theory which left it out would seem on these minimal grounds to be inadequate.

The second assumption, which is here offered as a major guiding hypothesis, is of vast scope and cannot therefore simply be taken for granted. It is the view that *prescriptiveness may be built varyingly both into the ethical theories and into the lives of men to which the theories refer and apply.* This presupposes a sufficient psychological and cultural plasticity in men, but it need not assume an unlimited plasticity nor any particular psychological approach.

An outline of the evidence. The evidence for the general hypothesis comes from many different fields—the comparative study of ethical theories, the lessons and insights of the psychological and social sciences, historical studies of changes in conceptions and categories, whether cultural, evaluative, or theological, comparable issues in the social normative disciplines such as law and education. The following outline does not so much prove or establish the hypothesis as indicate the kinds of materials that incline towards it.

1. The primary diversity of theories which we have examined itself suggests some such hypothesis. For it points to a sensitive diversity in the experience of prescriptiveness. It is hard not to say that there must be some truth in all the theories, for when

[34] T. H. Huxley and Julian Huxley, *Touchstone for Ethics* (New York, 1947), pp. 116-17, 252.

such refined and skilled observers of consciousness and its products tell us what they discover, they cannot be going wholly astray. But this means treating their accounts as primarily descriptive, as if they were informants about patternings of human life and feeling and thought. It therefore means curbing their universal pretensions. For example, if the legalist approach says that some people find imperative quality tied to law or rule, I can say, "Show me the people and I will see if it is so, but it sounds plausible. For anything important enough to constitute a rule would probably be important enough, on genetic or pragmatic grounds, to have grown or to be felt with an element of command attached to it." But if it is asserted that this is the correct universal account, I can say, "It does not fit me. I have never been able to see why 'mustness' must be tied to rule rather than to particular. The question is one of fact or of desirable policy, not of metaphysics." [35] The reader is invited to apply this method of analysis to the remaining theories and see what a variety of types exists within the Western ethical tradition alone.

2. There is considerable psychological ground for expecting diversity. The emotional side of life is not tied down to a limited organic expression. As Zilboorg points out, we are sad all over and gay all over; similarly, for love, hatred, sense of guilt and remorse, esthetic pleasure, egoistic and altruistic propensities, and so on.[36] And where there is localization, it admits of different forms. For example, anxiety and libidinal energy are seen anchored to all sorts of external objects, bodily parts, ideational complexes and symbols, varying experiences. There is no reason why such a phenomenon as an experience of prescriptiveness should be limited to one unique pattern. Ordinary observation yields the same result in simpler terms. For example, there is a clear distinction between the passive way in which prescriptiveness is felt by some to come from authoritative command outside, and the active way in which others feel it as a decision willed from within.

3. One suggestion that emerges from studies of personality and culture is that the way in which prescriptiveness is experi-

[35] For a fuller treatment of this specific question, see *Ethical Judgment*, pp. 41-50.

[36] Gregory Zilboorg, *Mind, Medicine and Man* (New York, 1943), pp. 47-48.

enced and handled is a function of the type of self which has been developed, and this in turn seems to be psychologically and culturally variable. For example, one society may build isolated or separated selves, another may build selves that are almost consolidated. The former will think in terms of moral commitment of the self and see moral knowledge as coming from a component of the self, the latter as coming through teaching from the store of public knowledge.[37] (One is tempted to speculate that the contrast of an emotivist and cognitivist outlook may itself have temperamental or subcultural components.) Or again, there may be a change in a society over a long period of time, as in David Riesman's picture of the shift from the inner-directed to the other-directed, in his *The Lonely Crowd*.

4. Studies in the history of culture, ethics, theology, all combine to suggest that there are categorial changes in the centers or foci of prescriptiveness. Examples can be found in many different fields. The ancient stress on a *summum bonum* gave way to a subsequent stress on natural law, and still later to an individualistically oriented sense of obligation as emanating from the inner will. The sense of original sin can be contrasted with the modern optimistic humanist aspiration towards harmonious human happiness. On a smaller scale, we may compare the Aristotelian insistence that activity (*energeia*), not character, is the heart of the good (cf. his insistence in the *Poetics* that consequently plot and not character is primary in a tragedy), with the Stoic assertion of the primacy of virtue irrespective of what it issues in. On a larger scale, there is the marked diversity in the conception of God-man relations, with the prescriptive element taking on a different quality depending on the type of relation envisaged— for example, God's will as from without, demanding acceptance, or as found deep within when a man searches for his fundamental being, or in contrast with both, a stress on the fact of mutuality or of immediate presence.

[37] Such contrasts are offered by Wayne W. Unterreiner in his extremely interesting "Self and Society: Orientations in Two Cultural Value Systems" (Ph.D. dissertation, Harvard, 1952), which compares the value orientations of a Texan-American and Pueblo community. Cf. Evon Z. Vogt, *Modern Homesteaders* (Cambridge, Mass., 1955). For a basic study of the self in relation to culture, see A. Irving Hallowell, "The Self and Its Behavioral Environment," in his *Culture and Experience* (Philadelphia, 1955).

5. Among the social normative disciplines, law stands out as the almost natural parallel to ethics in structural problems. And there has been some attempt to use its lessons to support one type of theory of prescriptiveness—for example, a practicalist one, in H. L. A. Hart's essay, "The Ascription of Responsibility and Rights." [38] But if we look to the wider historical field of theories of the nature of law, we find exactly the same diversity as in ethical theory. The authoritative-prescriptive element is sought in legal principles, in ethics and natural law, in the will of the legislator, in the actual power of enforcement, in the social recognition of the legal system and its social functions, and so on. Similarly, we may look at educational theories and compare those which see education as handing on basic tradition to passive receptive minds with those that think in terms of individual growth and social experience.[39] It becomes clear that ideals of objectives and conceptions of foci of effectiveness raise the same problems and contrasts as concepts of prescriptiveness in ethics. For the center of concentration varies from the objective demand of the subject-matter taught to the awakening aspiration of the individual. At stake here, too, are perhaps less theories than types of character and patterns of human value.

CONCLUDING RECOMMENDATIONS

If the concept of prescriptiveness can be varyingly built into ethical theory, and the phenomenon of prescriptiveness varyingly built into the lives and feelings and perceptions of men, then detailed attention has to be directed to the conditions under which each theory would be acceptable as sound policy in ethics. Since the purpose of the present work is not to advocate a particular location theory, but to restructure the general problem and to focus afresh on the conditions an adequate theory should satisfy, our concluding recommendation concerning procedure in this field of ethical theory will take the obvious major

[38] *Proceedings of the Aristotelian Society,* 1948-49. For a discussion of Hart's argument, as well as the general prescriptive thesis in relation to legal theory, see below, pp. 149-50.

[39] Cf. Theodore Brameld, *Philosophies of Education in Cultural Perspective* (New York, 1955).

illustration of cognitivism vs. practicalism. Quite simply, I want to indicate in bare outline under what conditions cognitivism seems to me to constitute sound theoretical policy, under what conditions practicalism. The conditions themselves may be classified broadly under the headings of methodological, factual, and orientational.

Methodological factors. To be acceptable, a cognitivist approach has to be possible. It presupposes the likelihood of developing a more or less systematic theory in the field of morality. Hence, methodologically it requires the articulation of a fairly clear concept of *moral experience*—whether by reference to a single quality, single feeling, family of qualities or feelings, or even a variety discoverably serving some definite purpose or carrying out a definite role. Secondly, it must provide some meaningful sense for *generalization,* either in terms of the reiteration of the experience or phases of the experience, or else by working out some novel notion of systematic patterning for its field, where 'patterning' is taken in a descriptive sense, not in the sense of imposing or forcing into a mold as a matter of practical will. This involves providing some more or less definite mode of *verification* for the generalizations which will not be simply an act of subscription or commitment.

Since on such a view the ethical judgment would have the status of a cognitive report, it would be especially important to distinguish the judgment from the act of will in making a decision or subscribing to a principle, or from any associated emotions and feelings expressed concomitantly. One would have to insist that even where they are a split second apart, the judgment is separable from the experience, and their interaction in practice or application is a genuine one, involving factors of interpretation, rapidity of internal communication, insight, perhaps some hypothetical elements. Thus application of moral knowledge would be genuinely application, and while it would provide opportunities for testing, as occurs in any applied science, it would not be simply making or constructing or willing alone. It would, indeed, always be possible to raise the question how knowledge of our moral experience is practical in its effect. But one can raise precisely the same question about expressing emotions, or even about acts of will. (It does sometimes happen, after all, that emotions become a substitute for doing, and that acts of will use up so much of a person's energy that he scarcely gets beyond them!) In short, the search would be simply for more intimate connecting mechanisms, both in the actor and the beholder, or the speaker and the listener.[40] And finally, a cognitivist approach need not fear that the status of ethical judgments would be reckoned as psychology rather than morality. For it is possible to see the difference in fields as lying primarily in content, not in the difference between a factual form of judgment and some other form.

The practicalist approach draws its strength in contemporary theory from the fact that these conditions have not been adequately met in cognitivist theories as yet. But in the long run more is required to establish its anticognitivism. It presupposes that these conditions will not and cannot be met, because it offers an alternative conception of the moral phenomena themselves. Their specific character (or a dominating part thereof) is emotive or volitional or practical in such a fashion that no determinate separation of judgment and experience is achievable; or, if achievable, only by rendering the cognitive judgment secondary and irrelevant to moral phenomena themselves; or, if relevant, only in virtue of the further practical functions of the linguistic expressions. Similarly, any adequate conception of generalization will be itself thoroughly permeated by the emotive or volitional or practical, so that no independent sense of its testing will be capable of elaboration. Hence, the methodological need is for some elaboration of a "logic of the will," on a quite different order from the scientific model of the cognitivist.

It follows from the analysis of this work that the alternative methodologies reflect two pictures of man, that these may be examined for degree of accuracy in factual presuppositions and for their orientational effect in human life, in so far as man is sufficiently plastic to be capable of taking either form.

Factual picture. The underlying factual presuppositions concern the goals of men, their constancy, the extent to which they are unavoidable or constitutive of human selves, whether they

40 This problem will be discussed further in connection with the analysis of the nature and scope of description. See below, pp. 174ff.

have parts or aspects that recur with some degree of regularity, so as to yield repeatable elements capable of generalization, whether there are determinate causal bases of all these factors that ensure stability. Further presuppositions concern the relation of knowledge and volition, or knowledge and emotion—whether there are definite connections under which knowledge is practical in its effects by its exhibition of consequences, relations, conditions, qualities of events and experiences, or whether the connections are basically indeterminate. Perhaps the issue may be summed up by reference to the Socratic quest of knowing oneself with its assumption that to know basic strivings is to follow their path. Is there a definite enough "oneself" to know, or is one so constantly being remade (including, of course, remaking oneself) that the very knowing is itself a process or refashioning or deciding? It need not be an all-or-none matter, but the difference of degree that emerges in the answer is itself enough to incline to a cognitivist or practicalist perspective. The area of advisable cognitivism in ethical theory as well as the area of acceptable stability in moral generalization in human life is thus in part a function of the correct picture of the "nature" of the human self.

Orientational factors. Within whatever margin of malleability there may be, what is the orientational effect of a cognitivist or a practicalist outlook, not merely held in theory, but embedded as a way of organizing moral phenomena in life experience? Which brings enhanced rationality, self-understanding and insight, sensitivity, community of purpose? Is either more likely to reflect or encourage a pattern of individualistic willfulness, or constant restlessness, or blind adherence to established self-patterns?

Take two extremes in the criticism of these approaches. The cognitivist will charge that practicalism tends to abandon rationality, that emotivism inclines to substitute ancillary practical techniques of influence by pressure, contagion, or seduction for rational deliberation, or that a commending view of the nature of ethical judgment puts into the shade the critique of the values that are being commended, hence engenders arbitrary willfulness. The practicalist will charge that cognitivism always binds a man to the past, that knowledge is always of what has gone by in active life and decision, that accordingly cognitivism shunts off the ever-present responsibility of present decision; the existentialist will add that the heart of morality is responsibility in the present.

Possibilities of a reckoning. Now it is no doubt possible for cognitivism to build in a safeguard in terms of secondary principles guaranteeing the genuine *testing* of principles in present experience to avoid an undue conservatism, and for practicalism to build in a conception of "good reasons" to avoid willfulness. To this extent, if it is possible for the two approaches to move closer together, the factual presuppositions of such moves must indicate some greater agreement on man's nature and self, and on the desirability of such orientational effects. One possibility is therefore a narrowing of the interval between the two approaches.

Another possibility is that the growth of knowledge of man in the human sciences will force decision on some of the factual propositions, especially concerning the extent of community and stability in aims. My own preference for some type of cognitivist formulation rests to some extent on the belief that the knowledge of man and society is still in the early stages, that the growth of the human sciences will be fruitful in making more stable ethical formulations possible.

Another possibility is that ethics will split up into two fields— *onlooker* ethics and *participant* ethics, with cognitivism constituting the theory of the first, and some form of practicalism the theory of the second. I do not think this is a wise course, because it would separate knowledge too sharply from action. I believe that knowledge has a vast role in individual human consciousness as well as in the "externals" of human life, that knowing is an inherent element in human rapport and not a withdrawal from it, that it is constitutive in human activity and not an isolated reflection, and that the dividing line between rationalist and irrationalist patterns runs deep through the interpretation of ethical categories; also that a participant ethics cannot escape a cognitivist tendency if it attempts to deal with judgment as well as phenomenon or event, since ethical judgment like esthetic judgment requires some 'psychic distance'; also, on historical grounds, I am suspicious of irrationalism in its voluntarist forms and of its obscurantist tendencies in modern times.

But all this constitutes a general hypothesis-configuration, and may be erroneous or oversimplified.

Another possibility is that the various approaches—legalistic, phenomenological, cognitivist, practical, etc.—can be fused into some synthesis which takes the best out of each. To some extent this seems possible, and the juxtaposition of views in the present work may incline in this direction. But I do not think it is wholly possible, because the factual presuppositions of the different views are to some extent in conflict. Here some will prove more nearly correct than others. But it is quite likely that in any case a general theory adequate in the long run will involve major conceptual transformations.

PART TWO

ANALYTIC METHOD

CHAPTER FOUR

THE ANALYTIC STANDPOINT

The problems to which analysis is applied in ethical theory are familiar, and many of them are quite standardized in terms of a number of competing answers. There is the general clarification of the meaning of ethical concepts and of how they are to be defined or used within the operations of the theory and in its application to moral issues. There are problems of the types of ethical assertions to be permitted, the status of axioms and rules, the theory of verification in ethics, questions of ethical reasoning and its nature, issues of decision and the theory of application, of the meaning of 'justification' in ethics, and so on. The study of logical coordinates in Chapter Two indicated the scope of some of these. Analysis inevitably plays a prominent role because ethics, like every other field that is being systematically explored, requires a conceptual apparatus, and a conceptual apparatus has to be clarified, sharpened, and refined, in relation to its use.

While analysis is as old as Socrates, and reflective thinking has been the core of philosophy itself, the nature of the analytic process and the delineation of the analytic standpoint have themselves been controversial questions. Especially in the twentieth century, we have become familiar with different programs of analysis offered as characterizing a distinctive way of doing philosophy, and sometimes presented as the most recent discovery of what philosophy itself is really up to. The general consideration of such programs is not our special concern in this book. It is perhaps sufficient to recall how influential have been Russell's method of logical analysis, G. E. Moore's commonsense mode of analysis, the logical positivist conception of the logical reconstruction of the language of a field, and currently the widely prevalent Oxford mode of use-analysis or ordinary-language analysis. Programs of analysis have had a very special effect in ethical theorizing. Because ethical theory is in such an unsettled state, they have tended to come in with a "new broom" attitude. Much of what has been going on is swept aside, and a new order is established. Often, a wholly new language for analyzing problems takes over, and jobs that have been done in the past have to be redone. Soon the new approach hardens into a functioning dogma, only to be overthrown in the next analytic revolution. There are gains in this process, no doubt, for new vistas open up, and often the novelty of the proceedings attracts the keenest minds. But there are losses too, not only in the break with continuity in the development of the field that jeopardizes results, but in the narrowing of outlook that often accompanies the intense concentration on the new aspects.

The claims for analysis as a distinctive approach with a very special character were clearly presented in Charles L. Stevenson's *Ethics and Language,* which exercised considerable influence in the development of ethical theory in the middle of the century. Analysis is described as a "narrow, specialized undertaking, requiring only close distinctions, careful attention to logic, and a sensitivity to the ways of language." [1] "The purpose of an analytical or methodological study, whether of science or of ethics, is always indirect. It hopes to send others to their tasks with clearer heads and less wasteful habits of investigation. This necessitates a continual scrutiny of what these others are doing, or else analysis of meaning and methods will proceed in a vacuum, but it does not require the analyst, as such, to participate in the inquiry that he analyzes. In ethics any direct participation of this sort might have its dangers. It might deprive the analysis of its detachment and distort a relatively neutral study into a plea for some special code of morals." [2] Yet analysis is not pursued without some values. For like all inquiry it shares "the evaluative considerations that directly concern and guide the process of inquiry itself." [3] Its neutrality lies in limiting itself to these values.

That analysis has primarily a linguistic-exploratory character, and is not an empirical type of inquiry, that it has its own inherent criteria of correctness, are views often stated in different ways. That it has a relative value-neutrality is sometimes nowa-

[1] Charles L. Stevenson, *Ethics and Language* (New Haven, 1944), p. 222.
[2] *Ibid.,* p. 1.   [3] *Ibid.,* p. 161.

days expressed by describing its aim as simply to clear up puzzlement. Perhaps most striking in recent presentations is the claim that in its newest forms analysis is dependent on no assumptions about the nature of the world; older forms of analysis are rejected, in Strawson's phrase, as "limited and theory-ridden." [4]

Our comparative study in Chapter Two implies a different picture. If there are always to be found in any ethical inquiry, logical, scientific, historical, and valuational coordinates, and any existent or proposed conceptual apparatus may be probed for all these aspects, then it is hardly likely that there will be any self-contained, neutral, distinctive, theoretically presuppositionless mode of analysis. The form of results that it prescribes and the criteria of correctness of an analysis will embody, directly or indirectly, some factual assumptions or theoretical assumptions, and will express purposes of a more general or a more specific type. Analysis as an enterprise is simply reflective thinking about a given material. Part of it consists in proposing more refined conceptual distinctions—usually elaborated from existent distinctions in other contexts or bodies of knowledge—which may serve some purpose in connection with the given materials. Part of it consists in bringing to bear factual knowledge to aid selection from among proposed constructions. And part of it consists in providing channels through which purposes may run if men—the analyst or other men—have them and put them into effect. On this whole approach, the analysis that one will offer at any time of analysis itself will reflect some theory of man and the nature of his thinking, the material of the specific field being investigated, as well as the current state of the growth of logic and its instruments.

In the specific studies that constitute the next two chapters, the contrast between these two basically different trends in understanding the nature and tasks of analysis will become clear from the different procedures and directions of ethical inquiry that they prompt. But I think something can be done in a general way by use of comparative method to make clear the problems in

[4] P. F. Strawson, "Construction and Analysis," in A. J. Ayer, *et al.*, *The Revolution in Philosophy* (London, 1956), p. 104. Cf. J. O. Urmson, *Philosophical Analysis, Its Development between the Two World Wars* (Oxford, 1956), pp. 165-66.

analyzing analysis itself. The effect of comparative lining-up is, as usual, to force attention on the implicit answers in a given image of analysis to questions which it may have underplayed or even wholly ignored. The underlying hypothesis is that many images of analysis are partial and incomplete, that by looking within them or into the way they are used, one can find the outlines of what is understressed or repressed. What we shall do, thus, is to construct a kind of profile-scheme embodying the different features that we may look for in a given image of analysis. Of course, we must not do this in such a way as to beg the question. If we ask of a given account of analysis that rejects empirical or theoretical assumptions, "Where are your empirical or theoretical assumptions?" as if we were asking of a drawing of a face, "Where are the ears?" we have stacked the cards. Our procedure is therefore very important. We have to gather our "features" from points that have on the whole been found in other images. And we have to introduce them as questions, not as demands, and pay special attention to the arguments of those who deem them unnecessary. However, we must not commit the opposite error of ruling out any images that might be dismissed offhand by special views as "obviously not analysis." Not merely Socrates' dialectical method—the prototype of analysis, devoted attention to which, in the western philosophical tradition, has produced extremely valuable insights—but also Aristotle's analytic procedures and even what Aquinas is up to when he appeals to authority to solve a carefully constructed problem, may be of help as data for the analysis of analysis, alongside of Russell and Moore, Wittgenstein, and current analysts.

WHAT IS THE CONTEXT THAT PROVOKES ANALYSIS?

This question may be dismissed by some simply with the statement that there must be something to analyze. But we cannot ignore the possibility that something may be learned about analysis by comparative survey of situations that especially precipitate it. There may be conflicts of belief with belief, of authority with authority, of belief with experience, of usage with usage. Or there may simply be doubt about the meaning of a term, a dissatisfaction with the way in which it is to be applied, an inability to explain something you know, a feeling that you must be making assumptions which have not been uncovered.

In the Socratic dialogues, the initial context is often a practical one: How should a man have lived to have peace of mind in old age? Can Protagoras teach virtue as he claims to? Does piety demand that Euthyphro prosecute his father for killing a slave? Aristotle relies on the general assumption that men desire to know. And, of course, with the growth of the philosophical tradition, there are the perennial philosophical problems that serve as starting points for repeated analysis. Even here, however, some see the context as an active desire to achieve systematic theory, others simply as the existence of perplexity and puzzlement.

Context questions may be simply questions of causal stimuli for analytic processes, but they may also provide implicit criteria of what would constitute a completed analysis or a satisfactory analysis. It is also possible that concentration on different types of contexts accounts for some of the different pictures of analysis.

HOW IS THE INITIAL QUESTION FORMULATED?

This covers such matters as the actual linguistic form of the question that launches analysis, or whether there is a standard form into which other preliminary questions are cast, and whether there are implicit in the early procedure any limitations on the type of answers permitted.

Socrates usually asks a question of the form "What is X?" (What is justice, temperance, knowledge, rhetoric, etc.?) Occasionally, there is a question such as "Can virtue be taught?" But this soon turns into a partial question of the usual type: It becomes "Is virtue knowledge?" and it is clear that if it is, then it is teachable; if not, then not. It is thus asking for a central property of virtue, not for a complete definition of the term.

In modern times, perhaps the most common formulation has been "What do you mean by X?" In recent analytic philosophy, as Urmson points out,[5] the slogan has become, "Don't ask for the meaning, ask for the use."

It is clear that many questions that appear to be about factual

5 Urmson, *op. cit.*, p. 179.

issues may be precipitating analytic rather than factual inquiries. When Aquinas, for example, asks whether angels are capable of feeling certain desires, he is, in effect, attempting to clarify the notion of an angel. (He is not so much deducing the properties from an assumed initial account, as trying to see which initial account is preferable.) Similarly, when in the wake of Newton's theory a question is raised whether there can be a physical point moving in absolute space if it is the only physical point in the universe, this is, in effect, asking for an analysis of 'absolute space' and 'motion.'

The early parts of the Socratic dialogues often give a clear illustration of the way in which there are implicit limitations upon the type of answer to be permitted. Socrates frequently receives a first reply which gives instances rather than general properties: he asks what is beauty and is told that a beautiful woman is a beauty. He patiently explains that he wants a general account or a set of properties, usually by appealing to the fact that there are other instances of the same concept, so that the concept cannot be identified with one exemplification. One wonders what Socrates would have said to someone offering the total set of instances as the extensional meaning of the term! In any case, it is clear that he seeks a general or universal form of answer. Even more, on occasion he rules out specific types of general answers—what we may call "consequential" types—in favor of "essential"types. When Euthyphro defines 'piety' as what is pleasing to the gods, Socrates wants to know the nature of what engenders divine pleasure, not merely the consequent feeling. Suppose Euthyphro had been existentially-minded rather than rationally arrogant, and denied that there was an intelligible inner order to Zeus's pleasure-responses; the only definition for 'piety' might then be simply what proved in experience to be pleasing to Zeus.

This brief supposition shows that quite different initial limitations from those demanded by Socrates may be found in different programs of analysis. To limit answers to the consequential type would be to follow the program of analysis implicit in the empiricist-pragmatic theory of meaning, according to which meaning is to be found in the particular experiences pointed to by the term being analyzed. This varies from empiricist emphasis on looking for sensory consequences to the pragmatic emphasis on experience in a broader sense.[6]

In Bertrand Russell's type of analysis, the limiting injunction for desirable types of answers is, "Wherever possible, logical constructions are to be substituted for inferred entities." [7] Taken with other assumptions, it produces a direction in analysis quite the opposite of the Platonic, one leading ideally to terminating atomic facts.

The different initial limitations on types of answers permitted may be regarded as providing, sometimes implicitly, *directions* which the analysis is to pursue. These suggest, but need not wholly determine, the outcome. For example, moving upward in generality tends to culminate in one principle, but could be pluralistic, or even endless. A movement to particulars may terminate in logically proper names, but it could go on indefinitely to relative simples.

HOW IS A PROPOSED ANSWER DEALT WITH?

On the face of it, this seems merely a question of technique. Does the analyst greet a proposed answer with the explosion, "Preposterous!" plus a bang on the table? The interlocutor may be prodded with the question, "Oh! Do you really think so?" or "Isn't it rather logically odd?" Or he may be asked about some fresh term in his proposed answer, "And what do you mean by that?" which would postpone the crisis. Such apparent questions of technique may, however, be of fundamental importance in determining the quality of the process. Socrates in particular does not deny the answer that is given to him; he helps the interlocutor to explore it.[8] It is crucial to his method that the decision

6 For a good illustration in a special field, see Justice Oliver Wendell Holmes' view that the analysis of a legal concept consists in washing it with "cynical acid" to remove its moralistic reference and concentrate on the operations of the law, and in seeing it from the "bad man's" point of view in terms of the losses or pains he anticipates ("The Path of the Law," in his *Collected Legal Papers*, New York, 1920).

7 "The Relation of Sense-Data to Physics," in *Mysticism and Logic* (New York, 1929), p. 155. At that point, Russell called this "the supreme maxim in scientific philosophizing."

8 The implications of such Socratic technique are carefully examined in

at each turning point be made by the other person, not by himself.

What every mode of analysis obviously has to provide is some way of rejecting a proposed answer. And a great deal can be discovered about the theory of analysis by paying close attention to its procedure at this point. In addition, in any analysis that takes the form of a dialogue there is a kind of pivotal tension built up as each turning point is approached. The skill of the analyst is seen in the way in which he puts his finger on precisely that material which will be recognized by the other party as being in conflict with the proposed answer. Socrates often starts with something that appears remote and is readily accepted, but soon it has implications that bring it into direct conflict with the answer that has been given. Contemporary analysts, from G. E. Moore to Gilbert Ryle or John Austin, have shown an almost uncanny skill at raising some point of usage which will play havoc with an answer that has already begun to settle down with smug finality.

The pivotal tension that forces a turning point is the dramatic focus of many an analytic method. In Socrates' case, it rests on the agreement that a contradiction is not to be allowed. There has to be motion one way or the other, or else some ambiguity will be discovered in one of the paths which led up to the impasse, and the contradiction avoided for the present by making a fresh distinction. F. M. Cornford points out that in many cases where Plato seems to be using an ambiguous term (as in some of the most difficult passages of the *Parmenides*) we must not assume that he is unaware of the problem; rather, he may be moving toward revealing the ambiguity precisely by showing that if the term is unanalyzed we land in contradiction.[9]

The dramatic character of the turning point often, however, throws into the shade extremely important questions concerning the type of data leading up to the climax, and the exact way in which decision is made. These are precisely the questions of the place of factual materials and of stipulations in analysis.

Leonard Nelson's essay, "Socratic Method," in his *Socratic Method and Critical Philosophy* (New Haven, 1949).

[9] F. M. Cornford, *Plato and Parmenides* (New York, 1957), pp. 111-13.

WHAT KINDS OF DATA ARE USED TO LEAD UP TO
THE TURNING POINT?

When the turning point comes an answer is rejected. (The answer to be accepted, if any, comes at the very end.) In witnessing the rejection, we become aware of the fact that forces of some type have been marshalled—either by open mobilization or in some disguised way. What kinds of data are these that an answer breaks upon them? What is it that you must not contradict? Is it some direct beholding, or intuition, as Moore sometimes seems to say, in effect, that if you can't see it, that's that; there is nothing more to be said about it? Or is it some set of authoritative usages? Is there a body of agreed-on phenomena—what everybody knows? Or is the stopping point some authoritative volume, such as the Bible and the church authorities in Aquinas, or the unabridged Oxford English Dictionary in some contemporary analysis? Or is the interlocutor or the skeptic directed not to his own usage or other people's, but told to inspect his own consciousness?

The study of the data that enter into a specific mode of analysis ought to establish how far there is reliance on factual assumptions. If there is, the study of the way the assumptions enter should show whether they are disguised or not.

In the case of Socratic method, Gregory Vlastos has shown clearly [10] how inductive processes enter to provide premises in the argument. Vlastos cites the inference from the greater-than-ordinary confidence that some specialists have (skilled divers or cavalrymen) to the general proposition that the wise are confident, and asks how Socrates knows that these odd cases are fair samples of a homogeneous class, even apart from assumptions about the psychology of these samples! Leonard Nelson takes the talk of weavers and blacksmiths by Socrates to be a deliberate attempt to block every effort to go straight to metaphysical problems and to be saying in effect that we must first learn the observed facts of everyday life.[11] The outcome would appear to

[10] In his Introduction to his edition of *Plato's Protagoras*, tr. Jowett, rev. Ostwald (New York, 1956), pp. xxxvi ff.
[11] Leonard Nelson, *op. cit.*, p. 15.

be the same in any case: without factual knowledge of some sort there would be no turning point in the analytic process. Vlastos, however, very correctly underscores the constitutive role of the Socratic claim of ignorance.[12] Socrates is not pitting dogmatic knowledge or incorrigible data against the proposed answer. The contradiction is engendered by holding the two propositions together, not by being sure that one is true. In this sense, the Socratic method is freer from reliance on *specific* facts than many other methods. But this does not mean that it dispenses with reference to facts; wherever a definite result has been reached there have been determinations of fact.

By contrast, Aristotle's analytic method, aiming as it does to get definite answers, is constantly enmeshing factual data in one form or another. At the beginning of his inquiry he gathers the *endoxa,* the current opinions on the matter held by common men, poets, and philosophical predecessors, including admitted fact and ordinary knowledge. He criticizes them in terms of a set of shortcomings. Some of these involve direct appeal to matter-of-fact beliefs, some to the fact that previous analyses do not cover the field comprehensively enough, some to the fact that usage of a term is different or wider or narrower than some proposed account allows. The outcome is supposed to be a set of concepts that fits the sound elements in all the *endoxa,* plus the further material that Aristotle has gathered.

Aquinas provides an interesting illustration because the data against which answers break are often authoritative sources. But this should not obscure the fact that he is carrying out a refined method of analysis. He lines up different views so as to exhibit an initial opposition on a particular point, then makes careful distinctions in the meaning of terms or in contexts of use and application, so as to see how far a decisive choice has to be made. A full exploration of his method cannot rest content with the fact that he appeals to authorities, but must see precisely what techniques he has for selection, for widening or narrowing the scope of a particular authoritative passage.

If Aquinas puts the appeal to authority in full view, and his selective apparatus in the background, and if Socrates has to be

12 Gregory Vlastos, *op. cit.,* pp. xxxi, xlv f.

probed deeply for underlying inductive processes, it may be that contemporary conceptions of linguistic analysis are similarly holding their authoritative decision-processes and their inductive processes deeply under cover.

Take, as an illustration, Nowell-Smith's use of the term 'logically odd' in bringing an analysis to the turning point. What factual assumptions are involved? We are told that "a question is 'logically odd' if there appears to be no further room for it in its context because it has already been answered." [13] Thus, to ask a man who says that he is having a nice smoke whether he is enjoying it is logically odd. Associated with this is the concept of 'contextual implication,' explained as follows: "a statement *p* contextually implies a statement *q* if anyone who knew the normal conventions of the language would be entitled to infer *q* from *p* *in the context in which they occur.*" [14] For example, if a man in ordinary life says, "It is raining," a hearer is entitled to infer that he believes it is raining. We shall see later that this definition is used to insist that certain kinds of information are not the content of ethical statements but only contextually implied by them. But in any case, it is clear that the proof that an assertion is logically odd would require evidence about the normal conventions of the language. And some of this evidence would be inductive evidence, or involve inductive evidence. Moreover, the effectiveness of this technique of achieving a turning point in the analysis would lie in the willingness of the interlocutor to abide by ordinary usage as against any feeling that it is inadequate or confusing. This last point concerns the act of decision, which we shall consider in the next section; however, the way in which the factual element enters is something we must still pursue. For, on the one hand, the analysts are inclined to deny with considerable plausibility that theirs is merely empirical study of usage, but, on the other hand, it would be strange

[13] P. H. Nowell-Smith, *Ethics* (Baltimore, 1954), p. 83. Statements are also regarded as logically odd. For example, we are told (pp. 177-78) that it is not logically odd to say, "This is the better wine, but I prefer that"; whereas it is logically odd to say, "This is the (morally) better course; but I shall do that."

[14] *Ibid.*, p. 80.

if the only kind of empirical assumptions involved concerned how words are used.

The claim that analysis is somehow a distinctively different process, *sui generis,* is commonly found. Gilbert Ryle, for example, carefully distinguishes 'usage' from 'use.' [15] To examine the usage of a term is to carry out a statistical anthropological or sociological survey, offering hypotheses for empirical testing. Clearly, analysis is not doing just that, even though it may begin by collecting some specimens of usage. It is showing the use, and in some sense determining the correct use. Similarly, R. M. Hare compares analysis to the attempt of people who know how to do a certain dance to formulate the steps of the dance. As they go through the motions and record them, they are not describing themselves in precisely the same sense in which an anthropologist would record a tribal dance.[16] For he would have no way of deciding who was right in case of a difference and would be limited to empirical description.

Let us see how departures from purely empirical description take place in analysis by working out a simple and partly hypothetical example. Suppose we are observing a community which puts to death anyone who has killed anybody. As analysts, we ask, "What do they mean by 'killing,' and what methods do they use to determine who 'killed' a given person?" To answer this we gather reports of their behavior in a variety of such situations. Presumably we must filter everything through reports, for if we observe and report we are scientists, not analysts. We would, in fact, feel more at home if we had a member of the group to talk to; it would then have more the appearance of dialectic and less that of a scientist offering a hypothesis to fit the facts of usage. Suppose we recognize, in either fashion, that these people mean by '*A* killed *B*' the following:

   (1) *A* deliberately wielded some instrument in such a way that after contact with *B*, *B* died; or

   (2) *A* had any physical contact with *B* after which *B* died; or

---

[15] "Ordinary Language," *The Philosophical Review,* LXII (1953), 167-86. Ryle points out that there can be no 'misusage' as there can be 'misuse.'

[16] "Are Discoveries About the Uses of Words Empirical?" in a symposium on "The Nature of Analysis," *The Journal of Philosophy,* LIV (1957), 744.

(3) *A* uttered certain ritual spells and *B* died before the third setting of the sun thereafter.[17]

If we limited our analysis simply to this account, it might seem to be purely descriptive. But it is possible that certain elements of interpretation and suggestion have already begun to enter. For example, if there is a tendency to interpret (2) as accidental killing as against the deliberate wielding of (1), it may be introducing a category more refined than the people concerned usually employ. Such categories may sometimes come from other usage of the people involved; they need not thus be entirely fashioned and imported from without. For example, the distinction between intended and unintended action may be made by the people in other contexts—e.g., between walking and stumbling— and be transferred now by the analyst. Even then, his work is creative from the point of view of the people, since there is no logical or moral mandate that a given distinction appear in two fields rather than one.

Suppose that in our analytic exploration with these people the distinction between intentional and accidental killing emerged as a product in our analysis. We might thus be carrying them over the path that mankind has long trod. At the very least, we are thus in effect showing them by comparison with other modes of classification that have been used elsewhere (or might be used elsewhere) how their own scheme (of lumping together 1, 2, and 3) might be regarded as putting together disparate elements and—in a neutral sense, of course—"confusing" them. An element

[17] Lest our example seem too remote and artificial, please consider whether *A* has killed *B* in the following:

A pulls away a life-belt from *B* in the water to support himself, and *B* drowns.

A gets to the life-belt that is floating in the water a moment before *B*, and swims off with it; *B* drowns.

A escapes from a threatening flood with the only available boat, on which *B* relied while he was helping others; *B* drowns.

A passes on germs to *B* unknowingly, and *B* dies of the disease.

A advocates a war successfully and *B* is the first one killed.

No doubt the reader can add examples indefinitely. Of course, he may prefer to carry out an analysis in which the question would no longer be whether *A* killed *B* but whether *A* is *responsible for* the death of *B*. How such a shift would be justified, and at what point, is a complicated further problem.

of suggestion has begun to enter. Simply to present an analytic scheme making a shift possible keeps it to a minimum. To urge the adoption of the revised scheme on grounds that it would clear up "ambiguities" or remove "paradoxes" (making sure these are *their* perplexities and not ours in the light of other usage in kindred or overlapping domains on our part) would be a stronger form, since it advocates the removal by them of certain states of mind which we assume they find unpleasant. To urge adoption on grounds of greater simplicity, effectiveness of application, etc., is a still stronger value-embodying suggestion. A more explicit and particular value-embodying suggestion would be to present a revised scheme as involving a greater humanitarianism or an ethics in which punishment is oriented to the degree of future danger anticipated, and so forth. The most extreme type of suggestion would be to urge the replacement of an old conception by a new one.

Suppose we criticized the third point which our descriptive analysis revealed. If we said that the use of spells was "not really killing," it would be suggestive in proposing the contraction of the concept analyzed. Or we might make a distinction between using spells which the other person knew of or suspected, so that we could regard him as killed by fear, and the cases in which as we would say "there was no possible relation." If so, we are questioning the people's implicit theory of causality, in which case the issue is a factual one or again, suggesting a revision of their concept of causality.

In actual analysis, the descriptive and suggestive elements may be difficult to distinguish. This is largely because the boundaries of the initial material that is being described are not always definite, so that a tentative description of usage at one stage may tend, by narrowing the field, to entrench the proposed description. After all, it is agreed that not all usage is clear-cut, determinate, and consistent. However, the interplay of the descriptive and suggestive aspects can be tracked down by keeping a close watch on the successive steps that take place.

The working out of our example seems to indicate that to describe usage will give you some data for the analytic process, but that such data need not necessarily *determine* your result. Note, however, two qualifications that are required. The further element *may* come from some goal that the analyst has in mind, so that he is, for example, making his decision among conflicting usages in terms of that purpose. And the fact that usage-description does not determine his result does not mean that a great part of his data may not be empirical. Clearly, the empirical assumptions that emerge in the process may be peculiar or appropriate to the specific subject matter investigated, and his contribution may be in discovering them. In our example, it looked as if where the analyst departed from pure description of usage it was precisely because assumptions about causality in human affairs indicated a need for distinction, or else assumptions about men's reactions to problems and what they would find unpleasant, or assumptions about presumed purposes, all inclined towards revision in the analytic result.

If we limit ourselves to the question of the kinds of data used to lead up to the turning point, and do not trespass, as we have begun to do, on subsequent questions of the process of actual decision or the goals of analysis itself, then a fairly clear answer has emerged from our comparisons. The kinds of data relevant seem in part to depend on how the initial question of analysis has been formulated and what restrictions in the mode of answer sought have been implicitly imposed. (Obviously, if you ask for the 'meaning' of an assertion, you are not asking for an empirical description unless you have previously analyzed the term 'meaning' in such a way as to yield that result.) But in all the different modes of analysis that have been proposed, it is likely that we will find among the influential data some empirical assumptions about the usage of terms, some empirical assumptions about events and processes in the world, as well as empirical assumptions about the purposes of men (in general or in the particular area of subject matter being analyzed) as well as about the aims of analysis itself. Some forms of analysis will, as we have seen, involve more specialized types of assumptions within this broad area—such as intuitive data, authoritative-edict data, or in the case of scientific materials, already systematized factual data. And some forms of analysis will have their own developed techniques for obscuring or pushing into the background data of one or another sort. Here an important part of the analysis of analysis is to dig out what is in the background and how it is kept there.

WHAT KIND OF DECISION-PROCESS TAKES PLACE?

In Socratic method, we have already noted that the actual decision falls to the man who is facing the contradiction: he asserted both sides and he must choose his direction, whether to follow one or else reopen one of the concepts and track down its ambiguity. In ordinary language analysis, alongside of the impact of language habits and factual assumptions there is either the implicit acceptance of the customary mode or a choice between two linguistic paths. How is the actual point of choice to be construed?

There are different ways with different consequences in which this can be done. If it is seen as pure volition, then emphasis begins to fall on its aim; for example, there may be a search for coherence or consistency of belief. The effect of the analytic process is then to widen the body of consistent belief. But decision need not be regarded as wholly arbitrary, and rarely is: it is felt as bound in some respect, whether to established fact or established usage, or obedience to some authority. This carries us back in part to the previous question of the kind of data involved—the appeal to ordinary knowledge or to observation, the introspective datum, a habit of usage or assent to accepted authority, the consensus of scientific evidence on matters of fact, and so on. The additional element here, however, is the weighing or selection or valuational choice of what data are to predominate. This decisional aspect seems therefore unavoidable, and it raises very sharply the question whether the decision process is to be construed as predominantly stipulative, so that in its outcome analysis would be primarily stipulation after a preparatory process deriving from multiple sources.

Many writers on the character of analysis tend to reject this possibility. For example, Ryle, in the article referred to previously, does not think analysis is simply laying down a norm in a prescriptive way, as a literary authority might prescribe the correct mode of expression. It is something distinctive, a discovery of rules of use which is at one time both discovery and ruling. Similarly, Hare, in the comparison of analysis to the attempt of dancers to formulate the steps of their dance, after pointing out that the dancers are relying on their memory, and that "it is not at all clear whether remembering something is making an empirical discovery," [18] even goes on to flirt with the Kantian synthetic a priori, and Plato's theory of recollection (anamnesis).

An interesting attempt not to set forth a unique or distinctive process, but to distinguish two different types of analysis, is made by S. Körner.[19] It is worth examining in greater detail because in departing from the view that analysis is a single type of process *sui generis*, it suggests a much more comprehensive perspective. The distinction Körner proposes is between *exhibition-analysis* and *replacement-analysis*.[20] The former aims at discovery and exhibition of rules for the use of words, and therefore combines rule-formulation which is neither empirical nor analytic (but apparently decisional) with empirical assertions about who has adopted the rules, and consequently the formulation of analytic propositions which embody the previous processes and present the results of the analysis. Replacement-analysis [21] involves criteria of defectiveness in rules, such as vagueness, internal inconsistency, etc., and some relation of replacement (in effect, a specified pattern of analysis; Körner illustrates with bilateral formal implications, or more or less clearly demarcated similarity). The problem of replacement-analysis is then formulated as follows: "given certain criteria of defectiveness and a replacement relation—to replace a defective set of rules by another which is not defective and stands in the replacement-relation to the original set of rules."

Körner's attempt to distinguish different types of analysis seems to me to be heading in the right direction in pointing to the different purposes involved. But I wonder whether beyond this the sharpness of the distinction can be maintained. He himself points out that quite often "putative exhibition-analyses are really examples of replacement-analysis, with both the criteria of defectiveness and the replacement-relation hidden from everybody, including the analyst himself." [22] What is more, replacement-analy-

---

18 Hare, *op. cit.*, p. 744.

19 "Some Remarks on Philosophical Analysis," *The Journal of Philosophy*, LIV (1957), 758-66. It is part of the symposium on "The Nature of Analysis" which contains Hare's paper.

20 *Ibid.*, pp. 762 ff.   21 *Ibid.*, p. 765.

22 *Ibid.*, p. 765.

sis will constitute a quite heterogeneous brood, depending on the criteria of defectiveness and the specified replacement-relation. For example, Körner includes in his illustration of criteria of defectiveness "metaphysical commitments of an undesirable kind." If this is so, is there any reason why defectiveness could not embrace different types of undesirable practical consequences? A rule might be regarded as defective if it could not be carried out (compare the use of "ought implies can" in ethics as a criterion for modifying moral rules), and the reason why it could not be carried out might take one from physical impossibility to undesirable social consequences! There could be statistical types such as "covers less than three-quarters of the initial material," or—to step boldly into criteria of improvement instead of criteria of defectiveness—methodological types such as "the constructs in the modified rules as compared to the original rules will accelerate the pace of discovery of new phenomena in the field."

On the whole, then, I should be inclined not to set up a classification of different types of analysis, but to suggest that analyzing refers to a whole range of reflective activity, that descriptive and suggestive components are to be found in different degrees in different contexts, and that the analysis of the analysis would do better to examine in detail the variety of contexts and the exact points of stress rather than to seek some distinctiveness and to classify kinds. At one extreme there would be the pure description of usage, as Ryle identifies it; it would be even more restricted if it limited itself solely to distinctions which were found in the consciousness of the users. The minimal form of the suggestive aspect would come with systematized description employing new concepts, but only for descriptive purposes. A bit beyond we might find the emergence of minimal regulative processes which ruled out "clearly incorrect" or even "borderline" cases, or "metaphorical usage." We have here the methodological processes through which value-elements creep into classification—perhaps unavoidably. Another step or two along the range and we begin to find additions suggested—as in the hypothetical example above, of the introduction of the distinction between intended and unintended killing; these may be felt only as natural extensions, or as just rendering more explicit what was clearly implicit. Still further on lies advisory analysis utilizing the "purely methodological criteria"—recommendations for adjustment to avoid inconsistencies, paradoxes, awkwardnesses, to increase simplicity, etc. Thus it continues till we come to those striking kinds of analysis which open up whole new avenues of thought and enable one to ask old questions in an entirely new way—what Hume did to 'cause' or Russell to 'number' or Einstein to 'simultaneity' or Hilbert to 'point' or what very much needs to be done to 'ought.' [23]

This seems to be the uppermost limit to what is regarded as analysis today. But it need not be. There could lie beyond, the more speculative reflection which fashions concepts not primarily to analyze existent material, but to cast a net for future materials that might profoundly recast present concepts. There are two reasons why such activity is not usually regarded as analysis. One is that it seems to resemble more what the pure mathematician does or the theory-construction of the scientist. (And many philosophers seem to be obsessed with the need to distinguish their activity from the scientists.) The second is that the very notion of analysis seems to imply the prior existence of a material to be analyzed. That is why the claims for philosophical analysis seem so often to present a rear-guard appearance of waiting on others to furnish data.

There is then no one account of the decision process or terminal point in analysis. How it utilizes various types of data, how it synthesizes, are to be understood in terms of its guiding purposes applied to the range of specific contexts. Clearly, then, the objection to regarding analytic decision as a simple type of stipulation once it goes beyond pure description is well grounded. But there is no ground for assuming that analysis is a unique type of activity, or that it lacks purposes, or that it uses a single standard for assessment of correctness. These questions bring us to the consideration of the purposes and goals of analysis.

WHAT ARE THE AIMS OF ANALYSIS?

Stevenson's formulation of analysis as a relatively neutral study with limited methodological aims of clear heads and good habits of investigation was presented previously. We may now ask how

23 For an excellent account of the impact of such analysis, see F. Waismann's essay, "How I See Philosophy," in *Contemporary British Philosophy,* Third Series, ed. H. D. Lewis (New York, 1956).

neutral analysis can really be, and how limited its aims. What would be the status of a statement to the effect that analysis is neutral? It may be a definition stipulating that analysis is a special type of reflection embodying only certain methodological values and involving only the application of logical distinctions and equipment. This is a highly abstract conception according to which the analyst would have to put an "if" before every factual assertion, and close his eyes to the possibility that he is having an effect upon the people whose usage he is analyzing, the scientific enterprise whose concepts he is refining, the person with whom he is engaging in Socratic discourse. Whether analysis as so defined has ever existed is an empirical question. Whether it can exist is also not a question of stipulation, but probably of psychology and social science. If analysis as practiced consists in dispelling naiveté, in bringing a certain intellectual sophistication, how can it be neutral except by being solitary, issuing in unpublished books or unactualized "conversations"? How could it be sure its effect was only good methodological habits? Socrates was wiser in regarding his effort as a branch of midwifery. In short, the value-content of analysis is to be discovered by factual investigation of the context of its operation, not by arbitrary definition or introspection of intent. Historically, the problem is, in effect, the scientific investigation of the role and efficacy of reflection.

If we line up comparatively the aims to be found in traditional modes of analysis, we find a considerable variety. Even in Socratic method there are different tendencies. The most obvious is the stimulation of the mind. The shock effect is well pictured in the Socratic dialogues. Leonard Nelson aptly says: "This method of *forcing* minds to *freedom* constitutes the first secret of the Socratic method." [24] But Socrates is also interested in the genuineness of the ideas produced. Similarly, in Plato as distinguished from Socrates, there is the double trend. At times, and especially in his *Letters,* there is the stress on the act of vision, which can only be communicated in a second-hand way. On the other hand, there is the outcome anticipated in many fields—as in the ideal society of the *Republic*—of a set of *clear ideas*. Even more, they are regarded as *truths*. Thus, the outcome anticipated from analysis may be anything from a roused spirit or a stimu-

[24] Leonard Nelson, *op. cit.,* p. 15.

lated mind, an act of vision, a set of clear ideas, to systematic knowledge of a set of truths. Or it may take a more limited form, simply a reconciliation of one's beliefs, say of Aristotle and the Bible.

Contemporary formulations have not been too far away from the older ones, although they have had their own specializations. There is an insistence on logical clarity, or an attempt to dispense with metaphysical entities—as in Russell's use of Ockham's razor to trim them out, in his theory of descriptions—or a therapeutic goal of removing a special kind of philosophic perplexity. Formulation of aims with reference to language has perhaps been the most common. But even here the goal of sharpening linguistic habits sometimes gives way to a goal stated in terms of clearer vision. As Wisdom says: "Philosophic progress does not consist in acquiring knowledge of new facts but in acquiring new knowledge of facts—a passage *via* inspection from poor insight to good insight." [25] And we have already noted Waismann's point about asking questions in a wholly new way as a result of seeing things differently.

There is a further aim in analysis which has been seriously underrated in the most popular accounts today. This is the use of analysis to help us discover underlying *factual* assumptions which we have not been aware of. Neglect of this sometimes leads to a misunderstanding of typical philosophical puzzles. Thus if a philosopher asks whether we *really* see the tree that is so obviously before us, we may feel that at best we are being forced into an unusual mode of speech. But the case may be far different. He may get us to agree that something has to exist for us to see it, and then ask whether we see the star whose light reaches us long after the star itself has exploded. When this shakes our composure, we are carried back to the tree before us. While one philosopher may indeed conclude that we do not "really" see it, another may instead simply lead us to recognize that a factual assumption underlying our judgment that we see it is that the time light takes to travel from it to us is shorter than that in which the tree could have "exploded." Many a time in philosophical analysis when the question has been pinpointed as one of queer usage, it turns out instead to be the perfectly serious attempt to adjust our ideas in the light of scientific advances, and to recognize factual assumptions that were unnoticed before in common inferences.[26]

A deeper probing of differences in aims assigned to analysis can be achieved by asking what specific form a mode of analysis expects to find for its results. This was prefigured in asking previously what initial limitations there were on types of answers permitted. We are thus able to see where there is an underlying theory of the world which guides the aims and formulation of the analytic process.

DOES EVERY MODE OF ANALYSIS INVOLVE AN UNDERLYING THEORY WHICH UNIFIES METHOD, GOAL, AND ANTICIPATED FORM OF RESULTS?

That some accounts of analysis have an underlying theory is clear historically. But whether this means that they are properly philosophically self-conscious or whether they stand condemned as "theory-ridden" is precisely the point to be determined.

Plato is the clearest example, in his familiar metaphysics of the soul turning towards the light, being freed by its endeavor toward the universal ideas, and culminating in the vision of the Good. Pragmatist, instrumentalist, and materialist accounts of reflective or analytic processes are often set in an evolutionary picture of man developing increasingly refined instruments of control. The Russell-Wittgenstein notion of a direction in analysis terminating in atomic facts, and an ideal language whose structure mirrors the structure of the world, is a familiar twentieth-century illustration. In contemporary forms of British analysis, there is also a definite expectation of what the results will be like. It is sometimes overlooked because of its pluralistic character. Perhaps it is best seen in Ryle's conception of "informal logics" [27] or unscheduled logics, or in the slogan that

[26] A. O. Lovejoy has called attention in his *The Revolt Against Dualism* (LaSalle, Ill., 1930), p. 19, to the shortcomings of the histories of philosophy in omitting the impact of such scientific discoveries as the fact that light has a velocity. A great deal of the contemporary perplexity about the nature of philosophical questions seems to me to stem from comparable neglect.

[27] Gilbert Ryle, *Dilemmas* (Cambridge, England, 1954), Ch. VIII.

Urmson gives as "Every statement has its own logic" [28] which warns us not to expect a few neatly tabulated tasks which all sentences perform. We shall see in the next two chapters how questions of definition and of reasoning in ethics were affected by what we may call this *fragmentarian* assumption. An assured plurality of contexts each with its own logic constitutes as much a definite thesis about the outcome of analysis as is an assured monistic principle.

The strength of this pluralistic assurance is one of the features in contemporary British analysis which makes us wonder whether the claim to discard older theories and not to be theory-ridden may not itself depend on some pseudo-theoretical surrogate in its own accounts. The formulations of the British schools are exhilarating: they convey the feeling of freedom, of shaking off rusting shackles. But we have to be careful to see whether, as in many a revolution, the freedom may lie merely in the interval in which older dogmas are overthrown, while new dogmas are fastening their hold in the name of freedom. Perhaps the fault with the older programs of analysis is not that they are theory-ridden (unless this term refers to a dictatorial predominance of untested theory), but that their theory was inadequate. And the fault with the new program may be that it is unaware of its underlying theory and so in danger of being uncritical.

If we couple with the assurance of pluralism the basic appeal to ordinary language, while no integrated theory emerges, there does seem to me to be a prominent guiding model that is being adhered to. When we ask why one should accept the normal conventions of ordinary usage rather than try to improve some of them—especially where the problems involved impinge on areas in which there has been advance in the psychological and social sciences—we meet with what seems an undue veneration of ordinary language. Sometimes the respect for common speech is justified by the argument that it is subjected to the severest test of constant use.[29] Respect grows almost into awe when J. L. Austin says: "Our common stock of words embodies all the distinctions men have found worth drawing, and the connections

28 Urmson, *op. cit.*, p. 179.
29 E.g., P. F. Strawson in "Construction and Analysis," *op. cit.*, p. 103.

they have found worth marking, in the lifetimes of many generations: these surely are likely to be more numerous, more sound, since they have stood up to the long test of the survival of the fittest, and more subtle, at least in all ordinary and reasonably practical matters, than any that you or I are likely to think up in our armchairs of an afternoon—the most favored alternative method." [30] Austin does go on to add, however, that we look "not merely at words but also at the realities we use the words to talk about: we are using a sharpened awareness of words to sharpen our perception of, though not as the final arbiter of, the phenomena." He even suggests the name of "linguistic phenomenology" for this procedure.

This passage in Austin seems to me the clearest reckoning with this powerful analytic trend that has had the widest recent influence in ethical theory. I should like to call attention to three points about it. (1) Apart from the evolutionary touch in the reference to the survival of the fittest, it is very reminiscent of Edmund Burke's veneration of tradition, or the defenders of the Common Law arguing against those who would introduce large-scale legislative changes. There are many things in the ordinary language school—its practicalism, as we shall see, comparing ethics constantly to judicial decision, its pluralism in the belief that there can be no unifying principles, and so on [31]—which make it sound as if its basic model were the Common Law as conceived by its traditional English defenders. Each corner has its own logical development which only the practiced can know; change cannot be forced, but occurs gradually, and any attempt to be wholesale is doomed to frustration. And so on. (2) The recognition that the movement is a kind of phenomenology cast in a linguistic form, seems to me to be basically correct. The conclusion Austin suggests—that it therefore provides a sharpened awareness and furnishes sensitive data—points to perhaps the greatest contribution of this mode of analysis. But the further qualification that the language is not the final arbiter of the phenomena, seems to me to be too often forgotten by the practitioners. It follows also that the limitations we shall find later on in discussing phenomen-

[30] J. L. Austin, "A Plea for Excuses," *Aristotelian Society Proceedings,* 1956-57, p. 7.

[31] See below, pp. 147ff.

ological description [32] apply also to the results of this analytic method. It furnishes data which are the beginning of inquiry, not the end, and which serve as only partial verification because linguistic analysis is not the sole source of data. (3) The only alternatives considered are ordinary usage (tradition) and arbitrary (armchair) rationalism. The advance of systematic science in the study of man, which is neither purely phenomenological description nor a priori rationalism, is not considered. Here we find the greatest weakness in the analytic schools. The impact of scientific materials in ethical theory is ignored or glossed over, and no channels are provided by which it can be brought into consideration. [33]

WHAT CRITERIA OF CORRECTNESS IN ANALYSIS ARE INVOKED?

If, as I have suggested seems likely, any program of analytic method rests ultimately on some theoretical view of man and his world, we can understand why the doctrine of what constitutes a "correct" analysis has been the Achilles' heel of any analytic method that thinks it is self-contained. It would carry us too far afield here to explore this problem in comparative detail. What we would have to show is that the criteria suggested on any given view reflect the implicit guiding purposes or aims, and the implicit underlying theory.

On our account, there is no single property which makes an analysis correct. Since the enterprise of analysis is taken to coincide with reflective thinking about a given material, correctness will be determined by the purposes guiding the inquiry and the material on which it is directed. Thus if it is simple descriptive analysis, the criteria are those of induction. If it is straight suggestive analysis in the light of certain purposes, the criteria are those of success in achieving the purposes. An analysis is factually well grounded if the factual propositions or assumptions it in-

[32] See below, pp. 169ff.

[33] An increasing realization of the inadequacy of the appeal to common speech when any serious decision has to be made between competing theories of mind or personality or moral outlooks is found in Stuart Hampshire's recent *Thought and Action* (London, 1959). Cf. pp. 155-56, 234.

volves are true. It is logical if the elements into which the concept is resolved can by the rules set up yield the concept whose analysis they purported to give, or if the axioms offered to systematize a set of propositions do yield them by logical derivation.[34] It is a fruitful analysis if it furthers the aims of the inquiry in terms of the traditional values of science. It is otherwise useful if it provides in any of myriad ways for the furtherance of accepted social ends, institutional enterprises, or other shared values.

Such a conclusion does not mean that analysis as an enterprise becomes merged with fact-finding, or with pragmatic evaluation. It does mean that there is no separate material cut off as its domain, and that it carries on its work in cooperation with other approaches and that it must be conscious where it is making assumptions whose justification lies in the application of these other approaches. The distinctiveness of analysis is no other than the distinctiveness of human thinking, which certainly stands out among the events of the world.

Analytic labors thus play a central role in the refinement and development of ethical theory, even though they do not define its character in unique and solitary splendor. Ethical theory has suffered from the isolation of analysis. We shall see in the next two chapters that different dogmatisms were forced on it in the name of what was taken to be the last word in logic and the theory of analysis. Today we are in a thawing-out period. The purpose of this analysis of analysis has been to try to consolidate the liberation and prevent the freezing of a new orthodoxy. If analysis is simply another name for many of the operations of reflection, then, as we have suggested, it must be carried on in intimate relation to other methods, and allow the greatest freedom in devising techniques for dealing with analytic problems in ethical theory.

The studies that follow in this part deal with two samples of analytic problems—the problem of the definition of ethical terms, and the theory of ethical reasoning.

[34] Here especially it is important to note that the correctness of one analysis in this logical sense need not mean the incorrectness of a different one. Both may do the same job in different ways.

CHAPTER FIVE

DEFINITIONAL POLICY IN ETHICAL THEORY—A REASSESSMENT

I

Some of the most crucial analytic issues in ethical theory during the past half-century have centered around the problem of the definability of ethical terms. Answers have ranged from outright rejection of the possibility of defining basic ethical terms to proposed definitional equivalents. Involved in these controversies are the major questions of how moral judgments are to be verified and whether they are really capable of verification at all. What policy is most desirable on this issue of the feasibility of definition at the present stage of analytic progress in ethics?

It is more than fifty years since G. E. Moore's *Principia Ethica* sounded the keynote of indefinability—at least for whatever be taken as the basic ethical concept—and gave it a form that was to carry all before it for decades. I need scarcely remind you that to say that a theory committed the *naturalistic fallacy* was to blackball it from the clubs of those who counted intellectually. Friedrich Waismann, in his recent magnificent paper on "How I See Philosophy" has called our attention to that sudden "breaking through to a *deeper insight*—which is something positive—not merely the dissipation of fog and the exposure of spurious problems." [1] The question is asked in a new way, and its light goes into the inmost recesses of philosophical history, long-standing issues are dissipated, and all is crystal clear. So it was with Moore's analysis. Now it could be seen why 'good' could not be defined as 'object of striving' or 'what I approve of approving' or 'pleasure' or 'what God wills' or 'where history tends.' 'Good' was indefinable. It designated a simple quality to be directly apprehended. All you had to do was imagine the object of which it was asserted

[1] *Contemporary British Philosophy*, Third Series, ed. H. D. Lewis (New York, 1956), p. 470.

as if it were a world of its own, hold it up like a jewel in the light—the light of your own vision—and simply look. One's judgment in looking was final, for the property was self-evident; if another disagreed, well, you could not force him to see it as you did, but you could stick by your guns. Other theories about 'good' were really proposals to correlate some natural or metaphysical property with this indefinable quality; the burden of proof was on them, but the decision was always one's own. (For of the good one remains oneself the proud beholder.) At one blow the ethical theorist was emancipated from theologian and utilitarian, from Marxian and Spencerian, from scientist and Bradleian. How permeating was Moore's influence can be seen in the way in which Charles L. Stevenson, in his earlier article on "The Emotive Meaning of Ethical Terms," [2] set it down as an initial requirement that the goodness must not be verifiable solely by use of the scientific method.

Moore's arguments for his position have not on the whole proved to be strong ones. Too many strands were mingled.[3] His underlying theory of definition—that definition is separating into parts, and therefore the ultimate simples cannot be defined—fitted only one type of definition, what Richard Robinson in his long listing of types in his book, *Definition,* calls an "analytical definition." Moore did nothing to show that this type was here the appropriate or relevant one. At most he objected to the synonymous type by arguing that if we identify 'good' with 'pleasant' our definition is reduced to a tautology, "Pleasant is pleasant." He added the logical demand that since 'X is good' and 'X is not good' are contradictory, any analysis of 'good' should not remove the incompatibility between the resultant analyses. This rules out oversimple interpretations—'good' cannot be interpreted as somebody approving since 'A approves of X' and 'B does not approve of X' are quite compatible—but it does not rule out complex naturalistic types, such as what a man would feel under

[2] *Mind,* XLVI (1937), 14-31, reprinted in *Readings in Ethical Theory,* ed. Sellars and Hospers (New York, 1952).

[3] Only a brief summary of his arguments and their outcome is here given. A more systematic reckoning, set in the context of an analysis of Moore's ethical theory, is to be found in my "The Logical Structure of G. E. Moore's Ethical Theory." See especially pp. 151-56 in the essay.

specified ideal conditions or what any man would desire for its own sake under specified (non-question-begging) conditions, nor theological types or even historical-evolutionary or utilitarian theories.

Moore's comparison of the simplicity of good with the qualitative simplicity of yellow, his special methodological intuitionism, and his view of good as a non-natural quality, constituted a complex of mixed metaphysical-epistemological argument for the indefinability of 'good.' Retrospectively, this whole phase of his thinking stands out as a British branch of the continental phenomenological movement, focused through linguistic sensitivity. Actually, the general gap between a Moore-type intuitionism in this area and an ethical naturalism is considerably narrowed by contemporary conceptions of the phenomenological field, as studied in Gestalt and descriptive phenomenological approaches.[4] These carefully distinguish reports of properties within the phenomenal field, as an independent descriptive variable, from correlation of these properties with physiological, psychological, and behavioral properties. Thus the presentational elements in ethical intuitionism have become separated from the claims of self-evidence or immediate certification. And the naturalistic theses become translatable into hypotheses about the dependent and representative character of the phenomenal in relation to organism-environment processes.

No doubt, the best known of Moore's arguments is what has come to be called the *open-question* argument, "that, whatever definition be offered, it may always be asked, with significance, of the complex so defined, whether it itself is good." [5] But he does not explain what 'significance' here means or how it is to be tested. Actually, the regress argument had from the beginning more the character of "surely this isn't what we mean!" than that regress is impossible. If we use throughout the same sense of 'good'—say approval, for simplicity's sake—then there is no theoretical objection to asking whether one approves of one's approving of one's approving. (And the answers might alternate in a particular case.) If the sense is changed, then obviously all that has been shown by the argument is that there are changing defi-

4 See below, pp. 169ff.
5 *Principia Ethica* (Cambridge, England, 1903), p. 15.

nitions of ethical terms, not that they are indefinable. Or again, if the insistence is ultimately that any naturalistic analysis, in Moore's sense, is not an analysis of 'good' but of the psychological phenomenon of *finding-good,* then this issue is bridged by recognizing that such an argument means a stipulation to the effect that the ethical term be used only of some quality or complex within the phenomenal field, and not for any correlation of field-property and psychological property. The question of the merit of such stipulation is a distinct one. Actually, Moore does not press the regress experiment far. Instead, he appeals to the reader to look into his own mind and confess that he had something simple and different in mind by 'good' when he embarked on the experiment. But if some convinced hedonist had said he found no difference between 'good' and 'pleasant,' he would have gotten short shrift from Moore, no matter how correctly he described his own state of mind!

The strongest point in the open-question argument is the insistence that any *equation* of the ethical term with any matter of fact description leaves meaningful statements in which the term may be used, which yet are not simply redundant.[6] This may be granted as a necessary caution. For it serves to keep the ethical concepts open against identification with what may prove to be a limited subject matter. But this recognition that a naturalistic interpretation gives a partial definition does not imply that something different in kind is left over which must be given non-naturalistic force. The ethical concepts may be open concepts in precisely the same sense that many scientific concepts are.[7] Thus the relation of 'obligation' to any naturalistic interpretation in terms of a specific type of feeling may be like that of 'intelligence' to a set of tests. The "ultimate" definition of 'intelligence' is not yet available, not because it is intrinsically indefinable or because it is also an honorific term, but because we do not yet know the terms that will enter into a theory of the nature of intelligence that will be adequate to the phenomena

[6] Moore himself throws in the pragmatic argument that if we start without a definition we'll have a more open mind! (*Ibid.,* p. 20).

[7] Cf. Carl G. Hempel, *Fundamentals of Concept Formation in Empirical Science,* "International Encyclopedia of Unified Science," Vol. II, No. 7 (Chicago, 1952), 28-29.

involved or even whether we are dealing with a family of phenomena rather than a single set. Where we have a term in a field
with a number of current theories, such as 'state' or 'capitalist
economy,' then major definitions reflect the competing theories.
And so in analysis of 'good' it is not surprising that historically
proposed definitions reflect underlying conceptions of man and
his nature, and society and its nature. An adequate definition of
'good' will require adequate theory in the human sciences. Mean-
while, 'happiness,' 'object of desire,' 'object of reflective approval,' etc., remain so many proposed operative indices to be
tested not by a correlation with some indefinable sense of 'good'
but as any operations or tests are refined and altered in scientific
investigation. And the case of 'ought' is precisely similar.

Time and analysis have unwound the strands in Moore's argument. But what is most surprising is how resistent the concept of
a naturalistic fallacy has proved, even while its foundations were
crumbling. It is a problem of intellectual history well worth
looking into, for it may contain helpful lessons in a reassessment
of definitional policy in ethics. Why then, did Moore's conclusion remain so widely accepted, although the arguments proved
some unclear, some beside the point, some simply dogmatic assertion? First, there was an unusual delay in coming to grips with
it. When Frankena published his well-known article on "The
Naturalistic Fallacy" in 1939, he could still say that "in spite of
its repute, the naturalistic fallacy has never been discussed at
any length." [8] The naturalists and idealists and the rest went
on doing their work, but they were regarded as old hat, and
under permanent indictment for lack of sophistication. An occasional voice had complained, as C. G. Field did in 1932, of the
open-question argument, "I have never been able to find any
plausibility in this argument," [9] but he went unheeded. So, insofar as I can see, did Frankena's riddling,[10] or that in other works,

8 W. K. Frankena, "The Naturalistic Fallacy," *Mind*, XLVIII (1939), reprinted in Sellars and Hospers, *op. cit.*
9 "The Place of Definition in Ethics," *Aristotelian Society Proceedings*, N.S.
XXXII (1931-32), 92.
10 Frankena makes it perfectly clear that whether the naturalistic fallacy
is a fallacy is precisely what is at issue between intuitionists and nonin-
tuitionists, and therefore it cannot be invoked to settle the issue; also that

such as John R. Reid's book, *A Theory of Value* (1938). Perhaps it was because the growing emotivist theory needed the protective insulation of Moore's disposal of naturalistic approaches; this had set it going in a new and interesting direction and it was too early to stop. Or perhaps it was simply that antinaturalist theories hesitated to throw over so well capitalized and flourishing a theoretical establishment! It was much easier to shift the arguments and maintain the weapon. One could always invoke the current slogans, "You can't derive the 'ought' from the 'is,' " or "The *prescriptive* is one thing, the *descriptive* another," or "How can a *fact* imply a *value?*" and say that this was what Moore had really been aiming at.

When the literature on the theme began to grow after the late thirties, reconsideration tended to take its stand on some such broader ground. A good example is Arthur N. Prior's *Logic and the Basis of Ethics* (1949), which is almost wholly devoted to this theme. He shows that a naturalist who is bold enough and tough enough can extricate himself from Moore's trap, but behind it lies the more basic fallacy. For the essence of the naturalistic fallacy, says Prior, is the claim to deduce ethical propositions from nonethical ones.[11] He shows that there has been a continuous battle on this issue of the autonomy of ethics in British ethical theory over the centuries, so that Moore wasn't so original, but he was fighting the good fight.

The emotive theory simply assumed that Moore had rightly seen the impossibility of a purely cognitivist definition of ethical terms, but had not realized that the force of ethical terms came from their emotive function.[12] The broader prescriptivists or practicalists carried this mode of analysis further. For example, Hare says: "Moore thought that he could prove that there were no such defining characteristics for the word 'good' as used in morals. His argument has been assailed since he propounded it,

---

if it rules out a definition of 'good' it rules out all definitions of any term whatever. And all this apart from any lack of precision in the concept of the fallacy itself.

[11] *Logic and the Basis of Ethics* (Oxford, 1949), p. 95.

[12] Cf. J. N. Findlay, "Morality By Convention," *Mind*, N.S. LIII (1944), 145: "That moral judgments are emotional is the truth which really underlies Moore's well-known doctrine of the 'naturalistic fallacy.' "

and it is certainly true that the formulation of it was at fault. But it seems to me that Moore's argument was not merely plausible; it rests, albeit insecurely, upon a secure foundation; there is indeed something about the way in which, and the purposes for which, we use the word 'good' which make it impossible to hold the sort of position which Moore was attacking, although Moore did not see clearly what this something was.[13] Nowell-Smith in a similar vein takes even the intuitionist exploitation of the naturalistic fallacy argument to embody a sound insistence on the autonomy of morals, but interprets this autonomy in terms of the distinctive function of moral language—"expressing approval, praising, advising, exhorting, commending, or appraising." [14]

Please note that contrary to some current interpretations, I do not regard the ordinary language approach in problems of ethical theory as making a sharp break with the emotive theory. The informalists (to use Philip Blair Rice's apt term) simply took seriously the view that the meaning of ethical terms was to be found in the way they were used—this corresponded with their shift from asking for the meaning to asking for the use—and set about gathering the specimens. The results they so patiently accumulated with the zeal of linguistic empiricism led them further and further away from the emotive theory and the Moorean base. They reached a point which is a philosophical correlate to the process of deeper insight breaking through which I quoted from Waismann: it is what happens when what had seemed so crystal clear suddenly becomes so terribly complex. This, too, is a wholesome process, as we can see by its results.

Now what about the naturalistically-minded ethical theorists? How have they reacted to the charge of committing the naturalistic fallacy? In fact, a wide variety of attitudes is to be found. At one extreme is the feeling that a great deal of fuss is being made unnecessarily, and that energy had better be spent on the real work of getting to know about man and his values and the complex ways in which they shape up into different patterns,

13 R. M. Hare, *The Language of Morals* (Oxford, 1952), pp. 83-84.
14 P. H. Nowell-Smith, *Ethics* (Baltimore, 1954), p. 181. See also his analysis of the naturalistic fallacy, pp. 32-34, and the treatment of intuitionism, pp. 36f.

and just how they find expression in action or in linguistic form. "In passing," says Stephen Pepper in his recent naturalistic study of value, "it may be remarked that an ordinary empiricist would not regard Moore's 'naturalistic fallacy' as a fallacy at all, except as a question-begging epithet illicitly tossed by Moore at critics who are not impressed by his linguistic perform-ances." [15] In the central range among the naturalists are many who feel that the naturalistic fallacy charge contains serious warnings against a narrow interpretation of ethical terms, but that greater analytic care can avoid its implications without sur-rendering definability; thus, for example, Hourani argues that if ethical terms are complex, their parts in analysis may be non-ethical and the whole still maintain a distinctively ethical char-acter.[16] At the other extreme are those who believe that the con-ceptual framework of a naturalistic ethics has to be recast so as to give a greater prominence to the noncognitive functions of ethical judgment revealed in the prescriptive development from

[15] *The Sources of Value* (Berkeley, 1958), p. 20. Note, however, that Pepper does credit Moore with stimulating greater analytical rigor, although he regrets that it did not go directly in the direction of "accepting 'good' as indeed ambiguous, as a term referring to a collection of natural entities more or less closely connected and requiring only to have their connections discriminated and described" (p. 30). It should also be pointed out that Pepper did not make such criticisms without having first paid attention to the theory of definition and attempted to work out the theory of what he called the descriptive definition. (Cf. "The Descriptive Definition," *The Journal of Philosophy*, XLIII [1946], 29-36.)

It is interesting to note further how peremptorily Ralph Barton Perry disposes of the intuitionist indefinability thesis, in his last major work on value: "If unanalyzable value is *there* within the range of intellectual vision, it should be possible, after a reasonable amount of effort, to bring it into focus. He who fails to find it cannot but conclude that there is no such thing; especially when the authors of the doctrine do not agree among themselves on what they find" (*Realms of Value* [Cambridge, Mass., 1954], p. 9).

As a further sample, take the view of Dewitt H. Parker, that Moore's theory "has in my opinion lain like an incubus upon ethical discussion for the last half century. One could, in fact, say of him what James said of Brad-ley, that 'he messed up philosophy to such an extent that it would require a generation to get it straight again'" (*The Philosophy of Value* [Ann Arbor, 1957], p. 40).

[16] George F. Hourani, *Ethical Value* (Ann Arbor, 1956), pp. 38-39.

Moore's analysis. Thus Rice worked out a balanced set of ethical concepts duly stressing each aspect in turn.[17] But others incline toward the view that while the framework of a naturalistic ethics needs to be developed in the light of the growth of knowledge, the prescriptive side belongs rather to the theory of application.

There are a great many side-arguments on the naturalistic fallacy which arise in the exchange of those relying on the argument to safeguard their own position, and those attacking it or criticizing its component theses. I cannot resist pointing to one type, which I should classify informally as the two-can-play-at-that-game argument. Here is the way it shapes up. The intuitionists dispose of the naturalists by a naturalistic fallacy indictment. No sooner are they safely in theoretical power than they are themselves indicted by the prescriptivists—and on the same charge. For example, Nowell-Smith points out that the intuitionist theory involves a special moral emotion of obligation on intuiting the obligatory character of an action, and asks, "Does it follow that I ought to do the action towards which I feel the emotion?"[18] But even the prescriptivists are not safe. For they rely predominantly on the analysis of common usage. And as Paul Kurtz points out in an illuminating paper on "Naturalistic Ethics and the Open Question," they themselves go from what linguistic usage *is* to how ethical terms are *to be* understood![19] Somehow one cannot help thinking that there is something wrong with a charge that can so readily go all the way round. A fitting conclusion to this circle is to be found in Peter Glassen's recent article, "The Cognitivity of Moral Judgments,"[20] in which he gathers all sorts of ordinary uses of moral terms which are clearly intended to make assertions. ("*Moral discourse is redolent, so to speak, of cognitivity.*") Accordingly, he concludes, putting

17 First outlined in Philip Blair Rice, "Ethical Empiricism and its Critics," *The Philosophical Review*, LXII (1953), 355-73. It was developed in his book, *On the Knowledge of Good and Evil* (New York, 1955), which is, in effect, a study of the consequences of the naturalistic fallacy analysis. For a brief summary of his solution and a suggested critique of it, see above, pp. 61, 69.

18 *Op. cit.*, p. 40f. In short, all one has to do is to find a gap, and the charge becomes possible. The only trouble is that once you begin looking for gaps, you may find more than you expect.

19 *The Journal of Philosophy*, LII (1955), 124-25.

20 *Mind*, LXVIII (1959), 57-72.

the words into the mouths of those who engage in moral discourse, "It is certainly true that we cannot tell you in other words what we intend to assert by our moral judgments, but that's what you philosophers are here for, to find out." Aristophanes could have had a lot of fun with this notion of the Demos as linguistic legislator and with the plight of the linguistic analyst caught in his own reverence for ordinary language. But there is a more serious side to the question. Perhaps the only way out is to keep on going, beyond what people say and beyond what limited contextual assumptions they make to the fuller study of their needs and aims and beliefs and their interrelations. But this is another story.

I have sampled at perhaps greater length than was necessary the different lines of argumentation over the naturalistic fallacy, and I come now to the answer I want to suggest to the question why the naturalistic fallacy accusation remained so strong and impervious to criticism. If it were simply an intellectual question of a position resting on its logical merits, I do not think it could have resisted the lines of criticism we have noted. It was always turning into something else—whether the qualitative study of the phenomenological field, or the prescriptive emphasis of the emotivists and the analysts, or the logical problems of deducing an imperative from an indicative—and though these questions could perfectly well have been explored on their own and were so explored, yet the frequency with which they were tied to the Moorean base seems to have been more than accident or piety. The key to our problem lies, I think, in the prominence of the open-question argument within the naturalistic fallacy complex. What is common to the protean forms in which the argument was transformed is the securing of a kind of *autonomy effect* for ethics. I do not think it is very helpful to state this as a doctrine or thesis,[21] in terms of one or two assertions. If it is to undergo a logical analysis, it would carry us rather into the whole theory of reduction in the logic of the sciences, and the various ways in which terms and laws in different fields may be related. Nor does it simply embody a methodological lesson, keeping a concept

[21] Cf. David Rynin, "The Autonomy of Morals," *Mind*, LXVI (1957), 308-17. See also the criticism of this article by Peter Remnant, *Mind*, LXVIII (1959), 252-55.

open so that it shall not shortsightedly be equated with a narrow set of observable entities, for this lesson allows the possibility of eventual though unlikely completion. What we have here is, rather, a valuational element, an effect to be secured and maintained at all costs, something that will not be surrendered no matter how strong the argument may seem to be against it. But it would be too easy to call it dogmatism or dismiss it as irrationality. I am dealing now with a pervasive mode, not with the special factors of given individuals or groups in various local situations in the past half century. Such persistence must have some basis to which it is clinging.

Now if the core of the naturalistic fallacy argument is a valuational attitude, what can it be? Early in the century, a self-styled reactionary like T. E. Hulme welcomed the school of Moore and Husserl for its break with the subjectivism and relativism of humanist ethics: "In as far, then, as they free ethical values from the anthropomorphism involved in their dependence on human desires and feeling, they have created the machinery of an anti-humanist reaction which will proceed much further than they ever intended." [22] And no doubt the forging of an anti-scientific ideology in our century has used many and varied strands, sometimes perhaps against their will. But *Principia Ethica* seems to point in another direction. Here Moore seems to have framed the situation of ethical judgment in such a way as to give a central position, from which it could not be dislodged, to *individual libertarian strivings*. I think I was on the right track some fifteen years ago, when after an attempt to formalize the structure of Moore's ethical theory,[23] I suggested that his notion of the indefinability of 'good' and what I called the "isolation-test," by which the individual determined for himself after isolating the object he was inspecting as a world by itself, were tailor-made to an exercise of individual judgment that should not be bound to any definite quality of existence. At that time, what struck me most was the way in which Moore used this potentially critical and liberating framework to enunciate a practical conformity. I sought the elements that produced this effect. But I think it was the liberating spirit that influenced

22 T. E. Hulme, *Speculations,* ed. Herbert Read (New York, 1924), p. 63.
23 "The Logical Structure of G. E. Moore's Ethical Theory," esp. pp. 170ff.

Russell's early Moorean attitude in ethics, and that stands out in Keynes' autobiographical recollections. And while at times it has been an arbitrary individualism and even had a petulant quality, yet I would want to suggest that a critical individualism in judgment has corresponded to a basic social and individual need in our century, and this is the real source from which the naturalistic fallacy accusation has derived its hold.

If there were time, I would wander among the philosophers of our century and try to spot how this libertarian striving entered into very diverse forms in ethical and even in epistemological and metaphysical discussions. As it is, I can only point to the constant stress on the changing, the new, the emergent, the possibility of going beyond any existent form, the need not to commit ourselves wholly to what is. This stress crosses philosophical lines as well as political lines. Nor shall I enter into a sociological analysis of this libertarianism and ask where it reflects a reaction to the social pressures of large-scale organization in the modern world, where an obscurantist reaction to the strides of science, where a genuine realization of human beings about the possibilities of a creative role on the face of the globe.[24] My problem now is definitional policy. I conclude then the purely historical part of my reflections by venturing the thesis that we will never lay the ghost of the naturalistic fallacy accusation until we recognize that it has this value-element, that this has been the source of its attraction, and that all the confusion it led to can be avoided only by separating this element and acknowledging its merit, accepting it as a common purpose, and having it built into definitions of ethical terms or systems of ethical terms at the appropriate place. In short, instead of letting this purpose operate surreptitiously as an obstacle to definition, it can be given its place as one of the built-in elements.

Such a proposal ought not to surprise us. There are constitutive purposes in scientific work—the so-called "pragmatic reasons" which vindicate our choices in terms of fruitfulness, systematic power, simplicity, experimental possibilities, control-possibilities, and so on, to which we appeal in preferring one to

----

24 In another context—see *Anthropology and Ethics*, pp. 164-67, 237-39—there is some consideration of this inherent *restlessness* in ethical theory today.

another proposed definition. There is no reason why the same should not hold for ethical definitions, except for the greater complexity that comes from the fact that ethics attempts to evaluate purposes as part of its job. This makes it more difficult, involving as it does the possibility of a (nonvicious) circularity, but it need not change definitional policy. David Rynin once suggested [25] that in ethics we could use as one criterion of acceptibility the extent to which our formulations made moral judgments more interpersonally communicable and socially verifiable. This is a frank purpose which has a conceivable alternative —to make ethics more mysterious and incommunicable. I see no theoretical issue here—a man can say, "Down with science," when the truth hurts or when he becomes frightened of its practical consequences. This does not make the definitions in science unstable because they have been geared to revealing rather than obscuring. Ethics, too, must become less fearful at the mere possibility that someone will disagree. Let him go his own way and work out his own framework, if he can.

How then shall we meet this libertarian demand in the analysis of ethical terms? It can be taken care of in a dozen different ways and should not be charged against indefinability alone.[26] There could be an agreement that the definition, though accepted, could be revised whenever there was major change in the body of knowledge (as happens in scientific concepts) or in basic shared purposes of men. The libertarian element could be centered in the mode of verification of value statements rather than in the fundamental definitions, by giving verification by the individual a prominent place. Or the principle that every man decides ultimately for himself could have an important place in the value content. Even a factual indeterminacy could secure a libertarian result: for example, Bentham, although he defines 'good' in terms of pleasure, is unready to generalize too much about what would give individuals pleasure because he assumes an almost indefinite variety in the sensibilities of men. And, of course, as a last resort, one might enshrine within the ethical theory a right of

[25] "Definitions of 'Value' and the Logic of Value Judgments," *The Journal of Philosophy*, XLV (1948), 281-92.

[26] For some discussion of the way in which values can be conveyed in different parts of the formal structure of an ethics, see above, pp. 36ff.

ethical rebellion, as Jefferson enshrined the right to revolution in political theory!

An objector might very well argue at this point that even if the naturalistic fallacy is disposed of, and the is-ought slogan is disarmed, there remains the prescriptivist objection to the definability of ethical terms: their force is practical or prescriptive, and this is not to be expressed in definitional form but only by seeing their manifold ways at work. I cannot here undertake to cope with this thesis in its full extent. Its intransigence on the question of definition rests in part on a narrow view of definition, which I am about to suggest is rapidly going by. It rests in part on the dogmatic assumption that the prescriptive element *is* the primary "meaning" of ethical terms, rather than a concomitant or an application problem; I should maintain on the contrary that the prescriptive element can enter in different ways and it is a policy decision as to how ethical terms are to be construed.[27] The prescriptivist objection to such a treatment would rest on the view that the character of ethical terms is to be determined by the analysis of ordinary language and its uses; some of the difficulties this would produce, we have already noted.[28] It is also possible that the contrast of the prescriptive and the descriptive has been oversharpened; in part this has involved an extremely narrow sense of 'description.'[29] And finally, there is the perennial question how far ethical judgments can become "scientific." But since this is a major point to be settled, it cannot be prejudged by ruling out forms of definition on the ground that they might make ethics more scientific. Although this is a bare indication of the issues in a vast problem, let me assume that the objections to the possibility of definition have been at least temporarily set aside.

II

If the sentence of indefinability has now been revoked, ethical theory faces the task of defining its fundamental terms at an extraordinarily propitious moment, for changes have been going

[27] For a full treatment of this problem, see above, Chapter Three.
[28] See above, Chapter Four.
[29] See below, pp. 164ff.

on in the theory of definition itself. The theory of definition is wide open today, and it would be folly to make a specific account of the nature of definition the basis for a limited treatment of ethical terms, as for example, Moore did by concentrating on analytic definition into ultimate parts and disparaging synonymous definition. I need not go far into the history of definitional theory. Let me remind you simply that when the classical notion of definition as giving the essence lost ground as metaphysical, it was succeeded by what for a long time appeared to be a perfectly clear distinction between stipulative definitions and ostensive or extensional types, with "real" or "structural" or "theoretical" definitions thrown in for good measure, whether to appease the craving left for essences or to recognize that as a matter of fact people often asked for definitions that should certify that they embodied the results of the established sciences. In the current controversies about analyticity, even the apparently simple synonymous definition is being asked to produce its credentials and show how synonymy is to be determined, with the implication that it is being assigned a Herculean labor. It is a commonplace by this time that the definition in which the right-hand side provides the necessary and sufficient conditions for the use of the term to be defined is to be recognized as an ideal rarely achievable in empirical science—rather a mathematician's hope—and by no means characteristic of conceptual clarification processes whether in ordinary discourse or in the workaday life of empirical inquiry. New attempts have been made to work out modes of clarification or specification of meaning of which the traditional definitional form will be only a limiting case. What is characteristic of many of these attempts is the controlled fusion of many elements—an effort to see how stipulative and empirical and purposive aspects, and even reference to contextual presuppositions and conditions, are functionally intertwined in the actual operations of clarification of terms.[30] And

---

30 For surveys of definitional types and concept-formation problems, see Richard Robinson, *Definition* (Oxford, 1954), and C. G. Hempel, *Fundamentals of Concept-Formation in Empirical Science* (Chicago, 1952). Abraham Kaplan's "Definition and Specification of Meaning," *The Journal of Philosophy*, XLIII (1946), 281-88, is a good example of the attempt to project a mode of clarifying that is "processive" rather than oriented to outcome of

of course the current British trend that is so influential in these problems, as well as in ethical issues, is adding its weight to break down the simple belief in definitions and to substitute the exploration of usage and the fragmentarian contextualism that gives up even hope of a definitive answer to the question "What is such-and-such?" To adapt Ryle's use of the phrase 'unscheduled logics' to our present problem, we may speak of 'unscheduled modes of defining.' At a time when types of definition are proposed in which extensional identity is the most that is required, and not always even this,[31] the very term 'definition' has come to mean, in many logic texts, little more than a set of forms and techniques by which one might try to make terms clear in discourse or in various fields of inquiry.

Not all the tendencies in contemporary definitional theory are, however, so dispersive. There is one approach of tremendous importance which has been explored in relation to theoretical terms in the sciences. The contemporary reaction against a narrow empiricism or a narrow operationalism which identified the concept with a set of observation-terms or operations has brought a revived appreciation of the role of theoretical constructs. Attention has fastened on their unifying character, the fact that they have to be understood in terms of the whole theory of which they are a part and may not be eliminated as equivalent to some set of observation-terms, the problem whether they are to be given a realistic or an instrumentalist interpretation, how they maintain an "open" character, the way in which deductions from the theory in which they occur are assigned coordinative or applica-

---

inquiry. Max Black's "Definition, Presupposition, and Assertion" (in his *Problems of Analysis* [Ithaca, 1954]) formulates what he calls a "range definition" which starts with typical or "clear" cases and maps variation in constitutive factors; it is an interesting example of a bold attempt to break through by fashioning new instruments rather than simply being critical of the old. In the main stream of logical formulations, Carnap's "Testability and Meaning," *Philosophy of Science*, III (1936), 419-71, and IV (1937), 1-40, constituted the recognized breakthrough. In such forward movements, it is often more important that the issue be raised and something tried out than how successful the specific proposal may be.

[31] E.g., Nelson Goodman, *The Structure of Appearance* (Cambridge, Mass., 1951), pp. 4-5; cf. his "On Likeness of Meaning," *Analysis*, X (1949), 1-7.

tory procedures, and so forth.[32] Now while the best illustrations of such constructs come from the most highly systematized parts of physical theory, controversies about their role have been recurrent in psychology as well. Whatever be the outcome of contemporary attempts to analyze these problems, it is clear that theoretical constructs are not indefinable, nor are they completely or exhaustively definable but they do maintain a unified character. We shall have to ask whether some uses of some ethical terms may not best be understood in the light of these issues.

This whole situation in definitional theory—without venturing predictions about its outcome or hypotheses about its causes—leaves us extraordinarily free today in ethical theory. We can determine definitional policy without a coercive model. Whatever its nature, morality does stand out as one domain of human life. Its analysis need not be limited to following the lessons learned elsewhere; on the contrary, it may provide data, uses, problems that may be the basis for fresh lessons in the theory of definition in terms of its unique elements. This does not mean abandoning well-tried insights and launching out wholly on one's own. But it does mean keeping our eye on our own area, feeling bound to no one theory of definition, but consulting all the theories as if they were proposing different types of definitions, and then trying to see how serviceable these types turned out to be. One might begin, for example, with a list of the types given in Robinson or Hempel or Copi,[33] or any of the current logic books, and simply try them out. One might look for synonymous definitions and use the current controversy as a warning to be as precise as possible about how we were judging synonymy. One might map contexts

[32] For a brief analysis of theoretical constructs, see L. W. Beck, "Construction and Inferred Entities," *Philosophy of Science*, XVII (1950); reprinted in Feigl and Brodbeck, *Readings in the Philosophy of Science* (New York, 1953), pp. 368-81. For a study of some of the logical problems involved, see C. G. Hempel, "The Theoretician's Dilemma," in *Concepts, Theories, and the Mind-Body Problem* (Minnesota Studies in the Philosophy of Science, Vol. II), ed. Feigl, Scriven, and Maxwell, pp. 37-98. See also Ernest Nagel, *The Structure of Science* (New York and Burlingame, 1961), Chs. V-VI.

[33] Robinson, *op. cit.;* Hempel, *Fundamentals of Concept-Formation in Empirical Science;* Irving Copi, *Introduction to Logic* (New York, 1953), Ch. IV.

of usage and the logic of 'wrong' without assuming that it will spread in so many directions that no systematic theory of wrong will emerge. One might look for an "implicit definition" of 'good' without worrying whether this type should really be regarded as a definition or the offering of a "model" or "interpretation." And so on. Thus, after listing some of the standard types, one might very well try one's hand at new types, fashioned for our own purpose in ethical theory. It is this creative exploratory task that I should like to illustrate in the remainder of this paper. Let us start with the more standard types, as they are found here and there in ethical writings.

Synonymous definitions. We could stipulate that 'good' is synonymous with 'worthwhile,' and that 'bad' is synonymous with 'evil.' I don't know if we could get away with it. 'Worthwhile' calls for something further—worthwhile *having* or *experiencing,* or what not. If it is synonymous with 'good,' then the formation-rules for subjects in sentences in which 'good' is a predicate term or occurs as an adjective, will have to be more limited than they usually are. I suppose "He's a good man" could be construed as saying that he is worthwhile knowing, and so on, but it looks as if complications will arise. And as for 'bad' and 'evil,' let me remind you that between these distinctions Nietzsche, in his *Genealogy of Morals,* found the whole difference between the heroic concept in which 'bad' means contrary to the interest of the class, and the mass concept in which 'evil' connotes sin. Presumably these last two examples—'bad' means contrary to the interests of one's class, and 'evil' connotes sinful—are either *nominal definitions* (stipulated verbal equivalences) or *lexical definitions* (reported customary usage). There are plenty of such a type strewn around in ethical theories.

How about *operational* or *coordinating definitions,* or *empirical indices,* or the like? Take, for example, Brandt's instructions when he asked twenty-six Hopi informants to express views about the morality of some thirty types of conduct, and explained 'wrong' as referring to what the informant would feel guilty about, what he would advise his children against, and that for which he would criticize other parties if it would be safe to do so! [34] Or take Sartre's test for a truly moral decision about 'wrong'

[34] Richard B. Brandt, *Hopi Ethics* (Chicago, 1954), p. 153.

tematize the field, and test competing definitions in the usual logical-scientific fashion. It is obvious that we will not have a complete account of any of the basic ethical terms in short order. They are at present indefinable except in one of the numerous partial ways, not because of an inherent indefinability but perhaps because we do not know enough about the phenomena, the processes, human life and human history, human possibilities of variation, and so on, to give us an answer. What we should want to put into a definition of a theoretical sort would be the terms that would enter into a more complete theory of man, life, and society. Note also that we should not be alarmed by the fear that this makes the good "purely a scientific matter." For how scientific it makes the good depends not on our using a parallel mode of definition to concepts in scientific study, but on how amenable the material will prove to scientific progress. It is by no means wholly clear how far health will turn out to be "purely a scientific matter" although we may suspect this may be so. And the situation is less clear in the case of democracy.

Let me now suggest a few less common and some "unscheduled" types or techniques of definition which may be helpful in our domain, affixing homemade or borrowed names to them.

A minimax definition. Here we list extremes precisely because we do not have an exact value. It is like the solution that *x* is less than 7 and greater than 2. Thus to define 'good' in terms of what pleases is too wide, to define it in terms of object of desire is too narrow; to define it in terms of what we would desire or else desire to continue if its termination were contemplated would be closer. And so on. I think that when we ask for the mark of the 'moral,' this type of definition may be the best we may be able to get at the present state of knowledge.[39]

A family definition. It might turn out that we could not provide a single definition but had to furnish a family of types with only a family resemblance. We would face such a problem in defining a term such as 'skill' if we were not satisfied with a simple synonym; probably we classify broad types and select salient characteristics from each. Sometimes we would have a cabinet-family, with each separate part supervising a special do-

---

[39] Cf. *Anthropology and Ethics,* Ch. II.

main. To take a rough example, the defining mark of 'good' in the division dealing with the individual's needs might be satisfaction; in dealing with social matters, the widest possible harmony; in dealing with long-range evolutionary periods, some criterion of progress. There might or might not be unifying relations. It might turn out that morality rested on there being on the whole a sufficient coincidence to keep going, and that where there was a real clash morality might be impossible. These are separate issues.

Or again, the family might consist in a set of definitions from different perspectives. A modern survey of a college asks what it looks like from the point of view of students, of faculty, of administration, of alumni, of the public, and so on; different criteria obviously may arise in each, although there may be mutual sympathy and overlapping. So too, the meaning of 'ought,' of 'good,' and the rest may vary from the perspective of participant chooser, of recipient, of subsequently affected (the younger generation), of general spectator critique.[40] This does not have to be so, but it may very well be so, and it ought to be explored to the fullest. One of the useful techniques here is personal-pronoun analysis— e.g., the difference between "I ought to do this" and "He ought to do this." It may very well be that a requiredness-vector phenomenological account fits the first person and a more utilitarian account the third person.[41] Again, what unity can be achieved in such studies is a subsequent question.

Equilibrium or *homeostatic definition.* This is another possibility in which some type of equilibrium situation is described, maintaining a given form, and 'good' is defined in terms of the maintenance of the form, and 'right' in terms of the rules required by the system to keep it going. This is the modern respectable type of definition that replaces the ancient, no longer respectable teleological type. Its use in current treatment of "teleological mechanisms" and "functional theory" seems pretty widespread. The medical concept of 'health' may perhaps best be defined in some such way. Of course, to prevent the system from being closed—that is, to maintain the autonomy effect—there would have to be some way of construing the notion of "shifting to a

[40] Cf. below, pp. 233-35.
[41] Cf. the somewhat different analysis in Nowell-Smith, *op. cit.,* pp. 193-97.

higher level." Otherwise, such a type of definition would seem to have the same limiting effect as the older ethical theories that defined in terms of a fixed human nature.

Genetic definition is an interesting type which incorporates some sort of causal account.[42] Thus J. S. Mill's implicit definition of 'good' seems to me to be not simply the inherently pleasurable, but that which is such *or* which has come to be such according to the laws of psychological association; this is suggested by his discussion of virtue. Spinoza uses this type of definition, for example, when he says, "Love is nothing else but pleasure accompanied by the idea of an external cause." [43] Definitions of color-terms frequently incorporate the differentiating physical causes, and definitions of such psychological terms as 'guilt-feeling' may add the genetic source or differentiating personality factors to the phenomenological delineation. The interesting point about genetic definitions then, is that they may cross levels and present a configuration of elements drawn from different fields and sciences. Of course, the relations of the parts are empirical, and it is always possible to say, "Couldn't you *imagine* yourself seeing green and investigating its physical conditions and finding them different from what you had thought they were?" And if you said "yes," it will be argued that you must *mean* something by 'green' which doesn't involve the physical conditions. But this only shows that there are different senses of 'green,' one purely phenomenological, the other involving phenomenological-physical correlations with all the tentative elements that arise in correlation. The reasons for using this second type of definition are, of course, another matter, to be explored in terms of the way definitions function in further inquiry and application. For example, a genetic definition of 'guilt-feeling,' which incorporates the psychological-developmental conditions correlated with specific qualities of the phenomenological picture of the feeling, may be used to fashion a concept of 'unconscious guilt-feeling' for describing what is going on in some persons. Now insofar as psychological terms enter into many different accounts of ethical terms, it is quite possible that we will misunderstand the more complex accounts if we do not pay close attention to the nature

[42] This type is discussed in Robinson, *op. cit.*, pp. 99f.
[43] *Ethics*, Part III, prop. xiii, note.

and role of such kinds of definition. Complex theories that define 'good' and 'right' in terms of the reactions of ideal and normal observers would have to specify the psychological attitudes and conditions for their observers, giving the definition the appearance of something like the genetic type.

A complicated and potentially valuable form is what we might call a *developmental definition*. It gives an ordered family type. For example, one might ask, as Erikson does,[44] how good and evil enter the baby's world, and look for marks to recognize it in terms of the child's perspective. Then one might go on to trace the proliferation of marks. We don't know the phenomenology of the infant, so the earliest marks might be what is swallowed or what is spit out, what produces a smile as against what produces crying. And so on, through whatever identifications might occur, to the development of the ego and its ways. (Actually, Erikson starts with the biting stage.) Interestingly enough, the use of such a procedure in ethics seems to me to be discernible in Aristotle's *Nicomachean Ethics*. In the earlier stages, Aristotle speaks of the noble (*kalon*) when he is looking at the moral good from the point of view of the child whose mark is the praise he gets from the authoritative figure or model. Only when reason flowers does Aristotle begin to speak of the good (*agathon*). How successful a developmental definition could be depends on how determinate and established is the underlying theory of development. It could also be used on a social level, if one found, as Julian Huxley for example claims, that ethics played a different role in different eras of human development. Huxley suggests a survival role first, involving a stress on solidarity, a class-domination and group rivalry role thereafter, and now a more complex type stressing provision of universal material and cultural opportunity.[45]

Santayana in his chapter on "Love" in *Reason in Society*, has love in the individual's life cycle go through the stages of parents, wife, children, ideas. If this is a "law" of human development, then the definition of 'good' might involve a parameter corresponding to the stage of development, unless, of course, one defined it in terms of a constant quality in the feeling and systematized the variety as successive objects of attraction. Which

[44] E. H. Erikson, *Childhood and Society* (New York, 1950), p. 74.
[45] Huxley and Huxley, *Touchstone for Ethics* (New York, 1947), pp. 116-17.

procedure might best be followed would depend on the results of the actual analysis of the material.

Another type of definition, useful in scientific work, is *definition by successive complication*. William James defines 'good' for a single sentient being in a moral solitude, by saying that what he feels good he makes good.[46] Then he complicates this by the introduction of a second wish and a second sentient being. Let me give a more complex analogy. We can define 'democracy' by a set of simple procedures for expression of the common will in the usual town meeting situation of old New England. Now increase the population, add representative techniques, but at each step maintain a connection with the previous account, so that what was seen as the content of democracy could be achievable now in a more roundabout way. As the scope is increased, new interests enter—regional, national, global—and the actual picture of democratic procedures becomes modified. Whereas at the beginning, the town meeting technique stood out as the defining mark made possible by a basic identity of interests, at the end the notion of a common will indirectly expressed by complicated techniques may stretch thin and cover chiefly the aim of maintaining harmony and modes of resolving potential conflict. But the continuity in successive definition is not wholly lost. Perhaps such a procedure applied to 'good' might turn into a developmental definition or else simply yield a family type, just as the complication of operations extends the meaning of 'number' in the history of mathematics. But it would be worth trying to experiment with such a mode of definition for both 'good' and for 'ought.' In the case of obligation-terms it might serve to do justice both to the inner-psychological phenomena of conscience and the political and juridical use of 'rights' and 'duties' in a moral sense, in a more unified way than is customarily the case.

There is another type which I should be tempted to call *definition by multiple coincidence*. Take, for example, Blackstone's much-criticized definition of 'law' as "a rule of civil conduct prescribed by the supreme power in a state commanding what is right and prohibiting what is wrong." What, it is said trium-

46 "The Moral Philosopher and the Moral Life," in *The Will to Believe and Other Essays in Popular Philosophy* (New York, 1956), p. 190. For discussion of this formulation, see below, p. 134.

phantly, if the sovereign commands what is wrong? Now I have no defense to offer for Blackstone, and for all I care, you may share Jefferson's most vituperative attitude which, if I remember aright, he seems to reserve for Blackstone and for Hume, together with Burke. But does the fact that the tests diverge in one context alter the fact that *where they coincide* you can get results with either one? Spencer, in his evolutionary picture, seems to say that we will have a good society when the actions that are altruistic are also egoistic, and vice versa. We might ask for a more refined definition in terms of motives, so as to be able to distinguish them even where the acts coincide, or perhaps we could use the fact of the motives diverging as a mark of the less good society. In any case, I seem to discern a type of definition in which 'good' could be defined for a limited or perhaps ideal range as: what you desire to achieve, would feel guilty about not aiming at, would bring the greatest happiness of the greatest number, would be what a man of practical wisdom would recommend, would be the sort of thing that a categorical imperative would be very categorical about, or what a disinterested observer would sympathize with, and so on. Oh, happy area in which the results of all the tests coincided [47]—even if with only an extensional near-equivalence! In any case, once we can conceive of such, we can explore what makes them fall apart beyond this common area. This is a roundabout way of seeking a comprehensive theory of man and his world which would make some kind of theoretical definition possible.

Perhaps instead of speaking more generally of theoretical definition, one might invoke at this point the idea of 'good' as a theoretical construct, functioning in the way suggested earlier. Its fuller theoretical formulation could not, of course, be given because we do not have the comprehensive theory of man and his world referred to. This would certainly be "open" enough! The various tests mentioned would function quite literally as tests, or coordinative definitions, or operational indices, or whatever you wanted to call them, and could be studied in their correla-

[47] In terms of Max Black's "range definition" mentioned above, this area would provide the clear cases or mountain peaks from which we would begin the study of variations. It could do this too, but my interest here is rather in seeing how we could move toward a theoretical definition.

tion and discrepancy, and refined or revised. The logical status of the ethical terms, at least, would be clear. How far such a solution to the definition problem in ethics might prove fruitful, it is too early to say. Perhaps not for all ethical terms, nor even for all uses of 'good.' It might, however, suit the notion of 'the good life' which keeps bobbing up at crucial points in ethical writings. In classical writings it was the usual starting point for ethical reflections. But even in contemporary works where you least expect it, it may come in to do what looks suspiciously like a theoretical mopping-up job. For example, Nowell-Smith says at the end, "What sort of principles a man adopts will, in the end, depend on his vision of the Good Life, his conception of the sort of world that he desires, so far as it rests with him, to create." [48] And although he adds, "Indeed his moral principles just *are* this conception," we are left wondering whether they may not be expressions of the conception or attempts to articulate it; not merely whether there is a field of study of forms, unities, diversities, qualities of attraction, causes, and so on, of men's conception of the good life—for this would be readily granted—but whether ethical terms may not more appropriately be defined by references to this whole field of study and its systematization, rather than in the prevalent linguistic mode. But this again is another story, and it cannot be prejudged. In any case, the possibility of treating some uses of 'good' as involving a theoretical construct cannot be ruled out.

Briefly then, to conclude. I regard the chapter in the history of ethics opened by the naturalistic fallacy accusation as ready to be closed. Its libertarian aspirations can be maintained in any sensible present-day ethical theory. The fuss over the "is-ought" slogan is (hopefully) giving way to the larger job of mapping what kinds of relations and gaps, what specific reductions there may or may not be. The theory of definition in contemporary philosophy is no longer restrictive and should encourage freedom of speculation about forms of definition in ethics. There is still a bias against definition on prescriptive grounds and on assumptions about ordinary language, but it is no longer strong enough to hold back experimentation. My suggestions about unsched-

48 *Op. cit.*, p. 313.

uled modes of defining have been guided by the belief that there is no reason to treat ethical concepts as constituting an utterly distinct category or to make a sharp break in the seam of the fields of human inquiry. Ethical inquiry needs to learn how far the scientific temper, scientific methods, scientific results, can help it in its theoretical problems. Artificial barriers to such inquiry should be removed. This is of course a policy decision and does not guarantee how far the efforts it is proposing will succeed. Our emphasis should fall on getting to work, rather than proclaiming intentions.

CHAPTER SIX

ETHICAL REASONING

Our second sample of analytic problems is taken from current controversies about the nature of reasoning in ethics. There have been serious claims that reasoning in ethics has its own special forms and is not of the same type as is found in scientific or ordinary-life inquiries. The problem before us is therefore whether we ever support ethical conclusions validly by reasoning which is neither deductive nor inductive. How shall we estimate current approaches to validity-models other than the established ones, in reaching such conclusions as "This is wrong," "Such-and-such is good," "I (he) ought to do this," and so forth? Let us first consider briefly the established models and the objections urged against them.

I

The familiar deductive model assumed a deductive system with moral universals as axioms, types of cases as theorems, and individual cases as exercises. Breaking faith with another is wrong, not keeping a promise is breaking faith with another, therefore not keeping a promise is wrong. This proposed conduct is breaking a promise; therefore, it is wrong.

Historically, the deductive model has exercised great fascination in ethical and legal theory. In recent times it has been widely rejected. But the desire to employ it is no more blameworthy than the drive towards mathematical system in physics. It can be rejected only by showing that it is premature, or by establishing that the conditions for its successful application do not hold in the field under consideration. For ethics, the points of special difficulty in the application of the model may be summarized briefly:

(a) Are there moral universals to act as premises? Most ethical systems find some meaningful sense for universals—for example, as prima facie duties or as invariant elements in moral reckoning.

(b) How will universals be certified? There is the familiar historical succession of methods—revelation, intuition, induction, Kantian universalization, arbitrary commitment or postulation, historical growth into firm acceptance. Here, shift to an inductive model is likely, as substitute or supplement.

(c) In individual cases, how shall we determine which rule to invoke? Where there are a limited number of writs in law or commandments in morals, this seems a simple question for a filing clerk. But obviously the existence of several possible subsumptions opens the way to alternative judgments. Particularly striking problems appear as conflicts of prima facie duties, resolvable only by special criteria of relevance, an ordered hierarchy of principles, a set of weights and measures, or some type of established routing system.

(d) Further difficulty may arise in interpreting the rule in relation to the particular facts. Does the stringency of a promise carry over to an implied promise? Can we appeal to a person of "normal sensitivity" in human relations? And so on through hosts of issues, familiar enough in law and moral casuistry.

Loss of faith in the deductive model is the equivalent of a general hypothesis that such difficulties will remain stubborn. This hypothesis is inductively grounded, or else deduced from a special theory of man asserting endless spontaneity and novelty in moral decision, or in any case the metaphysical uniqueness of each decision.

II

As two samples of the inductive model, let us refer briefly to Bentham and Dewey. For Bentham, moral judgments are ultimately inductive generalizations about what yields the greatest happiness, either in classes of situations or particular situations. Clearly, such an approach is not hostile to large areas of "deductive system" within human life; it all depends on the stability of the conditions about which generalization is made. Dewey's is a looser pluralism: every situation in which a moral question arises will be found on investigation to be already structured in terms of strivings and issues with alternative paths functioning as hypotheses for resolving the underlying problem. Thus appraisal is possible: moral knowledge consists of principles serving as instruments and continually subject to revision. Ethics will classify typical situations and where they are more stable, provide rules; where there is less stability, it will provide at least flexible tools for analysis.

Leaving aside the question whether the inductive should be construed as a special case of the deductive with certain types of assumptions about the constitution of the field, or whether it is "genuinely" different, as outside our present concern, we find voiced in contemporary ethical theory three major objections to the inductive model. For brevity I shall call them the *field instability argument,* the *naturalistic fallacy accusation,* and the *prescriptive emphasis.*

(a) Is there really the stability, the maintenance of a continued identity in the situation, which the inductive approach requires? Clearly, Bentham oversimplifies man in setting up pleasure as the single over-all goal, and he manages to get along only by keeping the term vague and stretchable. But does not even Dewey take for granted too readily the stability of the problem-situation and its well-structured character? May there not be an inner flux making most problems so multistructured or fleetingly structured as to be practically structureless? This would out-Dewey Dewey in its pluralism, yielding again an extreme pluralism, or at least an inevitable contextualism in the moral field. It offers itself as an inductive rejection of the inductive model for ethics.[1]

This *field instability argument,* in my opinion, points to the ultimate basis of decision concerning the established models in ethics. Where a field is sufficiently determinate to support generalizations, verification takes inductive forms. Where it also supports stable definitions with well-demarcated modes of application, greater use of deductive form is possible. The question of other validity models arises only when the field is not sufficiently determinate. In short, I take the contemporary search for fresh validity models to reflect the present immature state of the human sciences. To give way at this point to the field instability argu-

[1] The problem of the nature and sources of indeterminacy is discussed in greater detail in my *Ethical Judgment,* Ch. IV.

ment is like assuming in pre-Socratic days that the conflict of physical theories makes advance in physical science impossible and necessitates an extreme Heracliteanism. Instead, I should propose the following methodological policy: as far as possible, emphasis should fall on achieving greater determinateness by scientific investigation, by sharpening concepts, and by clearer articulation of values applied. To seek new models of validity is to accept the indeterminate character of the field in the existent state of insufficient knowledge, loose concepts, and unexpressed valuations.

(b) The inductive model requires that ethical terms be in some way linked with existential qualities, relations, or processes. This has usually taken the form of an ethical naturalism identifying 'good' in terms of pleasure, satisfaction, desire, or aspiration, and 'ought' in terms of selected sentiments or feelings. (Inductive intuitionisms are possible, too, but rarely come furnished with a sufficiently determinate mode of cognition, and on the whole intuitionism has preferred to claim certainty.) Now ethical naturalism, as we have seen in considerable detail in the preceding chapter, was long rejected by many as committing the naturalistic fallacy. If our analysis of the arguments underlying the naturalistic fallacy accusation and our study of its outcome have removed this obstacle to definition,[2] it is clear that an open character may be maintained in ethical concepts without forcing an abandonment of the inductive model. This does not guarantee that the inductive model can be successfully employed, but it does mean that it cannot be declared inherently incompatible with the nature and function of ethical terms.

(c) The third objection to the inductive model regards it as ignoring the fundamentally prescriptive character of ethics. Induction is concerned with generalization as a basis for prediction. Such results constitute a science, not an ethics. Reflective description, however valuable, is not moral judgment or decision. The prescriptive element is central to ethics. Take the legal analogy: induction will tell you the trend of judicial decision, if you are a lawyer wanting to predict which way the judge will go. But what will the judge himself investigate when he is in the act

2 See especially pp. 114-15.

of deciding? Even if he looks within himself he is not merely describing his past trend of decision but determining where he is to go. The demand for a first-personal rather than a third-personal logic of ethics reflects, no doubt, the crisis of decision in our times.

This argument has been one of the most characteristic of recent trends in ethical theory. The central conflict of a cognitivist and a prescriptivist approach which it involves has been considered in Chapter Three. But its special impact on the problem of ethical reasoning may perhaps best be brought out by looking at the way in which the established models have been abandoned.

III

The break with traditional models was carried through by the emotive theory, following Moore's critique of naturalism. Stipulating that ethics must not be psychology, affirming that ethical discourse functions in significant part emotively, and sharply separating descriptive statements embodying beliefs from expressions of attitude, Stevenson provided such ethical interpretations as: " 'This is wrong' means *I disapprove of this; do so as well.*" [3] The emotive theory thus embodies the *naturalistic fallacy accusation* and the *prescriptive emphasis*. Its unique turn is the interpretation of the prescriptive as the emotive functioning of ethical terms. The *field instability argument* is also developed in a special form: the connection of belief and attitude is construed as causal, not logical, so that, except for means-ends appraisal, the issue of how far difference of attitude is rooted in difference of belief replaces the search for "sound reasons" for a moral judgment. But it is assumed in effect that difference of attitude has an element of arbitrariness so that it is not wholly rooted in difference of belief.[4] It is not surprising therefore that on the ques-

3 Charles L. Stevenson, *Ethics and Language* (New Haven, 1944), p. 21.

4 It is not always realized how extensive is the reliance of the emotive theory on particular psychological and causal assumptions to fortify its field instability basis. It is interesting to note that when Stevenson came to defend his formulation of the theory against criticism, it was to the factual assumptions that he appealed: "My methodological conclusions center less on my conception of meaning than on my conceptions of agreement and

tion of ethical inference Stevenson finds it "wholly impracticable and injudicious" to sanction a sense of 'validity' from factual reasons to moral conclusions. The emotive theory thus created a vacuum in the field validity models which moral philosophers, if not nature, could not fail to abhor.

One direction towards restoration of validity concepts is the attempt, noted in an earlier chapter,[5] to work out a logic of the prescriptive element itself. Everett Hall's *What is Value?* suggested substituting legitimacy-values for truth-values and regarding value as that which makes a legitimate sentence legitimate in a way analogous to that in which fact is what makes a true sentence true. Hall's justification for a logic of normatives is ultimately the metaphysical belief that value, like fact, is a category and that the structure of the normative sentence in an ideal language reveals the structure of value. R. M. Hare's *The Language of Morals* worked out an analytical model on imperative lines resting on the view that the only way moral judgments can be seen to guide action, as they are obviously intended to, is to recognize that their function is to *commend*. Deontic logic, on its formal side, has recently grown to large proportions. But on the whole, it has been too busy with its technical development to offer any answer to the question of the form that ethical reasoning will turn out to take. If it succeeds completely, it will bring back the deductive model into fresh repute, yielding variants differing in type of syntax. But the interpretation of its primitive idea—whether 'moral permissibility' or 'moral acceptability' or 'mor-

---

disagreement. If the solution of normative issues requires agreement in attitude, if the relation between attitudes and beliefs is causal and possibly subject to individual differences, and if rational methods can effect agreement in attitude only through the indirect means of altering beliefs, then the essential features of my analysis remain intact" ("Meaning: Descriptive and Emotive," in "A Symposium on Emotive Meaning," by I. A. Richards, Max Black, Charles L. Stevenson, *The Philosophical Review*, LVII [1948], 142). Clearly, we need a full scientific study of the phenomenon of holding a belief, including the determination whether it has unavoidable emotional or motivational components. And we need a full scientific study of having an attitude or expressing an emotion, including the determination whether it has cognitive or motivational components. See the references in note 27 below.

5 See above, p. 61.

ally mandatory'—will still remain a problem.[6] Moreover, forms akin to deontic logic are being developed with skill in such different directions that one cannot be sure that the most useful system may not be one employing a term such as 'better' as fundamental,[7] capable of a descriptive interpretation. In any case, it is quite possible that approaches along any of these lines may be driven to invoke some variant of inductive models when they come to consider how normative or imperative sentences are "justified" or "established."

The second and major current movement to establish validity models along nontraditional lines stems from British analytic circles. Overlooking differing tendencies within the movement, I shall call it the *good-reasons approach*. While it shares the prescriptive emphasis with emotive theory, it refuses to abandon the conception of some sort of validity in ethical inference. It reminds us of the stubborn fact that we do offer factual statements as reasons for moral conclusions and regard some reasons as better than others. In practical judgment, says Hampshire, there are patterns of argument "which may be described as more or less rational in the sense that they are more or less strictly governed by recognized (though not necessarily formulated) rules of relevance." [8] S. E. Toulmin's *The Place of Reason in Ethics* (1953) was perhaps the clearest first sample of this approach in book form.

The good-reasons approach redresses the extremism of the emotive theory by taking seriously the idea of the function of ethical discourse. It exhibits a wide variety of uses to replace the oversharp dichotomy of informative and emotive. Hare distin-

---

[6] See, for example, Arthur N. Prior's complaint with respect to one system of deontic logic, that a proposition that we have an obligation to escape from the sanction turns ultimately into "necessarily if you escape you escape." He adds, "Really this system is not about ethics at all—it is about the technique of escaping from something you fear, and that is all there is to it." He points out further, however, that the notions involved are broad enough to cover 'being perfect' as well as escaping from what we fear. ("Escapism: The Logical Basis of Ethics," in *Essays in Moral Philosophy*, ed. A. I. Melden [Seattle, 1958]. pp. 145-46.)

[7] For the rise of such systems, see below, p. 263.

[8] Stuart Hampshire, "Fallacies in Moral Philosophy," *Mind*, LVIII (1949), 471.

guishes commending from commanding,[9] Falk, guiding from goading.[10] Hampshire stresses the function of practical judgment from the agent's point of view rather than praising or blaming from the critic's.[11] Hart stresses the ascriptive function of language in claiming rights and assigning responsibilities.[12] Attention has also been called to ceremonial use, performatory use, and so forth. Nowell-Smith lists as some uses for value-words, "to express tastes and preferences, to express decisions and choices, to criticize, grade, and evaluate, to advise, admonish, warn, persuade and dissuade, to praise, encourage and reprove, to promulgate and draw attention to rules; and doubtless for other purposes also." [13] Even within any given function, analysis is to be carried out in terms of particular contexts. Thus in the decision situation, Toulmin distinguishes reasons for a particular act under an existent code, reasons for altering or maintaining a code (for example, in terms of lessening suffering), reasons for trusting a man recommending reforms, and so on.

There is indeed a sense of liberation conveyed by the mandate to go ahead and analyze diverse functions and use contexts. The result is not unlike the early stages of the search for specimens in a descriptive science. New finds are announced (or here old uses brought to analytic light) with every other issue of *Mind*. And each new context undermines an old theory which is seen to have generalized the limited results of some narrow context. Construction of general ethical theory gives way to mapping diversified contexts and their implicit validity standards. One is tempted to map deliberately as many contexts as possible for intensified exploration of the use of ethical language, and along multiple bases of division. For example, over and above the many contexts referred to, there are varieties of sociological relation contexts which may have significant differences, such as relations of adult and child as contrasted with relation of agemates (compare Piaget's treatment in his *Moral Judgment of the*

9 R. M. Hare, *The Language of Morals* (Oxford, 1952).

10 W. D. Falk, "Guiding and Goading," *Mind*, LXII (1953), 145-69.

11 Hampshire, *op. cit.* For fuller discussion of the relation between the on-looker's and the agent's perspectives, see below, pp. 233-35.

12 See below, pp. 148-50.

13 P. H. Nowell-Smith, *Ethics* (Baltimore, 1954), p. 98.

Child).[14] Even in adult-child relations, the teaching situation may differ markedly from that of exercising authority. Similarly, there are sanctioning situations among adults, group decisions on policy, intercultural comparison situations, and hosts of others. There are whole types of approaches not yet explored. For example, consideration of moral *questions* would reveal aspects of meaning quite different from the lordly imperative that so readily offers itself when we consider the authoritative *answer* form. An expanded good-reasons approach thus pays close attention to the facts of the moral field, although filtered through linguistic usage.

IV

When all these patterns of good reasons have been delineated, what is to be concluded about ethical reasoning? Have we a multitude of validity models which are ultimate in the sense that they are not reducible to the deductive or inductive form, nor in fact to one another? Such ultimacy is not, we are assured, a metaphysical assumption of the sanctity of ordinary language but a belief, like Ryle's, that its "logical powers" are "unscheduled" and irreducible.[15] Or have we rather just a survey of local moral dialects, a set of contingent linguistic structures? Why insist on ultimacy? May there not be invariant elements in good-reasons contexts to support inductive generalizations, or even a systematic theory providing a "real definition" of good reasons for deductive purposes? In physics, we would not stop the search for a unified meaning for 'satisfactory explanation' when we learn that explanation involving action at a distance troubled the Newtonian era, but seemed the very prototype of satisfactory explanation to scientists in Helmholtz's time.[16] Only by assuming that a unified theory of good reasons is impossible or improbable can the approach remain content with contextual validity models of a nontraditional type. Let us consider

14 Cf. above, p. 64.

15 Gilbert Ryle, "Ordinary Language," *The Philosophical Review*, LXII (1953), pp. 167-86.

16 Cf. Philipp Frank, *Modern Science and Its Philosophy* (Cambridge, Mass., 1949), pp. 211ff.

briefly three grounds for such an assumption, the first two of which rest on the *field instability argument,* and the third on the *prescriptive emphasis.*

(1) One is a thesis of the permanent plurality of contexts.[17] But the various contexts are contexts of human psychological and social functioning, and may be both causally and purposively unified. Thus, learning contexts are integrated into adult aim contexts, and first-person decision contexts already embody a self as first person that has many social components. Even in strictly ethical terms it may not be easy to keep contexts apart. For example, take Toulmin's contexts: the realization that a particular act would fall under the accepted code may be the very point at which the code itself is brought under critical revision. Contextual pluralism may fit for equilibrium analysis but not for understanding change or development. The final decision concerning an ultimate contextualism therefore waits on the fuller scientific study of the interrelation of areas and contexts in human life.

(2) A second ground is the belief in an ultimate indeterminacy in the actual content of the good reasons found. This issue is again empirical. Toulmin himself assumes removal of unhappiness and promotion of happiness as a general ground in justifying codes. Similarly, Baier has argued for the objective universal character of "it will cause me pain" as a good reason (prima facie and presumptively) against doing the act.[18] The content of good reasons may turn out to have a unified structure; this depends on the extent of unity in human nature and life as exhibited in the results of the contemporary sciences.

(3) It may be claimed that the concept of good reasons will resist systematization because of the prescriptive character of ethical terms. If this is ascribed to the multiplicity of practical functions, then we are back to the previous grounds. It may, however, be thought to be inherent in the *activist* character of the decision process.

Perhaps it is best to pursue the whole problem of the conditions that would render a unified theory of good reasons unlikely by particular example. I take H. L. A. Hart's influential paper

[17] Cf. above, p. 107.
[18] K. Baier, "Good Reasons," *Philosophical Studies,* IV (1953), 1-15.

on "The Ascription of Responsibility and Rights" [19] because its excellent formulation of a limited problem and its coordination of legal and ordinary usage will enable us to sketch the issues rapidly and on a wider canvas. Certain legal concepts—contract, property, trespass, criminal liability—are often treated as if they were descriptive, as if we could state necessary and sufficient conditions for the existence of a contract. When we try to do so we end up by citing leading cases with a wide-open *etcetera*. Moreover, the concepts are *defeasible* in the sense that even where the standard elements of a contract seem to be present, a whole host of "unless" conditions (no duress, no immoral purposes, and so on) open up ways in which existence of a contract may be subject to "defeat." Hart maintains that ordinary sentences such as "He did it," "This is yours," as well as the concept of *action* generally have a similar character. His fundamental point is that such concepts are not used to describe, nor again emotively, but to *ascribe* rights and responsibilities, and to *claim* rights, *recognize* rights, and so on; this is all part of *judging* in the practical sense of deciding.

Among Hart's reasons for rejecting a descriptive interpretation of these "defeasible" concepts, the chief seems to be the existence of an indefinite set of "excuses" and the apparent impossibility of furnishing necessary and sufficient conditions for application of the concept. But are these reasons adequate? The indefinite set of "excuses" may be cut down by the growth of knowledge. For example, although voluntary action is a concept admittedly used historically to cover what is not excused as involuntary, it may acquire a positive content with a growing psychology; at least the types of involuntariness may be cut down to a limited set. In another context, excuses may be cut down by stipulation on grounds of social policy; as, for example, in determination of liability in workmen's compensation. Again, the fact that the ideal of necessary and sufficient conditions is not achieved does not rule out descriptive intent; many obviously descriptive terms in scientific use—'life' for example—cannot as yet meet it. But even if necessary and sufficient conditions were furnished for legal and ethical concepts, Hart would regard it as mistakenly "identifying the meaning of a non-descriptive utter-

[19] *Proceedings of the Aristotelian Society, 1948-49.* Cf. above, p. 78.

ance ... with the factual circumstances which support or are good reasons for the ascription." [20] His basic contention is therefore in effect a stipulation that legal concepts are to be given a meaning in terms of judgment as act, not cognitive assertion, just as the good-reasons approach holds that ethical concepts must be given a practical-decision meaning. But once again it is hard to see why the appeal to actual use should be felt as sufficient justification for the stipulation. For example, Nietzsche claimed that causality judgments were in effect seeking to hold nature responsible, to blame it for what was going on. Would this be other than an anthropomorphic irrelevance in scientific judgment, even if it were psychologically accurate? Hart's assignment of primacy to the ascriptive function of certain concepts may therefore be seen as more than use-analysis; it is also a policy recommendation requiring justification in terms of the given state of knowledge and implicit social valuations. We may conjecture that these are the kind that might be offered in contrasting a case law system with a rationalistically inspired code—that life is too complex, changes will be gradual, etc. But a fragmentarian use does not of itself justify a fragmentarian policy. And a recommendation to use a common law model [21] for problems of validity in ethical reasoning requires fresh justification.

Before we leave the legal analogue, let us note that attempts to provide a volitional logic of legal decision or to point to volitional factors as indispensable are by no means new. In the twentieth century alone, Wurzel attempted to add "projection" as a kind of ethical volition to subsumption and analogy in juridical thinking, Cardozo enunciated a method of sociology, Jerome Frank reduced legal logic to psychological stimulation, and so on.[22] That such accounts may correctly analyze the way in which decisions happen to be reached or may conceivably be reached does not constitute fresh validity norms; it gives them a status

[20] *Ibid.*, p. 189.

[21] Cf. above, pp. 107f.

[22] Karl Georg Wurzel, "Methods of Juridical Thinking," in *Science of Legal Method*, "Modern Legal Philosophy Series," Vol. IX (Boston, 1917); Benjamin Cardozo, *The Nature of the Judicial Process* (New Haven, 1922); Jerome Frank, *Law and the Modern Mind* (New York, 1935).

as psychological description. Their logical function would be either that of pointing to value premises required in argument, or else proposing methods of settling indeterminacy points in the traditional models; in the second case the methods themselves would require normative evaluation.

But even the fundamental fact that the business of the judge is to decide does not justify the prescriptive emphasis in the interpretation of concepts. That the role of judicial theory is to guide decision need not entail that it is any the less theoretical. (That physics may be pursued in order to enhance control over nature does not imply a control reference in analyzing 'motion' or 'energy.') We must distinguish between the *act* of deciding and the *cognitive content* of the decision. There is a margin of choice in the way decision may be construed. We may put the judge's fiat into the decision and regard the cognitive content as reasons with the good-reasons approach, or as steering devices with the emotive approach. Or we may keep the fiat outside and regard the decision as a cognitive conclusion that such-and-such is according to or contrary to law; the fiat is then seen as a volitional supplement. I am not insisting that the second course is correct, although among theoreticians it has probably been historically the more frequent. But I am maintaining that the general choice of the former—putting the fiat into the judgment and insisting that the concepts in the judgment have some fiat reference and are uniquely practical—is a kind of conceptual voluntarism not dictated by science, history, or partial coincidence with usage in a given historical context. It therefore requires justification. And in ethics at least, as a decision in methodological policy, the cognitivist approach is not to be so readily cast out.

V

Let me now apply this conclusion to ethics and show why a just recognition of the practical role of ethics in guiding conduct does not necessitate a predominantly practical interpretation of ethical concepts. That ethics involves a prescriptive element somewhere or other is clear. But it is by no means clear that "it is the distinguishing characteristic of practical judgments that they have a prescriptive or quasi-imperative force as part of their meaning." [23] The emotive theory locates the prescriptive element in the broad area of meaning as expressive or emotive meaning. Hall locates it in the syntax. The varied functions we have looked at in the good-reasons approach locate it in the pragmatic functioning of ethical terms. But Moore locates it in the field of ethical "vision" as the quality good; Köhler and the Gestalt approach generally locate it as a vector in the phenomenal field. I am not raising the issue here which is a "correct" location; it may be that these are actually different experiences in human beings, or again that they are different stresses in a common more complex experience. But it seems perfectly clear that moral judgments can be and have been formulated in such a way that the prescriptive element is part of the phenomena designated. A cognitivist approach, whether naturalistic or non-naturalistic, therefore cannot be accused of leaving prescription out.[24]

Take, for example, Hare's concluding warning that "moral philosophers cannot have it both ways; either they must recognize the irreducibly prescriptive element in moral judgments, or else they must allow that moral judgments, as interpreted by them, do not guide actions in the way that, as ordinarily understood, they obviously do." [25] But how do they? Guiding is a complex business, and commending (Hare's candidate) is only one fashion. Ultimately, to understand what guidance is we have to examine theories of learning and motivation in psychology, teaching in education, influence in political science, and so on. Here there seems to be a major shift emerging. The mechanistic model spoke of conditioning in learning and the pressure of drives and desires in motivation, of indoctrination conflicts in education, of political ideals as instruments to gain control over men. (The moral analogue is clear in the commanding, expressing, subtle "persuading" and goading of the prescriptive emphasis.) Now we find the Gestalt concept of comprehending meaningful relations, the psychoanalytic concept of insight as contrasted with "rationalization" and the recent emergence of the ego-concept in psychological thinking, the educational em-

---

[23] Stuart Hampshire, *op. cit.*, p. 478.

[24] This whole issue of variable location for the prescriptive element was developed in full in Chapter Three above.

[25] Hare, *op. cit.*, p. 195.

phasis on critical judgment, and we may even hope to see political ideals interpreted in terms of the human aspirations of subjects rather than the power interests of rulers. Similarly, in ethical theory, I think we are approaching the point where we will reinstate as the primary context in which one receives guidance that in which one *learns* or *comes to see clearly*. For it is a simple fact that when men are helped to see clearly what they want and what activities will bring what they want, and what the consequences of their action will be and what they will want in the subsequent conditions, then they have received guidance.

This should not be misunderstood. It does not minimize the element of subscription or commitment involved in decision as an act, whether commitment to a specific course of conduct or to a principle. What enters into ethical judgment on this view is not the act of commitment but the discovery that you are committed. The question whether a man who discovers he is committed will in fact act along those lines is a further distinct issue. Socrates thinks he who knows his own good will do it and Dostoevsky thinks one might want precisely for this reason to do the opposite; [26] nor need we regard this issue as undecidable. But even to guide is not to determine, nor is to commend to force. There is a gap not only between decision and action, but also between judgment and decision-as-act. Moral judgment is no more (and no less) practical than science is perceptive; science uses and learns from each fresh perception, and moral judgment uses and learns from each fresh decision.

The chief objection raised to such a direction of ethical theory concerns the content of the cognition. What does moral judgment judge to be the case if it is cognitive? What is the content of the ethical learning which guides conduct? We need not settle such an issue here. But it is decidable, and there are plenty of candidates. Many are traditional, such as what will produce happiness, or realize the self (in some empirical self-conception), or conform with the demands of certain obligation-feelings (e.g., guilt-feelings), or cohere with one's basic aspirations or existent system of strivings, or what would be approved or disapproved under specified ideal conditions, or be desired for its own sake under definite conditions. Traditional conceptions are being deepened

26 See his *Letters from the Underworld* (Everyman ed., 1913), pp. 25ff.

by the growth of psychological and social science; for example, by phenomenal field study, by psychoanalytic depth study and theory of personality development, by social psychological study of the self, by anthropological comparison of moral experience, by socio-cultural functional studies of morality, by historical dynamic studies of change in the content and form of moral elements. Candidates in a sophisticated contemporary naturalism may therefore involve configurations of such diverse elements, rather than the simple introspective "approval" of earlier theories. To decide among all these candidates is a theoretical problem of analysis, coordinating scientific materials and theory of ethics aims. And to assign primacy to cognitive content and the learning context as the core of guiding practice need not entail neglect of the various other types of content and their respective contexts.

In such a decision, scientific considerations may enter more deeply than we have the habit of recognizing. For example, emotive theory with its denial of the validity concept for ethics rests on a sharp separation of belief and attitude. This assumes the arbitrary character of emotion in relation to cognition. If however, emotion is found to have an inner motivational character in a pattern of human goal-seeking, then would not the emotive theory resting as it does on the sharp distinction prove somewhat barren? [27] Similarly, to say that an ethical judgment is a decision, not a perception or a cognition of relations, clearly embodies a very special theory of the role of will in relation to intellect. This ought to be rendered explicit for scientific criticism.

Valuational elements may also enter into methodological decisions in ethical theory. Stevenson treats the choice of methods as normative, and Hare might be led to commend some theories as well as conduct. And good reasons can be found for the habit of looking for good reasons. In any language, some area of choice

---

[27] Cf. R. W. Leeper, "A Motivational Theory of Emotion to Replace 'Emotion as Disorganized Response,'" *Psychological Review*, LV (1948), 5-21. For a theory in which the cognitive element is more central, see R. B. Brandt's summary of a field theory of the emotions, in his *Hopi Ethics* (Chicago, 1954), pp. 311ff. For a criticism of the psychological assumptions of emotive theory, see V. J. McGill, *Emotions and Reason* (Springfield, Ill., 1954).

between theoretical elements will be found to involve valuation. Here—especially if ethical theory be found historically always to have had some practical role—it seems thoroughly permissible to offer common purposes or needs as bases for decision. That one theoretical formulation will bring men closer together to face common tasks, or that it will widen the area of basic agreement, seems to me to be a "sounder" ground for theoretical preference or methodological policy than contingent usage, although secondary to the role of correct scientific assumptions. Formally, such valuations would appear as stipulations on a meta-level about the definitions and tasks of ethics. But their justification would repeat the ground we have here covered in outline.

The conclusion pointed to by these somewhat varied analyses is that the attempt to introduce new validity models in ethical theory rests either on too hastily accepted assumptions that the established models are unavailable, or a premature pessimism concerning the growth of the human sciences, or a narrow conception of the practical which ignores the thoroughly practical efficacy of cognition and reflection.

VI

Even at the risk of repetition it is worth adding a few general reflections on the logic of the argument that morality is practical, not theoretical, *and therefore* its fundamental terms require a prescriptivist interpretation; they must not be robbed of their normative force. I have been suggesting that this argument is a non sequitur; granted the practical character of ethics, the decision whether to cast its theory in a prescriptivist vein or in a nonprescriptivist vein is to a great extent a scientific one of *how practicality is to be achieved*. And to answer this requires knowledge about the human field—including men's aims, conditions of life, possibilities of knowledge, and the structuring of human and social relationships.

More than the interpretation of ethical terms and the mode of reasoning are involved if practicality permeates the whole framework of an ethical theory. Let us look back to the emotive theory which incorporates practicality throughout.

Its stage-setting is practical in the sense that it focuses on interpersonal influence processes and disagreement in attitude. There is no gainsaying the tremendous practical importance of such disagreements in the pre-World War II period of the growth of emotive theory. Moral discourse is thus seen as an attempt to resolve disagreements in attitude. Its instruments are emotions expressed in discourse; its aim is to change opposing attitudes.

Ethical concepts are interpreted in terms of their practical function. The magnetism of 'goodness' comes from the fact that the emotive element is placed *within* the meaning, not outside as concomitant or consequent. As a result, generalizations in ethics are simply generalized expressions with only the minimal cognitive element that lies in recognizing that the speaker (oneself) has these attitudes.

Any methodological concept of validity is sharply distinguished from deduction or induction, as we have seen. The use of a pattern of deciding is primarily an *advocacy* of a method of deciding, not a reasoning from factual premises to ethical conclusions.

The criterion of success or effectiveness is obviously practical, too. A normative issue is "solved" not in the scientific sense in which a solution of a problem is a true answer to the questions posed, but in the practical sense of resolving disagreement. An opposing attitude is dissolved or changed, and practical agreement is achieved.

The practical reorientation throughout the theory is thus apparent. And it is this attitude that persists through all the changes brought about in the various forms of prescriptivism.

Now how practical is it to gear every part of theory so closely to practical functions? What would happen if other practical fields—medicine or engineering or law or education—did the same thing? Take, for example, medicine, and think of it in its full historical development. Its task is practical and moderately well defined in terms of the goal of health. And although there have been all sorts of interpretations of health, there is a fairly clear set of indices embracing absence of pain, ability to function, absence of disabling anxiety, and even more abstract conceptions of generalized well-being. Now suppose an early medical theorist said to his colleagues: "Medicine is a *practical* science.

Its basic task is to cure the sick. Therefore, medical concepts should be reoriented to be practical—that is, curative. 'Ill' is a gerundive term meaning primarily *to be cured*. Any medical assertion therefore requires reinterpretation to see its curative effect." At first he might be tempted to assign to medical discourse a soothing emotive role with respect to the patient. But this might remind him too closely of witchcraft and primitive medicine by incantation. So he would probably recall that the context of medical discourse is primarily among medical men themselves, and thus carry out his translations as addressed to colleagues. For example, diagnosis terms classifying illness would be clarified as 'to be treated by purging,' 'to be treated by blood-letting,' 'to be treated by diet,' and so on. To translate a medical illness-term as 'having such-and-such symptoms' or 'having such-and-such going on within him' would be tabu; it would be branded as a layman's fallacy of descriptivism, equating a genuine (curative) use of medical discourse with a secondary—purely theoretical—usage. Concomitant conclusions might be reached by our practicalist regarding treatment itself. Since medicine is a practical science, not a theoretical science, it is a mistake to use inductive models. There is too much individual variation. It involves rather a practical skill and practical perception. And he would clinch his argument with: "Do you really expect medicine to operate with general theories and systematic laws, and make automatic subsumptions?" If it were not anachronistic—for we are speaking of an *early* practitioner—he would have added: "Your hope is as futile as Napoleon's naive faith that his Code would require no commentary or interpretation."

No proof is, of course, intended by this analogy. There may very well be domains in which such a mode of construing a field has merit, though medicine scarcely seems any longer to be one. And yet, I have occasionally come across psychoanalysts who argue almost in this fashion in objecting to any attempts to render their field more scientific! Our concern here is simply what is entailed by the admission that moral philosophy is practical. All I am trying to show is that nothing short of the growth of a field, and the study of its phenomena so as to see what factual-causal assertions can be made indicating the degree of order there discoverable, can in the end determine for us what is the *most prac-

tical way of construing the field, its concepts, its methods, and its sense of its tasks. There is nothing in the idea of being practical which prevents the most practical course from being the sharpest theoretical formulation of concepts and methods! The history of the sciences and mathematics, as well as the relation of basic research and practical technology in modern life ought to serve as the strongest evidence—at least up to the present.

The history of medicine shows the field widening as the conception of the human being and his world undergoes transformation. Temkin points out that ancient and medieval medicine kept the field narrow because it was assumed that there was a beneficent plan working in the world, so that curing was at most removing a block from nature's operations, but after Descartes began to think of the body as a machine, and faith was lost in the beneficent operations of nature as such, the realm of possible medical interference became much broader.[28] In modern times, we can see how the growth of psychology has brought mental phenomena within the ambit of health judgments, and the consequence has been the growth of psychiatry and the approach to a unified whole-man conception of the field of medicine. Even broader pastures lie ahead as the role of social and cultural factors in health comes to the fore.

Why should one expect to find normative force in ethical *language?* Compare linguistic judgments of praise and blame, virtues grounded in habits of decades, institutional educational policies and procedures with all sorts of interlocking sanctions. Will you look for normative force in the first, rather than in the second or third? Is it surprising that Aristotle ties his ethics into politics and deals liberally with education and law, and that Dewey focusses on problems of social change in response to conflicts and demands of given periods? Even if morality proved wholly an art, if no generalizations were possible, field instability and field complexity rose to a maximum,—that is, even if all the conditions warranting a prescriptivist approach were fulfilled —why the focus on language rather than the act of deciding? This is the kind of thing an existentialist view like Sartre's seems to be aiming at, chiefly because it considers all systematization as a type

[28] Oswei Temkin, "Metaphors of Human Biology," in *Science and Civilization,* ed. R. C. Stauffer (Madison, Wisconsin, 1949), pp. 179ff.

of enslavement by the past, including one's own past. But such a "practicalism" carried through consistently would have to refashion its concepts in terms of psychological results of the study of choice and decision as phenomena. The normative force would lie in the phenomenon of being a man in the human predicament.

The linguistic focus is not inherently an improbable one. Language *is* a powerful factor in human life. Word and thought have strong relations. The definition of man as a linguistic animal or a symbol-making animal competes with that of him as a rational animal. Men build up systematic patterns of words whose use sometimes makes a difference between love and hate, success and failure, even life and death. A great deal of moral training is through talk—in our culture—although in our more reflective moments we recognize the importance of example, habit, and the basic structuring of institutions. Once in a while I have the suspicion that the linguistic focus in ethics rests on the supposition that talk is the only instrument of morality!

Actually, the view that language is a powerful tool for moving men is not confined to ethical theory today. It is part and parcel of that wide movement which embraces everything from the most refined logical analysis of the language of mathematics and the illuminating cultural study of symbols, to the demagogy of politics and the latest tricks of advertising. In many of these areas there has been a tendency to conceive the influence from above, that is, from the point of view of the wielder; this ascribes greater power to the technique than it can really bear. A fuller study looks also from below; it shows the bases in men's constitution, circumstances, history, needs, aspirations, and so on, on which the wielding finds a field to work in. It shows also the limits of its power, and the basis of what success or failure it may have. I shall argue in Chapter Fifteen that in the case of ideals, the perspective from below is more revealing than that from above. In a sense, that is the general lesson that emerges here too about the relation of language and the whole context of men's psychological and social needs, capacities, problems. At least this is the hypothesis that I want to offer for the reconsideration of the linguistic trend of our time in ethical theory.

PART THREE

DESCRIPTIVE METHOD

CHAPTER SEVEN

THE DESCRIPTIVE STANDPOINT

In the good old days, before the twentieth century prescriptive revolution, the outline of the tasks of ethics seemed clear. As in every other theoretical discipline, it was assumed that ethics had its data, which it had to analyze carefully. These embraced moral phenomena, or moral experience, or moral feelings, or whatever other way you chose to speak about them. Moral inquiry would have to locate, isolate, and *describe*. To go on and explain was to offer some kind of theory over and above the descriptions, but that there was something to describe was not to be doubted. The eighteenth century might have gone too far in concentrating on the contours and relations of the moral sentiments, the Utilitarians too far in linking every moral phenomenon to the pursuit of pleasure, the rationalists and intuitionists too far in ontologizing the moral experiences. But they all agreed on data to be analyzed and described, and trusted in this core of basic phenomena and the spirit of rational interchange to correct one another's exaggerated interpretations.

The contemporary insistence that the function of ethical terms is primarily practical—expressive, persuasive, commendatory, and so forth—and not descriptive, has, as we have seen, been accompanied with the assumption that to engage in description would yield science, not ethics. The language of moral functions has replaced that of moral phenomena. To see what place descriptive method has in ethics today is thus a task that has to be carried out afresh, beginning with the very meaning of 'description.'

THE MEANING OF 'DESCRIPTION'

In ethical theorizing, contemporary writers rarely stop to ask what is meant by 'description.' [1] They tend on the whole to carry

[1] A spirited reopening of the whole question of the meaning of 'describing' is to be found in S. E. Toulmin and K. Baier, "On Describing," *Mind*, LXI

over an account of it that is pervasive in the current intellectual climate. This is not unreasonable, for after all a treatise on ethical theory is not to undertake the burden of analyzing all philosophical concepts. But there is always the possibility that the standard picture may be begging certain questions, and this means that some parts of it may have to be reopened. Now the standard picture of description today does seem to me to incorporate two distinguishable elements that have quite different import. One is that description is an *enterprise* of a quite special sort; it has a definite aim—that of coming to know what is going on, what is the case, what is true of a given area. (I multiply expressions because I do not want to get caught in the problems of a particular formulation.) In this sense, of course, the purpose embodied is not to evaluate or appraise, any more than it is to clarify meaning or find causes. It is quite possible to employ a single term which stretches far—such as to 'judge' in the sense of making discriminations—and so to assimilate different enterprises by speaking of 'making factual discriminations' and 'value discriminations,' but perhaps such a habit of stretching concepts is one of the sources of confusion.

That describing entails a distinctive standpoint in the sense suggested is an important thesis in this volume; but this does not carry with it the second element in the standard picture, which refers to the kinds of terms that constitute a descriptive account. The standard twentieth-century picture until recently embodied the long-standing tradition of a narrow sensationalistic empiricism, strengthened by the dominance of positivism. Descriptive accounts were in principle analyzable into complexes of sense-data or sensory experiences. They were to be sharply distinguished from interpretation; in fact, all theoretical concepts would be in principle translated into sets of observation-predicates. This whole

(1952), 13-38. Their concern is chiefly with the specific contexts in ordinary usage in which one is said to 'describe' rather than, e.g., to 'declare,' 'tell,' 'record,' 'report,' 'account for,' 'soliloquize,' 'inform,' etc. (p. 25). They expect that such differentiation will eliminate the pitfalls into which one falls by making a technical term of 'description' "to cover any sentence which can be spoken of as true or false" (p. 29). What I call the standard picture here overlaps to some extent with what they call the technical use. But my concern in what follows is not with ordinary usage, but with the different modes of describing found in the several sciences.

type of analysis has been severely shaken in the internal developments of the philosophy of science, and the ensuing liberalization is intimately involved with that indicated in the treatment of definition in Chapter Five. Sensory experiences have been pushed back into the role of elements verifying an assertion rather than ultimate constituents of the object of the assertion; the scope of theoretical elements has come to be regarded as penetrating rather than purely ancillary.[2] There is no longer any inappropriateness if we say that an account which uses dispositional terms ('fragile,' 'sharp,' 'likable,' and so forth) is a descriptive account.[3] Of course, there remains the task of distinguishing the upper limits of a descriptive account; one would not want to assume, going to the other extreme, that every theoretical assertion was to be regarded as descriptive. But this ceases to be an all-or-none question, and becomes rather the problem of analyzing the way in which the theoretical concepts of a field function in the body of statements of the field, at the particular stage of development of the system.

Obviously, it is not our present task to go into the philosophy of science generally, nor to adopt dogmatic solutions for ethics for problems that are the subject of controversy in the theory of science. But we are compelled to note that the pat standard accounts can no longer be simply taken over as authoritative. Accordingly, let us summarize a few conclusions about description, basic to the sense in which we shall speak of descriptive method in ethics:

(1) The adoption of a descriptive standpoint does not carry with it any automatic account of the kinds of terms that are constitutive of a descriptive report. The scientific role of the sensory is obviously central, but any *equation* of descriptive and sensory would have to be established independently.

2 See, for example, the references on theoretical constructs, above, p. 127, n. 32. For changes in the theory that identified meaning with mode of verification, on which much of the twentieth-century sensationalist theory rested, see Carl G. Hempel, "Problems and Changes in the Empiricist Criterion of Meaning," in *Revue Internationale de Philosophie*, January, 1950; also, A. J. Ayer's Introduction to his *Language, Truth and Logic* (New York, 1946).

3 This point is sketched in penetrating outline in relation to ethics, in Israel Scheffler's "Anti-Naturalist Restrictions in Ethics," *The Journal of Philosophy*, L (1953), 457-66.

(2) The entry of theoretical elements does not of itself render an account nondescriptive. If 'likable' and 'pleasant' are permissible, so are 'horrible' and 'satisfying.' One would then have to ask whether there are uses in which 'desirable' would be permissible, avoiding of course the questions of ambiguity that are often charged against Mill in this context. Even ethical terms of high generality might turn out to have a descriptive meaning, and even if 'good' were taken as a theoretical construct, it could still have descriptive components.

(3) The field of ethics would be one among many in which lessons might be learned about the relation of descriptive and nondescriptive elements. It would not be bound to accept as authoritative any general thesis about description based only on other fields. In short, its needs and problems as a field of inquiry constitute part of the evidence for or against any general picture of the nature of description.

(4) The frequent charge that if a term is descriptive the assertions involving it are scientific, not ethical, fails on two grounds: (a) 'descriptive' is not to be equated with 'scientific.' For example, a historical report is descriptive, but this is so even if the view were to hold that history is not scientific. In short, descriptions are the kinds of materials that science may systematize in its own ways, but there is no a priori guarantee that a given class of descriptions will become the subject of successful scientific inquiry. Even if this prove true for every possible description, this universal scope of science is itself a scientific hypothesis, not an analytic truth. We cannot then equate 'descriptive' and 'scientific'; but we can say that every description may enter into a theoretically possible scientific investigation. (b) Similarly, we cannot equate 'descriptive' with 'nonethical.' We can say, with an eye on the distinction of standpoints, that description is not evaluation, but we cannot beg the question in advance that ethics does not engage in both enterprises; in fact, we shall even argue later that it is concerned with the causal-explanatory enterprise as well. But what is more relevant here is to note that the scope of evaluation and of description may coincide or overlap, that the actual goings-on may be the same in spite of the difference in enterprise. Perhaps this point can best be made clear and explored after we have looked at the different modes of description.

MODES OF DESCRIPTION

Modes of description can be classified in many different ways. Sometimes one is concerned with the observation-source and maps the different kinds—sensation, memory, introspection, phenomenological report.[4] Sometimes different modes become classified as methods, especially in the controversies of schools within a growing science—for example, behavioral and phenomenological methods in psychology. Sometimes the emphasis falls on subject matter in the familiar sciences, so that we have the physical descriptions of the natural sciences, the individual-descriptions of psychology, the group or social descriptions of the social sciences, and historical description. Our concern here is not with systematizing this area, but with picking out what is useful for ethical inquiry. I should like, therefore, to comment on four modes of description, which we shall later see will help us pose the problem of directions of development in ethics. These are: behavioral description, phenomenological description, social description, and historical description.

Behavioral description has had its fullest development as a technique in psychology. It is a familiar story how the behaviorist school in psychology began as a revolt against introspective approaches and the traditional teleological modes of describing human action. Its aim was to make psychology scientific, in the sense in which it conceived the physical sciences to be the prototype of science. It is not our task here to reckon with the gains and losses of this chapter in the history of psychology, but to note the concept of behavioral description to which behaviorism has given sharpest form. Behaviorism sought to describe human action purely in terms of overt observable behavior sequences and expected that laws of human action could then be discovered to relate the impinging physical "stimuli" to the behavioral "responses." Thus hunger would be described not in introspective terms of a feeling of a specific type of discomfort in a region of the body, nor in teleological terms of a desire for food, nor in physiological terms of the contractions going on in the stomach. A behavioral description would specify the amount of food eaten

4 Cf. Henryk Mehlberg, *The Reach of Science* (Toronto, 1958), pp. 110-19.

when presented, or the persistency of selection of paths of action terminating with the food, or the time lapse since previous eating.

It is difficult, of course, to restrain the concept of behavioral description within its original limits, although the strictest of behaviorists are sometimes surprisingly rigorous. There are at least several directions in which it tends to stray. One is toward physiology, which can easily be reckoned as internal behavior, unless one has rigidly drawn the line at the skin. Certainly, if the aim is scientific observability, there is no reason why muscular contractions and glandular secretions should not enter into the descriptive picture. But the behaviorist insistence on the distinction between behavioral and physiological is conceptually salutary, since it shows that the same term—'hunger'—can cover different operative meanings, so that any assimilation of the two is a scientific correlation of separate variables. (How far there should be a *general* distinction between the two kinds of description, rather than caution in particular cases, would of course depend on how consistently they could be kept apart at the borderlines, and how great is the area of vagueness; also on how far reference to the physiological would be required to explain or systematize the narrowly behavioral.) A second tendency is to assimilate the domains of the introspective and the mental to some extent, by allowing verbal reports as linguistic behavior. How successful this really is depends on how adequate the behavioral analysis of 'meaning' and symbolization processes proves to be. Otherwise, this becomes a backdoor way of admitting what was excluded. A third drift, not always explicit, is toward the social. The ordinary use of terms in the human situation practically invites such extension. For example, a little boy is said to run out of the house on Saturday morning with a catcher's mitt; he joins other boys and they play baseball. This clearly sounds behavioral, but even apart from the teleologically tinged language, there is a distinct reference to social and cultural patterns. A social behaviorism which tries to apply a behavioristic approach in the social sciences, often operates on the assumption that a reduction could be carried out in principle to a complex pattern of individual behavioral responses.

The fourth direction is of central relevance to ethical description. It is a conscious development—best seen in E. C. Tolman's work [5]—directed toward fashioning responsible behavioral criteria for concepts of purpose and purposive behavior. That behavioral description can use such concepts responsibly, and with careful differentiation in verification, seems beyond doubt. The remaining issue is whether in human action other descriptive methods (introspective, phenomenological) are not required to give a *fuller* picture of what is going on.

In any case, the role of behavioral description in ethical description would seem to be a sufficiently definite one so that at least some behavioral reference would be required in the verification of value descriptions.[6]

Phenomenological description, or as it is often called, *phenomenal description*, has come into renewed prominence in contemporary thought. It has been developed in the wider context of contemporary phenomenology, utilized in scientific movements such as Gestalt psychology, long been implicit in literary description of human relations, employed as a basic technique in existentialist accounts, and occupies a central place in some schools of psychiatric theory. What was once regarded as the "merely phenomenal" has now gained a new respect, and is set perhaps upon a career of aggrandizement.

---

[5] In his *Purposive Behavior in Animals and Men* (New York, 1932). See also his "Behaviorism and Purpose" in his *Collected Papers in Psychology* (Berkeley and Los Angeles, 1951).

[6] It is worth noting that it is not logically impossible to deny this. It would be the thesis that "Man *A* has value *V*" is compatible with any and every possible mode of behavior on the part of *A*. We can indeed readily conceive of *A* having the disposition to behave in a given way, but being, through coincidence, so completely frustrated that it would not issue in behavior even under any conceivable (not merely actual) situation. But this gives us too wide a scope. For example, if the inhibiting factor is an incurable neurosis, we might imagine it cured, in a contrary-to-fact conditional. Ultimately, the issue of the suggested irrelevance of behavioral description becomes involved with that of policy in defining or analyzing 'having a value.' It may be that the irrelevance thesis is advocating instead that we *define* 'having a value' in terms of intra-organic description, or more likely in terms solely of phenomenal description. The grounds for such competing policies have to be considered by comparing and evaluating the different methods. Another possibility of a less drastic sort is that we are merely being warned of the dangers of relying solely on behavioral description.

In the ethical tradition there is, of course, a great deal of description of ethical feelings and sentiments. Such descriptions have often been taken to refer to "subjective" experiences or reactions, thus tying ethics to a special type of epistemological theory. A unique contribution of contemporary phenomenology is the effort to get a type of presuppositionless description of experience. Phenomenology, as Marvin Farber describes it,[7] "knows nothing and presumes nothing about persons; it raises no questions about myself or other human being, and makes no hypotheses. A phenomenological description deals with the given in the strictest sense, with experiences just as they are in themselves. The thing-appearance is analyzed, e.g., and not that which appears in it; and all apperceptions by means of which the appearance and that which appears enter into correlation with the ego, to which something appears, are rejected. The elucidation of knowledge that results from this analysis is simply adequate intuitive abstraction, which brings the general essence of that which is fixated phenomenologically to evident consciousness." The body and the empirical subject are also, of course, "put out of play," eliminated and "bracketed." [8] All that is left is the phenomenological (or phenomenal) field.

While the philosophical accounts raise issues of the nature of the "essences" directly intuited, and question whether existence can be effectively "bracketed," scientific use of phenomenological inspection has more or less swept these problems aside and concentrated on the aspect of strict observation. It is in this purely scientific sense that this approach will be referred to in this book. Perhaps the clearest illustration is to be found in the procedure of the Gestalt psychologists. Color, for example, is studied as in the visual field. It is where it "appears"; there is no question of its "real" location elsewhere. Changes in the field as other objects enter are mapped; figure-ground relationships simply are "there." The success of the descriptions and formulation of laws in this phenomenal field has acted as a kind of model in the attempt to extend a similar descriptive method to dealing with the emotions, to social psychology, and to ethical qualities. Its immediate consequence in social psychology, for example, has

---

7 *The Foundations of Phenomenology* (Cambridge, Mass., 1943), p. 183.
8 *Ibid.*, p. 526.

been a greater attentiveness to possible individual differences in the "meaning" of similar behavioral responses. An affirmative answer to the question, "Would you mind living next door to a Negro?" [9] may mean anything from a fear of risking lower status in the eyes of friends or a belief that property values may decline to a direct personal affective reaction.[10] Similarly, contemporary phenomenological psychiatry stresses the importance in dealing with a patient, of trying to find out not so much what feelings introspection will produce, but in great detail how the world appears to him—whether it is closed, depressing, without future, threatening, whether other people are seen as hostile or friendly, and so on.[11]

In ethics, certainly such notions as obligation, conscience, sympathy, envy, love, call for careful phenomenological description, so that their differences can be noted and specific phenomenological definitions formulated before correlations are sought with behavioral and causal elements. Obviously, we have to know the specific qualities of a man's conscience before we can seek to relate it to familial situation or social patterns of authority, or personal conditioning experiences, and so forth. In general, the phenomenologically-inclined philosophers have shown great sensitivity to finer shades, coming up with problems and relations that a behavioral approach tends to overlook. One has only to glance into such works as Max Scheler's *The Nature of Sympathy* or Nicolai Hartmann's *Ethics* to see what a mine of suggestive and subtle differentiation is to be found. But one has to be careful always to separate the phenomenological description from collateral conceptions of the nature of science, assumptions about reality, and even hasty assumptions about the invariance of the particular structure that the writer finds in the phenomenological field.[12]

9 Cf. Gordon Allport, "Prejudice, A Problem in Psychology and Social Causation," in *Toward a General Theory of Action,* ed. Talcott Parsons and Edward A. Shils (Cambridge, Mass., 1951), p. 372.

10 For a general exploration of the phenomenological approach in social psychology, see R. B. MacLeod, "The Phenomenological Approach to Social Psychology," *Psychological Review,* LIV (1947), 193-210.

11 E.g., J. H. Van Den Berg, *The Phenomenological Approach to Psychiatry* (Springfield, Ill., 1955).

12 For a brief presentation of some of the problems in the phenomenologi-

Actually, the use of phenomenal description should carry with it no special philosophy of reality. Whether the phenomenal field is to be construed in subjective terms, or as a quality of material process, is a separate question. Similarly, any question of the "reality" of a particular phenomenological description goes beyond this description to correlation with some physical or other existential account. Georg Lukacs tells of a conversation with Scheler on this question: [13] "For example, he explained, phenomenological researches could be made about the devil; only the question of the devil's reality would first have to be 'bracketed.' 'Certainly,' I answered, 'and when you are finished with the phenomenological pictures of the devil, you open the brackets—and the devil in person is standing before you.' Scheler laughed, shrugged his shoulders, and made no reply."

Which terms relevant for ethics can best be defined behaviorally, which phenomenologically, cannot of course be decided in advance of concrete study. It is probable that in so complex a field a constellation of phenomenological and behavioral elements will be required for most terms. Nor in calling special attention to these should we ignore the possibility that other descriptive approaches may occasionally prove relevant—for example, organic physiological description. Some psychological terms occurring in ethical discussion, such as 'tension' may require the physiological over and above the overt behavioral and the phenomenological in order to achieve a fuller understanding.

The third mode of description on which I should like to comment is *social description*. It is clear that in the social sciences—sociology, anthropology, economics, etc.—there is a great deal of description of institutions and the way they work, and of cultural and societal forms. Much of this, too, in recent times, is concerned with values and norms. How far is such description to be regarded as distinct from the behavioral and phenomenal types which are usually treated as descriptions of single individuals? Profound differences may follow if we cast an inquiry in terms of the single individual and in terms of group patterns.

cal approach—in connection with Karl Duncker's thesis of ethical invariance—see my *Ethical Judgment*, pp. 193-98.

[13] Georg Lukacs, "Existentialism," in *Philosophy for the Future*, ed. R. W. Sellars, V. J. McGill and M. Farber (New York, 1949), p. 574.

And yet there has been too ready a tendency to assume that if we work hard enough at it, we can exhibit the latter as a complex set of the former. Such programs of reductive analysis used to be more popular when the narrower empiricism identified the meaning of a concept with the way it was verified. And clearly, statements about social patterns are verified by observations on individuals. The difficulty with the reductive programs has been, on the whole, that they have remained programs, and not achieved results. And so other ways of treating group-pattern concepts are being tried out—as theoretical constructs, or as referring to emergent qualities or systems of relations, and so on.[14]

Take, for example, the description of the language of a given people. There is obviously a sense in which it deals with the verbal behavior of individuals, and so requires behavioral description. And on some interpretations, 'meaning' would involve some reference to phenomenal description. But is it not in some sense obvious that the description of a language is the description of a *social* pattern in communication? Perhaps this is obscured by the fact that an individual can make sounds by himself. Take, as another example, the description of a kinship system. Does it not require a constant eye on many people in interacting social processes and become pretty meaningless if referred only to the individual? And yet the verification is in terms of many instances of individual behavior. I am not undertaking here to analyze the logic of the whole problem, simply to suggest the problem. As we shall see, we will ask later on whether the very data of ethics should not be construed as social and cultural, rather than as individual.

Historical description does not raise new questions of logical principle over and above social and cultural description. But it does point to questions of time, growth, development, change. Values may be compared diachronically in a given tradition, as well as cross-culturally. Are there basic age-parameters in value-description for an individual, or epoch-parameters for a culture? Even in dealing with ethical concepts, the question how far the temporal permeates is not always obvious. I can be pleased for a moment and have a perennial desire. Can I assume an obligation

14 See, for example, Maurice Mandelbaum, "Societal Facts," *The British Journal of Sociology*, VI (1955), 305-17.

in a split second? How long does it take to grow a binding basic commitment to a way of life? Are these causal questions, or part of the syntax of the term 'commitment' and 'obligation'?

HOW FAR CAN DESCRIPTION BE EXTENDED?

It is possible that some philosophic readers may become impatient by this time and wonder what all this talk of description has to do with ethics, relevant though it may be for sociology or psychology in describing an individual's or a people's values. But actually, there are two separate questions. The first is how far description can be extended. The second is how much of this extended description is relevant for ethics.

Suppose one were to argue that by being an onlooker the reporter renders himself incapable of making moral assertions. Has this marked off a forbidden territory? Take, for example, Stuart Hampshire's distinction: " 'I decided that x was the right thing to do' is a descriptive statement, true or false; but 'x was the right thing to do' is a practical or moral judgment, right or wrong." [15] Does this mean that a reporter is always, so to speak, looking from outside, and never gets an inside view?

A first temptation might be to nibble away at the distinction. Why does Hampshire use the past tense in 'x was the right thing to do'? The event has gone by. Is the judgment a rededication? If not, then may it not be a self-reporter's assertion that the act conformed to the standards set by the self? 'I decided that x was the right thing to do' seems clearly descriptive. But what about 'It is my decision that x was the right thing to do'? In one sense this may be definitely expressing a present deciding, not reporting it.

The purpose of such erosion would be to establish that we are not dealing so much with different types of statements as with different functions or activities.[16] And so our reporter need not worry about the fact that practical decision as activity is not itself describing; he can always press on to describe what is going

[15] "Fallacies in Moral Philosophy," *Mind*, LVIII (1949), 482, n. 1. Cf. Nowell-Smith's analysis of 'he ought' in his *Ethics*, pp. 195-97.

[16] This seems to be recognized by Stuart Hampshire in his recent book, *Thought and Action* (London, 1959), e.g., p. 142.

on when the practical deciding is taking place. The scope of his reporting thus becomes unrestricted. For there is no practical act of whatever sort that is invoked as the interpretation of 'x is right' for which one could not set up the corresponding descriptive statement regarding the person concerned or uttering it: 'A finds x right (or decides that x is right) at time t.' The descriptive standpoint thus can transcend any evaluation with the descriptive report that the evaluation took place.[17] Even where the reporter is the person himself telling about his own decision, we can distinguish the instant-after report from the act of decision. This type of parallelism holds whether the moral utterance is itself taken to be cognitive or prescriptive. If it is cognitive, it is already describing—say a phenomenal quality in the field—and then the parallel description is a description of a quality being apprehended. If the utterance is taken to be prescriptive—for example, to be commending—then the parallel description is that so-and-so is now commending such-and-such.

Perhaps all this is obvious and might have been granted to begin with. But it is not without important consequences. For if reporting is possible at all points, the moral decision is reduced to an act or event; it is not a unique type of judgment in any sense that needs a logic of its own, of some special practical sort. Instead of a logic of the will, the real question becomes that of exploring the effects of a realization of a self-report and how quickly it can be communicated to oneself in action. At this point, the descriptive standpoint has passed over from sheer reporting to offering itself as a way of formulating and dealing with problems of ethical theory. It now becomes a complex form of cognitivist or descriptivist thesis in ethics. As such, it is to be judged by what it can accomplish. And in the light of the extent to which such a standpoint has been disparaged, it is worth noting, at least, that it has some distinct advantages. It is potentially wider, setting the occurrence of the decision in contexts, relations, causes. It includes the phenomenal attitude as part of the picture and need not be reductive. What is more, it does not close the

<hr>

17 Comparably in the evaluative standpoint, as we have already seen in discussing the libertarian claim embodied in the naturalistic fallacy accusation, it is possible to transcend any description with an evaluation of the situation described.

possibilities of change because—the process being temporal—
where a man is his own onlooker, the result may be a changed
situation for subsequent choice. It cannot even be closed by describing the pattern of interaction between the prior report and
the subsequent choice, because this is a fresh description, and so
this pattern can itself in principle become an element in subsequent action. Hence, the descriptive standpoint, by taking time
seriously, does not close freedom of action. A full descriptivism
thus maintains the autonomy effect.

Descriptive method, we may conclude, whatever be the outcome on the other questions raised, need set no limit to its scope;
nor need one fear in pressing it as far as it will usefully go, that
one is engaging "merely" in science, not in ethics. It is the results
achieved that will decide where to draw lines, if at all. But mean-
while, a fresh question comes into focus: are there any distinctive
grounds in terms of initial data on which to delineate sharply
what is in the domain of ethics?

WHAT ARE THE DATA OF ETHICS?

In a well-known and often-discussed passage, W. D. Ross says:
"We have no more direct way of access to the facts about right-
ness and goodness and about what things are right or good, than
by thinking about them; the moral convictions of thoughtful and
well-educated people are the data of ethics just as sense-perceptions are the data of a natural science." [18] Now Ross's position is
quite clear because he makes it clear in the rest of his writing.
But really, the notion of 'data' is not as transparent as one might
think. I should like to distinguish three meanings, and comment
on each.

(1) By 'data' of ethics one may mean terminating points which
are unshakable, in verifying ethical statements. The comparison
to the role of sense-perceptions in natural science suggests this
sense of what has simply to be accepted. Actually, Ross's view
ends up with something more comparable to the older conception
of mathematics—prima facie duties serving in an axiomatic way.
Others have stressed more the hard incorrigible character of particular judgments of obligation. In any case, we need not dwell

[18] *The Right and the Good* (Oxford, 1930), pp. 40-41.

long on the familiar intuitionist position. By affirming—one might almost say stipulating—the *hardness* of its data, it simply shifts dispute, where there is a dispute, to whether the observer has been thoughtful enough, or well-educated enough, or trapped in ethnocentrism, and so forth. (Similarly, in science one might question the observation on several grounds—ability of the observer, special interfering circumstances, futher refinement of the observation-datum by discovering unexpected complexity, adequacy of tools, discrepant observations by others under apparently similar circumstances, etc.) E. F. Carritt, in his claim that the verdicts of our moral judgment have the status of knowledge, allows *trying to doubt* as a way of probing the hardness of the data. Thus one finds it illuminating to doubt successfully that it is wicked for women to smoke, "but one may try for a lifetime to doubt the obligation to pay one's debts and have no success." [19] A wider historical search may, however, find others being more successful—for example, the oppressed in various ages whose perennial cry was the cancellation of debts, or revolutionaries, or a statesman altering the value of money and inducing inflation on economic principle. Of course, it is open to Carritt to argue that those who act on principle here do not believe that they are really in debt; they think nothing is "really owed." But such an approach would suggest that the hard data were turning into formulae functioning in a conventional fashion—a sad ending for indubitability, though not an infrequent one. But the lines of criticism of intuitionism are too familiar to require recounting at this point.

(2) By 'data' of ethics one may mean in the second place, the mass of phenomena that constitute the broad area of inquiry. In the sense in which all knowledge comes from experience, one might—to use Ross's analogy with sense perception in science again—say that sense experiences constitute the initial data of scientific inquiry. Of course, others might say that in this sense gross phenomena and not sense experience constitute the data. Similarly, in locating the mass of phenomena for ethics, one might throw broad boundaries around the phenomena of aspiration and desire, of discrimination and obligation, of praising and blaming and holding responsible, of claiming and assessing, and

[19] *Ethical and Political Thinking* (Oxford, 1947), p. 44.

so on. Such data would not be hard, but very soft; it would always depend on the subsequent conceptualization of ethical inquiry how much would be permitted to remain at the end.

(3) By 'data' of ethics, one may mean in a third sense some selection from the mass described in (2) which should act as the *starting point* of theoretical reflection or inquiry. In this sense, starting points carry no aura of indubitability. But they do have pretensions of delimiting what is to be regarded as "distinctively ethical phenomena (or situations, problems, experiences, functions, or uses)." Here, however, there is a proliferation of marks of the moral which focus different descriptive methods and different analyses of what we have examined as the locus of prescriptiveness. To discuss these would, in part, recapitulate that treatment. Let me then rest content here with a summary tabulation of the candidates:

(a) Phenomenal marks of the distinctively moral:

   a directly apprehended quality of requiredness

   the quality of precedence or decisiveness characterizing one rule in comparison with competing ones

   the characteristics of superiority and legitimacy in a prescription.[20]

(b) a set of distinctively ethical terms:

   in English, clearly, 'good,' 'ought,' 'duty,' etc.[21]

[20] The first two, with reference to Gestalt psychology and to positions taken by Maurice Mandelbaum and C. I. Lewis, are discussed above, pp. 57f., 65f. The last is a view presented by John Ladd in *The Structure of a Moral Code* (Cambridge, Mass., 1957), pp. 84-85, 101-7; Ladd explicates superiority as a claim of sufficiency, ultimacy and priority, and legitimacy as involving justifiability, intersubjective validity, and foundation in reality. Although these are complex notions, and Ladd's analysis is presented as an explication of moral discourse, I should be inclined to reinterpret it as I have done in the above classification as constituting a phenomenological analysis of the field when a man recognizes a moral obligation. Whether this description contains ethnocentric elements is a separate question.

[21] The difficulty here is that every such term is found in uses that the theorist would not want to call 'moral' or 'ethical' and so a supplementary criterion of ethical as against nonethical use of distinctively ethical terms is required. This carries us into the next group. Nevertheless, the occurrence of the terms themselves can operate as a starting point in the sense of a

(c) a set of distinctively ethical uses for ethical terms:

to express certain emotions

to commend

to decide or subscribe to courses of action and principles
to persuade [22]

(d) a set of behaviorally and phenomenally described activities
or functions:

valuing (whether being pleased by or having an interest in,
etc.)

appraising

reflective concern with the whole of life

evaluating and ascribing obligations [23]

In the light of these many candidates, there is no adequate
ground for decisive judgment. In fact, since they overlap, and
their relations have not been adequately explored, there is no
reason why different theorists should not try them all out without prior commitment to any one. It is almost like the early stage
in the development of the data of the theory of electricity: some
investigators explore attraction-and-repulsion phenomena, some
thunder and lightning, some light, some magnetic phenomena,
and so on. Eventually, we know, some of the phenomena will be
declared collateral effects, some very special applications; the field
may divide into two major areas and there may be a unifying

plunging-in point. For the problem of ethical terms on a cross-cultural basis,
see May Edel and Abraham Edel, *Anthropology and Ethics,* Ch. X.

[22] For a brief sketch of the diversity of uses proposed, extending beyond
the range here indicated, see above, p. 146.

[23] The first represents the broad family of traditional naturalistic approaches. The second is Dewey's stress. The third is offered as a criterion by
A. MacBeath in his *Experiments in Living* (London, 1952). An interesting
example of the fourth is Alexander Sesonske's recent *Value and Obligation*
(Berkeley and Los Angeles, 1957), which takes expressing evaluations and
ascribing obligations to be *functions* in human life performed by ethical
statements. Since he denies one-one relations between the functions and specific ethical terms, he is able to point to the functions themselves in their
human social setting as the primary focus of ethics. Thus, although he begins
with ethical language and appeals to usage as part evidence for his conclusions, he goes far toward bringing the linguistic digression in contemporary
ethical theory back to the older naturalistic mainstream.

theory, embodying some construct not originally envisaged. To waste energy in claims of primacy at this stage of the development of ethical theory is folly—once the claims of indubitability have been separated off, and it is recognized that we are dealing only with data as starting-points in the sense of jumping-off places.

Of course, starting points are not *mere* starting points; they embody hypotheses of directions of fruitful development. But in this sense, surely the more the merrier, since we shall be less likely to miss promising clues. What must be separated out, however, are any theoretical assumptions that a starting point may implicitly contain. For example, the phenomenological approach in ethical theory seems often to take for granted the uniformity in the structure of the phenomenological field. A careful analyst such as Maurice Mandelbaum will note the hypothesis involved: "there is probably no fundamental, irreducible heterogeneity in the moral experience of different persons, whether they be members of the same or of different societies." [24] He appeals to two lines of argument to support this. One is the occasional penetration through what appears to be ultimate diversity, to find a common core of moral experience. The second "would consist in the attempt to show that all men share the same type of moral experience through an analysis of the nature of that experience. If such an analysis were adequate to the cases upon which it was based, and if it could be seen to apply not only to those cases but to all others which might be cited, then there would be ground for a justified belief that all men share the same type of moral experience." [25] But how could we know when we had analyzed ourselves and a given number of cases, and had a result adequate to these cases, that it was an analysis of "the nature of that experience"? Surely this phrase simply covers the hypothesis of universal uniformity, which a limited set of cases would not by itself establish. Even if, as Brandt maintains in his *Hopi Ethics*, the Hopi turn out to have the same type of moral experience as we do, does it follow from these two cultures for the whole world in all human history? Only two possibilities occur to me by which one might support Mandelbaum's second form of

[24] *The Phenomenology of Moral Experience* (Glencoe, Ill., 1955), p. 234.
[25] *Ibid.*, p. 235.

argument. One would be if there were evidence for a physical or physiological correlate of the moral experience in the individual, and independent evidence for the occurrence of this correlate in human beings.[26] The second would be a belief in some logic of the "pure" case.[27] But we could not know we had a pure case of moral experience from which a universal could be established unless we knew we had all the factors analyzed and knew which were present in pure form. This would mean, in effect, an already developed ethical theory far beyond the present state. The only remaining possibility I can see would be one that Mandelbaum obviously does not intend—the kind of defiant postulation which Vivas exhibits when he says of primitives: "If they are human, they are moral, and if they are not moral, they are not human—and this by definition." [28]

A somewhat different path for the descriptive study of morality was followed in *Anthropology and Ethics*.[29] While the kind of phenomena pointed to in the several starting points would be fashioned as proposed indices for the presence of the moral, the phenomena described would be regarded as social and cultural, not purely individual. Thus we compared the morality of a people to the religion of a people, which was a complex involving elements of ritual, belief, attitude, emotion, practice, and so forth, whose study had progressed by drawing a wide circle and comparing these various phenomena in different cultures. Similarly, we pointed to the broad area of goals pursued and avoided, rules enjoined, character traits praised and blamed, lines drawn around the group of those who "count" and those who are held responsible, ethical terms employed and ethical statements organized, modes of justifying, types of sanctioning activity, sets of feelings drawn into these operations, modes of deciding, and so on. Such phenomena were explored, and clues suggested for relating them to needs and phases of social process. The underlying thesis was that any delineation of a "distinctively ethical"

26 Köhler's work on electric currents in the brain might suggest this as a speculative hypothesis—but purely speculative at this point.

27 Compare the arguments of Kurt Lewin in his *Principles of Topological Psychology* (New York, 1936), p. 8f.

28 Eliseo Vivas, *The Moral Life and the Ethical Life* (Chicago, 1950), p. 106.

29 *Op. cit.*, Ch. II. See also below, p. 208.

would emerge from the results of such a descriptive enterprise, in terms of the theoretical unities that were discovered and elaborated, rather than out of initial rough delineation of data or concentration on some limited set of operational indices.

Such an approach is, of course, to be judged not in terms of its program, but in terms of the progress it makes in increasing understanding, and in fruitful outcomes. What is important to note here, however, is that there are no sound a priori objections to such a project in the logic of the enterprise. The setting of the stage for ethical theory in terms of the lone individual engaged in apprehending or deciding [30] is a traditional way of doing it, but it may very well be an ethnocentric way in an individualistically oriented culture. It has much to be said for it, as a policy decision, but equally there is much to be said for trying out a basically sociocultural stage-setting with the individual finding his place within it. There is, on the one side, the fact that society is composed of individuals. But the body is composed of cells, and one does not therefore turn descriptive psychology into the study of the interaction of cells; the best approach is the one that works out best in terms of advancing understanding and knowledge. More central is the fact of individual consciousness, intimately involved in individual decision. But cultural patterns and social forces enter deeply into individual decision, even into patterns of individual revolt against social constraints. Should the social be relegated here merely to a "cause" of the individual, whereas the phenomena studied should be primarily decision-acts themselves? It is possible, but the opposite is possible, too. Acts of perception are individual and acts of speech are individual, but neither science nor linguistics has so far been fruitfully reconstructed as a complex of perceptions or as a complex of vocal utterances. Promises to do this have been plentiful, as we have seen, but performance is another matter. What is more, there need be no uniform decision for all domains. Religion on the face of it is a highly personal thing, and William James, who embodied so clearly so many of the central values of our culture, is quite understandable when in his *Varieties* of *Religious Experience* he lays the stress in religion on personal emotional ex-

[30] For the concept of a stage-setting inherent in every ethical theory, see above, pp. 21ff.

perience. But the approach of Santayana who (in his *Reason in Religion*) sees religion as a social form performing certain functions in individual life shows—I think there will be basic agreement on this among historians and social scientists—a more fundamental understanding of the framework in which the actual phenomena can be analyzed and systematically related, with James's emphasis as one of the phenomena involved. In the field of art phenomena, a separate theoretical decision has to be made, which seems at present more controversial. In the field of ethics, we are suggesting, it is time to explore more intensively the neglected alternative.

The logic of the question does not then preclude any of the paths considered. There is a logic for reduction to the individual —in the sense of a formulation of conditions under which it would be justified and conditions under which it would not—and similarly a logic for the study of emergent qualities, a logic for the treatment of complexes. In each of these there are numerous problems of analysis, as the philosophers of science in the contemporary world have discovered. Ethical theory cannot wait for the answer to all these questions, nor need it wait. It should be sensitive to the problems and results, and ready to try out alternative paths, even exploratory speculative ones, as we suggested in the comparable question of definition.

On an over-all view, there have been four major new approaches in the twentieth century development of ethical theory from a descriptive standpoint. One has been the attempt to unify all the phenomena under a sweeping general concept of value.[31] A second has been the growth of the phenomenological approach to description. A third—and perhaps the most prominent—has been the vast linguistic inquiry into the use of ethical terms; even though it saw itself as anti-descriptivist in theory, its accomplishment in descriptive terms, once we recognize the unrestricted scope of the descriptive standpoint, was to lay bare the variety of phenomena centering about the use of these terms. The fourth is the social or group approach to the description of moral phenomena. The first has been well conceptualized in phi-

[31] For a brief sketch of the development of this attempt, see Krikorian and Edel, *Contemporary Philosophic Problems* (New York, 1959), Introduction to the selections in Part IV.

losophy, and recently has emerged in sociological and anthropological exploration of values. The second has been promising but has not been carried very far. The third has been well developed but not systematized. The fourth has been moving ahead, but is not conceptually rigorous. All deserve the most careful treatment in extended studies. In the limitations of this part, I shall take two samples. One is a brief study of the value concept and some less recognized conditions for its use as a unified concept. The other is an attempt to provide a conceptual framework for the sociocultural descriptive approach to ethics.

CHAPTER EIGHT

THE CONCEPT OF VALUE

The term 'value' has a wide range of current usage in philosophy and the sciences. Descriptively, a man's 'values' may refer to all his attitudes for or against anything. His values include his preferences and avoidances, his desire-objects and aversion-objects, his pleasure and pain tendencies, his goals, ideals, interests, and disinterests, what he takes to be right and wrong, good and evil, beautiful and ugly, useful and useless, his approvals and disapprovals, his criteria of taste and standards of judgment, and so forth.

Parallel to this descriptive usage lies the realm of normative usage. Men do not merely have values; they also make value judgments assessing their values. For in every self-conscious choice that the individual makes, in every creative act as well as every criticism, whether economic, moral, aesthetic, or any other, there are assumptions about what is desirable as well as desired, preferable as well as preferred, appropriate standards as well as functioning standards, and so forth. The same is true of social decisions, even as embedded in the normal functioning of social institutions and agencies.

VALUE PHENOMENA IN ALL AREAS OF HUMAN LIFE

Studies of values and valuation-evaluation processes carry us into all areas of human life. In political theory, conceptions of public welfare cover a vast valuation structure including, for example, assumptions about the respective merits of public ownership and private enterprise, or what is the desirable distribution of tax burdens. Major decisions of guns or butter, war or peace, stand out as value problems in public consciousness. Even so apparently neutral a question as size of holdings to be permitted in a newly reclaimed agricultural area is full of value implications. Will it open the way to family farms or industrial farming?

Which is desirable? Some have even urged that the family farm be America's slogan in facing the problems of Asia. One has only to open a book like Lilienthal's on the TVA [1] to see how every step in such an enterprise made decisions among alternatives about desirable qualities of life and interpersonal relations, as well as about material welfare: the desirability of "active daily participation of the people themselves" as well as the social benefits of a "yardstick" for electricity rates, the growth of knowledge about soil conservation as well as spurring on new industries, revitalizing community life as well as extending power facilities.

Legal philosophy has underscored with increasing clarity the role of values in judicial process. It is seen that in finding, interpreting, and applying the law, a judge is not engaging in a mechanical process, but in a determination, within narrower or wider limits, of desirable social policy.[2] Thus, decisions as to the meaning of 'due process,' 'person,' and 'liberty' as used in the Fourteenth Amendment helped shape the form of our economic life. Similar decisions about the compatibility of expressions in the Smith Act and the McCarran Act with the freedoms of the First Amendment are really value judgments about how broad or narrow is to be the pattern of American social liberty today. Administration has the same value character as legal decision, whether in private or public agencies. A planning agency locating a housing project reckons with health, costs, beauty, social relations, etc. Too often it forgets to reckon with the population being displaced and unable to afford the new houses. Similarly, the very definition of a 'slum' implies standards of desirable human living conditions.[3] A manager determining the efficiency of his plant in the usual terms of minimizing cost is actually making decisions which will affect the durability of goods for consumers and the health of workers.

In economic theory we may think of the notion of 'just price'

[1] David E. Lilienthal, *TVA, Democracy on the March* (New York, 1944).

[2] Morris R. Cohen, "The Process of Judicial Legislation," in his *Law and the Social Order* (New York, 1933).

[3] Allan A. Twichell, *An Appraisal Method for Measuring the Quality of Housing: A Yardstick for Health Officers, Housing Officials and Planners.* Pt. I: Nature and Uses of the Method (American Public Health Association, Committee on the Hygiene of Housing, New York, N.Y., 1945).

as an ancient theologism. But if we control prices or wages, there are value decisions of scales and merits; if we do not, it is likewise a value-determination of policy. For it implies the desirability of operating on a free-market conception in the case of prices, or on the basis of collective bargaining or tests of economic power in the case of wages. Value has, of course, long been a fundamental category in economic theory, whether the underlying purpose has been to find a more constant element beneath temporary price fluctuations, or to explain 'exchange-value' by reference to satisfactions, or to provide a basis of justification for patterns of distribution. Economic analyses of value as reflecting labor, human preferences, scarcity, have had serious implications for value theory in general.

Many fields today make decisions revolving about personality values. Educational theory, for example, has posed the value contrast of stern discipline and personality growth, a conflict too often resolved by leaving the former in practice and relegating the latter to public pronouncements of educational officials. Various forms of counseling embody conceptions of ideals—mental health, family welfare, vocational suitability—whose detailed value study is the object of increasingly careful analysis. Questions may be raised as diverse as the role of aggression in relation to mental health, the desirable conditions for permitting divorce, the degree to which limitation of job opportunities by racial discrimination should be a basis for guiding a person away from a particular field. And, of course, moral philosophy itself in its analysis of virtue-patterns is intimately concerned with evaluation of character as well as goals.

All aesthetic studies from daily book and art movie reviews to exalted controversies concerning classicism and romanticism are fundamentally value studies. This includes hypotheses concerning the significance of the White Whale in *Moby Dick* or the perennial appeal of *Oedipus Rex*. It includes detailed discussions of Mona Lisa's smile or Cordelia's long absence from the middle part of King Lear,[4] as well as debates concerning how far literary criticism should depart from strict analysis of text. It embraces Beethoven's creative process as well as his notes on his intent.

4 Arnold Isenberg, "Cordelia Absent," *Shakespeare Quarterly*, Vol. II, No. 3 (1951).

Even the philosophy of religion can scarcely describe the properties of God without finding that in reconciling God's omnipotence, omniscience, and goodness with the existence of evil, it is taking some stand on such issues as the degree of resignation or hope appropriate to man. Or, if it considers the religious emotions, it finds itself assessing the emotional needs of man. Its very theory moves in the domain of values.

I have wandered over the field with little system or completeness in order to suggest that in the current sense of the term 'values' there are values and implicit valuations everywhere, and there are value assumptions in almost every human study. Self-consciousness on this is growing constantly. Witness, for example, the increasing realization in the social sciences today that the work of the social scientist cannot be value-free. His work as a scientist not only deals with values, it necessarily embodies values. Valuation is a constant dimension of all human existence. *Value* as a philosophical concept has thus been elevated to a fundamental category, alongside of *existence*.

It may be fruitful briefly to compare these categories. 'To exist' has meant everything from 'to be a form of matter,' 'to be a space-time event,' 'to be a conscious experience,' to an undefined operator in logic. And if one wishes to study existence, one studies physics, psychology, history, etc. Perhaps the general category of existence serves as a reminder of the unity in physics, psychology, history, logic. But the discovery that there is such a unity is not a metaphysical assumption; it is the scientific discovery of the evolution of matter, the emergence of life, of consciousness, of social groups, of a historical mankind. Perhaps the story of value theory is the same. Let us look at it briefly.

INTERPRETATIONS OF THE VALUE PHENOMENON

Facing the vast field of value phenomena, value theory has been tempted to make its treatment wholesale, not retail. It has tended to assume that value is a unitary quality, phenomenon, experience, process. It has therefore attempted to locate, catch, chain and describe the phenomenon, raising epistemological and methodological questions about how this is to be done. This approach is most clear in the notion of *generic value* as expounded, for example, in Perry's *General Theory of Value:*[5] "No one would be disposed to deny that there is a common something in truth, goodness, legality, wealth, beauty and piety that distinguishes them from gravitation and chemical affinity. It is the express business of theory of value to discover what this something is; to define the genus, and discover the differentiae of the species." It has further assumed that evaluation thereafter consists in some comparative measurement of height or degree, or estimate of commensurability, of the properties thus discovered.

A few samples of the directions taken in contemporary value theory may be of use. Hartmann[6] leaves 'value' undefined, presupposing a human sensitivity towards it which grasps values intuitively. He gives value a slightly ethical cast by construing it as an 'ought-to-be.' G. E. Moore[7] uses the more traditional ethical term 'good' but the effect is the same as Hartmann's; the term is treated as indefinable, designating a simple quality, and the goodness of anything is apprehended intuitively. Thus there is no subordination of aesthetic value to moral value, or of any field to any other. W. Köhler[8] interprets value in terms of a generic concept of *requiredness*, a quality found directly in the field of awareness of a particular context, what he calls the "phenomenological field." We see directly that a note is right, that a necktie does not match a suit, that an action is improper, that purple fits between red and blue. Köhler expects logic as well as ethics and aesthetics to be developed from one common principle. R. B. Perry[9] identifies value as any object of any interest, and regards a man's interests as empirically observable. Laird[10] employs a general idea of *election* which extends beyond the human and living domain. He reminds us explicitly that: " 'By no endeavour, Can magnet ever, Attract a silver churn,' understood quite simply and literally, is a perfect illustration of the principle." Stevenson[11] analyzes value expressions in terms of emo-

5 Ralph Barton Perry, *General Theory of Value* (New York, 1926), pp. 4–5.

6 Nicolai Hartmann, *Ethics* (New York, 1932).

7 G. E. Moore, *Principia Ethica* (Cambridge, England, 1903).

8 Wolfgang Köhler, *The Place of Value in a World of Facts* (New York, 1938).

9 R. B. Perry, *op. cit.,* Ch. V.

10 John Laird, *The Idea of Value* (Cambridge, 1929), p. 93.

11 Charles L. Stevenson, *Ethics and Language* (New Haven, 1944).

tive meaning, in which the response or the stimulus is a specific range of emotions. He accordingly denies that value expressions are propositions capable of scientific verification. Dewey [12] finds distinctive valuation propositions only in *appraisal* of means in relation to ends (to which scientific evidence is directly relevant), not in statements of enjoyment or prizing. C. I. Lewis [13] in contrast, has value statements terminate in prizings and disprizings of the presented content of experience. Urban [14] traces the development of the value concept in consciousness from desire-satisfaction through life-conservation to self-realization. Clark Hull [15] offers *primary need,* scientifically defined in terms of states of the organism whose continuance and/or intensification would endanger survival of organism or species, as the key concept for the explication of value.

Perhaps we are amazed as we remember the breadth of valuation phenomena at the arrogance of contemporary value theory. It is almost like Thales assuming that there is a single nature to all existence phenomena with their qualitative diversity and rashly assigning the unity to water; or Heraclitus to the fire-flux; or Pythagoreans to the number system; or Empedocles to the hot, cold, moist, dry; or Democritus to the atoms. The enterprise of value theory has developed a momentum of its own, and on the whole there has been little questioning about its legitimacy. Occasionally voices are raised wondering whether it is worth adding an abstract concept over and above the special ones such as the moral, the aesthetic, the economic, the physical, etc., or perhaps whether any unity actually required cannot be provided by the ethical alone. That the mere existence of analogous fields is not in itself a sufficient justification for the enterprise of value theory should be obvious. Simply because the sky is blue and the sea is blue and there are aesthetic reactions to blue and I may feel "blue" does not make a general theory of blueness fruitful in rela-

---

[12] John Dewey, *Theory of Valuation* (Chicago, 1939).

[13] C. I. Lewis, *An Analysis of Knowledge and Valuation* (LaSalle, Ill., 1946).

[14] W. M. Urban, *Fundamentals of Ethics* (New York, 1930), pp. 16–20. Cf. his earlier *Valuation: Its Nature and Laws* (London, 1909).

[15] Clark L. Hull, "Value, Valuation, and Natural Science Methodology," *Philosophy of Science,* XI, No. 3 (1944), 127–41.

tion to all these special areas. Such unity needs to be discovered or justified. Of course there is an obvious sense in which generic value is meaningful if it is identified with some property that defines the distinction between the living and the nonliving, e.g., the general appetancy of life, or any teleological behavior. But this is only a first step. We need therefore to explore the question:

Under what conditions or assumptions does *value* constitute a single phenomenon, and *valuation* and *evaluation* prove to be unified processes?

CONDITIONS FOR UNITY IN VALUE PHENOMENON

Stipulation alone cannot render *value* a useful generic concept. We must find either a central quality in conscious experience, or a central tendency in human appetition, or a unifying psychological, cultural, social or historical pattern which gives a central quality to valuation.

Insofar as a central quality in conscious experience is concerned, neither the indefinable intuitable quality of Moore nor the requiredness of Köhler has been generally agreed upon. Some, such as Bergson,[16] find instead a fundamental cleavage between obligation and aspiration. The burden of proof—given such diverse phenomena as sense of duty, pleasurable aesthetic feeling, conation or aspiration, sense of logical connection—falls on those who assert the unity. They must show that they are not fitting all these into the pattern of any one by diluting it; also that fruitful specific studies may be opened up by the general unification.

There is, moreover, a theoretic hesitation today in accepting accounts of value phenomena purely in terms of contents of consciousness. This stems from the growing awareness of the complex relations of consciousness to life processes—organic, psychological, social, and historical. Hence, even if some unity is discoverable in conscious awareness, we are prone to look beyond and not be satisfied until it is related to dynamic processes on these other levels. However, if no unity is discovered in conscious-

16 Henry Bergson, *The Two Sources of Morality and Religion* (New York, 1935).

ness, it is still possible that one may be discovered in terms of dynamic organization on some levels.

The search for unity in the value concept through a central tendency in human biology or psychology is probably most prevalent today. This is accentuated by an individualistic orientation: biological assumptions in value theory have tended to center on the unfolding of impulse in the organism rather than the evolution and development of the group; hence, identification of value with survival-impetus, and the hope that proliferation of values can be explained in terms of a complicated conditioning process somehow generating secondary needs. Such secondary needs presumably cover what in ordinary discourse we would call culturally and historically shaped goals. To insist that the unification is a biological one is therefore either simply stretching biological language or else presupposing the *future* discovery of empirical relations between levels, for which there is as yet insufficient evidence. It is arbitrary postulation to assert that because man is an organism and all activity has a biological basis, therefore all aesthetic, political, religious, moral valuations *must* have a biological *import* which only lack of knowledge prevents us from tracing. One might as well define values from individual desire to national aspirations in terms of a presumed movement of protons and electrons. The hard-won lessons of the sciences of man concerning the relations of levels should not be surrendered in value theory.

The search for some kind of psychological unity is an old story. Plato offered it, and he was, after all, in his conception of a single Idea of the Good embracing beauty, morality, politics, economics, religion, the first to offer a general theory of value. (Aristotle, incidentally, was the first to oppose it by insisting that goodness, like being and unity, was not a real genus but had only a kind of analogy in the different fields.) In Plato's *Symposium*, Eros is the driving force in the soul seeking that ultimate Good; beauty, knowledge, creation (whether of children, books, or laws) are all stages or phases of the single unified search. Freudian theory today is a good illustration of such a psychological thesis which, if granted, would warrant a unitary treatment of value phenomena. It might be theoretically possible for Freudian psychology to give a picture of the career of libidinal energy of the individual so as to exhibit his actual economic, religious, aesthetic, moral attitudes as a function of the stage of his psychic development in relation to the problems he has encountered. In spite of its serious effort, it does not seem likely that this will be done without bringing social factors so far inside the structure as to make it no longer a purely psychological framework. Nevertheless, the evidence of contemporary psychology on the dynamic unity of personality is one of the bases of justification for a unified value concept.

A cultural basis for a unitary value concept is suggested by the anthropological concept of a culture pattern.[17] In fact, this notion has come to have almost a value connotation itself. For some anthropological accounts see a common ethos or value configuration expressed in bodily activity, art, education, interpersonal relations, and many other fields.[18] There are extensive contemporary inquiries in this direction, both critical analyses of pattern concepts and field investigations of values.[19] To act as a basis for a unified value concept, a systematic unity would not only have to be descriptively determined in the life of different peoples but shown to be grounded in invariant social demands and processes; otherwise it might be an accidental feature of particular peoples under special unifying conditions.

There may also be a historical basis for unity in the value concept. This would assert that the unity of the value concept does not rest merely on the fact that men may find some uniform qualities in consciousness, nor merely that man is a single animal species seeking survival, nor merely that men have psychological needs and drives, nor merely that cultures have unifying value-configurational tendencies. The unity currently sought in the value concept reflects, over and above these, the fact that the

17 E.g., Ruth Benedict, *Patterns of Culture* (New York, 1934).

18 E.g., Gregory Bateson and Margaret Mead, *Balinese Character, A Photographic Analysis*, Special Publications of the New York Academy of Sciences, Vol. II (December 7, 1942); Margaret Mead (ed.), *Cooperation and Competition among Primitive Peoples* (New York, 1937).

19 Clyde Kluckhohn, *et al.*, "Values and Value-Orientations in the Theory of Action," in T. Parsons and E. A. Shils (eds.), *Towards a General Theory of Action* (Cambridge, Mass., 1951); Ethel Albert, "The Classification of Values: A Method and Illustration," *American Anthropologist*, LVIII (1956), 221-48.

historical career of mankind on the globe, building on these materials, has increasingly taken a unified form. It has faced man with what is almost a single world system in which every phase of life has been drawn increasingly into a common pool of decision. It has posed common problems for mankind and imposed the task of working out criteria for their satisfactory solution.

This historical approach to the unity of the value concept finds considerable corroboration, I believe, in the formative stages of modern value theory. Bentham, if any single philosopher, is the true father of modern value theory in his assumption that all values are exchangeable into the one currency—in his view, *pleasure*. His psychological hedonism may be comparatively trivial as a basis. The historical strength of his theory comes rather from the way it reflects the growing aims of life in the middle class of his day—the accumulation of wealth and the translation of every particular value-quality into exchange-value expressed by money.[20] Thus the basis of his general use of a value concept may be summarized briefly as follows. When the world became integrated into a single system so that everything, no matter how different, had its price in the single world market, then a general theory of value (seen by him as a generalized moral science) was necessary to attempt to render commensurable what had hitherto been isolated and disparate (and in his eyes, capricious selection). All values were thrown into a single market. Their separate qualities became relegated to individual appreciation (consumption), their exchange value became their generic value.

The historical unity of the value concept today need not have the same simple basis that this hypothesis envisages in the case of Bentham. The economic, political, cultural, moral, intellectual problems of the contemporary integrated globe have both sharpened and matured. It is possible that a unified value concept today may come to represent on its theoretical side, the growing unity of the knowledge that we have of man. And as a normative concept it may reflect to a greater degree a growing unity of aspiration pattern underlying the contemporary world.

[20] See the treatment of this question in Chapter Two, pp. 29ff.

To study value phenomena on all these levels provides a unity for the value concept which is full-bodied rather than simply abstract or formal, thoroughly empirical rather than simply intuitive, and comprehensive rather than reductive. Value is not equated simply with expressing emotion or being interested or feeling a tug. Man's value experience is not cut off from the whole of his living activity and turned into some form of immediate presentation unrelated to dynamic processes—organic, psychological, cultural and historical. Nor, on the contrary, does the study of value operate on a reduced biological or psychological level, defining its cultural and social dimensions by stipulation in terms of the lower level. The ideal for value theory is, therefore, to find the unity of value in the most systematic historical evolutionary picture of man from his emergence on the globe to the present day, through the various stages of his development, with whatever knowledge we have or can acquire of the appearance of the various value phenomena and processes of valuation and evaluation, the changes in these phenomena, the conditions (biological, psychological, social, and historical) of their appearance and their change. The pattern of unity is thus to be read from the *results* of the inquiry, not from initial qualitative starting points, methods or conceptual tools. If this is so, then the unity of value theory is intimately bound up, almost step by step, with the advance of the sciences of man.

THE VALUE CONCEPT AND THE DESCRIPTIVE STANDPOINT

Although at the outset of this chapter we distinguished the descriptive usage of 'value' and its normative usage, it is clear by this time that the general approach inherent in the development of the value concept has been descriptive. The occurrence of evaluation is not ignored, but dominant interest lies in the fact that every act of evaluating, every act of setting up or using a standard, may itself be described. Thus the materials that an evaluative approach might jealously guard as its private preserve become assimilated into the content of description. If we are doing a fuller study of contemporary general value theory, we would find ample evidence of the way in which descriptive attention to men's standards in comparing, reconciling, and integrating their values not only rounds out the field but in return furnishes an armory of criteria for evaluation upon which evaluative method can then draw in use. In Bentham, there are the familiar measures of the felicific calculus—intensity, duration, purity, and the rest. In R. B. Perry, there are intensity, inclusiveness, preference. Of course, to have described and systematized is not equivalent to accepting. For accepting is a category within the evaluative enterprise, not to be confused with description of accepting.[21] But the ideal of unrestricted description, as we saw, is to cover the whole ground. From its point of view, the evaluative standpoint is reduced to the act of selection, with the describer ready to pounce on it once it is over and describe it as fresh data!

It is interesting to note that the recent rise of anthropological and sociological concern with mapping the values of groups has explicitly embraced evaluating as an aspect of its descriptive concern. Thus Clyde Kluckhohn, presenting a definition which became the basis of extensive values studies, says: "A value is a conception, explicit or implicit, distinctive of an individual or characteristic of a group, of the desirable which influences the selection from available modes, means, and ends of action." [22] He adds that it is not merely a preference, but felt or considered to be justified. This aspect of the value concept is on the whole stressed in most of the recent social science treatments of the subject. In this respect, the social science use has pointed up the evaluative element more sharply than the philosophical use in general value theory, in which value is broadly equated with interest or pleasure or desire, and their objects. In the end, however, the result is the same. The evaluating function in the philosophical account is carried out in the theory of comparative value which elaborates the criteria for choosing among values, or else by a subtheory of obligation, which tells which *should* be preferred and why. The descriptive function in social science

[21] Not to mark where the shift in enterprise takes place is to open oneself to the charge of smuggling in values or engaging in what Stevenson terms 'persuasive definition.' See his penetrating discussion of this in his *Ethics and Language*, Ch. IX.

[22] Clyde Kluckhohn, *op. cit.*, p. 395.

accounts is often broadened by using a concept of *norms* as customary approved modes of behavior and feeling.[23] In any case, the whole enterprise is fashioned for and carried out within a descriptive framework.

[23] I have shown elsewhere in a sample survey of psychological and sociological writings that there is an inverse tendency in the use of 'norm' and 'value.' Writers who use the first broadly use the second in a narrower evaluative sense; the converse tendency is found among some scientists and of course, more often among philosophers to whom 'norm' usually connotes 'ought.' ("The Concept of Levels in Social Theory," in *A Symposium on Sociological Theory*, ed. Llewellyn Gross [Evanston, Ill., 1959], esp. pp. 189-92.)

CHAPTER NINE

A CONCEPTUAL FRAMEWORK FOR SOCIO-CULTURAL DESCRIPTIVE APPROACHES

We noted at the end of Chapter Seven that a promising descriptive approach to ethics was found in those views that treated moral phenomena as basically social in character. Our aim in this chapter is to work out a conceptual framework from the descriptive standpoint to do justice to such views. A framework of this sort will have to show how a domain of moral phenomena is delineated, how ethical theorizing is related to moral phenomena, how moral concepts and theoretical ethical concepts are introduced, how typical issues of ethical theory can be understood in this framework and in what way their solution is advanced thereby.

Social frameworks can be either socio-cultural or socio-historical. It is obvious that there is some sense in which moral codes grow up and have their existence in a matrix of human social activity, and that ethical reflection grows out of problems within and with respect to moral codes. We do not, however, know enough about this growing up as yet—the development of culture over the past 25,000 years in intimate detail—to fashion a conceptual framework that will reflect clearly demarcated stages of historical development. Accordingly, we shall concentrate on a socio-cultural framework of a more abstract analytical sort, which leaves room for historical relations and socio-functional relations as empirical specializations.

There are two central features in the framework to be proposed here. The first is that it is *descriptive* throughout. It may be describing behavior. It may be describing codes as existent documents or as ways of reacting whether with obedience or defiance. It may be describing theory as ways in which men think and the utilization of their thinking in interpersonal and social relations.

It may be describing the phenomenal field and its properties. In all these cases, it is concerned with given individuals or groups at given times in given places, or invariant aspects or abstract phases of their experience and reflection.

The second feature is that it employs the concept of *levels*. It distinguishes a ground-floor level of conduct and its associated elements of feelings, desires, and purposes; a moral level corresponding roughly to codes and code-oriented action and attitude; and an ethical-theory level consisting of ethical theorizing and whatever human processes and phenomenal qualities can be found in association with it. We shall often refer to these, for brevity's sake, as the first, second, and third levels respectively.

The concept of levels as it has been dealt with in philosophical discussion is a very complex one.[1] In the sense here intended, we are concerned with what may be called "instrumental-functional" levels, that is, ordered hierarchies of instrumental relationships between distinguishable human activities or phases of activity. The reason for dealing with levels in this sense is an obvious one: whatever the disputes about morality, there is general agreement that it operates in human life to guide conduct, and whatever the disagreements about the nature of ethical theorizing, there is general agreement that it helps morality, at the very least by giving us an understanding of it. In economics, one can map the relations of the levels of consumption, production of consumable goods, production of instruments of production; in educational life, teaching students, training teachers, developing the theory of education. So too, with our set in the ethical domain, of conduct, moral pattern, and ethical-theory levels. (There is, incidentally, no sanctity intended for the number three. How many levels are needed is always to be determined for the particular inquiry.)

In economics and education, the initial defining relations between the higher level and the lower are obvious; they are clearly service relations. Once the levels are set up as separable processes

---

[1] For a study of the concept and its utility, see my essay, "The Concept of Levels in Social Theory," in *Symposium on Sociological Theory*, ed. Llewellyn Gross (Evanston, Ill., 1959). Four senses of levels are there distinguished, and the present scheme for ethical description is suggested in a brief sketch (pp. 181-183) as illustration of one type.

of human activity, or as distinguishable aspects of a single activity, we can study their mutual influences, how far they draw on the same basic resources, where they get in each other's way, and so on. So, for example, the allocation of resources toward consumption or production or long-range preparation for future production, is one of the most serious issues of modern life in underdeveloped countries. Again, the development of the technology of production actually changes what is consumed, and the development of the theory of teaching changes the curriculum. There are also reciprocal influences. The exact pattern of inter-influence is always an empirical question, to be studied in each particular field for the period involved. Changes in the pattern of interinfluence may occur over time. Even the initial defining relation may be transformed. Thus if one sets up the moral level over and above the general conduct level by using some repressive function as a defining mark, it does not follow that even if repression may always continue in morality to some degree, it will maintain a central position as man progresses; it may instead become a peripheral relation with more rational types of functions playing a more central role.

What are the defining relationships in terms of which we may distinguish our levels in the ethical domain? What areas of fruitful research can such a conceptual framework open up? And can it help at all to clarify the kind of theoretical problems with which moral philosophy has been concerned? These are the questions to which the present chapter attempts an answer in an experimental mood.

THE GROUND-FLOOR LEVEL OF CONDUCT AND
ITS ASSOCIATED ELEMENTS

Conduct in the sense employed here is not to be equated simply with observable bodily acts in sequence. It refers to bodily behavior systematized in terms of direction or goal-seeking, or what is in some other sense "meaningful." Conduct may be studied by reference to conscious elements in goal pursuit, using techniques of introspection, phenomenological report, interview, etc. Or operational concepts may be developed to deal with data observationally as by the various behaviorist approaches to purpose. It is worth noting also that conduct need not be construed along the lines of a single model. Its "meaningful" element may consist in its involving choice between alternatives or conformity to norms, as well as being determinate patterning of goal-striving. All such concepts for differentiating conduct from mere behavior would require separate detailed explication.

The description of conduct is sometimes a simple matter and sometimes it requires extended study. A man might, for example, enter in his diary at night the account of his day's doings, prefatory to reflective comments upon them. Studies may be made of a nation's food habits over a given period, by sampling home cooking and receiving reports of restaurant sales and patrons' selections. The Kinsey reports—to take a large-scale ambitious project—sought to map the sexual conduct of Americans in as purely behavioral terms as possible.

That patterns of conduct are not simply "observed" has become increasingly clear in critical social theory. Numerous problems of method, both theoretical and practical, center about the task of achieving accurate description of such patterns. There is, in the first place, the problem of the very meaning of 'pattern.' This is, in some sense, a theoretical construct involving the selection of features from the continuum of conduct. For our purposes we may regard 'pattern' as designating a systematic order among recurrent elements in conduct, not as an ideal type or a governing norm, or a determining mold. (These characterizations may, however, arise in special relations of the individual and the group.) Thus the term is being used in a neutral sense, as one might think of a language as a pattern of the speech of a people. There are, in the second place, numerous issues of technique and interpretation in the use of practical methods—introspection, interview, case-study, participant-observer, statistics—that have been so intensively explored in the psychological and social sciences. Obviously these are important questions, and equally obviously the further refinement of these methods—including guards against the surreptitious intrusion of value elements—is the task of these sciences.

It is quite possible to step down below the ground-floor of conduct to a basement and sub-basement. One might, for example, step down to the level of physics, and regard patterns of conduct as interpretations of, abstractions from, emergents out of (whatever one's favorite language) physical motions. It may be that only ignorance prevents us from going all the way down to the protons and electrons, to what some semanticists picturesquely call the "unspeakable" level. The judgment that such descents are not required for the study of morals and ethics is not, however, a priori. It embodies the recognition that morals and ethics deal with whole people or persons in the everyday sense of the terms. For example, one does not assign moral attributes to an organ or part of a body. A man may be called virtuous, but not so a brain or a heart; a stomach may be unruly, but scarcely vicious. Yet these speech habits may reflect cultural patterns; Plato speaks of the virtue or excellence of an eye, using the Greek equivalent of 'virtue' (aretē). If, however, man is a unified physiological organism and a unified psychological personality, then there is no need to go below the ground-floor level of conduct as a first level. Basement phenomena must, however, always be attended to for their possible relevance at special points, especially in connection with issues of causality.

Even where conduct already includes the relation of act and goal actually sought, systematic understanding requires reference to many associated elements. (We may know what a person ordered in a restaurant, but this will not tell us whether his selection was based on health or taste.) All the wider relations of the act and the goal, upon which further direction of future action and goal-seeking may depend, can be understood only if we know the wider context of conduct—the feelings of men concerned, their desires, tensions, problems. There is no point in standardizing some concept on the first level to cover all these alongside of 'conduct.' Such a term as 'desire' is useful where there is a high degree of consciousness of what is sought. The behavioristically-inclined may think in terms of 'tension-patterns,' the logically parsimonious in terms of 'potential goals' alongside of 'actual goals.' What is required for our purposes is simply the recognition that alongside of conduct, associated elements of feeling, appetition, tension, etc., are required to understand changes in conduct-pattern and especially to take note of the important phenomenon of *compromise* in human life.

In fact, actual conduct is often compromise. If people in a

restaurant order more beef stew than porterhouse steak, it may well indicate that it was the cheaper, not the preferred food. Independent inquiry is needed to ascertain the direction of major desire. Without some type of distinction between conduct and desire, the assumption too readily creeps in that whatever prevails in conduct must have been the most desired, whereas it may have been simply the most tolerable of a limited set available at the moment. This assumption is sometimes writ large in the conservative use of a sociological functionalism: it is argued that since the existence of a social institution is evidence of its serving some need, it is thereby in some sense justified.[2] Close attention to the limitations of compromise promotes a view of tension points, which may open the way to an understanding of dynamic elements and help explain otherwise unpredictable change. It also provides, thereby, a fuller picture of the first level for purposes of evaluation.

THE MORAL PATTERN

The second level in our conceptual framework we shall call 'the moral pattern' of a given people. The term 'pattern' is perhaps unusual in such a context, but it helps us remember the descriptive standpoint of our framework. 'Moral judgments' might be misleading, since it concentrates unduly on discourse, which we may construe as partial evidence for the existence of the pattern. 'Moral norms' might do, but the term 'norms' is used very widely with varied connotations, and so we shall use it only when the context makes its meaning quite clear. Perhaps the nearest equivalent term to a moral pattern would be to speak simply of the existent morality of a people. Take the example of a moral pattern expressed in a code—say the Ten Commandments. This code contains injunctions to the Hebrew people; they are told to adhere to one God, not to use graven images, not to blaspheme, to rest on the seventh day, to honor parents; to abstain

[2] Cf. Dorothy Gregg and Elgin Williams, "The Dismal Science of Functionalism," *American Anthropologist*, L, No. 4, Pt. I (Oct.-Dec., 1948), 594-611. See also Robert K. Merton's account of the conservative and radical uses of functionalism in his *Social Theory and Social Structure* (Glencoe, Ill., 1957), pp. 37ff.

from killing, adultery, stealing, false witness; not to covet what is one's neighbor's. We shall see later in greater detail what a moral pattern may include. In general, it involves a selection of types of conduct, desire, feeling, interpersonal or group relations, certified as moral or criticized as immoral. But what are the marks by which this certification is carried out, and what are the steps in concept-formation which issue in a descriptive concept of the moral level? Let us build up the concept gradually.

It is generally agreed, even where the nature of morality is analyzed in different ways, that its relation to the conduct and desire level is one of *regulation,* of guidance and control. The proposition that every society has some form of regulation is either empirical, or—if the notion of maintaining and transmitting its pattern is included in the conception of a society—it is analytic. It can then be established empirically that regulation takes many different forms under different conditions—from coercion to persuasion, and from complex social organization to prediction of what experience will reveal that the individual will want. If one had found uniformly but a single mode of regulation, that mode might have been substituted for the initial generic term. Also, if it should ever be established that underlying the regulation there is always one single central problem—suppose one found overwhelming psychological evidence that aggression is the central problem of human relations, and that regulation in effect turned out to be repressing aggression—then this relation of the second to the first level can become a part of the initial definition of 'moral.' In this way, the growth of knowledge about the actual functioning of what we may at any point call 'morality' may help to clarify and alter our differentiating idea of it. But no such unification has yet been established.

The next step involves a kind of parting of the ways in the conception of the moral level. We might simply equate the concept of a moral pattern with *any* mode of regulation, or else with just some determinate mode or modes. To follow the first path, after the previous agreement that every society has some mode of regulation, would make the statement "Every society has a moral pattern" analytic. To take the second path would make the statement empirical; we should then have to be able to conceive of a society lacking in morality, irrespective of the question whether such has existed. Although some writers find solace in the thought that one could definitionally ensure the existence of morality in every society, the second alternative is clearly scientifically preferable, since we know that morality is not the only pattern we are interested in, and that we will want to differentiate it at the very least from the legal pattern.

The next step is perhaps the most difficult one. Having decided that not all regulation modes would constitute the result a morality, we have to decide which would, or else which would not. At this point, philosophers often proceed to look for one differentiating property or one set of properties, or take it for granted that it would always have to be the same set of regulation modes intended. These are, however, further assumptions which should be rendered explicit, and once explicit, it can be seen that they need not hold. We could have a conception of a morality in which the particular set of regulation modes (in each case short of the total conceivable or actually found) might be regionally or culturally variable, and the only unifying element might be that the regulation was relatively successful. Nevertheless, a few properties have been suggested, and it seems likely that some of these will do—that is, do in the sense of helping to develop a *fruitful* concept.

One such property is the negative one of excluding regulation by sheer coercion or fear of violence. This is the familiar idea that morality must somehow operate from "within" a person. This probably accounts for the unwillingness of theorists to say that a society which regulated the relations of members wholly in terms of fear would have a "fear-morality"; they would rather say it had no morality. A comparable problem arises about the typical philosophic charge that Hobbes denied morality rather than advocated an "expediency-morality." Please note that I am not trying to settle such a question by an appeal to usage; usage is part evidence but not determinative. If it were, we could really settle the question! But for my part, I think the reason it cannot be settled—apart from the textual question of what Hobbes meant, which is controversial enough—is that we have not a sufficiently clear idea of expediency, and that it will not be clear enough (apart from some usual contexts) until we have much more knowledge about the "self" and the part that different types of desires and emotions play within it, how it grows, what is "inside" it and what is "outside," and how such questions are determined in individual development. The contemporary psychological study of "internalization" processes in individual personality development, in spite of competing hypotheses about the mechanisms, seems to have gone far enough to make the idea that morality is something within a person a fruitful defining property. But it is not wholly clear that this may not involve ethnocentric concentration on the individual's feelings.

Another suggestion of a different type may be extracted from Redfield's use of the phrase 'moral order' to refer to bonds among men and binding sentiments, especially as they appear in religion.[3] He contrasts this with the 'technical order' where utility and coercion are the predominant relations in human affairs. It is possible that a distinction between binding and nonbinding in this sense may prove more fruitful than one between internal and external, or there may be partial overlapping. There are also questions whether the technical order may not turn out to have its own conception of the individual and his goals, so as to be able to be reckoned as a different kind of morality (a "success-oriented" one, but quite relaxed by contrast with a folk-binding type.) But to pursue this here would carry us too far afield.

A third property implicitly suggested by much of ethical theory is that the kind of regulation constitutive of the moral level has to involve some element of discourse. (We forego the extreme formulation that it is regulation *by* the use of words!) This suggestion has much to be said for it—at least as a mark that is a necessary though not a sufficient condition—in the light of contemporary realization of the importance and penetration of language in human life. It is strengthened by modern naturalistic interpretations of the development of self-consciousness as arising in the social communication of men, and by the realization that the emergence of self-consciousness marks a genuine critical point in human development. Once this suggestion is adopted, it is then a matter of *empirical* discovery that many societies in which such regulation (regulation involving discourse) takes place use distinct terms for this type of regulation, or at least that there are felt distinctions in the usage of terms.

It is by some such use of differentiating criteria and by empir-

3 Robert Redfield, *The Primitive World and its Transformations* (Ithaca, 1953), pp. 20-21.

ical survey invoking them, that we determine the various constituents to be listed as the content and structure of the second level. There follows an exploration using some of the constituents in the attempt to find others associated with them. The net result is a rough outline of a morality or moral pattern—not all of whose constituents are necessarily found everywhere—held together by the fact that broadly speaking, enough of them function in some configuration or other to secure the regulation effect. The following array of constituents is empirically discoverable in this fashion:

Selected *types of acts or desires* whose performance or possession is enjoined or forbidden.

Selected *character traits*, dispositions to patterns of action, feeling, desire, interpersonal relations, which are cultivated or avoided, praised or blamed.

Selected directions in conduct or *goals,* and ways of achieving goals or *means.*

These may be regarded as the content of the morality. Then there are numerous constituents that make up its structure:

Invariably there is some implicit or explicit conception of *the scope of the community of those who count,* as well as of *the marks of a responsible person.*

Invariably there is some *set of concepts* to be found in the pattern for referring to the constituents.

There is always some *scheme of organization or systematization:* for example, the morality is cast in discourse as commands or as universal laws; organization also involves unifying emphases, modes of reasoning, procedures of application, methods and scope of decision.

Often there is some selected *type of justification* resorted to when questions of uncertainty or criticism arise: for example, religion, tradition, protection, or welfare.

Usually there are some *types of sanctions,* rewards and punishments, attached to some or all of the preceding constituents.

All or some of the above are found in specific configurations associated with selected *types of feeling,* such as guilt, shame, remorse, respect for authority, pride, etc.

This outline of the constituents of a morality is explored in considerable detail in *Anthropology and Ethics,* where our aim included a study of the coordinates to be employed if one were setting out to map moralities. It would be unnecessary repetition here to go over this ground. Note, however, that once we have this wider picture of what constitutes a morality, the very properties that helped us build it up may be brought under scrutiny, refined, and even discarded as initial oversimplification. We also look for, but do not necessarily find, unifying properties for all moralities as so described. This is why we have to employ such a general term as 'selected types of. . . .' It allows the possibility that the mode of selection or procedure or unifying property may vary in different moralities. The central mark in one morality may be "what your conscience tells you," in another, "what tradition has given us," in still another, "what preserves the tribe." The answer need not even come from a single constituent—the first is from the feeling and emotion group, the second from a justification constituent, the third from a goal constituent.[4] It is such possibilities, not just appeal to lack of knowledge, that makes one hesitate, as we have seen, to accept the insistence of some philosophers in our tradition that what they offer is *the* mark of the moral,[5] and insist instead on formulating the relation of the moral level to the conduct level in such a way as not to foreclose the results of much-needed further empirical inquiry. It is important to note, however, that this openness in the general criteria does not mean that there may not, *in a particular morality,* be the sharpest separation of the moral and the nonmoral. Our western morality, for example, makes very sharp divisions between moral and nonmoral goals, moral and nonmoral attitudes, and so on, using sometimes feeling tests, sometimes phenomenal qualities, sometimes religious ideas. But how sharp the distinctions are will itself be a feature of a given morality, *to be empirically determined.* Sharp distinctions and soft gradations will be different configurational properties.

TRANSITION TO THE ETHICAL-THEORY LEVEL

Since we are dealing with levels as phases of human activity related in an instrumental-functional way, the most obvious phenomena on our third level are men reflecting or theorizing about the moral level, and producing theories in discourse or in books.

[4] This embodies the lesson that moralities shape up in different configurations. Cf. *Anthropology and Ethics,* Ch. XIV.
[5] See the discussion of data, above, pp. 176ff.

(More subtle phenomena will be examined shortly in dealing with the phenomenal field of individuals.) To see the defining marks of this level, we have to discover or specify its relations to the moral level. Fortunately, we are in a more familiar area in dealing with ethical theorizing, for on the whole it is a more recent cultural product and history can tell us something about the way it arose. Such an account helps us locate the points in the moral level at which the growth occurs, in short, the "budding off" points for ethical theorizing.

Ethical reflection is prompted because problems arise in the application of nearly every moral code, because conflicts exist in the life of society or stem from economic and social change, because men learn that there are varying moral ways and so alternatives may exert some appeal, and for a host of other reasons.

Application of a moral code is simple only in a simple society. Even there Solomons are at a premium. For moral rules are difficult to interpret and they come in conflict with one another. Thou shalt not steal. But what is stealing? A Spencer talks at times as if taxation were a form of robbery to be put up with for the sake of protection. The slaveholder regards freeing the slaves as confiscation of property; the advocate of liberation sees the existence of slavery itself as a stealing of human labor. And what of the theory of "exploitation"? The history of the Ten Commandments in Hebrew literature is itself an imposing illustration of the role of interpretation in applying a moral code. Any developed legal system, for that matter, shows exactly comparable problems.

Conflicts of all sorts give rise to strains within the morality. The growth of cities makes inroads on a rural morality, the growth of trade on a peasant morality, the growth of slavery on the morality of both master and slave. By the time that conflicts assume major proportions in the life of a society, ethical reflection has usually worked out formal modes of justification for one side or the other.

The sense of variety in moral codes usually becomes provocative in an atmosphere of dissatisfaction with the old ways, at least in their restrictive aspects. Herodotus and the Sophists in the ancient Greek world, the Skeptics in ancient Rome, the Encyclopedists in eighteenth-century France, the sociologist and anthropologist in contemporary America have all used comparative materials from different societies to shake the dogmatism of one's own ways.

The demand for understanding and evaluation grows in its own right with the development of knowledge in all aspects of human life. In that sense, ethical reflection on moral ways is probably unavoidable.

If these brief considerations are to the point, the ethical-theory level functions in three ways: (a) to extend or reshape the morality in its application; (b) to justify or criticize the morality in its relation to the guidance of the conduct level; (c) to mediate between the morality and the growth of human knowledge. These functions are by no means cut off from one another. To see their respective weight in a given society is an empirical question; to determine which is to have a primary place or how they are to be combined at different times is itself an evaluative question.

The budding points in the morality for the growth of ethical theorizing, corresponding to these three functions, are usually its scheme of organization and systematization and its modes of justification. In well-developed philosophical traditions, this is where we see philosophers taking hold. In primitive societies, wherever there is quasi-philosophical elaboration, this is where the elders as philosophers will weave their patterns.

So far we have spoken of the ethical-theory level without specially distinguishing between the theorizing as human activity set in an existential context, and the theory as product, as a more or less well-defined set of assertions capable—as the philosophical tradition shows only too clearly—of being dealt with apart from its context. A comparable distinction holds between the moral process as a set of phenomena of human behavior and attitude and the moral code as a set of assertions or injunctions (depending on the form it takes). There are many problems in ethical theory for the analysis of which one would have to distinguish very carefully whether one was talking about an ethical utterance, the meaning of the statement, the act of assenting to the statement, and so on. Consideration of such problems in general will be found in Part Four. In our present discussion, the context will make clear what is intended—that is, where we are using the term 'ethical-theory level' in its most inclusive sense, and where, for example, we are discussing the relation of ethical theory as product and morality as product.

How sharply a particular ethical theory is intertwined with or separated from a particular morality is a factual question for the specific case. Take, for example, the moral code of the Decalogue. One may start from the scheme of organization and look to the way the content was cast, the way in which the sanctions were invoked, the factual setting implied in the document. Thus the content is cast as commands of a God who has a special relation to the group concerned ("I am the Lord thy God, which have brought thee out of the land of Egypt, out of the house of bondage"). There shall be no worship of idols: "for I the Lord thy God am a jealous God, venting the iniquity of the fathers upon the children unto the third and fourth generation of them that hate me, and showing mercy unto thousands of them that love me, and keep my commandments." The Sabbath day is justified by being modeled on the Lord's resting the seventh day after creating the world in six. Parents are to be honored "that thy days may be long upon the land which the Lord thy God giveth thee."

Now since organization of the morality is in terms of conformity to God's commands, ethical reflection will want to know what sort of God we are dealing with. Is God simply a possessor of power jealous of worship, or does he embody a perfection appealing to us as a model? M. Lazarus, in his *The Ethics of Judaism*, minimizes the imperative form, in favor of a model interpretation.[6] The fundamental law rather than will or command says, "You shall be holy, for I am holy." As biblical interpretation (not as Kantian predilection), Lazarus affirms the view that "God is the lawgiver but he did not promulgate the law as his pleasure or as an arbitrary or despotic command; and man is not to obey it as such. It is law for man, because he recognizes in God the prototype of all morality, because God is the creative force back of the moral order and moral purpose of the world." To determine what is the actual ethical theory implicit in the Decalogue is a question of text and history. What ethical theory it is *desirable* to associate with a definite morality is a quite different question.

In contrast with this intertwining of the morality and its ethical theory, consider how sharply they may be separated. Suppose

---

[6] Philadelphia, 1900, I, 112, 115-16.

we have the familiar moral pattern of traditional rules whose violation is associated with guilt-feeling; alongside, suppose we have an ethical theory in which morality is seen as an effort of a group to maintain cohesion for survival purposes. The integration and justification of what is moral is thus in terms of group-survival value. The specific rules will be justified or criticized by this standard, even the occurrence of guilt-feeling as an internal sanction will be evaluated as a useful or harmful property of human nature or development. The conclusion might be that we ought to use survival-value as a direct criterion for selection of acts and goals to be certified as moral, or else that we ought to let well enough alone. In either case, the distinction between the moral and the ethical-theory level is clear.

The degree of distinctness that may emerge between moral patterns and their associated ethical theories is seen in the fact that various ethical theories may be found with the same moral pattern and different moral patterns with the same ethical theory. Thus a morality of honesty may be certified on an ethics of God's will or of general happiness. Conversely, God's will in an ethical pattern does not determine what morality God is taken to will: it may be a social cooperative order or an individualistic success order. General happiness as an ethical principle has appeared with the same variety. It does not follow, of course, that there may not be determinate relations (whether logical, psychological, historical) between some particular moral patterns and particular ethical theories. That is a distinct issue.

THE CONTENT OF AN ETHICAL THEORY

What we find in a given ethical theory will, of course, depend on the complexity of the morality with which it has been associated, and the degree of reflective sophistication that it embodies.

In an ethical theory of a more developed type there will usually be some account of good and evil, analyzing the meaning of the terms and clarifying and refining the ways of identifying and certifying goals and means as good or evil, also the ways of comparing, ordering, and systematizing goods and evils, determining which goods are to be regarded as ideals, and—in general—how they are to be evaluated. For example, goods may be evaluated by reference to an ethical conception of man's end or purpose in the world.

There will be a theory of rights and wrongs and obligations, performing scaling and evaluative functions in that area comparable to the ordering functions in the theory of good and evil. For example, duties may be measured by their contribution to general welfare or the degree of their relevance to some religious framework.

There will be a theory of virtues and vices, and their mode of assessment.

There will be some theoretical interpretation of the particular feelings that have been stressed in the given morality—such feelings as conscience, shame, sympathy, sense of responsibility, and so forth. Witness how, for example, the feelings of conscience in the Western tradition take shape as a sense of sin and grow in Western ethical accounts into the voice of God or the commands of universal reason.

Another element will be some theory of sanctions and the particular way in which they are patterned; compare the ethical role of heaven and hell with the systematic utilitarian reduction of all sanctions to measurable feelings of pleasure and pain.

There will also be some theory of methods of decision, assessing their reliability. Compare in the Western tradition the conflict of intuitive, authoritarian, and empirical methods, or on a less sweeping scale, the various estimates of the reliability of the moral feelings as guides to conduct.

There will also be extensive analysis of moral concepts and critical consideration of methods of dealing with moral issues, correlating these with reflective consideration of other areas of human life.

Implicit in a great many of these elements of an ethical theory is some view of man, the nature of human relations, and man's relation to the world. This picture of existential conditions constitutes another and very central element to be looked for in analyzing an ethical theory; we may call it formally the *existential perspective* of an ethical theory. It was compared, in Chapter Two,[7] to a theatrical stage, which specified the setting and dramatis personae of the moral process. The hypothesis was offered

7 Pp. 21ff., above.

that every ethical theory embodied an existential perspective. For example, an ethical theory associated with the moral pattern of the Ten Commandments would see the stage set clearly in the relation of God and the Hebrew people. Certain features of the actors are also described or assumed. God tells the people what kind of a god he is; it is taken for granted that men have certain fears, want a long life, etc. This constitutes one type of supernaturalist existential perspective. Other ethical theories embody biological stages (set in terms of groups struggling for survival, or organisms maintaining their balance), or psychological stages (set in terms of individuals equipped with certain drives or needs) or socio-historical stages (set in terms of assumed historical-developmental patterns), and so on, as well as various combinations. It should be noted that an existential perspective is an element within the ethical theory, not to be confused with an external analysis of historical causes and social significance of a given theory.[8]

That there have been different ethical theories in human history is obvious. The variety of ethical theories is probably smaller than that of moral codes, just as the variety of grammars (as well as purposes served by language) is smaller than that of languages themselves. It is, in fact, possible that ethical theories may on examination constitute a limited number of species, as kinship structures apparently do, but it is not necessarily so. The variety of ethical theories is one of the chief factors prompting the use of comparative method to codify, analyze, and evaluate ethical theories themselves.

It is important, at an early point in the development of comparative theory, to resist any premature tendency to typology. It would be easy to choose some methodological difference such as empirical versus intuitionist, or some metaphysical difference such as naturalist versus supernaturalist, or some stress difference in analysis such as teleological versus deontological, and classify along such lines. Such classification may be relevant for specific purposes. But the very advantage in thinking of theories as prod-

8 For a systematic analysis of the concept of an existential perspective, a classification of existential perspectives, and the outline of evidence to support the claim that every ethical theory embodies an existential perspective, see my *Science and the Structure of Ethics.*

ucts in an ethical-theory level consists in underscoring the existential-historical character of the materials with which we are dealing. An ethical theory is thus always *of* some society or group or writer, anchored to and analyzed out of existent materials, even where it happens to be a projection of a possible pattern or proposed as a universal pattern. Any satisfactory typology will probably reflect the outcome of the analysis of the full range of materials and the types of conclusions reached about them. The classification of ethical theories can be no more a priori or semi-a priori than a classification of languages.

IS A FOURTH LEVEL IN THIS CONCEPTUAL FRAMEWORK DESIRABLE?

There is a well-established practice in many fields today of allowing meta-theory to rise above any theory that is being considered, as in the case of meta-mathematics or meta-science. But meta-ethics has been the subject of special controversy. Usually, it is proposed from an analytic perspective, embracing the consideration of meanings, methods, modes of justification, which we saw in Part Two to be the enterprise of analytic method. It has, however, in the usual accounts of its status, been sharply separated from normative ethics, and so assigned a methodological neutrality.[9] Do we need a new level for this?

Setting apart normative ethics parallels our separation of the moral pattern from the ethical-theory level. But the ethical-theory level, as we have seen, embraces a picture of the world and man as stage-setting. And we have had frequent occasion to note that the theoretical constructions of ethics embody valuational or purposive elements of a general or a specific sort. If one thinks in terms of rising to still higher levels, it is important to recognize what may be a distinguishing complication in the ethical field. In other fields, the recognition of purposive elements in theoretical construction may have less serious impact; for although decisions do have to be made on the meta-level, they may be made on "pragmatic" grounds. Now pragmatic grounds embody special classes of purposes, as in the familiar appeal to providing greater systematic power, fruitfulness, etc. But in ethics, any appeal to

9 See above, p. 86.

purposes seems to take us down to the lower levels again, the very ones from which we are trying to rise. If meta-ethics deals with the conceptual tool-factory of moralities or normative views or with the analysis of ethical theories, then let us press the analogy. A tool factory is built on terra firma; it uses the same raw materials that otherwise might go into consumer goods; it takes up part of the general budget. Decisions with respect to tool manufacturing may take the form of: don't go beyond a certain production point because it will limit consumption, or, don't develop these specific tools because they are usable only with a high degree of standardization of product, and this is aesthetically unsatisfying, or it will dull men's initiative. Such statement of reasons is almost parallel to what we saw in locating prescriptiveness: don't locate prescriptiveness there because a life lived on such a theory will make men too passive. In ethics, it would appear then, that some decisions in any conception of meta-ethics are made *on the basis of the kind of purposes about which a stand is likely to be taken in the moral patterns or normative theory which the meta-ethics is analyzing,* or even lower down on the conduct-desire level. It does not follow that because meta-ethics would have this character it would not be worth pursuing. (One might as well say that tool factories are not worth building.) On the contrary, it is extremely clarifying to see what lower-level purposes have risen to governing position in the higher domain, how they gained their office, and what the consequences are of their rule.

A further caution in setting up a meta-ethical level is not to assume that its properties will parallel those of a meta-mathematics, any more than those of the latter are like those of meta-science. For example, meta-science has been defined by some as a science of science, and so would include the sociology of science, whereas meta-mathematics is not usually taken to include the sociology of mathematics. The point is simply that there is no one meta-approach. It can be analytic, descriptive, causal-explanatory, evaluative. One has always to be very clear about the way in which one is fashioning the higher level.

Therefore, while there is nothing to preclude mounting to a fourth level in the framework we have developed, once the cautions are made clear and the fact that it would not have a unique or distinctive character, there seems little reason for developing it separately. There does not seem to be any fresh servicing or functional relation to the third level that calls for the extension. The mere fact that one can compare ethical theories, or that one can be critical about ethical theory itself, is not enough; one can moralize about moralizing, for that matter. The kind of activity—analytic or theoretically evaluative, and the rest—does not seem to be very different in type from what has been going on below. It is better therefore to see such activity more modestly as simply the self-conscious pursuit of ethical theorizing in a systematic and comprehensive way. And this characterization holds for the type of philosophizing that is being done in this book.

We turn now to some of the uses to which our framework, preliminary as it is, can be put in the extension of research and the clarification of ethical theory.

SOME AREAS FOR EMPIRICAL RESEARCH

Since the framework is descriptive in intent and refers to bands of phenomena, questions of origin, distribution, interrelations, and development, all take an empirical form. In this way the framework encourages research into a variety of problems.

The need for origin and distribution studies would be generally granted. This is not a matter of schools; for example, an ethical realist like Carritt will not hesitate to say: "Since men were once infants and mankind has presumably been evolved from animals, it would seem that as we became rational we became obliged and more obliged as we became more rational; that with the senility of the individual and the race obligations must decay, and that when we fall asleep they lapse into the night of not being." [10] Whether it is rationality or repression or social need that makes us more moral, the problems are certainly there, and only genuinely scientific study, historical and genetic, will solve them. Some among the totality of phenomena in our field no doubt had an earlier origin than others. Persistent tendencies tantamount to desires and aims are clearly prehuman. How about a rudimentary sense of wrongdoing? Is the sense of obligation a pan-human phenomenon or a specially cultivated one under special conditions? Can we find typical crystallization processes, criti-

[10] E. F. Carritt, *Ethical and Political Thinking* (Oxford, 1947), p. 141.

cal points, integration processes, both in individual development and in the development of mankind? What changes arise when the third level emerges? And so on. Clearly we do not have many of the answers, but to formulate the search from a "levels" approach, with a clear differentiation of phenomena, helps us to avoid simplism in research.

There are other ways in which level mapping can help us pinpoint issues of origin and distribution on a smaller scale. For example, when we delineate the levels in a particular society we often find some twilight zone between the first and second levels. For example, in American sexual morality, premarital sexual relations on the part of males are, verbally at least, immoral. But the phenomenon is not only widespread in practice, but even regarded as a mark of manliness and often encouraged within the given age-group. Should it be classified as part of the "functioning" morality in contrast to the "verbal" morality? Or should it be left in the category of widespread immoral but fairly widely accepted behavior? Some part of such problems may be resolved by distinguishing subgroup distribution, and finding out whether the behavior is immoral but accepted in one and accepted as moral in another.[11] Even the former should not, however, be regarded as showing a merely "verbal" character in the moral rule. Instead, analysis is required to discover the social conflicts underlying the contradiction, and the particular balance achieved, whatever the stability or instability. Such situations may well indicate beginnings of change, or "mutations" out of which change may come on the moral level if the conditions generating the problems persist.

Comparative study of content moving from level to level gives us another insight into developmental patterns and poses problems of explaining the processes involved. For example, in the Western world, the rise of egoism from an antimoral policy on the first level to a respectable way in which the public welfare was advanced by each looking out for himself (self-regarding duties on the second level) to the very theoretical foundations of

11 Kinsey's data, for example, suggest class-differentiation. For a sketch of the general question of normative variation and evasion problems in American society, which distinguishes deviant behavior, institutionalized evasion, and cultural fiction, see R. M. Williams, *American Society* (New York, 1955), Ch. X.

a utilitarian ethics (third level), is an astounding success story intimately intertwined with the social development of Europe and the modern world. The constant tendency for concepts like 'harmony,' 'rationality,' 'loyalty,' to rise from the first or second to a ruling third level is noticeable enough to tempt a theory of the circulation of the élite among ethical concepts.[12]

The functional interrelations of the several levels constitute a broad area of much-needed research. The functional relation of the second level to the first was defined purely in general terms as "regulation" with certain minimal properties, but the actual exploration of the relations of moralities to conduct may find a variety of psychological and socio-historical forms of regulation. The moral pattern provides rules, maxims, models, types, in the fashioning and channelling of conduct and desire. These may operate through engendering fears or hopes, love or guilt, through repression or providing expectation; through strict indoctrination or widening of opportunity. Through its relation to conduct patterns, the moral pattern may also be geared to serve varieties of social, economic, political, cultural, needs. This "gearing" relationship requires careful exploration; there is no reason to expect that the affiliation of morality to various phases of human life has been less complicated than, say, that of law or religion. The same may be true for the several relations of the ethical-theory level and the moral level, and perhaps even of the ethical-theory level and the conduct-desire level. What problems on the conduct-desire level, for example, have sometimes produced those tensions in the moral level that made the ethical theory work out complicated systems of interpretation, and fashion deductive systems? Under what conditions does ethical theory get pushed so far into problems of comparative value that theoreticians begin to wonder whether they ought not to refashion their purest ethical concepts so as to make 'better' rather than 'good' or 'ought' their basic notion? [13] What role do ethical theories play in

---

[12] I have elsewhere called attention to their progress from the status of empirically discoverable values to unavoidable values to structural properties of moral activity, and indicated the changes in their logical character as they rise; see "The Status of Key Concepts in Ethical Theory," *The Philosophical Review* (May, 1945), 260-70.

[13] See below, pp. 262ff.

those historical crises where justification battles with criticisms of a morality and whole ways of life are in the balance? What are the concrete forms that the third function—that of mediating the growth of knowledge for the morality—takes when cultures meet and acculturation gets under way or when science grows rapidly to take a dominating place in a changing civilization?

The relations of the ethical-theory level and the moral level have too often been construed simply in terms of the logical relations between their products as statements. That is, of course, one possible type of relation. For example, it is possible to conceive of the role of an ethical theory as simply that of filling in the gaps in a moral code by making it more self-conscious and more systematic. On such a view the ideally developed moral pattern would be formulated in a tightly knit system of propositions in which the distinction between moral and ethical portions would be simply that between lower and upper regions. Thus in a unified Benthamite system, such judgments as "Killing is wrong" and "In a legal system security rather than equality ought to be the primary aim" would be in the lower moral region of theorems and corollaries, whereas such judgments as "Every man counts as one," "Where the amount is the same, the pain of loss is greater than the pleasure of gain," "Intensity of a pleasure is one measure of its value," "Pleasure is the good," would be reckoned as ethical postulates. The outcome is a rather over-rationalistic conception of the relation of ethical and moral patterns, but it is one conceivable relation. Attention to functional relations, however, shows that this is only one out of many, and if it is propounded as the *desirable* type, it requires justification as against alternatives.

Functional relations studied over a temporal span lead to broad historical researches. Questions thus arise of the interaction of levels in the historical process, both with one another and with other phases of social activity.

If the moral and ethical-theory levels have a relative independence, then the question of their social power and relationships requires study. This constitutes part of the general question of the dynamics of social and cultural equilibrium and change. What are the causes of change in the upper levels? How are such changes related to transformations in social conditions, that is, to transformations of man's conduct and desire and their determinants? Moral rules, for example, are often found to reflect practice. Sometimes they arise from hardening or crystallization processes in conduct. They may undergo change as the modes of social activity alter. Sometimes parts of a moral pattern are abandoned and merely given lip-service. Idealist philosophies of history have given a primary place to the development of ethical ideas. Materialist philosophies of history have seen ethical theories as reflecting changing material conditions. These questions can be raised with respect to specific ethical elements as well as to general configurations. In type they carry us into the whole problem of the relations of attitudes and ideas to social and historical conditions, and so to the exploration of the causal-explanatory standpoint in its relation to ethics.[14]

THE SPECIAL VOCABULARY OF THE THREE LEVELS

A quite different contribution of the proposed framework is that it may help us bring some order into the kinds of terms employed in ethical discourse. Because it is a descriptive framework, it must pay attention to the actual use of language for ethical purposes, whether it be the traditional terms that have been carrying the job or fresh terms from all sorts of other fields entering to take over one or another task. And because it is a levels-framework, it can help avoid the confusions that come from terms that are employed on several levels, or that are in the process of moving up from one to another. Let us therefore briefly sort out some of the typical vocabulary of the three levels, indicating the kinds of problems and confusions that may arise.

It follows from the initial description of the ground-floor level that psychological and socio-cultural terms such as 'goals,' 'aims,' 'desires,' 'wants,' 'drives,' 'pleasures,' 'pains,' and, in general, terms indicating direction of striving and more or less simple feelings belong to the vocabulary of this level.

[14] This is the subject of Part Four. And beyond that, of course, lies the whole class of studies that would arise about our levels if we attempted to *evaluate* the types of functional and dynamic relations of levels; for example, if we made such statements as "Ethical theory has been too content to follow; it ought to lead." Such problems of evaluation belong to Part Five. Compare also a few suggestions offered above, pp. 52f.

There are, however, some terms very appropriate to this level which have acquired an ambiguous status. One such important concept is that of 'ends.' In the simple first-level sense, it is synonymous with 'goals.' But in such expressions as 'the ends of man' in the teleological sense of 'what man is ultimately intended for,' it has clearly been elevated to at least a second level. Again, there are other terms such as 'need' which seem to straddle levels, indicating both existent drives or tendencies and some justification for their satisfaction. And even relatively straightforward terms designating a feeling or emotion may edge over to an upper level. Compare, for example, 'pleasure' with 'happiness,' or 'anger' with 'indignation.' Pleasure as a feeling associated with reduction of tension, or anger as an emotion in the context of goal-frustration are obviously on the first level. But happiness is sometimes given a more special status in which it ceases to be descriptive of a state of feeling and functions as a psychological surrogate for the good. And indignation almost seems to contain a specifically moral element. In fact, Westermarck rests his theory of ethics on the special status of such emotions as indignation.[15] Similarly, 'approval' can be found on both of the first two levels.

All such concepts which have a secure footing in the first level but which come close to the second level or pass over into it, or straddle both levels, or are ambiguously used for separate phenomena in each of them, require careful analysis in the contexts in which they are to be employed. Continuing the analogy in the term 'ground-floor,' we may think of these as *mezzanine* or *escalator concepts*.

On the whole, the vocabulary of the first level is so rich that there is no reason to encroach on higher levels for first-level description. Only confusion can come, for example, from speaking of 'what is good for a man' and meaning only the man's goals in his pattern of desire. Even to use 'instrumentally good' as an equivalent for 'useful for a specific purpose' is to invite ambiguity. There is considerable justification for adopting such a stipulation as G. E. Moore's that 'good as a means' involves the judgment that the effect produced will itself be good.[16] And, of course, the term 'value' by crossing at least two levels has

15 Edward Westermarck, *Ethical Relativity* (New York, 1932), Ch. III.
16 *Principia Ethica*, p. 82.

sometimes made one's desires seem automatically self-justifying by their mere occurrence!

If we turn now to the vocabulary of the moral level, we find that the central terms occurring in English have been fairly standard. 'Good' and 'bad' or 'evil' are usually applied to goals and means included in the moral pattern; sometimes also to characterize persons or dispositions. 'Ideals' refers to special types of goods. 'Right' and 'wrong' are usually applied to the selected types of acts or desires enjoined or forbidden. In similar ways, although in complicated relationship, we find such terms as 'ought,' 'should,' 'duty,' 'obligation.' The generic terms 'moral' and 'immoral' are also applied to conduct. 'Virtue' and 'vice' are used of the selected character traits.

Subsidiary expressions arise from the term 'worth' or the use of the suffix '-able'; for example, 'praiseworthy' in the sense of 'ought to be praised,' or 'desirable' in the sense of 'ought to be desired' or 'worthy of desire.' In such connections, the gerundival form, such as in 'to be desired,' often functions without the 'ought.' Many of these conceptions are capable of analysis in terms of the fundamental moral concepts, but in the contemporary flight from moralistic language the secondary expressions tend to take over the field. 'Desirable' is often found in such a position. The theoretical import of secondary expressions is not to be neglected. There has, for example, been some difference over whether 'What shall I do?' is equivalent to 'What ought I to do?' or whether it functions as an even prior indication of a practical decision-situation.

A wide range of concrete moral vocabulary fuses the general moral element with some indication of descriptive first-level content, whether of types of conduct or of character or of the emotion or feeling involved. The specific virtues and vices stand out most markedly in this group in our morality—for example, 'honesty,' 'courage,' 'cowardice,' 'miserliness,' and so forth. Such lists are to be found in most traditional ethical treatises, such as Aristotle's *Nicomachean Ethics* or the *Deontology* ascribed to Bentham. Terms indicating some specific acts of conduct are fairly common, though less frequently tabulated. They appear as nouns or verbs—'lie,' 'theft,' 'adultery,' 'murder'; or on the acceptable side, 'help,' 'charity' (as act, not spirit). Some of these have a straddling or what I called a mezzanine character in that in some uses they are almost wholly descriptive of conduct and so would belong to the ground floor level, while in others they are moral terms. On the whole, there do not seem to be many goal-words for what is to be striven for or avoided, on the moral level; one thinks of such general terms as 'riches,' 'prosperity,' 'happiness,' the last of which, as we have noted, has a many-level character. With respect to feelings and emotions as they enter into moral judgment, there is a wealth of evaluative adjectives—'admirable,' 'contemptible,' for example—which serve in the moral judgment.[17] And there are no doubt many other areas which can be explored for moral implications of terms—e.g., motives and personality traits ('well-intentioned,' 'spiteful'); the language of estimation ('sound,' 'well-done'); the language of comparison, even apart from comparative and superlatives of fundamental terms, like 'better' and 'best' ('higher,' 'superior'), and so on.

The vocabulary associated with methods of decision and application and with sanctions, lacks the richness and precision found in some of the other elements. Terms like 'properly,' 'duly,' 'correctly,' 'reasonably' occasionally carry a moral connotation; the last, in fact, seems almost to be bordering on the third level. Similarly, one may be told to settle a question by consulting his 'conscience' or presenting it to some moral 'authority.' In the field of law, this whole phase is more explicitly systematized: for example, the concept of 'due process' refers to the legal procedure for determining legal relations, and the law governing procedure is itself a branch of the whole law. In this area of a morality we find also the language of 'rights,' 'claims,' 'responsibilities,' 'excuses,' and so forth, much of which is only beginning to be mapped with sensitivity, especially in the current studies of the British analytical school.

One fundamental lesson in this whole area has been that of coming to terms with varying usage, fine shades, contextual differentiation in the use of the same terms, and so on. Emphasis has shifted from finding the meaning for terms in isolation to

---

[17] Richard B. Brandt has carried out an interesting classification of this phase of the moral language in his "Moral Valuation," *Ethics*, LVI (1946), 106-21.

seeing them in their whole functioning. And classification tends more and more to follow lines of different function, rather than just the different terms.[18]

The vocabulary of the moral level here considered is, of course, drawn from our own tradition.[19] Students of other cultures have the task of identifying the moral concepts there employed and making sure they are not too hastily translated into an equivalent of our own. They also have the task of deciding how far a line can or should be drawn in a particular culture between a moral and a nonmoral use of terms probably spanning more than one field—for example, 'tabu' in Polynesia, or 'dangerous' among the Navaho; just as in our usage we distinguish between the religious and the moral element in the concept of 'sin' and the use of 'right' in morality and arithmetic.

If we turn now to the vocabulary of the ethical-theory level we find, of course, the central concepts of the moral level. It includes, for example, the concept of virtue and vice but has little occasion to employ the whole brood of specific virtues and vices.

A second part of the ethical-theory vocabulary is constituted by terms that come from the philosophy of science and epistemology. For example, the ethical tradition speaks of the moral 'law,' and of morality as expressing man's 'nature.' Occasionally, philosophers have distinguished between 'natural' and 'nonnatural' qualities (preparatory to describing the moral as nonnatural). The analysis of such problems involves applying to ethical theory the lessons of the philosophy of science and epistemology.

The language of any special field from biology to theology may, of course, enter into ethical discourse. A theory may base its conception of 'good' or 'right' in concepts of biological 'drives,' psychological 'interests,' or theological 'divine beings,' and so forth. Often, the language of an ethical theory provides the quickest clue to its existential perspective.

When content terms of the first level turn up in the vocabulary of ethics, we have to be careful to note any shift in meaning, in

18 This lesson is a central one in Alexander Sesonske's recent *Value and Obligation* (Berkeley and Los Angeles, 1957).

19 For a discussion of the problem on a transcultural basis, see *Anthropology and Ethics*, Ch. X.

the use of the terms. For example, as indicated above, the term 'end' has a first-level meaning simply as 'goal'; it also turns up occasionally on the moral level as a 'worthy object of striving.' And it sometimes appears on the ethical-theory level in the contrast of end-centered and law-centered systems, as well as in the interpretation of 'the good life' as 'men's ends in life.' Even 'love,' 'harmony,' 'reason,' which may refer to first-level feelings and activities, sometimes emerge as central ethical-theoretical ideas. But once they are recognized as third level, we have to be aware of subtle shifts in their meaning. 'Reason' on the first level refers to a process of thinking, while on the third level it may embody a host of built-in values.

PHENOMENOLOGICAL ASPECTS OF LEVEL-DIFFERENTIATION

We have next to see how level differentiation can furnish clues for more extended and refined phenomenological description in the field of ethics. Phenomenological fields are individual, whereas our framework was set up as socio-cultural description. We have, therefore, to recall the relation of individual to group discussed above.[20] We saw that properties of groups concerned individuals in their interrelations. Properties of individuals could be appealed to for verification of statements about groups without the procedure thereby constituting a reduction. But we may now offer the further heuristic principle that where group patterns have been discovered, there are likely to be individual phenomenological elements corresponding to them. This is not necessary, nor always so, but it is worth looking to see how far it extends.

Take, for example, the act of having children as a content element whose levels position is to be determined. Behaviorally, we can describe the widespread desire to have children, and so recognize its place as a first level phenomenon. But in some societies we find that it is a moral duty. People may say this about it; it may also be inferred from their attitude to children as evidenced by phenomenological reports: children are literally beheld as "a duty and a responsibility," sometimes even such rather than "a delight." In such cases, phenomenological reports of individuals serve as part of the evidence for level location. But

20 Pp. 172f.

the duty to have children may be associated with quite different ethical theories. Sometimes there is a religious ethics in which God commands it; sometimes a nationalist ethics, in which it helps in the expansion of the fatherland; sometimes a group-survival biological ethics in which perpetuation of the species becomes an integral part of the ethical justification of moral rules and societal forms.

How would our heuristic principle apply to these three different situations? This principle may be amplified to specify that for every ethical element there is a corresponding possible (not necessarily actual) qualitative difference in the phenomenological field of the typical individual. To the religious ethical theory, there would correspond the view of children as carriers of one's religious obligations, the sense of being without children as a failure before God, the loss of children as a spiritual death. These would be permeating features of present feeling and attitude, not simply patterns of verbal expression or justification. To the nationalist ethics, there would correspond an actual seeing of children as "gifts to the country," "mainstays of the nation." To the species-perpetuation ethics, there would correspond some specific sense of one's children as "carrying on the human enterprise." It is not a simple task to map a comparative phenomenology of having children, but it is a task that is suggested by obvious cultural differences, as well as (in the Western tradition) in biblical attitudes and in that conveyed in many literary works.[21] Now when we go from possible phenomenological fields to actual phenomenological fields, we are concerned with existence and studies of distribution and incidence. Clearly, with respect to having children, there have been actual phenomenological fields corresponding to religious and nationalistic ethics; perhaps to a more limited extent corresponding to a species-survival ethics, since the "carrying-on" feeling is probably more specialized than to involve mankind as such. But these are questions requiring empirical determination.

We have then a new area of exploration which our framework has indicated. It can operate in a double way—using ethical-

21 For example, in Euripides' *Medea*, where the importance of children is a recurrent theme, culminating in Medea's murder of her children to take revenge on her husband.

theory differences, where found, as clues for differences in phenomenological quality, and conversely, where the latter are more available, using them as clues for ethical-theory differences. In addition, we may distinguish cases where the ethical theory reflects features of the existent morality from cases in which the theory arises first and the phenomenological field undergoes subsequent conforming changes.

This mode of investigation can be applied directly to traditional ethical theories. We can take a Kantian theory or a Benthamite theory, and ask what the phenomenological field of a man would have to be like, if he embodied in his reactions the orientation specified in the theory.[22] Clearly, if there were a man who felt—corresponding to Kant's theory—that he should pursue happiness because it was his duty, rather than because he wanted to be happy, his would be quite a different quality of living from that of the more carefree hedonist. On some elements of ethical theories—such as the structure assigned to obligation-feelings—we are likely to find fairly accurate correspondence between theoretical accounts and phenomenological qualities of conscience.

Character traits raise similar issues. Humility, for example, is simply a first-level trait in some. It is a virtue in others, or again a vice in still others. Elsewhere it may be the key to an outlook in which the individual's absolute obedience and acceptance expresses a relation to the divine. Here we may expect to find, and do find, a corresponding ethical theory.

Feelings, too, sometimes show a close correspondence of theory and phenomenological field. For example, Benedict points out that in America "we do not expect shame to do the heavy work of morality"; we leave that to guilt-feeling, whereas the Japanese pattern harnesses shame to the work of morality.[23] Shame would accordingly belong to the ground-floor level in America, although it is increasingly coming to occupy the mezzanine. For, as Benedict suggests, its role is increasing, while that of guilt feeling is diminishing. But this, she adds significantly, is commonly interpreted as a relaxation of morals. In Japan, however, shame would

---

[22] Robert Redfield characterized this procedure in conversation as bringing the philosopher as *informant* to the anthropologist.

[23] Ruth Benedict, *The Chrysanthemum and the Sword* (New York, 1946), p. 224.

be in the upper levels. Benedict's formulation even suggests it belongs to the third level; for she says: "Shame has the same place of authority in Japanese ethics that 'a clear conscience,' 'being right with God' and the avoidance of sin have in Western ethics." In these Western parallels guilt-feeling is not simply a selected feeling on the moral level, but involves some elaboration of that feeling in the light of a theological perspective.

Sanctions constitute a fruitful field for phenomenological distinctions. There are first-level sanctions which are felt to be part of the ordinary mechanics of the world, as we regard germs causing illness or other people getting angry and striking one. Some specific sanctions are incorporated in moral codes, so that the code tells you how to treat the violator. For example, it may be wrong to offer food and shelter to one who has killed a member of the in-group, or one may be enjoined to turn the other cheek and forgive those who have hurt you. Further sanctions for failing to apply these sanctions may raise difficulties. If you give food or shelter to a killer of a member of the in-group you will get leprosy, or Zeus will throw a thunderbolt at the village; if you do not forgive your enemy you are hardening your heart and may be damning your soul. The first of these seems to be going back again to the first level; the last (and probably Zeus as well) points to a third-level sanction.

Let us take a final example from the area of justification. Compare the relation of religious goals and secular success goals. On the face of it, one would be likely to think that the religious framework would serve as justification in the ethical theory, and the search for happiness or success as a central part of the moral obligations or goods. Such it is, for example, in Paley, who defines his fundamental ethical concepts in terms of God's will, but decides that what God wills is in fact human happiness.[24] So too, in the earlier development of the Protestant ethic, it is a man's duty on earth to make the most of his powers and opportunities. As the seventeenth century English minister, Richard Baxter, put it: "If God show you a way in which you may lawfully get more than in another way (without wrong to your soul or to any other), if you refuse this, and choose the less gainful way, you cross one of the ends of your calling, and you refuse to

[24] William Paley, *The Principles of Moral and Political Philosophy* (tenth American ed., Boston, 1821).

be God's steward, and to accept His gifts and use them for Him when He requireth it: you may labor to be rich for God, though not for the flesh and sin." [25]

In a treatment of the ethics of the Hupa-Yurok, Walter Goldschmidt underlines their similarity to the Puritan ethic. Both share "the moral demand to work and by extension to the pursuit of gain, the moral demand of self-denial, and the individuation of moral responsibility." [26] In both too, there is the relation of success to religion. Among the Hupa-Yurok, a daily religious ritual serves as a sanction in the moral pattern. It involves going through a narrow oval opening in the sweathouse, and as Goldschmidt says, "Only a lithe, naked, sweaty body could work its way through this opening. It is obvious that any indulgence in food or sloth would make egress impossible." [27] The overt purpose of this ritual, we are told, is to ensure luck for the individual in his economic pursuits. At this point, the two ethics—to judge from the material in Goldschmidt's account—would seem to diverge. The one justifies the religious ritual by the wealth it will yield, the other justifies the achievement of wealth by the evidence it will furnish that one is destined to be saved. The conception of the individual who is responsible may also be different. Of course, it is possible that they all come to the same thing in practice, but unless this is an empirical thesis that some ethical theories serve as "rationalizations," the decision would have to be made in terms of the actual phenomenological differences of the people concerned. Such a study would be revealing, not only across cultural lines, but even in the history of the Protestant ethic itself.

THE REFINEMENT OF THEORETICAL ISSUES

Let us now see what happens to familiar controversies of ethical theory when they are cast in the terms here developed. Take, for example, the standard controversy of deontologism versus teleologism—the question whether obligation or goal-pursuit is

25 Quoted by Max Weber, *The Protestant Ethic and the Spirit of Capitalism*, tr. Talcott Parsons (New York, 1930), p. 162.

26 "Ethics and the Structure of Society: An Ethnological Contribution to the Sociology of Knowledge," *American Anthropologist*, LIII (1951), 513.

27 *Ibid.*, p. 515.

to be given a primary place in the analysis of moral judgment. It is one of the vast issues that requires a full treatment of the whole range of ethical theory. If it is posed as a problem of analysis, it is easy to see that analytically we can fashion all possible combinations—priority to the deontological, priority to the teleological, equal status to both, and many variations. But these, if fashioned in this speculative way, would have a purely speculative status of *possible* ethical theories. By taking a descriptive approach we could next see that some of these combinations have in fact been found on the ethical-theory level. So far, it would seem to be only a roundabout way of saying that there have been theoretical oppositions on the question. It has not yet located the difference in *what the theories assert*. But in fact it has advanced the solution by indicating—what a fuller analytic examination would be required to show in detail—that the solution cannot be found in analytic terms alone. How far, then, the issue is to be resolved in descriptive terms depends upon the particular form in which the argument is advanced. Take a common contemporary form of the deontological claim that teleological analyses of 'ought' do not conform to moral experience, that the proper place of teleological considerations is in dealing with the justification of obligation judgments.[28] Descriptively, this is equivalent to the assertion that deontological elements are always to be found on the second level and teleological elements are never to be found on the second level. When so formulated, it is clear that the view has to establish that *there never could be* a human being or a people in whom the direct moral experience had a quality of "this is the best possible thing in the situation." [29] In short, we have here a thesis involving comparative study on the three levels, bringing us back to the attempts to establish a uniform universal structure for moral experience. But even that would not be enough, since this might be an accidental structure dependent on historical factors pervasive only up to this point. Hence the thesis involves further assumptions about the causal-

[28] This is found in such varied accounts as Maurice Mandelbaum, *The Phenomenology of Moral Experience*, and John Ladd, *The Structure of a Moral Code*.

[29] As a matter of fact, Kurt Baier so translates the obligation judgment in his *A Moral Point of View* (Ithaca, 1958), pp. 86ff.

explanatory account of moral experience, or else it has a large gap. Finally, it may of course be meant as a policy decision not to recognize an experience as distinctively moral if it is teleological. But this would be an evaluative judgment equivalent to setting up a specific narrower characterization of the second level, and so would require justification in terms of prior-established knowledge from a descriptive and causal-explanatory standpoint. As against this whole approach—which may of course be correct, but which I suspect is ethnocentric to a strongly guilt-oriented tradition—one might set up the second level, as we have done, in an open manner allowing that both teleologically-tinged and nonteleologically-tinged experience can occur on the direct moral level, look for samples, try to find causal conditions, and make evaluative theoretical decisions such as not to foreclose both possibilities.

Such lines of argument would have to be repeated for each form of claim in the deontological-teleological controversy—for those who would force the deontological, for example, simply into the mold of a means-judgment; or those who, like Prichard in his *Moral Obligation* would insist that obligation has a self-justifying character and so belongs, in our terms, on the third level as well as the second, or those deontologists who would force all teleological judgments into simply first-level happiness-pursuit phenomena, as Kant often appears to do, and so on. In all these cases, concentration on the descriptive standpoint, and on looking for second-level phenomenological correlates of third-level theories, helps clarify the problems and show what to look for in order to resolve them; beyond the descriptive, there are clear lines to possible claims about the causal and the evaluative.

Take another example, from a theoretical issue of a more recent vintage, that emerged as the prescriptivist movement was in its ascendant phase—the attempt to distinguish sharply between two kinds of ethics, *spectator ethics* and *agent ethics,* and to assign primacy as ethics to the second. "The typical moral problem," Stuart Hampshire wrote in an influential article in *Mind,*[30] "is not a spectator's problem or a problem of classifying

30 *Mind,* LVIII (1949), 468. This central remark of Hampshire's was quoted on p. 60, in the general discussion of the locus of prescriptiveness. The relation of this position to ethical reasoning was discussed on pp. 145ff.

or describing conduct, but a problem of practical choice and decision." John Ladd takes up and elaborates Hampshire's distinction.[31] He finds the spectator approach to be ethnocentric, "for not only is it not to be found among the Greeks but I find nothing resembling it in Navaho culture." In noting the prevalence of the spectator approach in Western thought, Ladd refers to the formulation of ethical judgment in terms of what an impartial spectator would feel; he points out that among the Navaho such a judicial-decision attitude would not occur; the function of a judge there is not to decide what is due but to conciliate parties and restore harmony.

How can our descriptivist levels framework help analyze such claims? In the first place, we must be quite clear what is meant by 'spectator' in these claims. It is not the spectator as *reporter* or onlooker that is here intended,[32] but the spectator as *critic* rather than participant. Nor is the issue that of descriptivism versus prescriptivism, because it is easy to give the critic's assertion also a prescriptivist interpretation, to suggest, for example, that when he asserts a moral rule he is really subscribing to it, not describing it.[33] The difference between the spectator as critic and the agent must then lie in the *type of context* referred to. The spectator seems to be engaged in guiding by setting up standards or strengthening virtues, whereas the agent seems to be deciding particular what-to-do's. Why should the context of the last-mentioned be given a prime place, as the typical moral problem? Is it because other contexts are held to be primarily a means to practical particular decisions? This is so, of course, in the sense that morality is intended to regulate conduct, but why should morality be identified with immediate conduct-determinants rather than with the more generalized principles that systematize the regulating mechanisms? What is more, conduct is itself intended to achieve goals, and so we come again to a teleological approach as fundamental. Or is the reason for the primary place of the particular decision to be found in a narrow practicalism, as if one were to say that the primary scientific situation is one of

31 *The Structure of a Moral Code* (Cambridge, Mass., 1957), pp. 70ff.
32 Cf. p. 174.
33 Cf. Hare, above, p. 60.

observation, not of theory-construction? Or again, is it a deonto-logical bias, reckoning anything beyond the immediate decision as part of the justification picture?

Once again, if we formulate the issues in the descriptive-levels framework, we can see that on the third level we find both spectator-theories and agent-theories. The question is which has correlates on the moral level—in short whether we find both types of moralities. Here the answer seems readily available. Ladd's own explanation of why the Navaho do not develop a spectator morality in terms of their institutions, also explains why in the complex western tradition a spectator morality at various points makes sense. It can also be used to explain why under certain conditions of large-scale social transformations and the need for critical decision, an agent-perspective should loom larger. The conclusion would not be that there is a distinctive moral context, but that there are many contexts in terms of which ethical concepts may be analyzed, that the decider-agent's and the spectator-critic's are two central ones, and that whether one of these or conceivably some quite distinct alternative is assigned a primary place in a given culture depends on the forces that push one or another context into a prominent position. The question of adequacy of a particular second-level pattern is a further evaluative problem which may not yield a single deter-minate answer for all conditions.

Thus once more, analysis paves the way, and a descriptive approach helps reformulate the theoretical question, to separate what is a matter of evidence about the occurrence of patterns on the several levels, and to set forth beyond that what are issues of causal explanation and further specific evaluation. The under-lying thesis of this chapter is then, that a descriptive framework set in socio-cultural terms, and carefully distinguishing levels of phenomena, stands the best chance of clarifying some of the per-sistent and tangled problems of traditional ethical theory.

PART FOUR

CAUSAL-EXPLANATORY METHOD

CHAPTER TEN

THE CAUSAL STANDPOINT

While there is general agreement that some description enters into ethical theorizing, causal studies have not been so welcomed. Sometimes, of course, they are frankly rejected as irrelevant. Causality is usually tied to the natural world, and views of man which deny that he is part of nature are prone therefore to reject the ethical relevance of inquires into the natural world. More surprising, however, is the apparent disregard of causal studies even among many philosophers whose general approach to the study of man is a scientific one. If you press the point that surely everything has a cause which it would be interesting to know, they nod. They will agree that ethical phenomena, whether behaviorally or phenomenally described, may have physical, biological, psychological, social, historical causes, just as a color has appropriate physical and retinal conditions, pain appropriate external and brain conditions, guilt-feeling appropriate psychological and historical conditions; even conscience may be explored for its causal basis, and so may the holding of a particular ethical theory. But when you are through with your recitation, you encounter a special gambit: The whole world is turned over to science, but only provided it will then go away and not bother us in ethics! For if we pay attention to such things, aren't we in danger of committing the *genetic fallacy?* And what respectable philosopher would want to encourage such a substitution of causal source for analysis of meaning or judgment of truth or worth?

Such protective insulation produces its own nemesis. Theoretical approaches show a certain sensitivity and if they are snubbed they become overaggressive. Their repression makes them strike out against ethical theory as a whole, and soon they are explaining it *away* (rather than simply explaining it); various theories are explained as ideologies reflecting social interests, or defenses against one or another type of anxiety, and so on. The merits of ethics and the causal study of man are both lost sight of in this conflict.

Let us then start with a basic reassurance. It is not our intention to mislead anyone into committing the genetic fallacy. A question of the truth of an opinion is not to be shunted aside by talking of the causes of holding the opinion. We shall explore this point in detail in the next chapter. But similarly, there is no point to using the genetic fallacy accusation so blindly as to prevent inquiry about the ways in which the causal standpoint may be relevant for ethics. The answer is not to be a wholesale yes or no, but a making of many distinctions and an indication of different respects. And surely this is close to the analytic temper!

I have been talking in this conciliatory fashion because the issue here is one that apparently rouses considerable feeling in many philosophical quarters. If we put aside the world-outlook antagonisms involved in some of this feeling, and the hardened attitudes of different schools, and approach the issues using the method of comparative ethics, we may find that there are causal assumptions of one or another type involved in many ethical theories. The issue seems more properly to be what kind of causal assumptions to use. For after all, is not the appeal to emotions and their effects, to feelings and their constancy, to a definite type of human nature and its expression, really an appeal to a constant underlying order in terms of which moral processes can be assumed to go on in an established and dependable way? Paul Kurtz has put the issue with clarity in a recent paper. He points out that among writers on ethics—

> . . . most of the prevailing discussions of human motivation are limited to surface questions: Is reason, desire, or emotion central in choice? Can cognition control behavior? What is the relationship between belief and attitude? Do ethical judgments have a descriptive or imperative function? Many writers refer to Hume's claim that reason by itself moves nothing without feeling or sentiment; others express their faith in reason and cognition.
>
> Actually, the problem of motivation is only part of the broader question: What are the *determinants* of human behavior? But, as the social sciences indicate, there are undoubtedly many causal factors. Most of the theories of motivation have been

based on earlier limited psychologies: primitive hedonism and attitudinalism, speculative self-realizationism, or naive cognitivism.[1]

This view is relevant not only for those who ignore the causal standpoint but also for those who employ it while still insisting on its restricted role. For example, Richard Brandt, in his *Hopi Ethics*, assesses what anthropological field exploration can do for ethics. He notes that it can furnish wider descriptive data of moral experience, and it can help establish explanatory theories about moral experience. Thus, for example, it could put to the test a universal assertion based on limited experience of our culture, such as that all men have a definite moral reaction of a given sort, and it could help us test whether certain types of social structure such as the nuclear family are necessary to produce certain kinds of moral responses and feelings. But when we come to philosophical analysis of ethical concepts, he feels that there is little more than stimulation to be derived from the scientific studies.[2] In dealing with norms, later on, Brandt does insist that "A complete understanding requires an explanatory theory, in the sense of the natural sciences, both of the alternations of norms in time and of why particular societies have developed particular configurations of ethical standards."[3] In short, he has allowed the penetration of science through what we have called the moral level, but restricted it from moving up into the ethical-theory level.[4]

The thesis here to be advanced is that the causal standpoint has an unrestricted initial scope, just as the other methods have, and that it can in its exercise bring greater understanding in the various other enterprises in a number of different ways, without infringing on their autonomous operations. To explore these ways

[1] Paul Kurtz, "Need Reduction and Normal Value," *The Journal of Philosophy*, LV (1958), 556-57.

[2] Richard B. Brandt, *Hopi Ethics* (Chicago, 1954), pp. 5-12.

[3] *Ibid.*, p. 285.

[4] Some limitations may also arise from the fact that the particular kinds of laws he looks for are largely psychological, being concerned with the reactions of individuals living in a certain kind of world, so that social and historical inquiries would enter only indirectly into his formulations.

is the aim of this part. But let us first make some preliminary distinctions, especially about what is to be meant by the causal standpoint.

SOME PRELIMINARY DISTINCTIONS

No major analysis of the concept of causality will here be undertaken. It is not necessary for our purposes to go into philosophic controversies on this topic; whatever analysis of causality proves adequate for the psychological and social sciences and for history can be appropriated for our use of the concept.

Some will no doubt prefer to speak of theoretical explanations, rather than the causal standpoint. My preference is for the causal formulation, because I want to keep an eye on factors of time, development, career, occurrence. Dealing in terms of theoretical explanations carries us into systems of symbols and their relations. Causality is a rough concept, but it will do for our purposes; although I am assuming that any results of inquiry cast in the language of theoretical explanations can be translated so as to make the temporal context relations clear. I shall then speak of 'the causal standpoint' or 'the causal-explanatory standpoint.'

The causal standpoint involves, of course, paying attention to effects as well. Strangely enough, although there has been much aversion to causal analysis in ethics, there has been little reluctance in talking about effects. Ethical ideas are taken to have effects not merely on other ideas—it is quite respectable for one philosopher's ideas to *influence* a subsequent generation's thought —but also on action and feeling. In fact, a number of theories that eschew causal exploration in ethics as irrelevant even go so far as to give a central position in their analysis to expressive, emotive, and other effects.

The question naturally arises at this point: causes and effects of what? The answer can only be: of the phenomena that are described in the broad field of ethics. This means, in the light of our previous discussion of the descriptive standpoint and the levels formulation, all the phenomena of the moral level and the ethical-theory level; let us refer to them briefly as *moral norms* and *ethical ideas*. But surely, it will be said, this involves a confusion. Causality refers to events in time. Therefore, the phenomena caused are not moral norms and ethical ideas, but the existential events of *holding to, believing in, having feelings about,* or *symbolic discoursing about,* or *psychological acts expressing* moral norms and ethical ideas. The norms-in-themselves and the ideas-in-themselves are not part of the temporal stream. Of course, even here, further distinction is necessary; there may be temporal events mentioned in, referred to, or contained in the moral norms and theoretical ideas; for example, the norm that lying is wrong contains the idea of lying, and to tell a lie is an event in time. But this property is not transferable to the norm or idea.

Let us not underestimate the problem involved; it is nothing less than the nature of thought and its object. How easily one could fall back here into the old Platonic mode and think of a moral norm or an ethical idea as a nontemporal essence, over and above its temporal manifestations! Ethics would then be primarily concerned with essences, and secondarily with the particular essence-existence bundles of holding norms, believing ideas, etc. And causality would be concerned with the existential side, not the essential side. Even the non-Platonic ethical analysis readily falls into parallel modes of thought, because so much of ethical analysis starts with moral *judgments,* which are at the minimum *utterances* or *expressions* or *assertions.* And if there is one logical lesson which philosophical sanity requires, it is to make a sharp distinction between the *existential aspect* of the utterance or event and the *referential* aspect of an utterance as what it means or points to. Clearly, we are now coming to the problem that was hinted at above in formulating levels—the relation of level as a set of existent events and level as content asserted; for example, on the ethical-theory level, between theorizing as act and the content of the theory developed. For the purposes of the formulations at that time it sufficed to distinguish process and product—theorizing and theory—but now we have to go further. We have to look into theory itself and ask whether it may not itself be an existence-essence bundle. Let us then distinguish sharply between the *content* of the idea, and the existential *context* of the idea, and make it a major task in our present consideration to deal with the bearings that context may have on content.

If we continue to use the term 'idea' loosely, then 'content of the idea' designates the referent of the symbol employed, the meaning of the statement made, the object of the idea. 'Context of the idea' designates the existential act of a person holding the idea, the act of discoursing about it, the sentence as existent vehicle, the feelings in focussing on the content, the causes of any of these, the effects of any of these. And—to complete the picture —we must recognize that this includes concomitants as well as possibly prior causes and possibly subsequent effects. Thus the successs of an idea in swaying people is an effect (in part) of asserting it; the intention to sway them is usually a concomitant of asserting it. I shall use the term 'causal standpoint' to indicate this whole attention to causes, concomitants, consequences, and their relation to content.

RELATIONS OF CONTEXT TO CONTENT

I have treated this whole question of the relation of context to content in the theory of ideas in a previous study.[5] What I should like to do here is to reformulate some of the basic ideas there developed for our present consideration of the controversies in ethical theory.

Let us start off by separating from our problem the points upon which substantial agreement might readily be reached. The first is that we have a right to look for causal origins in dealing with the holding of ideas. Some may be skeptical about the possibilities of success in this venture; others may differ on lines of investigation to be pursued. But the meaning of the enterprise is not at stake. For it is a wholly contextual inquiry, since it looks for causes of the holding of ideas by particular individuals or groups. Thus it is up to the biographer of Kant to decide how far his ideas about ethics stemmed from a Pietist upbringing, how far they were an expression of a growing universalism in European culture, how far a reaction against French materialism and an effort to find an impregnable basis for religious sentiment, how far an expression of his own psychological rigidity, and so on.

It can also be agreed that the discovery of causality is important from the point of view of control. One can see green without

5 "Context and Content in the Theory of Ideas," in *Philosophy for the Future,* ed. Sellars, McGill, and Farber (New York, 1949), pp. 419-52.

knowing the physical and physiological conditions underlying it. But a knowledge of causality enables one to seek control of the appearance of green as well as to develop new shades of it. Similarly, a causal account of conscience might be helpful in stabilizing it, dulling or sharpening it, purifying it, or making it more widespread. Whether this could best be done by a "conditioning process" or an education "insight-developing process" would depend on the results of the causal investigation.

Another point of ready agreement is that the holding of ideas has functions, that in this sense ideas are used in many ways. Thus Kant's idea that religious conceptions express primarily ethical features and ethical needs was used by him as a way of providing a fresh support for religion when he thought the old supports were bankrupt. The same general idea has been used by Santayana to construe religion as a mythology helpful in organizing the regulation of human life. Ideas of natural rights have played a revolutionary role in one age, a conservative role in another. Historical and anthropological study shows the most varied relations that ideas may have in servicing areas of social activity. For example, a belief about the necessity for human sacrifice or the proper treatment of strangers or about the effectiveness of magic, may be found functioning to provide assurance about food supply or health, or play a part in maintaining solidarity or ensuring reproduction of the group, or avoiding in-group hostilities. In contemporary ethical theory there has been considerable concentration on an important subclass of concomitants and effects—that of expressing emotion, attempting to influence others, conforming to language habits, and so on.

We move on now to the area of major disagreement. How are we to understand the notion of the *content* of an idea or assertion once we wish to come to grips with it? There is hardly a turn we can make without seeming to beg the question. If we try to *locate* the content, we shall be accused of assuming it has a spatio-temporal existence, and so of "reducing" content to start with. If, on the contrary, we keep a sharp separation as if context and content moved in the realm of different entities, we shall be accused of some dire "category-mistake." Perhaps the easiest path would be to adopt a specific theory of the nature of thinking and work from it. And I should be ready to start with a broad naturalistic approach with an insistence that thinking is a part of nature and therefore all concepts in its analysis have to be understood in some fashion or other in terms of existential qualities and relations in natural processes.[6] But I am now trying to do more than trace the consequences of one among several theories that have been held. I should like to suggest that certain relations between context and content are increasingly coming to the fore and are applicable to many, if not all, different approaches. I shall therefore proceed by the technique of comparative method, to take several different approaches, and see the form that our problem takes in each. Let us take the phenomenological, the materialist, the pragmatic-instrumentalist, and the logical-linguistic-analytic approaches.

On a phenomenological approach, the distinction between content and context would appear as that between the phenomenal field and the scientific knowledge of the existence that has in its several forms been "bracketed." Our problem is therefore to see the different ways in which causal knowledge can effect phenomenal fields and phenomenal description and analysis. One way is that causal results can help extend phenomenal description. For example, causal analysis may sometimes serve to bring apparently outside phenomena into the ambit of moral phenomena. Thus an understanding of the causality of apathy may enable one to see it as a type of guilt conflict and thereby enhance, by more directed inspection, its phenomenal description. In such a process, causality provides the clues which description follows up. Thus Fromm uses a causal psychoanalytic theory to secure a clear distinction between anxiety and outgoing relationships in many character traits and feelings—e.g., between industriousness that is psychologically productive and industriousness that is anxiously keeping busy.[7] Thus what is at first appearance one trait becomes divided into two quite distinct phenomena. In principle, all such differences could be located by simple inspection of the phenomenal field by a sensitive probing; in fact, literary treatment of the human spirit has often anticipated such psychological refinement. But causal knowledge makes possible systematic exploration of

[6] See Ch. XIV ("A Naturalistic Account of Man") in my *The Theory and Practice of Philosophy* (New York, 1946).

[7] Erich Fromm, *Man For Himself* (New York, 1947).

the field, especially in areas where repression blunts ordinary awareness.

Can causal explanation, when one is aware of it, produce an effect within the phenomenal field? Köhler, whose interest in dealing with this question lies primarily in insisting on the objectivity of the phenomenal field, says categorically, "No explanation can change a phenomenon or its location." [8] But it looks as if he only means that it cannot revise a previous description. For he says subsequently: "Qualities belong where we find them. And no explanation or theory can convince us that they were not there where we found them—even if it should prove possible to shift them to another place under changed conditions of subjective attitude." [9] Therefore, if we waive consideration of the metaphysical issues in this context, the variety of effects which a knowledge of causality may have within the phenomenal field becomes an *empirical* question. Several such effects may be distinguished.

(a) The field may remain unchanged but actions, beliefs and attitudes associated with it may undergo alteration. For example, we act toward the "bent" stick partly submerged in water in the knowledge that it is physically straight although visually bent. Similarly, Kant, in urging us to avoid dialectical illusion, uses the analogy of the moon whose appearance is larger when it is at the horizon; we can correct unavoidable intellectual illusions as we correct unavoidable visual illusions.[10] Nietzsche gives remorse a similar status—a man is healthy "when his remorse seems to him like the action of a dog biting a stone." [11] The phenomenal quality is not denied, but its value status is altered. In the same way, "Ruskin has described with eloquent candor the change in his aesthetic experience of the same visible scene when he discovered that it was not a mist-wreathed Alp but a glass roof behind blue smoke." [12]

(b) The field may become extended as a result of the growth of

8 Wolfgang Köhler, *The Place of Value in A World of Facts* (New York, 1938), p. 71.

9 *Ibid.*, p. 82.

10 *Critique of Pure Reason*, tr. Norman Kemp Smith, p. 300.

11 *The Will to Power*, tr. A. M. Ludovici (New York, 1924), I, 191.

12 E. F. Carritt, *Ethical and Political Thinking* (Oxford, 1947), p. 178. The reference is to *Modern Painters*, IV. x, § 8.

causal knowledge. It is as if the screen widened and showed more. This is, of course, a partial change in the field, not a revision of the previously described field. For example, a man afraid of dogs sees a particular dog as threatening. At first, he may steel himself not to run away because he has learned there is no objective danger in the situations in which he encounters dogs, but the menacing object in the field remains. However, it is possible that with growing confidence or insight, the field may grow to include himself as a cowering figure. This shift reflects the fact that he is coming to realize that the qualities of the field are a causal function in part of his personality problems as well as the properties of the objects.

(c) It is possible again that the particular field pattern may completely break up and an alternative field pattern take its place. Insight achieved in the example of the dog should have this effect; the dog would no longer be menacing and might even be friendly. The causal force of acquiring knowledge in breaking up a phenomenal field is a familiar occurrence in cases of mistaken interpretation of symbols and correction of the mistake.

Such recognition of the ways in which context (causes and their knowledge) may influence content (the phenomenal field and its properties) does not mean their identification. In fact, their separation may help to clear up confusions in statements on the three levels. Suppose someone says that satisfaction of hunger is the end of eating. It may be either a causal or phenomenal assertion, and there are cases in which it would be true in the one sense but not in the other. We can distinguish phenomenally the cases in which we eat a steak to appease our hunger from those on which, while also hungry, we eat a steak to enjoy a steak.

The maintenance of the distinction need not, however, mean a metaphysical dualism. Köhler, for example, is quite ready to regard the phenomenal field as an attribute of electrical brain currents in the same sense in which magnetism is an attribute of electrical currents. In this sense, content becomes thoroughly "naturalized," and its relation with different context processes is a thoroughly empirical one.

The materialist interpretation of content draws the least rigid distinction between it and context. Perhaps it may even be regarded as largely a relative distinction. In the materialist mode, an idea reflects, represents, or corresponds to its object. But an idea as well as its object is regarded as a form of matter in motion or energy transformation—not merely in its vehicle, but, so to speak, in its very core. This need not mean the nonreality of the "idea itself," nor of the content-part of the idea. For a nonreductive materialism there will be emergent qualities of material process, and consciousness is regarded as one such level. Therefore, what we have in ideation is one set of qualified material processes reflecting some other set of happenings or qualities and their relations. This roughly characterizes the causal context. Now if we ask about the content relationship, we are asking about the degree of correspondence between the two terms in the reflection relation. Causally, every act of thought reflects some goings-on. But epistemically, the reflection can be very murky or very inaccurately representative. The contrast remains, then, but between the causal and epistemic standpoints. We need not here go into the question of the different kinds of correspondence that might be distinguished or the different tests for correspondence; these are problems of a materialist epistemology. The important point in our present concern is that a content-question is regarded as only a special way of studying a full-context situation, by seeing how one part mirrors or symbolizes the whole. The fullest picture of the content will therefore consist in the exhibition of the whole set of those material processes and their qualities that throw the reflection. If it is a very clear reflection, the problem of understanding its content from the effect is simpler. If it is a distorted reflection, figuring out the exact content may require extensive research. It can be begun from either end (that is a matter of research tactics)—by articulating the structure of the reflected picture, or, where we can discover it, studying the causal process which produced it.

Some such conception seems to me to be involved when materialist philosophers, such as Marx and Engels, take an abstract notion and delve into the social history of a period to produce its meaning. Thus they say of philosophic ideas: "All epoch-making systems have as their real content the needs of the time in which they arise. Each one of them is based on the whole of the antecedent development of a nation, on the historical growth of its class relations, with their political, moral, philosophical and other consequences." [13] A similar sense of content in relation to context seems to me to underlie the way in which Freudian psychologists probe layer after layer of content, distinguishing manifest from latent content, and finding depth below depth not merely as causes but as a complex mode of symbolization. As a matter of fact, discourse in the field of art assumes a comparable character when the "meaning of a work of art" is discussed in terms of "what the work is about" and this in terms of "what the artist is expressing."

The pragmatist treatment of content was cast in terms of an inquiry into meaning. Charles Peirce's original essay, "How to Make Our Ideas Clear" went further than to suggest a technique of clarification. On the contextual side, it regarded ideas as habits of action; on the content side it equated meaning with sensory effects—the sensory experiences pointed to by the term. In William James, meaning is clearly equated with effects in experience and portions of experience pointed to. In Dewey, the aversion to anything like the sharp distinction between context and content is early indicated; he regards it as a vestige of dualism. Nor is he intimidated by anything like charges of the genetic fallacy. Ideas are part of nature; they have effects and typical roles. What an idea is, is to be understood in terms of its role or function. It is not a copy function but "the prospective and anticipatory character that defines *being* an idea." [14] Thus it is only by paying attention to context and seeing the way parts of experience assume ideational character and service continued experience that we understand particular ideas. Their function is their very content. Thus in terms of our framework of analysis, the pragmatic movement and the instrumentalist philosophy can be regarded as denying the sharpness of contrasts between context and content. If a distinction is insisted on, it is one between the underlying causal problem-context, and the specific elements that point forward—the functional solution-discriminating parts. But of course criteria for success emerge in the process, and so one can distinguish description of context from appraisal of success.

[13] *The German Ideology* (International Publishers translation, New York, 1939), p. 87.
[14] John Dewey, *Logic, The Theory of Inquiry* (New York, 1938), p. 109.

The logical-linguistic-analytic way of approaching our present problem has an interesting development which is perhaps most instructive. For here we find the greatest precision, and the drawing of the sharpest boundary-lines. By focussing on linguistic utterances, this analytic tradition secured the advantage of the most definite starting-points for inquiry into meaning. All questions of meaning were questions of the use of language. Two types of meaningful utterance early distinguished were analytic statements (tautologies) and empirical statements (analyzable according to the earlier positivistic view into observation-statements or sense-reports). It is familiar history how this rendered meaningless statements of ethics, religion, metaphysics, and how this was modified by allowing them expressive meaning. In all these, one was dealing with the uses of language, and this corresponds to what we have distinguished as content. Context would embrace psychological and sociological assertions of causes—a legitimate scientific enterprise, but taken to be irrelevant to the logical reconstruction of the language of science, or to the pursuit of analysis.

To a considerable extent, the issues involved in this sharp form of the content-context distinction have been dealt with in the discussion of analysis in Chapter Four, and in the applications to definition and to reasoning. But it is worth going further into the historical shifts of this broad school of thought because it shows clearly the pressure that the problems of context began to exert on a view that regarded them as irrelevant to the logical reconstruction of the language of science. As long as the work concerned internal relations—the syntactical relations of linguistic expressions, and the semantic analysis of designation relations—there was easy going. But wherever discussion got close to the borderlines, trouble arose. Thus there was an early controversy over whether the analysis of empirical statements terminated in protocol *statements* (Neurath) or in incorrigible sensings or sensory *acts* (Schlick). The eventual outcome on the part of many was to challenge the sharp line between observation and interpretation. A readier resort to context might have led inquiry directly to the psychology of perception as part of a science, and the formulation of a policy decision about the appropriate points of termination on the basis of what psychology had discovered about sensory processes and qualities. But this would mean the frank use of outside context results for making inside decisions in the logical reconstruction. A second problem concerned the justification of basic rules—e.g., such questions as why make a sharp analytic-synthetic distinction, or why employ the verifiability principle, or basic inductive principles. Some tended to give a conventional status to ultimate rules, but others felt it necessary to look beyond convention to some type of pragmatic justification.[15] But even a general reference to practical purposes of life, knowledge, control, and so forth, cannot help showing that some of the decisions within the system are made in the light of outside (context) criteria.

A third point, more intimately related to ethical inquiry, is that already mentioned, of expressive meaning. This developed into Stevenson's conception of emotive meaning. In our formulation of context-content relations, this in effect took some of the context elements—certain types of concomitants and effects, whether of feeling or induced attitude—and placed them directly inside as the meaning of the ethical terms. In fact, the controversy over Stevenson's view has often been formulated as whether the emotive aspect belongs inside the meaning or is a concomitant effect.[16] (An important issue here would be what would be left if one took it out—i.e., the issue of what the cognitive approach claims to cognize.[17]) That the kind of pragmatic meaning given to ethical utterances by the emotive theory was in effect breaking down the sharp lines between context and content and called for a wider contextual exploration, was noted above, in the way in which British analytic ethics opened the door to a multiplicity of functions.[18]

Analyses of language also exhibited the same general broadening. The category of meaning gave way to the fuller examination of the semiotic situation—for example, in Charles Morris's be-

[15] Cf. Herbert Feigl's concept of *vindication* in his "De Principiis Non Disputandum . . . ," in *Philosophical Analysis*, ed. Max Black (Ithaca, 1950).

[16] E.g., Henry Aiken, "Emotive 'Meanings' and Ethical Terms," *The Journal of Philosophy*, XLI (1944), pp. 456-70; also his review of Stevenson's "Ethics and Language," *The Journal of Philosophy*, XLII (1945), pp. 455-70.

[17] See pp. 62, 153-54.

[18] See p. 146.

havioral study of modes of signifying and functions of signs in his *Signs, Language and Behavior*. Logical analyses turned from the narrow confines of intensional and extensional relations to presuppositions and contextual implications.[19] An excellent comparative reckoning with the whole situation today is to be found in two recent papers by Frankena.[20] Keeping his eye on what is going on when a man makes an utterance, both in him, his hearers, and the neighborhood, and trying to overlook no communicated element, Frankena is led to distinguish nine different factors "each of which may be and has been referred to as the meaning or part of the meaning of the utterance." [21] We may summarize these by elaborating on an illustration he uses for one of them, a case in which a speaker says to a hearer, "You're late." We can then distinguish:

"The primary conceptual content symbolized, i.e., presented and evoked"—the event took place (the hearer arrived, for example), after some predetermined time.

A propositional attitude with regard to this—the speaker believes it true; it is uttered as an assertion, not a question.

Secondary conceptual content—the hearer has been willfully tardy or has done something wrong.

A propositional attitude with regard to secondary conceptual content—usually if the remark is a complaint, it is assertion,

19 E.g., Max Black, "Definition, Presupposition, and Assertion," in his *Problems of Analysis* (Ithaca, 1954); dealing with definitional theory, he suggests that where suppositions have to be expressed, they be put into a preamble, stating that whereas such and such is the case, the word shall be applied in a specific way. A use violating presuppositions would be null and void rather than false. Compare also, the running battle over Russell's theory of descriptions in contemporary analysis—whether we can say, for example, that "The King of France is bald" is false. If "France has a king" is part of the meaning, then of course it is false. If, however, it is a presupposition, then the original utterance is something else—whether null and void, pointless, or the like. Cf. P. F. Strawson, "On Referring," *Mind*, LIX (1950), 320-44; Bertrand Russell, "Mr. Strawson on Referring," *Mind*, LXVI (1957), 385-89; Stuart Hampshire, *Thought and Action* (London, 1959), pp. 200ff.; for significant banter on the topic, Arthur C. Danto, "A Note on Expressions of the Referring Sort," *Mind*, LXVII (1958), 404-07.

20 William K. Frankena, "Some Aspects of Language" and " 'Cognitive' and 'Noncognitive,' " Chs. VI and VII in *Language, Thought, and Culture*, ed. Paul Henle (Ann Arbor, 1958).

21 *Ibid.*, p. 138.

but in some cases, for example if the hearer has never been late before, the secondary content may be that something has gone wrong, and the propositional attitude almost interrogatory.

Emotions and conative attitudes expressed—indignation and complaint, something-has-to-be-done-about-it.

Emotional tone evoked in the hearer—something to feel sorry about, or apologetic.

Emotions and attitudes revealed—the speaker is impatient.

Other kinds of effects—it embarrasses the audience or rouses pity in them for the hearer. (Frankena illustrates other effects as remote as breaking glass and putting to sleep!)

The purpose—to assert authority, or reprimand, or to suggest that the hearer will have to work hard to catch up, etc.

In the light of these distinctions Frankena then explores the senses of 'cognitive' and 'noncognitive' and their dependence relations. Many of the common oversharp dichotomies crumble as a consequence. For example, it is seen that a sentence may be cognitive not merely in virtue of its conceptual content (functioning as a symbol) but also in virtue of the emotions and attitudes it reveals (functioning as signal).[22] In this sense, to say "Hurrah!" teaches that the person who utters it is pleased about something; it is in this context that the example of exclaiming "You're late!" which we have elaborated, is offered as revealing impatience.

It is important to note how wide is the field of meaning once the doors have been thrown open in this way. What is revealed depends in part on the background knowledge of the hearer; a chance remark revealing impatience may be a personality symptom to the psychologist or a revelation of a typical role to a sociologist. For involved in the phenomenon of impatience is an underlying attitude to time, wasting time, keeping things going by being there at the right time, which is a fertile field for cross-cultural exploration. It is a common observation that punctuality is a virtue of prime importance in a complex industrial society, and that feelings about punctuality may go deep into the structure of personality.

It is equally important, however, to realize that the compartments set up are not hard and fast, that they assume different shape and marshal the content differently depending on the

22 *Ibid.*, pp. 163-164.

kinds of subsidiary criteria employed. For example, is the primary conceptual content of the utterance to be determined by the standardized ideas that would come to the mind of a man who was ignorant of the context, or by the man who knows the detailed situation and its background? In the former case, the criterion is the widest general conceptual element; in the latter, it may be what the speaker "has in mind" or what is "central in his consciousness." A man might actually "have in mind" when he says "You're late!" something like, "This is the last straw," or "You're wrecking the works, holding up production"; certainly, it would be quite different in the case of a husband speaking to a wife, a professor to a student, an officer to a soldier, an employer or foreman to a workman. And it is not merely the distinction between primary and secondary conceptual content, but that between the latter and what is revealed which may raise problems. Clearly, a symbol is not a signal, and the speaker is not *saying* even secondarily that he is impatient. But it is the application of the distinction that is difficult, and the material that is signalled in one context might be the subject of a secondary assertion in another use of the same expression. With a wider knowledge of context one is more likely to realize what may possibly enter as secondary content, that is, what images and associations will come to mind in the act of utterance and be evoked in the hearer.

Let us take an example in ethical theory of the difficulties that arise when the sharp rejection of causal inquiry meets the effort to broaden the area of meaning analysis. Nowell-Smith in his *Ethics,* early dismissed causal exploration. Criticizing the view that the phenomena studied by the moralist are reports of the moral consciousness, he points out that this would involve asking questions such as "Under what circumstances does such and such a moral judgment occur?", "What causes does it have?", "What effects?" and concludes that this is part of empirical psychology; "the moralist is not interested in describing, classifying, and explaining these judgments. He is interested in discovering whether or not they are *true*." [23] And yet it is a central part of his procedure to analyze the *jobs* that moral discourse is performing. This might seem to be describing a type of effects being secured. What is more, he employs in his logical analysis the wider notion of "contextual implication" discussed previously,[24] which involves some kind of factual generalizations about normal usage and people's habits of thought and speech. These steps toward the descriptive and the causal context are, however, obscured by the fact that the sharp distinction has been moved to a different point. The "no trespassing" sign is now placed not between philosophical analysis and causal inquiry as at the outset, but between meaning and contextual background in analyzing ethical terms. For example, Nowell-Smith says of 'good,' "the elements of objective fact which some philosophers insist on treating as part of its meaning are really part of the contextual background of its use." [25] But this assumes that there is a fixed material falling into each category, rather than that one would have to decide in different situations what was now taking its place as meaning, what as contextual background. But there is no real attempt to establish this theory of fixed jobs and separate residences for different kinds of material, or to show how one would decide what falls where. It is rather a deduction from the initial assumption that ethics must not run the risk of appearing to be psychology.

There is, however, a beckoning finger directed later to psychology: "Psychology is not as irrelevant to ethics as some modern philosophers insist; for, although moral judgments do not follow from psychological statements, we cannot understand what the terms used in moral judgments mean unless we examine them in the context of their use; and they are used either directly to express a pro or con attitude or to perform some other task which beings who had no pro or con attitudes could not perform or even understand." [26] This is taken to point to a study of choice, and Nowell-Smith expresses a general agreement with the great moral philosophers insofar as they held "that men choose to do what they do because they are what they are, and that moral theories which attempt to exclude all consideration of human nature as it is do not even begin to be moral theories." This leaves one puzzled; surely the relevant study of what men are is not exhausted for ethical theory purposes by the discovery that ethical discourse has a commendatory job to perform in a context in

24 See above, p. 95.   25 Op. cit., p. 164.
26 Ibid., p. 182.

which men have pro and con attitudes. Jobs and functions are not linguistic entities or properties of discourse, but aims of men, although they employ linguistic instruments. It was a step forward to think in terms of use rather than meaning, and a further step to move from use as typical or correct linguistic association to jobs or functions performed. But little will be gained from these advances if the inquiry is still to be strained through language-analysis rather than have the analysis take its place as valuable evidence in a broadened investigation. How compatible are Nowell-Smith's conclusions with his original dismissal of questions of cause and effect? Will the very moral judgments whose truth the moralist was said to be interested in become clear enough to ask whether they are true, unless there is some study of context in a much wider sense than has been allowed?

From this comparative survey of the four approaches, a fairly clear conclusion emerges about the desirable theoretical policy for ethics. The generally agreed-on purposes of ethics—to furnish some guidance for life—in the long run make it impossible to be satisfied with a narrow approach to ethical ideas. Those who delimit a small field of content and take their stand on this are sooner or later compelled to widen their field of inquiry. Thus the phenomenological approach cannot be content with merely phenomenological reports but has to relate them to causal contexts of comparative and developmental materials. The analytic tradition begins to import functions and effects and indirect contextual reference to expand its category of "meaning" or to be faithful to ethical usage.

At the same time, it must be noted that those who take a broad approach to the content of ideas are not released from the obligation of making careful distinctions within their schemes. The materialist approach has to distinguish the causal from the epistemic standpoint, and differentiate types and clarity of correspondence. The pragmatist-instrumentalist approach has to distinguish types of functions and degrees of success, and to set off the enterprise of appraising success.

One can, of course, start out in one way or the other for specific reasons—e.g., make a narrow content-stand to achieve initial clarity, or a broad content-stand to make sure no clue is left out. The choice—to take a political analogy—seems to be between a small territory with a very complex department of external affairs, or a broad territory with a complex department of internal affairs. In contemporary ethics, the dangers of being narrow have proved much the greater.

Although some distinction of context and content can thus always be drawn in each problem or investigation, there is not always, and need not be, the same distinction drawn for all problems or investigations. That is, there are no unique context-materials and content-materials—as for example in the metaphysical view that the former are material entities and the latter ideal entities, or in the view of analytical ethical theorists that descriptions can never be content in ethical judgment but must always be contextual implications. It is like an object on which light is cast; there is always an initial bright focus, and a wider range in shadow or in darkness. But the light can be moved!

In a less developed field such as ethics, where there is not a sufficiently established theory to tell us precisely what is relevant and what is not, there is considerable advantage in focussing on a wide context. Many of the boundary lines currently drawn are too narrow in their effect. It is therefore useful to think in terms of *extending or increasing the content of an idea* by materials furnished in the exploration of context. (This is the correlative of the familiar view that we "gain a deeper understanding" by seeing the full context.) It is not, however, to be taken as a simple uniform process, even in any one of the approaches we have considered. Let us briefly recapitulate its variety in general terms, before turning to selected illustrations. In phenomenological description, extension of content means clearer identification of an element in the field, or the breaking up and reconstitution of the field so that the succeeding one is wider, richer, or fuller than the earlier one. In the materialist approach, it means the wider spreading of the reflected side, so that it purports to give a fuller and richer picture of relations and elements in a wider stretch of existence. In the pragmatic approach, it involves bringing the instrumental relations of the field directly within the field. In the linguistic-analytic approach, it can perhaps take many forms, corresponding to the different types of results that we say may be produced by a completed analysis.[27] One might be the dis-

---

[27] See above, pp. 102f., on the range of analytic results.

covery of extensional equivalence in the uses of initially distinct terms (or some other looser type of connective relation) and a consequent use of one of the terms or a new term to combine the originally separate features. Another way in which the field might be extended, on the contrary, is by splitting a term, hitherto used to cover two inadequately distinguished phenomena, into two terms each applied to one of these. A third type might be, after examination of context in some of the senses such as Frankena mapped them, a meta-linguistic stipulation that fuses in the meaning of a term both its primary conceptual content and some of its expressive effect or propositional attitudes; the emotive theory of ethics, in effect, was doing something describable in this way. A much more complicated type would arise when context-exploration yielded purposes on the basis of which decision was made among competing analyses. And so on. It is perhaps less a question of standardized relationships than of creative ingenuity in fashioning new and useful ones.

SOME ETHICAL ILLUSTRATIONS OF CONTENT EXTENSION

How our understanding of ideas relevant to ethics is increased or extended by attention to context has already been illustrated to some extent, especially in Chapter Two, where the idea of *pleasure* gained in scope as the scientific, historical, and valua-tional coordinates of the theories that focussed on it became clearer.[28] Here I should like to take two brief case studies, one dealing with a concept of considerable relevance to the moral level and the other to the ethical-theory level, and suggest the way in which the growth of knowledge of context helps clarify internal problems in the delineation of the concept and the determination of its intrasystemic role. I take the concept of *love* to be considered in its psychological context and the concept of *better* in its socio-historical context.

Love plays a large role on the first level—that is, in human life and activity. It enters pervasively into the moral level, both as a

28 Cf. also "Context and Content in the Theory of Ideas," *op. cit.*, secs. 4-6, which deal with the kinds of occasions that call for extension, and the relations of phases of content once extension has taken place; illustrations explored include Aristotle's idea of the mean, Engels' treatment of equality, and the question of quality in pleasure in J. S. Mill.

good and as an index of moral interpersonal relations. Basic injunctions frequently include that one should love his fellow men. Ethical theories sometimes elevate love to a central position. Thus Socrates' famous speech in Plato's *Symposium* makes loving desire (*eros*) the very heart of the human quest for the absolute good. And in modern times we find occasional incorporation of the idea of love into definitions of the good. For example, Brentano decides that "We call something good when the love relating to it is right. That which can be loved with a right love, that which is worthy of love, is good in the widest sense of the term." [29] And Max Scheler, in *The Nature of Sympathy*, in effect equates love with the sense of value.

Now how can the familiar causal picture that Freud has given help the understanding of love on the moral and ethical level? What has the account of infantile dependence, of the demand for affection as a basic need, of the Oedipal stage and its passing, of sexual maturity and its tensions, of all the pitfalls in development and the types of neurotic adjustments, and so on, to do with the meaning of love and its moral relations? We must, of course, separate from such a causal account any moral or philosophical theses that may be associated with it in the literature—for example, that all value is an indirect pursuit of libidinal gratification, or that values are primarily means for release of tension, or that permissiveness in gratification is better or worse than discipline and restraint, and so on. These are separable debatable issues. Nor are we concerned with the particular developmental theses, as compared to alternatives in matters of scientific detail, important as these are for specific understanding. Our question is the general clarification of the meaning of love as a consequence of a causal-developmental account.

For one thing, the psychological causal-developmental account helps us mark out similarities and at the same time sharpen differences. It thus presents us with a clearer delineation of the phenomenon of love itself. What might be suspected on introspective or on phenomenological grounds, or even in terms of behavioral differences, becomes more clearly established when related to lines of development in personal growth. The love

[29] Franz Brentano, *The Origin of the Knowledge of Right and Wrong*, tr. Cecil Hague (New York, 1902), p. 16.

that crumbles suddenly, or the love that is imbued with hate, or the love that demands and drains but never gives or supports, the love that worships from afar but withers at close range, and countless other forms, are all suggested in literature, but they are not always understood. When the causal picture is rounded out, the task of sharper delineation becomes easier. Stressing the differences, some would then deny the name of love to some of these forms, but this may be underrating the developmental continuities. At any rate, one can differentiate the love that is primarily need or dependence, that which is primarily self-reassurance, that which is a basic demanding, and so on, from a more "essential" or "authentic" or "mature" type. Thus Erich Fromm broadly differentiates the anxiety-allaying relationship from the productive one, and defines love in terms of the qualities of affection, care, responsibility, that enter into the sense of the relationship.[30] Perhaps the chief success in the psychological causal account so far has been to set off the immature and the neurotic types from the more mature. The positive description of the mature has not, as yet, been so sharply worked out. The achievements even up to this point, however, are not to be minimized. It becomes less and less possible to think about love in the moral field or to employ the concept in an ethical-theory formulation simply in a generic interpretation of desire or attraction, without embodying the lessons that a psychological approach has carried through.

It is not, however, merely through the differentiation of quality that the picture of causality brings clearer understanding. The moralist or the ethical theorist cannot simply say that having been aided in sharply differentiating love from a host of pseudo-love forms, he can now retreat to the genuine feeling or quality and deal with it in isolation. It is not merely that to know what love is, we have to know what it is not; nor is it merely a question of knowing what might have been had developmental processes taken a different turn. Even though the causal analysis of love is far from complete, the very way in which it is pursued broadens the conception of love itself. Plato showed this structural insight when he treated love not as just a feeling or a quality of experience, but as itself a quest or effort of growth and striving. It may be that a fuller understanding of love as a human phenomenon

[30] *Man For Himself* (New York, 1947), pp. 96ff.

requires a more complete causal account of the growth of the self than is given in the psychoanalytic picture hitherto established. (It may, of course, also be the case that a socio-historical application of the causal standpoint is here required, too.) In any case, the very idea of love becomes more broadly understood as certain qualities and feelings in the relation of persons who have achieved a mature development and whose pattern of action toward one another has such and such a structure. (And this is without raising such further questions as the meaning of 'love' in an expression like 'love of truth,' and how a context-analysis of devotion to truth might help clarify this area!) Thus even a partial causal exploration, with a clear sense of the direction in which it is moving, points to the view that ethical terms are better interpreted as complex constructs concerning structural properties of life and process and feeling, than by reference to purely phenomenal qualities or introspective feelings.

We turn next to the second example, in order to illustrate how a very abstract ethical-theory conception and its role can gain in clarity by paying attention to the context of theorizing. An interesting strand in pure ethical theory of the twentieth century has been the rise of the concept of *better* to the position of candidate for primacy in the systematization of ethical language. I have not carried out a historical study of this problem, and so it may be that I have been misled by impressions. But it will serve, with this warning, as an example of the kind of inquiry I have in mind. What first called my attention to the problem was finding, in a close study of Aristotle's ethics, that he does not give the notion of *better* very much place in his fundamental framework of ethical concepts. There is, of course, a term for 'better' and he does have concepts for comparative ordering. But they are of a different sort. He furnishes an account of 'the good,' ascribes to it the attribute of being 'complete,' and uses proximity to the end as one of the ways of what we would call scaling. As he says at one point in the *Politics,* "that which is nearest to the best must of necessity be better, and that which is furthest from it worse, if we are judging absolutely." [31] But in actual use, we find him talking of what is incomplete or less complete, ordering by plac-

---

[31] *Politics,* 1296b8. For other rating techniques, see *Topics* III.

ing along means-ends relations, and in special contexts making special distinctions. For example, some goods are *prized*, others *praised*, and the former are therefore superior. If anyone had said to Aristotle that the fundamental concept of ethics was *better*, he surely would have regarded it as logically odd, if not actually theoretically subversive!

What do we find in the twentieth century? 'Better' stakes its claim early in the century. Perhaps the first clear proposal to elevate it to central position comes in A. P. Brogan's "The Fundamental Value Universal." [32] Brogan sets as his objective "to prove that the relation 'better' is a sufficient fundamental universal for the theory of value and that it is the only value universal which can be taken as fundamental. In other words, all value facts are facts about betterness." Since he dealt with this by definition and analysis, the most that he could really establish, as we have indicated sufficiently by this time, is the greater logical power or simplicity of his scheme, or else that it corresponded to the phenomenal field of his readers—that is, that it reflected accurately the emerging twentieth century consciousness. The detail of his formulations is beyond our present scope; perhaps it is sufficient to give his definition of 'good': '*A* is good' is equated with 'the existence of *A* is better than the nonexistence of *A*.' It is interesting to note that Dewey almost immediately accepted the point of view advanced by Brogan. Specifically placing himself on record as agreeing, he went on to add, "Upon this view, which I accept, liking would have to be understood as *preference*, selection-rejection, interest as 'this-rather-than-that.' The word bias seems to carry this on its face." [33]

How congenial such an approach has proved is clear on the present theoretical scene. Even apart from the weight of Dewey's general emphasis on the priority of preference—which concerns interpretation rather than the specific logical analysis—there are various indications of its strength. Among the systems akin to deontic logic, it has recently found representation in Sören Halldén's *On the Logic of 'Better.'* [34] J. O. Urmson's article, "On

---

[32] *The Journal of Philosophy*, XVI (1919), 96-104.

[33] John Dewey, "Valuation and Experimental Knowledge," *The Philosophical Review*, XXXI (1922), 334, n. 2.

[34] Library of Theoria, No. 2 (Lund, 1957).

Grading," [35] which is widely referred to in current discussion, sets its inquiry into grading procedures in general, and works up to regarding good as a grading label applicable in many different types of contexts. But perhaps the best evidence of having arrived is to be found in casual acceptance, almost as if it were the obvious meaning. Take, for example, the following from a recent work:

> "To say that this is a good spade is to say that, if I were choosing spades, I would prefer this one to most others, and so would other people. Moral evaluations, however they differ from nonmoral ones, agree in this. To say that a thing or action is good is, in part, to say that I and others would rate it more highly than others of its class; to say that a person is a good man is, in part, to say that I and others would rather have his qualities than those of most other men. The fact that 'good' carries with it a scale of preference has induced some philosophers, quite plausibly, to propose that the basic moral evaluative concept should be not 'good' but 'better.'" [36]

Now, in the light of this contrast of twentieth century proposals and the Aristotelian mode, how are we to decide whether 'better' is the primary ethical term? Clearly, such a decision is one of methodological policy. But what basis can we use for decision? To some extent, intrasystemic considerations of simplicity and convenience. But obviously, partisans of other notions can do as well and incorporate whatever advantages 'better' offers within their system. We have therefore to turn to context in one sense or another. We may turn to a generalized human psychology and argue with Dewey that preference is the fundamental feature of choice, and so a conceptual framework which reflects this is superior to one which does not. To pursue this would then take us into the psychology of choice. How adequate the conclusion would be I do not here venture to determine.

If we go not to the psychological context but to the socio-historical context, the program of inquiry takes a different form. This treatment of ideas in relation to their socio-historical bases was first developed on a large scale by Marx. It is quite a sep-

[35] *Mind*, LIX (1950), 145-69. For a basic criticism of this approach, see C. A. Baylis, "Grading, Values, and Choice," *Mind*, LXVII (1958), 485-501.

[36] Bernard Mayo, *Ethics and the Moral Life* (London and New York, 1958), p. 25.

arable contribution from many of his other theses, and one that is extremely suggestive. Take, for example, his discussion, in his *A Contribution to the Critique of Political Economy*,[37] of the way in which the idea of *abstract labor* develops:

> The indifference as to the particular kind of labor implies the existence of a highly developed aggregate of different species of concrete labor, none of which is any longer the predominant one. So do the most general abstractions commonly arise only where there is the highest concrete development, where one feature appears to be jointly possessed by many, and to be common to all. Then it can not be thought of any longer in one particular form. On the other hand, this abstraction of labor is but the result of a concrete aggregate of different kinds of labor. The indifference to the particular kind of labor corresponds to a form of society in which individuals pass with ease from one kind of work to another, which makes it immaterial to them what particular kind of work may fall to their share.

On this type of heuristic principle, when we find an abstract category rising to prominence in a society, we do well to look to institutional forms and socio-economic processes which act as a base for it and which render indifferent or interchangeable the specific qualitative forms that the category embraces. In our example, we would have to find something like this. Society is organized in such a way that men are finding it increasingly necessary to make comparative choices. Economically, there is a wide variety of goods not all of which they can pursue, but many of which are possible. They are no longer status bound in determining their mode of life. There is a common market which these goods enter, and what is more relevant, a common medium (money) so that they can be pursued without asking necessarily at each point which one is being pursued, and so that they can be compared in terms of that medium. Sociologically, status is ascribed in terms of wealth and getting ahead of others. This too involves comparison. Measurement is a standardized activity in many areas of production and of ordinary life. It enters into scientific work to the degree to which science has sometimes been conceived as dealing with what is measurable. Cost accounting and grading are pervasive. And so on. The general tenor of such

37 Tr. by N. I. Stone (Chicago, 1904), pp. 298-99.

an argument is clear. Is it surprising that the habits of mind engendered in so much of contemporary life are reflected in abstract concepts? Already in Bentham's day, the act of measuring permeated his conception of the felicific calculus. Now a more scientific view of measurement, as well as the intensification of the tendency over a century and a half makes the idea of the comparative a vigorous contender for conceptual primacy. In fact, the conditions that make measurement possible are construed as the mark of rationality. If a man behaved in such a way that the preference relation was not transitive, that is, if he preferred X to Y and Y to Z, but when faced with X and Z did not necessarily prefer X, he would be regarded as irrational.[38]

Whether such an analysis is a correct causal-historical account, is of course a matter of specific inquiry. The heuristic principle is to look for such bases—it would have to be qualified also to see whether it was intended largely for ideas about human affairs or all ideas in some respect—but it does not guarantee our finding them, nor, if we do, does it settle the policy question of adequacy in further theoretical use. Suppose, however, that it proved historically correct in this case. How would it serve as an extension of content? Clearly, it is not literally extending the meaning of 'better,' since there is an obvious general sense in which this term had somewhat the same meaning in medieval times and in ancient Greek as well. On the other hand, by exhibiting the variety of procedures for comparing and grading in the Aristotelian view and in the modern view, it is showing some contrast of meaning insofar as craftsmanship ideas of incompleteness or inadequacy and contemporary ideas of measuring-comparison are different, and operations or indices of application are not wholly irrelevant to differences in meaning. Perhaps it might best be regarded as a case of the complicated kind of extension of content mentioned above, in which the pragmatic bases of a meta-theoretical policy are revealed by context-exploration. A clearer understanding has been brought to the question "Is 'better' the primary ethical term?" For in the light of the context investigation it becomes, in effect, "Are there socio-historical processes of

---

[38] Cf. Oscar Lange's account of the postulate of rationality in his "The Scope and Method of Economics," *Review of Economic Studies*, XIII (1945-6); reprinted in Feigl and Brodbeck, *Readings in the Philosophy of Science*.

comparison and grading and measuring that so overshadow the qualitative aspects of the acts of choice in the modern world that we could do a more successful job with our ethical language if we gave them a primary place?" As so formulated, the question is not an easy one to answer. For example, someone might say, "No, let's not be so comparative in spirit, it's psychologically unhealthy!" I think Aristotle would have approved this kind of answer. For I can quite see him saying that to make 'better' the central concept of ethics is *unnatural,* which would mean for him—as in his economic doctrine—that the aggrandizing spirit of a competitive commercial economy is inferior to the well-ordered agricultural society. To repeat, the answer is not simple, but I think the question formulated in such terms taps more profoundly the human issues at stake than when formulated as conventional choice of basic concepts, or a question of intrasystemic simplicity. Of course, it is open to anyone to say that this is not the question *he* meant, in which case an answer to this is not an answer to his question. But it is *his* obligation to decide what *he* meant, and to tell us, if he wants an answer.

Of the two following chapters of this part, the next will deal with the problem of truth and the genetic fallacy because of the central place it has in the controversies of this area. The subsequent one will be an example of the significance that straight causality research may have for ethical theory.

CHAPTER ELEVEN

GENETIC INQUIRY
AND TRUTH DETERMINATION

That the causal standpoint properly employed does not commit the genetic fallacy can be shown in general as follows. The causal standpoint, as we have examined it, can produce three kinds of results. It can discover the causes and concomitant conditions of the holding of ideas, it can trace the effects and uses of holding ideas, and it can help extend the content of ideas. In the first two, there are no claims to determine the truth of ideas. In the third, there is a contribution to the clarification of what is to be adjudged true or false. Now the genetic fallacy consists in *substituting* context-inquiry for truth-determination or verification (comparably, for worth-assessment or evaluation). But the question of truth-determination cannot arise till we have the meaning of the assertion to be tested. (Comparably, the question of worth-assessment does not arise till we have a full picture of the situation to be evaluated.) Therefore, the contribution of the causal standpoint in extending content is *over and done before the question of truth (or worth) arises*. Therefore, it cannot be posing as a substitute.

All this shows, of course, is that the causal standpoint as worked out in the last chapter does not commit the genetic fallacy. The actual historical situation has been much more complicated. For there obviously have been attempts to work out genetic modes of truth-determination. These have come usually in the wake of great advances in the causal understanding of man and his works. Such advances shake up the whole arena of thought and beget fresh insights which are often overextended. In the last hundred years, the chief attempts at elaborating genetic inquiry into an epistemic doctrine have come from extending the work of Darwin, Marx, and Freud. There has been some repercussion also from the anthropological studies of cultural differences. From the evolutionary approaches has come the pragmatic view that man's intellect is a practical instrument that emerged in his evolutionary development and was primarily geared to the solution of practical problems; the overextension of this view was the occasional equating of truth with success. From Marxian theory came the realization that ideas arise and function in a socio-historical context; its overextension was the social relativization of the idea of truth in the social sciences. From Freudian theory came the probing into the emotional roots of thinking, and a fresh perspective into the role of ideational schemes; its overextension, in philosophy at least, has been the attempt to exhibit philosophies as primarily anxiety-allaying mechanisms. From anthropology came the outlook of cultural relativity; its overextension has been to turn truth into a local-cultural category. We cannot undertake the full-scale consideration of all these contentions here. But they cannot be ignored, for they usually contain an element of insight which will be lost if they are simply dismissed. Unless they are dealt with, they provide a perpetual encouragement to the effort we noted in the last chapter, to throw out the whole causal standpoint in the analysis of ideas. In short, while the last chapter was concerned with the exhibition of what the causal standpoint can legitimately do, and its defense against the purists, the present chapter is concerned with the analysis of those approaches that seem to me to overplay it.

Let us first dispose of borderline cases which may appear to be settling truth issues on genetic grounds, but which are really elliptical arguments. Some of them are simply showing that the idea has no cognitive content, or has only negligible cognitive content. These would be precisely parallel to the expressive analysis of ethical concepts which finds them simply a vehicle for giving vent to feelings; or, in Stevenson's emotive formulation, the actual cognitive content (as in the model "I approve of this; do so thou") requires little truth-determination if it is assumed that a man knows his own acts of approval. Now what if a social philosopher takes some of the Nazi assertions of race superiority coupled with an intuitive test of what is Nordic and what is not, and dismisses them as "sheer ideology" with the implication that once he has understood their social role as expressing certain sociopolitical interests, that is all there is to be said about it? He need not be committing the genetic fallacy, for his assertion may be simply elliptical for the judgment that the view is nonsense, or that it is not worth engaging in its truth-determination. But the causal standpoint is enlightening. A fuller treatment of such cases would have to distinguish the different kinds of assumptions involved: e.g., the ideological view is meaningless, or it has long since been discredited from a truth-determination point of view, or it is not worth the energy to investigate its truth, and so forth. But the existence of such cases is by no means equivalent to a general assertion that genetic-causal analysis is a mode of truth-determination.

In similar fashion, I think that many of the criticisms of evolutionary ethical theories as substituting evolutionary trends for ethical evaluation are often beside the point. I do not mean that such confusions have not been committed, but that an attempt should first be made to see in each case whether we may not be dealing with an elliptical argument. To say that what is most advanced along an evolutionary line is the best may already involve a prior definition of ethical terms by reference to specified human aims, a mode of differentiating basic from secondary aims, a historical generalization that secondary aims undergo transformation in the light of the state of possible achievement of primary aims, a general-direction thesis that the possibility of achieving primary aims is in fact constantly increasing. Even in Herbert Spencer's grandiose evolutionary picture, we find such strands as: an initial conception of the good and criteria for good conduct, projection of the idea of a complete life in a complete society, the empirical thesis that ethical views are adapted to conditions and the claim that a more scientific ethics belongs to a more advanced social state, a theory of the origin of feelings of moral-obligation in general, together with a background assumption of the direction of social evolution.[1] Whatever the errors of such a scheme may be, it is gross oversimplification to regard the argument as merely a genetic fallacy.

Among the attempts to work out some constitutive role for genetic analysis in truth-determination in the area of social thought, perhaps the best known is that in Karl Mannheim's *Ideology and Utopia*.[2] Mannheim generalizes the Marxian insight into the social and political interests underlying systems of

---

[1] See his *Principles of Ethics* (New York, 1896), I, 23-25, 73-74, 97-98, 124, 137-38.

[2] New York, 1936. See especially pp. 258ff., 266.

ideas. He points out that the unmaskers themselves have a social basis. He concludes that the social position of the observer enters intimately—unavoidably—into all social and historical knowledge. In his hands this passes beyond being a practical difficulty which one may hope to overcome by more assiduous investigation. He seeks a way out by a comparison of perspectives and a call for a more comprehensive view to be achieved by intellectuals who because of their own social position feel the impact of different classes. I have criticized this elsewhere [3] in the light of the view of the relation of content and context sketched in the previous chapter. One objection, of course, is that a genuine practical difficulty of gathering nondistorted evidence and determining relevance in any particular socio-historical inquiry is being elevated into an insuperable barrier of principle. This is not justified by the fact that defenders of objectivity are frequently lax in seeing their own biases; there can be an ideological use of objectivity itself. In general, it is bad policy to remove the distinction between a practical difficulty and a theoretical difficulty because it removes criteria of increasing success in overcoming the practical difficulty. Yet we do recognize that some accounts are grossly biased, and others less so. Why then follow what seems like a counsel of despair? But such a rejoinder is only preliminary. The real question is whether we can in fact make progress towards objectivity and whether this is itself meaningful. Here the central point of my argument is a logical one—that the very act of unmasking a view as partial is itself a contribution to the criteria of impartiality. The failure to note this seems to me to stem from the desire to find a general antecedent criterion for rationality rather than be content with the accumulation of empirical lessons that become established as criteria. The case in social-genetic inquiry is parallel to deciding that a man's evidence is unreliable at a given time because he was drunk or under the influence of drugs. If sobriety is another form of drunkenness, our original unmasking makes no sense. (Moreover, if we find definite laws relating to this man's drunkenness—for example, that he has a

[3] In "Context and Content in the Theory of Ideas," in *Philosophy for the Future,* ed. Sellars, McGill, and Farber (New York, 1949), pp. 442ff. See also the discussion of the question "Is Knowledge Itself Culturally and Historically 'Relative'?" in my *Ethical Judgment,* pp. 282ff,

clearer perception when he is drunk, or that he distorts always in a definite direction to a definite degree—we may use appropriate transformation formulae!) So too we can learn about the typical ideologies of particular classes over a long historical stretch, and so come to understand the kinds of distortions that have to be corrected in the use of evidence from such sources. The comparison of perspectives is liberating, not because one who is motivated to compare is himself straddling classes—which may be independently the case or not—but because the comparison increases the store of specific criteria in the bit-by-bit building up of a conception of an adequate base of judgment.

In recent years, attempts to work out genetic modes of determining truth and estimating worth on a psychoanalytic basis have come to the fore. It is therefore important to consider these carefully, as they seem to be making headway. I should like to take one of the most carefully formulated of these attempts and consider it at greater length. This is Lewis S. Feuer's paper, "The Bearing of Psychoanalysis on Philosophy." [4]

Feuer takes as his point of departure the principles of philosophizing stressed in different philosophical outlooks—"parsimony, continuity, verifiability, common sense"—and regarded as self-evident by their defenders. He takes this self-evidence to be psychological, not logical, and presents biographical data from Russell, Moore, John B. Watson, and others, to suggest that each principle expresses an underlying emotional standpoint, which he calls "the decision-base of the philosopher, that is, his configuration of feelings of affection and aggression, with their specific directions and intensities, in both their conscious and unconscious forms." [5] The various fallacies, such as the genetic fallacy, the naturalistic fallacy, and so on, sometimes serve as resistance-mechanisms, holding back scientific analysis. Analysis of emotional origins is not claimed as truth-determining in the case of scientific statements, but as applicable to philosophical principles, since these can be disposed of neither factually nor logically.

4 In *Philosophy and Phenomenological Research*, XIX (1959), 323-40. This was read at the December, 1956, meetings of the Eastern Division of the American Philosophical Association. My criticisms here are an elaboration of those I made at the time as commentator on this paper.

5 *Ibid.*, p. 323.

Feuer draws the distinction of the scientific and the philosophic here by reference to Freud's "reality-principle" and "pleasure-principle" respectively.

The way in which psychoanalysis is relevant in judging truth-claims is then formulated. "A philosophic doctrine is genetically 'explained away' when the primary determinants for its adequacy are found to be the outcome of projective motives." "Genetic analysis dissolves beliefs which are projective in origin; it reinforces those which are realistic in their derivation." [6] Feuer goes on directly to make interesting distinctions in the logic of genetic analysis: "A proposition is genetically self-consistent, or self-reinforcing, if its assertion, in existential form, constitutes a necessary part of the theory of its origin. A proposition is genetically self-inconsistent, or self-dissolving, if its denial in existential form, appears as a necessary component in the theory of its origin. A proposition is genetically neutral if neither its assertion nor its denial are part of the theory of its origin." Thus "an adequate economic explanation of the origins of the belief in the primacy of economic factors in history would be genetically self-reinforcing; on the other hand, such an economic explanation of a purely political interpretation of history would be dissolving in its impact." "The existence of God is genetically neutral with respect to both atheist and believer. For the psychological explanations of what makes a person either an atheist or theist themselves neither assume nor deny the existence of God." But "the theory of solipsism's origin denies solipsism by assuming the existence of the external world."

I think that this gives us the core of the argument, although it omits many interesting detailed points and illuminating flashes. Now there is one difficulty to begin with. It is not made clear whether philosophical views dealt with in the way Feuer proposes have any cognitive content and are statable as propositions. If to say they are not provable and not refutable implies that they are not cognitive, then there is no question of truth or falsity, and no need to think in terms of any kind of inconsistency. In this sense, the theory of solipsism's origin could not deny solipsism because there is nothing to deny. And if there is no question of truth or falsity, the kind of evaluation being performed is one of desir-

6 *Ibid.*, p. 333.

ability of attitudes. This might as well be discussed directly—on the psychological side at least—in terms of the theory of different mechanisms of defense. Here the core of the evaluation will lie in the grounds that differentiate realistic from neurotic or quasi-neurotic attitudes in general. For Feuer's thesis then to be a significant one about truth-determination, the philosophical utterances must be propositional in at least some moderate sense.

Even as a purely causal thesis dealing with philosophical utterances, however, it raises interesting questions. Of course, any light from any genetic inquiries applying authentic psychological and social theory to biographical data is to be welcomed. Feuer does offer numerous suggestions on the role of loneliness, desire for security, aggression, emotional resistances provoking anxiety, and so forth, in the causal origins of specific philosophical outlooks in particular philosophers. But this need not mean a stable correlation between psychological problems and philosophical forms of expression. For example, one man's solipsism may be an exalting of the ego, another's a resort to the infantile unity of the "oceanic feeling," another's some yet more varied motivation acting to rob the world of "reality." Even apart from the impossibility of putting philosophers of the past on the analytic couch to trace the many meanings they attached to specific ideational elements, there is scarcely the beginning of sufficient evidence on which to suggest types of correlations between motivation and doctrine.

A further difficulty is the question of how far psychological as opposed to more particular social and cultural accounts carry us in this domain. Feuer's suggestion that the psychological give the more universal causal components has some plausibility, but this very broadness may render them less available for explaining specific philosophical trends. Take, for example, solipsism, in the case of Berkeley's rejection of the reality of material substance, and consider the variety of theses propounded. Was it simply a keen logical sense which could not tolerate the fictional element in the Lockean something-I-know-not-what conception of matter? Was it the unconscious motivation that J. O. Wisdom has elaborated in his *The Unconscious Origin of Berkeley's Philosophy* —a desire to get rid of a poison within the body by philosophical incantation plus tar-water? Was it a desire to clear the world of matter, as Lenin has it in his *Materialism and Empirio-Criticism*, to make room for God? Was it an Irish nationalist feeling against those Englishmen—Newton and Locke—who robbed them of sensible reality in the name of insensible extensions and hidden mechanisms of the world? The Irish poet Yeats has called attention to an entry in Berkeley's own journal which suggests this.[7]

The same difficulties arise if the genetic inquiry is directed to function or use of the doctrine, not simply origin. For not only do philosophies change hands, but the motivation in use may come to differ from motivation in origin. Thus, whatever the origins of Berkeley's rejection of matter, he is explicit in using it thereafter to get rid in wholesale fashion of "all the impious schemes of atheism and irreligion" and thus saving the trouble of considering separately "every wretched sect." [8] Again, use of the verification principle to *avoid* certain issues, which Feuer takes to serve a repressive function because it makes statements about the possibility of immortality meaningless ("It tries to repress the death-anxiety with a grammatical rule" [9]), is more likely explainable in socio-historical terms or in terms of cultural conflicts about morality and religion. And while in a given behaviorist, the treatment of man as a machine may involve the desire to repress feelings, we cannot assume this to hold for the liberating social use of the machine model in the eighteenth century. Perhaps psychoanalytic investigation may make us understand today why one man sees automation as making man more machine-like, while another sees it as making the environment an extension of man and therefore the world more man-like. But even here there may be factual issues, such as different predictions about the probable limitations of social freedom involved.[10]

Feuer's procedure of evaluating a philosophical view genetically involves relating it to what he calls the *decision-base* of the

[7] "There are men who say there are insensible extensions. There are others who say the fire is not hot. We Irishmen cannot attain to these truths." From the *Commonplace Book*. Quoted in Yeats' Introduction to J. M. Hone and M. M. Rossi, *Bishop Berkeley* (London, 1931), p. 28.

[8] George Berkeley, *Principles of Human Knowledge*, § 92.

[9] Feuer, *op. cit.*, p. 325.

[10] That Feuer has not underestimated the role of socio-historical factors in a man's philosophy is to be seen in his admirable book, *Spinoza and the Rise of Liberalism* (Boston, 1958).

philosopher, specified as the feelings of affection and aggression which incline him toward the advocacy of particular philosophical principles. Now it is commonly recognized that philosophical choices—especially when such general principles as parsimony, continuity, verifiability, and so forth are involved—involve a set of purposes by which the principles are validated or vindicated "pragmatically." How far apart is such a pragmatic base in the operations of the philosophy of science from the decision-base proposed by Feuer in genetic evaluation? For the moment I pass over the fact that one is approached from the side of genetic inquiry, while the other is reached as a terminus in a logical reconstruction. The thing that strikes one about Feuer's proposed base is its narrow limits, even on a psychoanalytic theory. It is cast purely in terms of the emotions that are sources of anxiety and not in terms of those psychic ego-processes that establish contact with reality. Surely a decision-base should be wide enough to be capable of distinguishing between the *realistic* or *insightful* on the one hand, and the *projective* or even *neurotic* on the other. How it will do this will no doubt vary with the specific psychological theory, and it is too early to restrict such inquiries to one school of motivational theory. Feuer does, as we noted, use the mark of derivation from the pleasure principle and the reality principle respectively to distinguish between philosophy and science. I do not see on what psychoanalytic grounds it can be denied that a similar distinction can be made within philosophies. Even in Freudian terms, the distinction between defenses against anxiety and successful sublimations could be applied to divide philosophical principles rather than seeing all such principles merely as anxiety defenses. Or again, in the language of the more recent ego-psychology trends in psychoanalytic theory, why could not one ask which philosophies are grounded in the "conflict-free sphere" which includes development of perception, object-comprehension, thinking, and so on, as well as motor development? [11] Feuer's view that genetic analysis reinforces beliefs which are realistic in their derivation itself seems to call for this widening of the decision-base. But the more we go in this direc-

11 Cf. Heinz Hartmann, "Ego Psychology and the Problem of Adaptation," in *Organization and Pathology of Thought,* ed. David Rapaport (New York, 1951), Ch. XIX.

tion, the closer we come to precisely those criteria in perception, thought and action, which are appealed to in the philosophy of science—the pragmatic basis by which its general principles are vindicated. Thus less attention will be paid to the fact that the verification principle may serve some philosophers in an anxiety-allaying respect, and more to the long-range lesson that sensations and not feelings or emotions provide the most stable verifying elements for generalized systematization where the purpose is prediction and control.

When genetic analysis is taken in its full seriousness and when pragmatic vindication is tracked down by asking for a detailed picture of the needs which constitute the pragmatic base, it becomes possible to see the role that genetic analysis can play with respect to the truth problem. It turns out to be one that is surprisingly different from what has been claimed. But before we come to it, it is worth stressing that even if we stay within the confines Feuer has kept for his decision base, there is no need to formulate genetic criticism as if it were some distinctive mode of validity-determination which dissolves or genetically explains away certain philosophies by exhibiting their projective content. After all, whose beliefs are dissolved? The philosopher who remains purely within the terms of his philosophical theory can always reinforce it by reinterpreting psychoanalytic results in his own language, just as a religious ethics has no difficulty in offering a religious history to explain the revelation of its commandments. And the outsider can simply recognize that if psychological or genetic theories are accepted as true, they provide evidence against views that prove to be inconsistent with them. After all, solipsism is not strictly dissolved by being shown to express certain types of anxiety. Berkeley could have taken this very theory in his stride, as he could take Dr. Johnson's feeling of resistance on kicking a rock. More is involved in the refutation. What a refutation must show is at least: (*a*) that logical analysis finds no distinctive empirical consequences; (*b*) that conceptually the proposed solipsistic scheme uses 'sensation' as a category in an overextended sense (which in turn rests on philosophical generalizations about the desirable use of categories); (*c*) that the anxieties it expresses are not adequately coped with by such a categorial device (a lesson from psychoanalysis empirically established, about the difference between defense mechanisms and realistic handling).

What then is the role of genetic analysis, whether psychological or social, or, for that matter, biological, in relation to truth determination? I have already suggested it in discussing Mannheim's view and the way in which every act of unmasking a view means establishing a partial criterion of irrationality and so by opposites a partial criterion of rationality. Psychological unmasking can help in precisely the same way by building up empirical criteria in dealing with ideas for distinguishing the rational from the irrational. The same holds for other forms in which genetic analysis has tried to undertake truth determination. William James argues in his essay "The Sentiment of Rationality" that underlying the whole of truth-seeking is this effort to satisfy our sentiments. Such an approach is found in his familiar pragmatic conception of truth, that truth is the expedient in the way of our thinking. Actually, having discovered a sentiment-component in our drive for truth, he should have gone in precisely the opposite direction—the careful scrutiny of sentiments to discriminate which, as a policy decision, should be given a place in the meaning of truth and which should be excluded. Thus if the desire for stable order is involved, we would have to distinguish the exclusive insistence on universal or strict order and the acceptance of probable order. (Here the Deweyan revelation of the scope of the "quest for certainty" is psychologically helpful genetic analysis in refining the criteria of truth.) Surely, if we decided on pragmatic grounds that control as well as prediction belonged to the decision-base in dealing with ultimate principles of method, this would not mean giving free scope to a dictator to call true whatever increased his control! We should have to discriminate what kind of control is to come into the base and what is not.

Take another illustration, from anthropological theory. The variability of most elements of culture including the variation in beliefs and in languages, suggests that there may be variations in the fundamental categories in which experience is cast. Does this mean that truth is relative to culture? On the contrary, it opens up a new avenue for studying precisely how categories are related to language, and so sifting out divergences and projecting modes of convergence.[12]

A final illustration from the history of the sciences. As we noted above,[13] Philipp Frank asks what made the mechanical model seem unsatisfactory in one age, and later the very prototype of successful explanation. In doing this, he is not establishing a thesis of the historical relativity of theoretical truth in science. On the contrary, such inquiry is pointing to the need to study the history of science in a genetic spirit, in order to be able to prune off localisms and locate unavoidables.

Every fresh type of genetic analysis is thus a possible source for the discovery of our provincialisms, but also a source for techniques to overcome them. The positive contribution of genetic analysis to the truth problem is therefore to assist in the clarification of the *criteria* of truth (similarly, of adequacy or worth). It is an obvious lesson of contemporary epistemology that the concept of truth is no simple one, that the criteria for establishing truth become increasingly complicated as we move from singular descriptive propositions to theoretical statements. The search for criteria here becomes part of the delineation of method for truth discovery. The role of genetic elements in sharpening criteria of rationality is thus precisely parallel to the role of psychology and physics of perception in providing sharper criteria of adequate and dependable observation.

It is to be noted finally, that this outcome gives to genetic analysis exactly the same role that emerged in general in the last chapter. Where it is not concerned with frankly causal questions and questions of effects, uses, functions, it is concerned with presenting a clearer understanding of meaning. In this case, the concept whose content is being extended is probably best designated as 'the pursuing of truth.'

[12] The general thesis of the relativity of categories to linguistic processes of specific cultures was propounded by B. L. Whorf. See his *Language, Thought, and Reality*, ed. J. B. Carroll (New York and London, 1956), especially pp. 207-70, "Science and Linguistics." For brief comment on this general outlook, see my "Interpretation and the Selection of Categories," in *Meaning and Interpretation*, "University of California Publications in Philosophy," Vol. XXV (1950), esp. pp. 66-69.

[13] See p. 147.

CHAPTER TWELVE

SCARCITY AND ABUNDANCE
IN ETHICAL THEORY

So far, in considering causal-explanatory method, we have dealt chiefly with theoretical issues. The few brief illustrations offered took moral norms or ethical ideas and showed how they might be clarified by context-research. In this chapter, I should like to outline a type of case study which moves in the opposite direction. It starts with a clearly nonethical theme—a large-scale change in material conditions of human existence—and seeks in a historical and comparative way to suggest its effects on moral norms and ethical ideas. It hopes thereby to illustrate the desirability of more extended research from a causal-explanatory perspective in ethical theory.

The theme to be considered is that of scarcity and abundance. It is especially relevant to the atomic age. For although the destructive possibilities of the atomic age are at present uppermost in men's minds, there is a strong undercurrent of speculation about the constructive changes that atomic power will make possible in human life. The keynote of this speculation is the replacement of scarcity by abundance and control. It differs only in degree from the technological optimism that has characterized the past half century, but the difference is great enough to give the problem a central place in reflective thought. Neo-Malthusian pessimists may fear the rapidity of population growth and underscore erosion, devastation and wasteful exploitation of fundamental resources. But there are sufficient grounds for hope—if only war and self-willed destruction can be avoided—that abundance replacing scarcity will some day be the fundamental fact underlying all social, political and cultural life.

I

One has only to study the history of man to see how thoroughly men's relations, institutions, feelings, and ideas are permeated with the awareness of scarcity and the insecurity and strife that it entails. Moral philosophy is no exception. And while it is far too early to assess the detailed consequences of an abundance that is not yet and may not soon be achieved, it is not too early to reflect on the kind of role that abundance replacing scarcity can have in the formulation of ethical concepts and methods.

To assess the material conditions—social and organic—of ethical theory is a task that moral philosophers have been prone to neglect. It is well to be reminded by Morris R. Cohen of the immediate material bases of the very sense of values: "What makes it possible for us to carry on, instead of quitting as we can when we really want to, is not our guess as to the unknown goal, but rather the zest developed by our actual daily experiences, by our organic activities, by the light and warmth of the sun and air, and by the joys of human companionship. When the zest for life is really gone, all words of comfort or exhortation are vain. There is nothing to which to appeal. But wise reflection may fan the flame when it is low, illumine our labor, and increase the scope of our peaceful enjoyments." [1]

Let us look very briefly at the historical role of the scarcity concept in ethical formulations, and then in greater detail at the kinds of changes in ethical constructions that its replacement by an abundance concept might involve. The underlying ethical problem of what constitutes the good life when it has abundance at its command—in short, the objects of ultimate value for mankind—is not our present concern. But the shift in what appear to be means and material conditions will prove to be far-reaching, and its consequences extend into unsuspected areas.

The guiding role of scarcity in the formulation of ethical theory is an old one, although its operation has frequently taken a disguised form. A world of scarcity has been so pervasive a fact that it is accepted as the permanent background of the ethical scene. The setting seems so immovable that little thought is given to its cramping effect upon the action that goes on within the human stage and blame is channeled on other factors in the field.

Plato's *Republic* furnishes a classic illustration. Socrates constructs an ideal society, the simple city of simple tastes. Glaucon brands it a city of pigs. So Socrates enlarges it, adds luxury

[1] Morris R. Cohen, *The Faith of a Liberal* (New York, 1946), p. 7.

services, embellishments, professions, and concludes: "The country, too, which was large enough to support the original inhabitants, will now be too small. If we are to have enough pasture and plough land, we shall have to cut off a slice of our neighbors' territory; and if they too are not content with necessaries, but give themselves up to getting unlimited wealth, they will want a slice of ours."[2]

War is unavoidable, and this necessitates a warrior-guardian group, out of which is elaborated the familiar Platonic class-structure and cultural regimentation. Plato, however, does not attribute the characteristics of his state to the foundation of scarcity, but to the desire for luxury and the passions of men.

In ancient moral philosophy generally the influence of scarcity is refracted through such condemnation of the passions or else through a restrictive ideal of self-sufficiency. These two approaches are united in Epicurean and Stoic theory. Epicurus contracts desire by simplifying tastes and so attains security and peace of mind. The Stoics cut off the spirit from worldly attachments. One of the central components in the stress on intellectual activity in all ancient philosophy is its self-sufficient character. Its domain is abundant and completely accessible. Thinking is the activity in which a man relies most on himself, needs least of the world, trespasses not at all on his neighbor. Thinking unites men just as competing passions for limited objectives divide them. Thinking allows a constant accumulation for all. Hence the intellectual life is a safe investment—it never is precarious or at the mercy of accident.

With the break-up of the medieval outlook and the growth of secular aims, the acquisitive passions acquire respectability. But even the positive pursuit of power reflects in a fundamental way the setting of scarcity. For attention is focused on competition, and the "state of nature" is one of insecurity and the scramble for scarce goods. Hobbes is perfectly clear about the negative basis of the pursuit of power. When he endows mankind with "a perpetuall and restlesse desire of Power after power, that ceaseth only in Death" he adds: "And the cause of this, is not always that a man hopes for a more intensive delight, than he has already attained to; or that he cannot be content with a moderate

2 Plato, *Republic,* tr. F. M. Cornford (New York, 1945), p. 61.

power: but because he cannot assure the power and means to live well, which he hath present, without the acquisition of more." [3]

Even in so sophisticated a system as Kantian ethics, the insecurity of the natural world may be seen as a background. Kant's condemnation of the serpentine windings of utilitarianism clearly reflects the view that the consequences of action are in fact incalculable, so that security of judgment can be found only in the attachment of morality to pure principle. And his very moral argument for the existence of God rests on the assumption that the natural and social world cannot be made to guarantee the unity of virtue with happiness, which is the *summum bonum*.

Only with the flowering of pleasure theory in the school of Bentham is the hold of scarcity both in its condemnation of the passions and in its basic insecurity reaction consciously broken. The difference between ancient and modern pleasure theory, it has so often been pointed out, lies in the shift from a pessimistic to an optimistic outlook. It was, of course, a shift grounded in the promise of trade and industry, in the accession to dominance of the commercial and industrial classes, and the vista of the whole globe as a source of growing wealth and happiness. Bentham can be liberal to all desires. If he allows that "quantity of pleasure being equal, push-pin is as good as poetry," it is because he thinks the world has room for both and more. Abundance is specifically included by Bentham as one of the ends of civil law. If security, the major goal, is provided by protection of property, then abundance needs no special urging.

Desires extend with means. The horizon elevates itself as we advance; and each new want, attended on the one hand by pain, on the other by pleasure, becomes a new principle of action. Opulence, which is only a comparative term, does not arrest this movement once begun. On the contrary, the greater our means, the greater the scale on which we labor; the greater is the recompense, and, consequently, the greater also the force of motive which animates to labor. Now what is the wealth of society, if not the sum of all individual wealth? And what more is necessary than the force of these natural motives, to carry wealth, by successive movements, to the highest possible point?

[3] *Leviathan*, Part I, Ch. XI.

It appears that abundance is formed little by little, by the continued operation of the same causes which produce subsistence. Those who blame abundance under the name of luxury, have never looked at it from this point of view.[4]

Bentham's attitude toward abundance has two elements which are capable of leading in different directions. His fundamental this-worldliness, resting on a realization of the possibility of achieving increasing abundance, sweeps away the disparaging attitude toward desires which had thrived in a background of assumed inevitable scarcity. But his opposition to any organized or collective effort for achieving abundance and his general atomic individualism thwart the development of a fully self-conscious ethics of abundance. In fact, his conception of human nature is capable of sustaining the same type of ethics as the older conception of passion as evil. For with competitiveness and desire for indefinite aggrandizement postulated, the older absolute scarcity is merely replaced by an inevitable relative scarcity.

The Marxist philosophers, taking an international perspective and making collective social action the center of their thinking, gained a fuller vista of the possible role of abundance. They were prompted to this by their view of history as the growth of freedom and their stress on the fundamental part played by the mode of production in determining the character of human life. Engels epitomizes this realization in his *Anti-Dühring:* "In a society in which the motive for stealing has been done away with, in which therefore at the very most only lunatics would ever steal, how the teacher of morals would be laughed at who tried solemnly to proclaim the eternal truth: Thou shalt not steal!" [5] And in similar fashion, he greets the argument that the labor-time of the professional architect and the professional porter are equally valuable with a rejoinder that sweeps away the problem: "It is a fine sort of socialism which perpetuates the professional porter!" [6]

That the possibility of abundance is something seriously to be reckoned with in social and ethical formulations is now a common view. Some still hold to relative scarcity through competi-

4 *The Theory of Legislation,* ed. Ogden (New York, 1931), p. 101.
5 Frederick Engels, *Anti-Dühring,* tr. Burns (New York), p. 109.
6 *Ibid.,* p. 229.

tive desire. Thus Roscoe Pound, in his *Social Control Through Law,* makes it a premise of law that "as the saying is, we all want the earth. We all have a multiplicity of desires and demands which we seek to satisfy. There are very many of us but there is only one earth." [7] But the consequences of nation devouring nation in the attempt to encompass the globe are now too sinister, and the pursuit of global conquest by any nation will thwart the very abundance for which it may hope. Thus the promise of tremendously increased abundance for all mankind is the only alternative to total destruction.

II

Serious objections will be raised in ethical theory to assigning a moral significance to the transition from scarcity to abundance.

One objection comes from the dominant ethical tradition with its sharp separation of content from context. "What has abundance to do with moral truth?" it will be said. "It may determine whether men have the means to carry out what is right, but how can it relate to ends, or be in any sense determinative of what is right or wrong?" In this view, morality is regarded as the assertion of a set of truths which remain true whether they are applied or not.

Even under the objection, however, nothing prevents various truths from changing in relative "importance." The profound truths of one age may become the trivial truths of another age. "Thou shalt not scalp thy neighboring tribesman" once had relevance in America. No doubt it is even now a sound moral injunction. Nor is its content adequately disposed of by subsuming it under "Thou shalt not kill," which is still very pertinent. For scalping has a different social, psychological and ethical content; it differed from murder just as does our killing in warfare, and such differences can, as we have seen in Chapter Ten, best be discovered by careful attention to the causal context.

It should be noted further that the objector does not represent the unanimous verdict of the ethical tradition. A great part of naturalistic ethics does not make the sharp distinction of ends and means involved in his criticism, and would therefore readily

[7] Roscoe Pound, *Social Control Through Law* (New Haven, 1942), p. 64.

admit a developed technique of preventing or transcending problems as an essential technique of ethics.[8]

What is more, great or important means acquire moral quality in the very organization of human energy they make possible. When Henry A. Wallace, in his *Century of the Common Man* speech, offered the vista of a pint of milk a day for every child throughout the world, all the jibes of articulate reaction could not rob it of its spiritual quality as a symbol of the human love of the child and hope of the future.

A second objection hits at the very heart of the technique of abundance. For the essence of an ethical approach in terms of abundance is to solve moral problems by transcending them. The objector will deny that this is a genuine mode of ethical solution: to manage to avoid facing problems is not to answer them, it is to be lucky rather than moral. Therefore, he turns for ethical insight to the extreme case, the "marginal" situation, the choice which is individual and final, and cannot be subsumed under readily applicable general rules. For example, Jean-Paul Sartre, referring to the choices made by resistance workers in France under the Nazi occupation, says: "And the choice that each of us made of his life and of his being was an authentic choice because it was made face to face with death, because it could always have been expressed in these terms: 'Rather death than . . .' "[9]

This objection confirms as much as it refutes the underlying claims of an ethical approach in terms of abundance, for it focuses its special attention upon the unavoidable scarcities and insecurities of life. From one point of view in the moral economy at least, death is the scarcity of time, however much metaphysically it presents itself as the cessation of individual being.

A further assumption of the existentialist ethical analysis is the individualist character of morality. If, however, morality be regarded as social in its inmost nature, in the sense discussed in Chapter Nine, then the marginal case presents no problem in principle. How a man should behave in the face of death, where sacrifice is desirable, how a man should assume creative responsibility

8 See, for example, Dewey and Tufts, *Ethics* (rev. ed.; New York, 1932), Ch. X.

9 "The Republic of Silence," in *The Republic of Silence,* comp. and ed. A. J. Liebling (New York, 1947), p. 498-99.

in unique situations, are problems of concrete social evaluation. To focus them as primarily individual problems because the individual is the one who dies is to substitute psychology for morality. How a particular man deals with crucial situations enables us to judge the structure of his personality. Perhaps it is true that every man has his critical point, or breaking point, beyond which all moral quality disappears and there is simply struggle for survival—though for some the point is so high that death will first overtake them. And perhaps there is a correlation between a given man's critical point and the qualities of his moral feeling. But in principle to make this the central phenomenon of morality is as if one studied language as primarily an expression of individual emotion just because one does not speak unless one is "moved" sufficiently.

A third and more immediate objection at this point is the fear sometimes expressed that the technique of transcending ethical problems may adversely affect character. It is argued that if men are not hardened in the school of ethical torment they will be softer and unable to meet crucial problems, if they arise, without shock. This is a serious question, comparable to the issue in bringing up children as to whether the parents ought always to avoid saying "no" to the child by skillful steering and reconstruction of situations or whether they ought deliberately to allow some crucial negations to arise in order that the child should not become "self-willed."

This type of objection is to some extent a reflection of the era of scarcity itself. It has much in common with the claims that civilization makes men decadent. It seems to rest on the assumption that an achieved abundance is itself insecure, so that men should be ready for its disappearance at any time. But we do not now train men in the habits of the frontier wilderness, on the assumption that city life may suddenly vanish. So we must estimate realistically whether an achieved abundance is a temporary windfall or genuinely secure. In general, the ultimate effect on character of particular techniques for transcending problems is itself a problem of experimental psychology. If a utopian abundance makes life too easy and men in some definite sense "weak," then hardening processes can be incorporated into collective experience. At most, therefore, such types of objections provide certain cautions within an ethic of abundance, rather than grounds for general rejection of such an ethic.

III

Just as scarcity connotes absence of means and precariousness of realizing ends, abundance implies availability of materials, knowledge and control. We are not speaking of magical fulfillment such as Aladdin's lamp (or even Gyges' ring), but specifically of existent technology, attainable security, and the scientific inventiveness which reasonably assures progress and increasing control. It is not the static abundance of an agricultural community with rich soil on which a plentiful yield of traditional crops is assured, but the growing fields of applied physical science and social organization. Given such a background we may see at least three ethical consequences of abundance:

(1) It can prevent a scramble for scarce goods by providing enough of a given good for everyone's consumption. Thus it can remove many a basis for crime or strife.

(2) Where there are distinct and noncompeting desires which nevertheless conflict because of a crowded field, abundance may remove the ground of the discrepancy and allow each desire separate and diverse expression. For example, if materials are sufficiently abundant so that apartments have sound-proof walls, many an obvious clash is removed, hence many an ethical controversy or legal complaint.

(3) Knowledge coupled with resources makes possible more long-range planning and development of character, hence anticipatory prevention of desires and attitudes that are a source of frustration and conflict. Abundance means a higher quality of educational system, greater individualization, attention to personal and emotional problems, remedial treatment of criminality where it occurs, and hosts of reforms whose type and beneficial effects have long been clear to educators, social theorists and practical commissions of experts, but whose extension has always been thwarted on budgetary grounds.

The way in which obligations, virtues and vices shift as we go from scarcity to abundance may be seen in greater detail if we take one illustration of an already accomplished transition.

Water is a constant good both for drinking and washing. Yet how different are the duties and attitudes ethically relevant in a small community situated on a lake, in a larger community that imports its water as a commodity, and in a large industrialized city of today. In the first, the essential problems are those of avoiding pollution. Rules are directed to the individual; they are simple but strict. Without special problems of transportation, with direct resort to the lake when a pump breaks down, there need be no borrowing of water, no rationing of supply. In the second case, however, the problems of water resemble very much the current case of milk. Given the old-fashioned water carrier of many a European city of the past, the whole ethics of buying and selling, of property and theft, of quality of commodity, are immediately relevant. (If water cannot be diluted it can be polluted.) There is the ethic of charity, the virtue of gratitude; there is room for ethical problems of borrowing and of interest. And apart from all this there are additional calculations about the number of baths that can be afforded and the relative values of cleanliness and other achievable objectives with a given limited means.

In a modern city, the issues have been completely changed. At first sight water may seem to have been removed from the domain of moral problems. Given public fountains reasonably distributed, as well as public lavatories, the quenching of thirst and cleanliness (except as cleanliness depends on living quarters, clothes, etc.) are open to all, and each may take according to his need, not according to means or as a reward for work. Nevertheless, although moral issues are screened by the impersonal character of the relationship, there are very definite virtues and obligations involved in a number of different areas. On the technical side, there are problems of responsibility of technicians in care of reservoirs, in maintenance of transportation facilities, etc. These are the virtues of responsible workmen. There are all the obligations of a civil service system, an ethics of impersonal choice of personnel as against a partisan patronage system. There are problems of justice in fixing of wage-scales and conditions of work. From the point of view of supporting the system, different principles of taxation may be employed which raise quite different issues for consumers: water meters and payment according to amount used, special water tax, or support of water system from general tax fund. That such differences involve moral as well as economic components was seen, for example, in the discussions that centered around the Beveridge report on social security in England; it recommended financing partly through general taxation, partly through individual contributions in order to give the feeling of participation. (The whole issue of moral attitudes toward the general tax fund is well worth special study by moral philosophers.) Again, from the point of view of the consumer there are virtues of care and conservation involving fixing of leaking faucets, not wasting water, repressing of desire for a free flow in washing dishes as against use of a dishpan and curbing length of showers when the mayor warns that the rainfall has been insufficient to replenish reserves. These are problems of education, although some of them may be removed in turn by the technique of abundance—for example, the familiar automatically closing faucets in public fountains so that the problem of care itself disappears.

The above by no means constitutes a complete treatment of the ethics of water supply, but it is sufficient to enable us to offer preliminary generalizations about the typical direction of moral problems and the shift in ethical ideas in a situation of achieved abundance:

(1) The problems involved tend to be viewed as whole-society problems, whether the mechanism of accomplishment be state enterprise, co-operative enterprise, or competitive enterprise. This entails, as a minimum, social regulation of standards from a point of view of broad social welfare.

(2) Insofar as maintenance of abundance or productivity is a central task, many virtues and vices, duties and responsibilities will be oriented toward this end. The whole moral tone of these rules will depend upon the importance of specific ends in the scheme of life. Care, for example, may very well acquire the moral tone that thrift once had, as our technological system becomes more complex and a single slip may produce a plane crash or an explosion.

(3) Problems of distribution of costs or burdens become fundamental. These are in principle society-wide problems and not usually to be determined by the special character of the field

alone. Issues concerning the price structure in a society and the desirable extent of social control through subsidies, price-fixing, etc., as well as the questions of taxation referred to above, illustrate these problems.

(4) The greater the abundance the more the principle of distribution of the good tends to become "to each according to his need." This is clear in public drinking-fountains, in the modern theory of educational opportunity, and so forth. The judgment of need in the case of water is left to the individual, given complete abundance. This may be supplemented by guidance (as in health or vocational guidance). In such matters there may also be the democratic regulation of limits and standards, for example, of ability to become a doctor, or of social need for doctors. Again, it must be noted that water is a material quantitatively divisible, easily disposed of, and having uses by itself. Fresh problems of social relations would arise, for example, in an abundance of airplanes.

(5) If relative scarcity shows itself within a field of abundance, it may be dealt with by a subethic of of rationing, and does not entail abandoning the whole ethics of abundance. Numerous special principles require elaboration in such a subethic. There are, however, limits beyond which the system itself collapses. Yet even here, from the point of view of the ethics of abundance, general orientation should be toward recovery of abundance by increased productivity. In this sense, the ethics of abundance urges men to get together for the increase of the common good rather than regard as their central moral task the development of principles by which a limited good may be partitioned. Thus predatory habits are avoided by establishing the goal of abundance even in a period of scarcity. This is the point implicit in the common notion of replacing the struggle of man against man by that of man against nature.[10]

(6) The ethics of abundance provides no answer for situations of extreme scarcity. It does not itself tell men what to do in the typical textbook situation of two men on a log out at sea when one must let go or both will sink. It does, however, urge the manufacture of safer boats, the abolition of war and torpedoes,

[10] The ethics of abundance is to the ethics of scarcity as the abolition of the causes of war is to The Hague regulation of war practices.

and the development of scientific techniques in advance for emergency situations—a life belt for every man, inflated rubber lifeboats, and so forth. In this sense, the ethics of abundance is addressed to society rather than the individual alone, to educators and legislators and men who plan ahead. The situations of tragedy are not removed but the ethics that gives a central role to abundance aims to make them the exception rather than the type in terms of which moral principles are to be framed. In this sense, the traditional preoccupation of ethical teaching with "individual" rather than "social" morality reflects the ethics of scarcity.

(7) In general, an ethics of abundance takes a positive rather than a negative approach to moral questions. It is less concerned with telling men what they must *not* do than with working out positive opportunities for harmonious human happiness. Thus its interpretation of liberty will not be merely that social control over the individual is lacking, but that determinate conditions of human welfare be brought into existence. Its interpretation of equality will not be merely impartiality of treatment and the absence of discrimination, but the effective release of all men's initiative and capacities. This same approach, ethically and psychologically, will characterize the handling of the traditional problems of social philosophy.

It should be stressed in conclusion that to realize the possible role of abundance in ethical theory is not merely to attempt a portrait of a possible future. For the acquisition of abundance may begin to function as a present goal, acting because it is so vast, as a standard by which many of our present virtues, vices, obligations and responsibilities may be assessed. Thus awareness of what is possible may become a driving force in the midst of the actual. The realization that a great part of our morality is grounded in scarcity and the expectation that the achievement of abundance and social self-sufficiency will release untold human energies, generating a veritable flowering of human values, are twin pivots in the reconstruction of a moral outlook today. And they illustrate amply the paradoxical truth of human life that attention to material conditions provides the only high road to general enhancement of ideal goods.

PART FIVE

EVALUATIVE METHOD

CHAPTER THIRTEEN

THE EVALUATIVE STANDPOINT

The moving frontier of ethics is to be found in the enterprise of evaluation. Obviously, this is not an isolated or independent activity. It employs materials which can be analyzed, described, explained. As a human activity, its own results may be causal in revising the conduct or moral attitudes of those concerned, and it may itself be analyzed or described as a process. But *in its employment,* or *in its occurrence as an activity,* it is clearly distinguishable from analyzing, describing, or finding causes; it furnishes a distinct standpoint among those we are considering.

The complex theoretical problems that arise in the evaluative standpoint will be illustrated in the two studies of this part. One of these is concerned with the basic issue of the evaluation of ends. The second attempts an exposition on the ethical level of the way in which a single ethical category—in this case, the category of ideals—may be dealt with evaluatively in the light of analytic, descriptive, and causal-explanatory exploration. In dealing with evaluation, perhaps more than in any other part of the study of method in ethical theory, we become conscious of the vistas of effort opening up and realize that the title of this book must be taken with literal seriousness. We have not been furnishing an ethical theory ready for use, but doing only a preparatory investigation into the methods for constructing such a theory. In these introductory remarks, I should like to comment briefly on the following questions: [1] What are the occasions of evaluation? Who evaluates? What is the scope of evaluation? What is the conceptual apparatus of evaluation? Where does evaluation get its standards or criteria?

The occasions of evaluation. The evaluative standpoint may be adopted on any of the levels of phenomena we explored. A

[1] For a sketch of the problems of evaluation approached from another direction, see May Edel and Abraham Edel, *Anthropology and Ethics* (Springfield, Ill., 1959), Ch. XV.

study of its occasions would be a causal inquiry into the conditions under which we take up a selective, critical, weighing, judging, appraising attitude, and the typical objects towards which it is directed. Stated so broadly, evaluation in an implicit or explicit form is woven into a great part of our conscious activity. It parallels the wider area of values, rather than the narrower confines of morality.[2] Even the rudimentary value-experience of *prizing* is itself sometimes analyzed as a kind of holding on to, or electing, and so regarded as a kind of evaluating. (The relation between prizing and evaluating has had roughly the same philosophical vicissitudes as that between perceiving and understanding.) Again, that evaluating tends to shade into assessing and estimating and discriminating, means that the category will come to embrace many decision processes in all sorts of areas. How far a critical theory will want to render evaluation specific so as to draw sharper lines between evaluation and valuation, is a particular problem in fashioning the conceptual apparatus of the field.

Who evaluates? Formally, this is easily answered. Evaluating is done by persons, either as an individual process or as a group process. But this covers, of course, the central problem of what is a person. Let us admit that, in the long run, no satisfactory account of the evaluative standpoint will be achieved which does not have a coherent theory of the self, and the relation of persons in society.

The scope of evaluation. Correlative with the remarks about the occasions of evaluation is the recognition that evaluation as a process has unrestricted scope. The levels that description maps can be used as steps for a mounting or descending evaluative process. Conduct and desire can be evaluated in terms of their own aims, and these in turn from a moral point of view, and morality may be assessed from the point of view of an ethical theory. But both theory and morality may be assessed from some loftier perspective, or else for their impact on some range of conduct and desire. The self that is evaluating is always standing somewhere, but analysis is sometimes perplexed by its speed in moving about.

The unrestricted scope of evaluation is strikingly evident when

[2] See above, p. 185.

it goes beyond the content of a morality and questions its very form or categories. Thus Nietzsche sometimes condemns ideals as elements in a morality, regarding them as poisons occasionally needed as cures.[3] Similarly, one can ask for an evaluation of the category of obligation. Why have obligations? This does not mean denying their existence, or proposing their abolition, nor is it merely a causal investigation. It may be a search for a functional role that obligation has in human life. It is interesting to quote Nietzsche's sketch of points evaluating morality as a whole, in his *Will To Power:*[4]

> To what extent was morality *dangerous* to Life?
> (a) It depreciated the joy of living and the gratitude felt towards Life, etc.
> (b) It checked the tendency to beautify and to ennoble Life.
> (c) It checked the knowledge of Life.
> (d) It checked the unfolding of Life, because it tried to set the highest phenomena thereof at variance with itself.
>
> Contra-account: the *usefulness* of morality of Life.
> (1) Morality may be a preservative measure for the general whole, it may be a process of uniting dispersed members: it is useful as an agent in the production of the man who is a 'tool.'
> (2) Morality may be a preservative measure mitigating the inner danger threatening man from the direction of his passions: it is useful to *'mediocre people.'*
> (3) Morality may be a preservative measure resisting the life-poisoning influences of profound sorrow and bitterness: it is useful to the 'sufferers.'
> (4) Morality may be a preservative measure opposed to the terrible outbursts of the mighty: it is useful to the 'lowly.'

There is much to criticize in Nietzsche's conception, but it does convey a sense of the scope of ethical evaluation in putting on the scales the whole of morality as a human phenomenon. It may, of course, be deceptive, since he may really be evaluating only one form of morality—the Hebraic-Christian humanitarian tradition—in the light of an implicit alternative. In that case, we would have here the clash of moralities rather than the evaluation of morality as such.

We may go even further and ask the same question concerning

---

3 See below, p. 335.

4 *The Will to Power*, tr. A. M. Ludovici (New York, 1924), I, 219-20.

ethical theorizing itself. This follows from our analysis of ethics as a third level of describable phenomena. It then becomes a historical problem of assessing the trend of ethical theorizing and its benefits or disadvantages in the light of pre-assigned standards. Usually, distinctions are drawn and good theories set aside from bad. Thus Bentham saw ethical theories other than his own type as simply mistakes or misdirected formulations of the search for happiness.[5] Often, all ethical theorizing is taken to be for the good, as expressive of the inquiring spirit of man, or his spiritual needs. Sometimes, however, all ethics is taken to be bad. For example, Max Stirner, in his *The Ego and His Own,* sees ethical theorizing as an attempt to seduce the individual from attending to his own real interest—himself. Or Lewis Feuer, arguing that ethical modes of expression come into being to solve social antagonisms not by removing their causes but by moral coercion, predicts that ethical theorizing will disappear as an enterprise when social antagonisms are solved.[6] The estimation of the role of ethical theorizing itself is thus part of the theory of cultural integration and historical development, which itself embodies criteria of judgment. To determine the mode of evaluating ethical theories is clearly central to ethical theory itself.

Is there a limit to evaluation? The apparently endless scope of evaluation raises serious theoretical problems. It is not simply that there is so much susceptible of evaluation. For domains of analysis, description, and causal investigation are likewise apparently endless. The critical issue in evaluation appears to arise rather from the use of standards in the process of evaluation. Once these are described and analyzed, how shall they themselves be evaluated? In terms of other standards beyond? And so on ad infinitum?

The conceptual apparatus of evaluation. Clearly, a considerable part of the development of the theory of evaluation will be carried on from the analytic standpoint. This concerns the clarification of concepts and the refinement of methods. The discussions of definition and reasoning in Part Two illustrate some of these problems. But the actual working out of the conceptual

---

[5] *Principles of Morals and Legislation* (London, 1823), Ch. II.

[6] "Ethical Theories and Historical Materialism," *Science and Society,* VI (1942), 242-72.

apparatus consists in the study of the specific concepts—'good,' 'right,' 'ought,' and so forth. To undertake this task itself has not been the aim of this present book: our concern has been rather with the methodological basis from which it could be more satisfactorily accomplished.

One salutary tendency in the recent treatment of ethical concepts has been to emancipate oneself from the hold of specific linguistic terms and to realize that they have to be dealt with by reference to functions. Perhaps the most difficult question of conceptual apparatus that then arises is whether ascribing obligation is to be recognized as a function distinct from evaluation. There has been considerable inclination to do so.[7] It is not an easy problem; in fact, it is a perennial issue, being a contemporary version of what has been traditionally discussed as the right and the good. On the whole, however, I think a more satisfactory conceptual apparatus can be achieved by regarding obligation as dealing with applicational theory—the engineering of ethics, as it were—rather than by a sharp initial dichotomy within ethical theory itself. This approach would have to be justified by an extensive analytic, descriptive, and causal inquiry, and its resultant status would be a policy recommendation in ethical theory.

Standards of evaluation. The problem of standards is too often oversimplified. It is not just a question of finding a final place on which to stand. It is a complex inquiry arising in many different forms, in many different contexts. Are there ultimate moral laws to serve as ultimate standards? This entails an analysis of the concept of moral laws. Are there ultimate rational methods applicable in all ethical evaluation? This involves the analysis of rationality in ethical theory. Are there ultimate goals? The answer is part of the search for invariant elements in human striving. Is the search for ultimacy itself vain? This depends on how successfully an ethical theory can embrace the phenomenon of endless regression within its formulations. Is there any metaphysical way of transcending the process? The phenomenon of transcendence itself merits scientific scrutiny from several points

7 E.g., Henry D. Aiken, "Evaluation and Obligation: Two Functions of Judgments in the Language of Conduct," *The Journal of Philosophy*, XLVII (1950), 5-22; Alexander Sesonske, *Value and Obligation* (Berkeley and Los Angeles, 1957).

of view. Inquiry along the various approaches to the problem of ultimate standards leads to the heart of what is traditionally oversimplified as the problem of the relation of existence and value.

It is obvious then that a central study in the development of an ethical theory must concern itself with a theory of standard-formation. In the present book, there will be some indication of the problem of criteria and how they are dealt with in the task of evaluating ends and evaluating ideals. A general attempt to work out the concept of a dynamic standard for evaluation was made in a previous book,[8] employing the idea of a *valuational base* as a fusion of fundamental needs, perennial aspirations, discovered high values, central necessary conditions, and critical contingent problems. It was suggested that such a base, as the outcome of critical inquiry, answered the demand for a standard to diminish indeterminacy in ethical judgment, that there was a sense in which it was not arbitrary, but that it was open to modification in the light of further experience. In short, it functioned in ethics in a way somewhat parallel to that in which the accepted body of scientific knowledge functions in giving us a factual picture of our world. Methodologically, then, it was neither an absolute ultimate, nor an arbitrary product of the will. But the logic of its justification is a large task and, to be fully done, it has to be part of a fully developed ethical theory. For we must not overlook the problems that a theory of standards has to face. In pursuing the lines we have suggested, it must deal with situations of competing standards, with indeterminate situations or unstructured situations in which no standards are apparent, with the creative element in standard-formation, and so with the vast area of the traditional problem of free will. I believe that a theory of ethics embodying the conception of the valuational base will be able eventually to cope with these problems successfully, precisely because it makes explicit place for incorporating as part if its analysis the growing knowledge of man brought by the human sciences.[9]

[8] *Ethical Judgment*, Ch. IX.
[9] For some consideration of these issues, see my *Science and the Structure of Ethics*, Ch. IV.

CHAPTER FOURTEEN

THE EVALUATION OF ENDS

Sooner or later, every treatment of evaluative method has to face the problem of how we can evaluate ends. The treatment of ultimate ends, particularly, shows most clearly the conceptual apparatus with which a theory operates and where it goes to get its standards or criteria for evaluation. It will, accordingly, assist our exploration of evaluative method if we face this problem directly.

There is a long-standing and tediously familiar view that while *means* admit of evaluation because they can be assessed in terms of the ends to which they lead, the *ends* themselves—genuine ends, real ends, ultimate ends—do not admit of evaluation; they are simply held or entertained or pursued. Aristotle said that we deliberate about the means, but we wish for the end as an expression of the order of our nature. Medieval religious theory implanted ends in things, so that the very stone falling towards the center of the earth expresses thereby its love of God. Modern positivism, making short shrift of the metaphysical underpinnings, left ends without their credentials. They remained suspended, so to speak, in mid-air, held up by nothing, it is alleged, but the bare volition of the holder. Hence, they acquire an appearance of arbitrariness. If they are challenged by opposing ends, there is, in the trite phrase, nothing to dispute about. What is there left to say but that when we affirm ends—ultimate ends—our language is expressive, emotive, persuasive, ceremonial, or that we are engaging in any of a host of other practical functions that an eager analytic eye can readily discern, and that in consequence there can be no rational or empirical mode of validation for judgments of ends? Russell's optative formulation [1] is a simple illustration: to say that an end is good is simply to say "Would that everybody desired it!"

We are all familiar with the shape of these views in the social

---

[1] Bertrand Russell, *Religion and Science* (New York, 1935), Ch. IX.

sciences. Social science is regarded as value-free, and the prescriptive is somehow out of bounds. It is turned over to philosophy or to religion or to private volition or to intuition, and so on, and in each case it often falls victim to subjectivism, dogmatism, or arbitrary stipulation. Although it is fashionable today to blame the positivists for the outcome, they are, after all, simply drawing the conclusions of the fundamental picture of ends in the traditional philosophies, once certain metaphysical presuppositions are removed.

Whether our problem admits of precise formulation or whether it represents rather a contemporary mood—perhaps even now already swept aside by onrushing winds of doctrine—it is not easy to say. Sometimes, I confess, it seems to me, in Gide's *mot*, that everything has been said, but because nobody listens it has to be said again. John Wisdom has traced, with great insight, the way in which many provocative philosophical problems go through three stages. In the first, a thesis is declared outrageous, impossible, obviously false. In the second, it is proclaimed as obvious, necessarily true. In the third, it evaporates or is dissolved. Our problem of the evaluation of ends has gone through the preliminary steps. It was first felt outrageous to deny that there are ends "in the nature of things." Then it was felt truistic to assert with Poincaré that an ethical imperative could *not* be deduced from a scientific indicative for the obvious grammatical reason that an imperative does not follow logically from an indicative. Finally, after a whole quarter-century of methodological argumentation the question is reaching its breaking point, although it is not yet clear where we are going. The aim of this chapter is to help carry the problem through Wisdom's third stage. I propose to seek this reorientation, first by some preliminary skirmishing to find a weak spot in our predicament where the defenses may be broken wide open; then by suggesting what has to be done to reconstruct the problem; and finally, by indicating how possible objections may be met.

I

Let us begin the skirmishing with a philosophical fable. Once upon a time, a young philosopher was profoundly in love with a fair maiden. With the articulateness that philosophers sometimes have even in love, he lavished praises on her wondrous beauty, the luster of her presence, the grace of her every mood. It was almost as if he thought a goodly company of Platonic ideas had at last found exemplification without losing so much as an iota of their heavenly perfection. The maiden listened, pleased at first, but then with a deepening sorrow that welled finally into copious tears. He stopped in amazement and heard her say through her sobs: "You won my heart, but now I see you do not love me. You lavish praise on my attributes, but no portion of your love is conferred on my very self. Beauty is frail—your philosophic masters have made that amply clear. The light movement of my hand that so enthralls you will lose its grace with the heaviness of age. How can the luster of my eye survive the sorrows that life unavoidably brings? Go, love your Platonic ideas that you pursue in me. I will draw my heart back if I can, and hold it for one—if I am fortunate enough to meet and love him—for whom I am a person, and not an illustration."

The philosopher stood transfixed by this outburst. But at last he spoke up: "You, my beloved, are so right that I shall no longer even praise your wisdom. How could I have been so semantically incorrect as to confuse the multitude of adjectives with the noun. But I have not lingered on the semantic surface. Deeply have I probed the nature of my passion. I have bracketed irrelevancies, discounted instrumentalities, set apart collateral joys, even put aside drive satisfactions as too negative in their promise of the release of tension. The joy of our children-to-be is ultimately here as irrelevant as the envious glances of my confreres. I am certain of it now—it is you I love, and I love you for your own sake, not for anything else."

But once more the fair maiden burst into tears, and this time she sobbed even more disconsolately. "Do you mean," she said, "that when we are married and I say to you as wives do in all the best novels, 'Tell me why you love me,' you will be able to do nothing but repeat the fact—the *brute, arbitrary, contingent* fact? If your love for me has the character of an ultimate end for which no reason can be given, is it not then *irrational?* Has it not the ontological status of a *whim?* This is more than I can bear."

And because she was very beautiful, and because he was a gallant spirit, he saw no difficulty in her argument. Her tears called to him, he took her in his arms, and our tale had a happy ending. And so he remained on the level of a *practical solution* for the theoretical problem. And because his solution happened to be a happy one, he thought that the problem was somehow solved.

Somewhere in all the modern controversy about the arbitrary nature of ultimate ends, there has been a strange reversal so that a hitherto perfectly respectable criterion for the good—in fact, what was once regarded as the very definition of the good, that it was pursued completely for its own sake and not for the sake of something else—has been turned into a brand of unjustifiability, of arbitrary presumption.

Enough of skirmishing. Does ultimacy in an end betoken unjustifiability? This depends on what we are to mean by 'ends,' by 'ultimate,' and on how we are to construe the task of 'evaluation.'

II

In the philosophical literature on means and ends, I find three distinct senses in which the means-ends categories are construed. The first and most obvious is purely descriptive of a causal process in time. Some acts or states are steps directed toward other acts or states as goals; both have consequences. The implicit context is one of plans and purposes, or choice, or action analyzed in retrospect. These categories here employed may thus be termed 'steps,' 'goals,' 'consequences.' These are experimentally ascertainable descriptive concepts, whether behavioral or phenomenological. Thus to be pursued for its own sake would be a descriptive property of some goals, irrespective of further judgments of frequency, relatedness, or value. It might mean that they could be envisaged as isolated, as complete experiences in themselves, as being pure in the sense of containing no elements of steps to another goal, and so on. In the light of the claims so often made that no sharp distinction can be drawn between means and ends, it is important to stress that at least in the sense of step and goal one can offer behavioral indices and introspective tests of what would be a step without goal quality and a goal without step quality, whether or not pure samples can be found in human experience.

I find a second and distinct set of means-ends concepts in those philosophers who are attempting to interpret the lessons of contemporary psychology in our century. Take, for example, Dewey's familiar picture of the means-ends continuum and his persistent interpretation of all ends-in-view as really means—"means to unification and liberation of present conflicting confused habits and impulses." [2] I do not believe, as is so often alleged, that he is being merely hortatory, and setting up the pervasive goal of growth and expansive process as the one great end. There is this upward-and-onward element, and anyone who wants to stay behind is (in Dewey's own phrase) a "molly-coddle"; but there is more. Dewey is bringing in a new set of categories into means-ends theory to give a place to the insight of contemporary psychology that human behavior, and all qualitative distinctions that can be made in its description, involve an underlying dynamic tension-system. We shall not enter into controversies about the best characterization of this dynamical aspect—whether you choose to speak of drives, instincts, needs, or in Dewey's own more behavioristic concepts, of habit-configurations. Suppose we speak neutrally of 'drives' for the underlying dynamic element, and 'expression-objects' for the overt activities and qualities that express them in the behavior-experience continuum, without taking a stand on such contemporary psychological controversies as functional autonomy versus unavoidable drive-dependence, or specific determinate instincts versus generalized energy-patterns.

The use of the categories of drive and expression-object does embody the psychological thesis that drives provide the motor-power from which the intensity of held goals is derived; that the quality of a present goal depends on the state of the underlying drives and the pattern of their specific economy; that sometimes even where no present qualitative distinction can be found in the goals held, the underlying drive picture provides a basis for predicting subsequent qualitative emergence—e.g., that one man will tire of a goal when he achieves it whereas another man will increasingly relish it. Note too that in the social sciences we find a parallel way of thinking when social goals are seen as the expression of social needs, and when changes in social ideals are traced to historical transformation in social needs. The logic in the analysis of these social relations is more complex and more dif-

2 *Human Nature and Conduct* (New York, 1930), p. 229.

ficult, but in type it is parallel to drives and expression-objects. Whether we are dealing then with individual life or with social groups, an item in the behavior-experience continuum may be looked at in terms of its place in a step-goal-consequence framework or in terms of a drive and expression-object framework. The thesis that every item which is a goal is also an expression-object is clearly an empirical thesis, and that is why the two sets of concepts have to be kept analytically distinct.

I find a third sense of the means-ends notion which is frankly of a value type. This is seen in such expressions as 'the ends of life' or in the ready equation of 'a man's ends' with 'a man's conception of the good.' Similarly, a term like 'extrinsic good' is synonymous with 'instrumental good,' which implies that 'intrinsic good' is what has 'end-value.' It is not surprising that to say 'Pleasure is the end of life' is readily taken as if one had said 'Pleasure is the good.' The ancient philosophies, as our initial skirmishing indicated, regularly assumed the identity of 'the good' and 'ultimate end.' A great part of modern ethical theory has been concerned with separating them; witness, for example, Hartmann's insistence on an axiological domain quite separate from a metaphysical domain, or G. E. Moore's familiar concept of the naturalistic fallacy for any equation of 'good' with any psychological or metaphysical or, in fact, any descriptive term. Where there has been so much fire directed against a view we must recognize that it at least represents one tradition in usage. And so we distinguish as the third sense of means and ends that of 'cost' and 'value.' These are not wholly satisfactory terms, but they do have some advantage in their very bareness. Thus to speak of the cost gets rid of any temporal reference in the notion of the instrumental, and eliminates confusion with steps: for costs may be paid on the installment plan after value received, but there are never future steps for a present goal. Again, the term 'value' helps us maintain a certain neutrality in our present inquiry to the specific content or the specific type of ethical theory to which one might adhere. It has a certain disadvantage in that we shall have to speak of evaluating values—but this may prove to be an advantage in disguise.

We have replaced the means-ends categories by three distinct sets of categories—steps, goals, consequences; drive and expression-objects; and cost and value. I assume that these sets are relatively independent and not to be logically reduced to one another. For even if there is an empirical reduction, the concepts have to be kept logically distinct to be empirically related. If a metaphysical reduction is attempted—as, for instance, if one objected to drive-concepts as potentiality-concepts and sought to reduce them to phenomenal succession-patterns—then it raises still unsolved logical problems (for example, of contrafactual conditionals); in any case, such reductive attempts have not succeeded.

We began with the problem of evaluating ends; we now have before us the triple problem—the evaluation of steps, goals, consequences; the evaluation of drives and expression-objects; the evaluation of costs and values. And in each case the focus of attention is on ultimates.

But first how shall we understand 'evaluation'? Clearly, in the ordinary sense it is a process of assessing something against certain *criteria*. It is like measuring or grading or ordering. What criteria are and what they are criteria of, what they may be surrogates for, is of course the heart of the question. But let us first watch them in action.

Beginning then with *goals,* as the end-concept in our first conceptual set, there is no difficulty in seeing that goals are constantly evaluated. There are hosts of criteria, readily available and commonly employed, and there are rough judgments of relevance, applicability, and context. If a goal is isolable—that is, if it can be envisaged by itself, as a swim can be, but perhaps liberty cannot, for it involves a whole life-setting—we can inquire about its *purity* or *permanence* or about its *attractiveness,* holding it up like a jewel in the light, as it were. We can place it next to other goals and rate each for its *constructiveness* (support of other goals) or *conflict-potential*. We can put it in the context of required steps and unavoidable consequences and consider its *attainability*. We can regard it in relation to the person or group for whom it is a goal and ask what is its *area* (how much of their total set of aspirations it covers), or what is its *depth* (how fundamental the drives or basic the needs for which it serves as an expression-object). We could probe for its *role* and see whether it served as a whole-hearted aim, an internal conflict compromise, a frustration-reaction involving some mechanism of defense, or a symbol in consciousness for something other than its manifest content; we might even find modes of distinguishing *genuine* from *spurious* goals on this basis. And I suspect we will find that a much larger part of evaluating goals than we ordinarily think, consists not so much in assessing goals in isolation as in determining the desirability that one hold or pursue them.[3]

Now what about ultimate goals; how shall we recognize ultimacy in descriptive terms? An ultimate goal may be simply one that is sought for its own sake. If so, ultimacy is equivalent to the criterion of attractiveness of a goal in isolation. Then there is no problem about evaluating such a goal. For attractiveness is only one criterion, and we can ask all the other questions about it. (The question of evaluating attractiveness in itself, rather than the particular goal which is attractive, is a later one.) Suppose, however, that something more is meant by an ultimate goal; we must then look for a further experiential mark. For example, men often mean by an ultimate goal one they would rather die than give up pursuing. But clearly, one would not want to stop evaluating here. Socrates said he would rather die than give up his philosophical inquiries, and he did, but Nazism too could have its martyrs. As I have suggested elsewhere,[4] what may be labelled the Luther-phenomenon—here stand I, I cannot otherwise—which is certainly a clear mark of actual ultimacy, can be treated, as it is in conceptions of heresy, as a mark of corruption. Hence, its justification lies either in a morality of the exaltation of inner conscience, or in a psychology explanatory of its unerring accuracy under specified conditions. A large part of this continued evaluation will therefore use the criterion of *truth of underlying assumptions* and a whole host of other criteria that arise in knowledge-seeking contexts.

I need not prolong this search to show that somewhat comparable criteria and modes of application will hold for *drives* and

[3] Compare Aristotle's remark that we pray for what is good, but we should pray that what is good in general should be good for us. Compare also the important point made by Felix Kaufmann in the logic of science "that the process of validation is not related to propositions as such, but to the *acceptance* of propositions" ("Three Meanings of 'Truth,'" *The Journal of Philosophy*, XLV (1948), 344).

[4] *Ethical Judgment*, pp. 80ff.

expression-objects. Obviously, an expression-object could be evaluated by how effectively it gave expression, whether it helped express other drives at the same time, what element of the genuine or spurious was involved, whether it tended to appear in consciousness as a step or a goal, and so on. Similarly, we could ask of a drive whether it had a wide range of utility or a narrow and fixed path, whether it was readily harnessed for men's goals or proved recalcitrant, disruptive and frustrating. At this point, we forego the temptation to look for refined criteria. But it is worth noting what ultimacy here consists of. Ultimacy in the case of an expression-object would mean that this was a sole and indispensable way in which in fact an unavoidable drive could be satisfied. Ultimacy in the case of a drive would mean that it was a central and inherent part of the human make-up. But in neither case is evaluation compelled to cease and desist because it has come to ultimate ends. We could still see even a major drive— for example, aggressiveness, if one believed in Freud's death instinct—as something we were stuck with because it served some evolutionary purpose under far different conditions in pre-history but for which we are now paying a high price by giving it sublimatory expression at considerable cost. And so an ultimate expression-object could itself be abhorred, grudgingly accepted, welcomed, gloried in, depending on the outcome of detailed evaluation.

So far we have had comparatively clear sailing. But now we turn to the third sense of 'ends,' that is, values or goods. It is probably apparent from the above that we have been employing these terms in evaluating goals, drives, expression-objects. For every criterion used can be seen as a value in action. Is not attractiveness itself to be construed as the appeal of value? Permanence as a criterion presupposes values of security, familiarity; attainability, the value of achievement as such. Drives assume the values of survival, of life, of potential fulfilment. And many criteria involve the value of harmony, the greater value of the more over the less, and so on. Evaluation of values thus poses the problem of how one could evaluate the criteria that have appeared in the process of evaluating ends in the previous two senses.

In some cases, there is little difficulty, but in every case there is complexity. Take, for example, the criterion of attainability. How attainable must a goal be to be more worthy of pursuing? Some will want enough distance to lend enchantment —but for it to be out of sight is too discouraging. The proper degree lies somewhere between immediate grasp and impossibility. That too, will vary for different kinds of goals, perhaps for different kinds of temperaments. Before you are through you are plunged into problems of levels of aspiration, virtues of insight, the dangers of the carrot as a principle of motivation, and the history of the influence of remote ideals.[5]

Let us take so apparently simple a criterion as avoiding frustration, which certainly plays a large role in evaluating expression-objects. On the face of it, to be frustrated is a negative element. But consider it in typical human contexts, and you have to deal with everything from the character-problems arising from too much permissiveness in child rearing to the theories that artistic creativity requires a neurotic base—from Max Nordau's characterization of genius as a degenerative psychosis of the epileptoid variety, to current fears that to psychoanalyze is to normalize or mediocritize! I do not raise this to show that evaluation of criteria is hopeless—that would frustrate my own present thesis—but to show that there is a recognizable process of evaluation resting in part on the growth of knowledge about human beings by which value criteria are themselves considered and stabilized or refined. Even truth itself, which enters as a criterion at many points, has a long history as a value in which it became stabilized over such rivals as pleasant belief, traditional or accepted doctrine—to mention only a few simple contending criteria. Even now, there are cases of application in which doubts are raised. A psychologist may say of a particular person that he could not bear up under a knowledge of what is going on within him. An anthropologist points out that the belief of a particular people in a moral punishment theory of disease is so entwined with their social structure that it would upset some aspects of their social order if they suddenly accepted a germ theory. A government hints that the security of its people is bound up with their not knowing what is going on. But these

---

[5] For some discussion of this problem in the context of ideals, see below, pp. 343f.

are application problems; presumably the person making the declaration uses truth as the criterion to decide at least what it is that is to be withheld!

Or again, what of such criteria as purity or permanence? Aristotle took the absence of means components—what we have called step elements in a goal—to be a condition of highest value; Plato and Bentham thought the presence of instrumentality added to the value. There are obvious reasons why a goal that in fact arises perennially or is continually pursued or appears repeatedly as a focal aim in the lives of men should, other things being equal, have a high rating, but sometimes the lasting is deprecated in favor of the novel. Yet without going into detailed evaluation of each of these, we can see that the opposing criteria might be given each their own fields of application in a non-conflicting way. All this means continuous evaluation.

What could an *ultimate* value criterion mean? I can find at least three possible meanings—apart from simple intuitionist claims. One is a simply stipulated criterion which a man would hold to through thick and thin above everything else. A second would be a criterion that everybody would accept. A third would be a criterion in terms of which all others might be systematized. Let us consider each possibility.

Suppose a man said. "This evaluation of criteria is only a business of running around in circles. You end where you began, and that is stipulation. After all, criteria are innumerable. The world is full of possible perspectives. We could evaluate everything from the point of view of—say, whether Julius Caesar would have liked it." What could we answer? Well, first of all I would be inclined to say that he is not taking stipulation seriously enough. A human being making stipulation of an ultimate value criterion is an impressive phenomenon. A stipulation really held would turn out to be the coping-stone in a structure of desires, beliefs, ambitions, and identifications, which would themselves be capable of evaluation in manifold ways. Show me a man who seriously stipulates the Caesar criterion. He would be an extremely interesting subject for careful study. It is said of the historian Theodor Mommsen that he could never bring himself to write of the death of Caesar, and this accounts for the gap between the end point of his great *History of Rome* and the starting point of its successor. Compare this with the treatment of Caesar in Ferrero, for whom the approval of something by Caesar would seem almost an index of evil. Here, too, a whole network of belief and outlook, a whole social philosophy of freedom and hatred of the dictator lies behind the criterion. I doubt whether human life can show any really unrooted value stipulations, if by roots we do not mean simply causes, but underlying needs and purposes which the value stipulated helps to satisfy.

In the second sense, an ultimate value criterion is one that everyone would accept. Of the criteria considered, *attractiveness* would seem the most likely candidate for this position. Surely to find an end attractive in itself is all that can be said about its worth, *other things being equal*. William James argues that in a moral solitude—a single sentient being introduced into a lifeless world—so far as such a being "feels anything good, he *makes* it good." [6] In short, attractiveness-in-itself of the object needs no justification or further evaluation if there is no competing interest or second being. But suppose we wondered whether a single solitary desire could not be for evil? What line of argument would ensue? Would it make sense to tell the sole sentient being to repress his desire because he has some principle of growth unknown to him, which the expression of this desire might thwart? Or is this introducing a reference to effect on other potentially attractive ends? Perhaps so; I am not interested in denying that if you manage by hypothesis to exclude the possibility of *any* other criterion, you are left only with one. But we must recognize that we are dealing with only one sentient *act;* introduce a second act or a more determinate picture of the being and the first act has lost its power of making something ultimately good, for the second may reverse the first by feeling averse to what the first found attractive.

If we are dealing with a real human being, there is no point in denying that what is attractive is attractive and insofar, at least, a prima facie value criterion. But much more might be asked about it. For example, what part of the phenomenal field does it occupy? Can a value be so attractive as to enslave

---

[6] "The Moral Philosopher and the Moral Life," in *The Will to Believe and Other Essays in Popular Philosophy* (New York, 1956), p. 190.

or render fanatical? Is it a case of genuine attraction, or is there some underlying source for the attractiveness into which we do not have insight? Take even some immediate object of attraction and assume it genuine—say a simple pleasure. Are we not startled to find, in manuals of civilian defense, that poison gases have the fragrance of geraniums or of new-mown hay? It might have been that in human life the sweetest smells betokened the greatest dangers, that the most attractive persons were the most unreliable. In the light of threats of subliminal advertising, I can even conceive of a situation in which the criterion of subjective conviction might be the basis for questioning rather than accepting a belief! I do not raise such possibilities to frighten, but to show that we may be assuming connections in ordinary life which turn out, when laid bare, to be empirical rather than logical or phenomenological. The point is an old one, in spite of its new garb: Herbert Spencer speculated on what evolution might have been like if pleasure were the predominant mark of the unhealthy. Certainly a species in which the attractive does coincide predominantly with what conduces to survival has a tremendous evolutionary advantage.

Let us take an example of an end which has been powerfully conceived of as a good-in-itself and even at times as the highest and purest of goods. Aristotle, it will be recalled, gave this position to contemplation—to direct knowledge of the eternal necessities of the real, the ultimate confrontation of the divine. The intensity of the stress on the direct attractiveness of knowledge in all its purity is nowhere better portrayed than in the picture of Archimedes, the greatest engineer of ancient times, given by Plutarch in his "Life of Marcellus." After listing Archimedes' many practical accomplishments, Plutarch says: "He yet would not deign to leave behind him any commentary or writing on such subjects; but, repudiating as sordid and ignoble the whole trade of engineering, and every sort of art that lends itself to mere use and profit, he placed his whole affection and ambition in those purer speculations where there can be no reference to the vulgar needs of life."[7] Does this not suggest that the aloofness of the contemplative act may embody an aristocratic pre-

7 *Plutarch's Lives*, tr. Dryden, rev. A. H. Clough, (Everyman ed., 1910), I, 474.

dilection for thrusting aside instrumentalities? This would lead us to the whole historical-social assessment of the aristocratic outlook, in terms of its relations in human life and social processes. This would not, of course, belie the direct joys of contemplation—but these too would need analysis. How far are they expressive of a direct instinctual curiosity? Or have they some other basis? What, after all, is contemplation? It is not to be identified with the joys of discovery which a modern scientist might exalt. A whole phenomenology of contemplation is required, and each complex element as it appears would need further evaluation. If it prove, for example, that a sense of instrumentality corrupts the enjoyment of knowledge, we would have to ask whether and why this is universally so, or how far it expresses a particular cultural environment. Compare with this ancient attitude the challenge of St. Francis of Assisi: "Suppose that you have enough subtlety and science to know all things, that you are acquainted with all languages, the course of the stars and all the rest, what have you to be proud of? A single demon in hell knows more than all the men on earth put together. But there is one thing of which the demon is incapable, and which is the glory of man: to be faithful to God." [8] Or again, compare the Baconian maxim that knowledge is power, remembering—for it is too often the fashion to be unfair to Bacon—that he wanted experiments to give light as well as to yield fruit. Clearly, the attractiveness of knowledge in the one case is seen as the expression of a hardening arrogance, in the other as the striving for control. Similarly, for a Deweyan view of knowledge with its strong futuristic stress, with its practicalist tone, its evolutionary biological assumptions about the role of intelligence, and its psychological thesis that the apprehension of meaning and the joy it involves rest upon a consciousness of instrumentality relations. In all this, there is no denial of the value quality of attractiveness as such—for this is the sense in which it is an ultimate value here—but there is clearly a wide area for evaluation of whatever is found to possess this ultimacy, and so of the extended value relevance of the criterion of attractiveness itself.

In the third sense, an ultimate value criterion is one in terms

[8] Quoted in J. H. Randall, Jr., *The Making of the Modern Mind* (revised ed.; New York, 1940), pp. 100-101.

of which all other criteria might be systematized. Now such a theoretical possibility cannot be denied. It would have to be shown that all men at all times were implicitly using such a criterion in all their evaluations, that where they did not there was a discoverable distortion explicable as something other than a rejection of this criterion—for example, lack of knowledge, replacement of conscious by unconscious processes, compromise through giving up hope, and so on. It was in this sense that the utilitarians thought the maximization of pleasure to be the ultimate criterion because they assumed an invariant motivation of men in terms of a pleasure principle. The test of ultimacy here would be to show that the proposed value criterion entered as the central concept in a unified substantiated theory which would in fact explain in a systematic way the actual values found in the life of men, and what is more, that further inquiry would support the theory and future events confirm it. There may be ultimate value criteria in this sense, but candidates for this moral supremacy have not so far been very successful.

Suppose we had such an ultimate value criterion. Would it then be immune to evaluation? On the contrary, it would have achieved its position as a principle by proving its worth and power and role, and so far from being arbitrary, it would constantly be working for its living by providing a sustaining structure for the mass of goals and drives and expression-objects and other value criteria in human life. It would differ in scope but not in type from those values that acquire a position of unavoidability because their pursuit or achievement constitutes a necessary condition for the pursuit or achievement of *any* other value.

I conclude then that in any descriptive sense of 'ultimate' and for any of the three senses of 'ends,' ultimate ends admit of evaluation. Only if this is precluded by definition of 'ultimate'—in which case it is question-begging—does this not follow. But in that case, to say that ultimate ends are beyond dispute is, as Bosanquet long ago pointed out, to do no more than to reiterate that "at any moment we think what we think unless and until we see reason to think otherwise." [9] Or else it is as if we said, "Decisions cannot be disputed, because we have agreed that all dis-

9 Bernard Bosanquet, *The Principle of Individuality and Value* (London, 1912), p. 293.

pute takes place *before* they are made." Even suppose a systematization of value criteria was made in the deductive model, so that
we had staring us in the face the set of ethical axioms—the bare
ultimate stipulations that made up the bases of the system—so
that their proof was ruled out, there would still remain the possibility of what Herbert Feigl has called 'vindication' [10]—the justification of the axioms by showing the purposes underlying their
use as against possible alternatives. But, of course, you will want
to have these purposes systematized and added to the axiom set
itself. And the process will repeat itself. There is no guaranteed
end; the system is always less than on-going life itself, and so the
best that I think you can have at any time is what I have elsewhere called 'the valuational base.' [11] This is an interlocking
structure of human knowledge and human striving, embodying
fundamental human needs, perennial aspirations and major goals,
central necessary conditions, and critical contingent factors of a
given age. Just as the claim to truth or scientific adequacy on the
part of a principle or law in questions of factual knowledge implies prediction that that principle or law will be maintained in
the body of science as further data accumulate and further theoretical refinement is achieved, so the claim for ultimacy in ethics
involves the prediction that the given principle of value will remain in spite of all further growth of knowledge and valuational
experience. The valuational base is not transcended and judged
from some ultimate outside criterion, but it remains open, and
continued valuation and re-evaluation in the light of developing
experience is a permanent possibility.

III

It remains now simply to forestall three possible objections to
the position taken.

The first is critically analytic. "Your scheme," it will say, "has
no clear lines of authority. You evaluate goals in terms of drives
and values, drives in terms of goals and values, values in terms of
goals and drives and other values. This is worse than anarchy—

[10] "De Principiis Non Disputandum . . . ," in *Philosophical Analysis*, ed.
Max Black (Ithaca, 1950).

[11] *Ethical Judgment*, Ch. IX. See above, p. 302.

are there no fixed points, no imperative ought-to-be, no classical highest good, not even an identifiable if indefinable quality of goodness? Is there just a mob of criteria taking in each other's washing, without making up their minds what they are criteria of?"

Answer. The trouble with everybody living by taking in another's washing is not circularity or interdependence but non-productivity. There is no trouble if people do different jobs, which have direct relevance to the mass base of desires, interests, purposes, needs, joys, and so on, out of which ends in all their senses crystallize, which they help organize, and to which in turn they refer in evaluation, with which they interact, and which we can increasingly learn more about. At bottom, there is then a constant creative source. What degree of unity human life shows in ends, in evaluative processes, and in type of moral organization, cannot be determined a priori. It may be easier to draw a picture in a moral autocracy, but life may after all be unavoidably more basically fragmentarian. Is there more circularity in the interplay of criteria we have discerned than in the political processes of a democracy? Did not Aristotle think of constitutional government as involving citizens who rule and are ruled in turn? Abstractly, how could a man be both a ruler and not a ruler? Sometimes what is condemned in abstraction as circularity is thus really circulation of offices. It is the same with our criteria; they too are set in a temporal process and may play different roles in different contexts. And if there is any pattern in the whole process, it may turn out to be not a circle, but a spiral. That depends on whether the general effect is an increasingly productive one.

The second objection is cast in a cultural vein, with an analytic preamble. Is there not, it will be said, a gap in my concept of 'value experience' under which the arbitrary ultimate walks in through the back door? This argument points out that one's value experience is not without its cultural determinants, and so all we really have is the procession of historical ultimate values, whatever the precise cultural conditions. The medievals sought personal salvation as an ultimate. From early Protestantism through the rise of capitalism, one can trace the exaltation of individual self-assertion. Many a contemporary who thinks that he is making ends arbitrary by saying "My ultimate ends are what *I* want" is really asserting as an absolute the value of individual will-assertion, and this too is an ultimate historical value that rules its epoch. There is then an ultimate arbitrariness, but it lies in the parade of historical ideals; these, it is held, can be explained causally, but they cannot be evaluated.

Answer. This mode of analysis achieves profundity when it looks for the values underlying even the theoretical shifts in value theory! But it need not stop there. Why should the historical procession be seen as exhibiting the arbitrariness of ends? Can it not be seen instead as a large-scale process of the evaluating of major ends? Men tried a succession of major life-goals. In Mac-Beath's phrase, which he uses in the title of his book on primitive ethics, they were "experiments in living." [12] Now what the experiments proved may be a matter of dispute. Catholic social philosophy sees them as increasing deterioration of man frustrating his basic striving through overemphasis on the individual will and the counteremphasis on the abstract totality. The Marxians see them as successive stages in the effort of men to expand their productive power for material and cultural ends. There are different kinds of answers, but they all assume that men have some character and some needs and that they are in this changing historical picture attempting to satisfy their needs. And so there is a basis for comparative evaluation; however difficult the historical and cultural and psychological issues, it is too early to write off such human inquiries as inherently incapable of solution. As a matter of fact, does not the very occurrence of the sense of arbitrariness in a cultural context of power conflict itself provide some indication that pure power as an end is profoundly unsatisfactory to human beings?

Our last objection is cast in a metaphysical vein, in the existentialist mode. I have been dealing, it will be said, with *onlooker* ethics, not *participant* ethics. I have assumed that at any time men *have* ends which can be looked for, rather than *creating* ends in the act of choosing. This assumption is called the 'profound fallacy' of all intellectualist ethics and is held to vitiate the whole Western ethical tradition except the precursors of contemporary activism. [13]

[12] A. MacBeath, *Experiments in Living* (London, 1952).
[13] See also above, pp. 78-81.

Answer. I agree that evaluation is a process in which a man standing at one point in time looks forward, then asks, "Shall I jump? Which way shall I jump?" and that not to jump or to jump in a familiar way is a decision. Or at least it is capable of being seen as a decision, if you have decided to broaden this category to cover all conscious choice. (If it were a humble empirical category one could ask meaningfully, "Did he really decide, or did he just go along out of habit?" Our previous objector might remind us to inquire under what historical conditions men come to see every gesture as a momentous decision.) But no decision proceeds from a completely blank self. If I ask, "Who are you, who is deciding?" your answer will include some ends or values already, for you cannot give an account of a self without some directional momentum. Only if you say that you have no ends but simply desire to have some can your objection be a real one. And that it is not so is obvious. But I do not deny that in the act of choice you have the world before you, and for every end that I can find in you, you can ask whether to continue having it. But even if you take God to have created the world *ex nihilo,* it does not follow that you can create your choices so! To evaluate belongs to the pause before choice, no matter how close you draw them together. You can shuttle from choice to evaluation to choice, and you can even bring the patterns of shuttling into the area of evaluation. There is no ending to the problem because the widening of the area that evaluation covers is itself a large part of the meaning of freedom and of the creative openness we assigned to the valuational base because we find this libertarian striving in human life. But whether human life is like that or whether it ought to be simplified, more stabilized, and why, we leave to continued experiments in living, reflections on them, and fresh choices.

A final further reflection. Is not the picture I have given, according to which we always plunge, like Homer and the epic poets, *in medias res,* and find around us questions of scientific fact, of the nature of the universe and man, of abiding aims, of what can be achieved, and so on, an accurate representation of the way great choices in individual and cultural life, even in sharp changes and historical crises, are in fact inevitably made or capable of being made? Take India, faced with alternative paths. She may want Western industrialization, but perhaps not the Western family system, or Western capitalism for that matter, if she can avoid it. And why this, and not that? Is it not in terms of what she has been, and is, and what changes in institutions and aspirations have taken place, and what needs cry for satisfaction? She does not evaluate the totality of life at one blow and out of all context.

Marx wrote that no social problem arises on the human historical scene until the means of its solution are at hand. I think he was too hopeful—he was looking backward at societies that had changed and survived. A wider vista of biological evolution is needed to see the species that died out because problems arose for which there were no means of solution at hand. However, it may be true that no *evaluation problem* arises in human consciousness until the criteria for a satisfactory solution are at least dimly perceived—negatively if not positively. This need not be taken to preclude the speculative probing for justification of anything at all. But purely speculative evaluation must be content with hypothetical speculative criteria, which of course are legion. And if its probing is a tentative searching, it wants not definite answers but alternative sets of possible answers. This is an old story, long learned in the history of mathematics and of science. It is time to learn it in ethics.

CHAPTER FIFTEEN
THE THEORY OF IDEALS

As a case study in evaluative method, we select a specific ethical category—that of *ideals*. Because it is more specific than that of end or of value, we can give it detailed consideration in narrower limits and show how analytic and descriptive and causal-explanatory method play their part in making evaluative method more effective.

In human life, evaluation of ideals is given special urgency by the fact that a new generation is constantly growing up. Unless one is simply to equip it with older attitudes in spite of changing conditions, or unless one simply imparts a sense of momentous tasks to be done, leaving the content of these tasks as a kind of value-vacuum to be filled in by chance, careful attention to the nature of ideals and criteria for their evaluation are indispensable.

Reflective attitudes to ideals have varied between wide extremes. Traditional respect for ideals as basic spiritual realities is epitomized in the following story told by Pareto: [1]

> In January, 1914, the French Ministry succeeded in passing a bill appropriating 20,000 francs for a national funeral for General Picquart. A member in the Senate rose to inquire just what services the General had rendered the country. The premier, M. Doumergue, replied: "You ask me what services General Picquart has rendered the country! He believed in immanent justice and truth!"

In a similar vein but far different context, Fernando de los Rios, who served the Spanish Republican government in its unsuccessful resistance to the fascist revolt, once said: "If there are no Platonic ideals, then what did we fight for?"

[1] V. Pareto, *The Mind and Society* (1935), III, 1311. Quoted in Huntington Cairns, *Legal Philosophy from Plato to Hegel* (Baltimore, 1949), p. 19. Cairns also suggests the contrast with Sumner indicated below.

A contrasting conception of ideals is found in the sociological treatment of Sumner:

> Every group, in every age, has had its 'ideals' for which it has striven, as if men had blown bubbles into the air, and then entranced by their beautiful colors, had leaped to catch them. In the very processes of analysis and deduction, the most pernicious errors find entrance.[2]

And again:

> *Ideals.* An ideal is entirely unscientific. It is a phantasm which has little or no connection with fact. Ideals are very often formed in the effort to escape from the hard task of dealing with facts, which is the function of science and art. There is no process by which to reach an ideal. There are no tests by which to verify it. It is therefore impossible to frame a proposition about an ideal which can be proved or disproved.[3]

WHAT IS AN IDEAL?

Given such conflicting approaches to the nature of ideals, it is important first to clarify the concept of an ideal and the phenomenon of holding ideals. This involves use of descriptive and analytic method in a comparative way.

Phenomenal description of the ideal. Phenomenally viewed, the ideal falls somewhere along the range between what is urgent and what is wished for. Food is more than an ideal to a starving man; if one may hunger for the ideal one cannot be too ravenous for it. Nor can a pleasing fancy, something desirable if nature or others conspire to bring it about, be reckoned an ideal. Some drawing power is a minimum condition; it is the specific emotional tone of the ideal. The ideal does not simply command or affirm or reckon; it *attracts.* Plato's description of beauty, in the *Symposium,* as the pathway to the good, follows this approach, and the mystic tradition elaborates it. The ideal grips the whole soul; so deeply are we stirred by its faintest glimmer that, according to Plato, no man sees the good and yet chooses evil.

Nevertheless, an ideal cannot be regarded simply as a value that stirs us deeply. For the object of passion also grips the

---

[2] W. G. Sumner, *Folkways* (rev. ed.; Boston, 1934), p. 32 (sec. 37).

[3] *Ibid.,* p. 201 (sec. 203). Sumner, however, goes on (sec. 204) to show when ideals can be useful.

whole soul. If a distinction is to be drawn between the ideal and the passion—sometimes suggested by the saying that the ideal elevates and passions narrow the self—a more specific psychology is required. The general quality of dynamism is a partial, not a complete, answer to our question.

Characterization of ideals by type of content. Remoteness is commonly regarded as a central mark of the value that is an ideal. To pursue the ideal is to abandon the present for the future, the near for the remote, says Hartmann, who includes his discussion of ideals under a chapter entitled "Love of the Remote." [4] In ordinary usage, far-off values, goals approachable but not achievable, drawing men on but always out of reach, are identified as ideals. Santayana's paradox in his *Reason in Religion,* that the gods to preserve an ideal character must be nonexistent, that an ideal embodied is an idol whose feet of clay will be unmasked by time, entails such a conception. This approach is strengthened by the common contrast between the ideal and the real. Dewey, however, says, "The larger and remoter values of an act form what is ordinarily termed an ideal," and denies that ideals are "fixed, remote goals, too far away to be ever realized in conduct. . . ." [5] This reference to the larger values of an act suggests a second element of content sometimes considered essential—abstractness. Abstract values such as justice and liberty are regarded as ideals in a primary sense.

Both these elements add to our conception of an ideal. The content must be far enough removed from ready achievement to summon forth a man's energies over a period of time. But this need not mean that achievement is impossible. Nor is abstractness a necessary condition of every ideal. Many people's ideals are quite specific. To have a home and family is an ideal in most men's lives. And who has not heard of the ideal of three square meals a day? There is a moving story by the Yiddish writer, Peretz, of the man whose humble and uncomplaining life was the model of piety. On his death, the portals of heaven opened readily, and he was brought directly to the feet of the Almighty. To God's grant that he choose anything he wanted as a reward, he at first demurred, and then confessed that there was some-

[4] Nicolai Hartmann, *Ethics* (New York, 1932), Vol. II, Ch. XXX.
[5] Dewey and Tufts, *Ethics* (rev. ed.; New York, 1932), p. 301.

thing his heart had always been set upon. Could he have a white roll and butter *every* day?

Such ideals are neither abstract nor incapable of achievement. The further proposition that man's ethical nature is essentially restless, that ideality departs from what is possessed, is a separable question. Similarly, the normative judgment—that men should prefer unattainable ideals—requires independent establishment.

Logical formulation of the ideal. The ideal may also be characterized from a logical point of view. An ideal is formulated differently from an imperative or a rule. "Thou shalt not kill" is an imperative; "Killing is wrong" is a rule, while "Peace on earth" is an ideal. The imperative is a command, in this case a general one. The rule presents a universal or general criterion for choice in action or deliberation. The ideal refers to a proposed state of existence.

Characterization of the ideal by its role. Sometimes we recognize that an envisaged form of life is an ideal not by its logical formulation or its specific content, but by its role in the arena of choice and conduct. An ideal is thus a value which serves to organize other values, either within a given person's life or among men generally.[6] Whatever content is found to have such scope in particular lives is an ideal within those lives.

Valuational height as distinguishing mark. A purely valuational element may also be suggested for identifying ideals. So regarded, ideality characterizes the higher or greater as against the lesser values. Thus G. E. Moore says that when we call a state of things 'ideal,' "we always do mean to assert, of the state of things in question, not only that it is good in itself, but that it is good in itself in a much higher degree than many other things." [7] Even if ideals are otherwise identified, this question of their position on a scale of values remains a central one.

Summary conception of an ideal. On all these approaches the genus of ideal is *end or goal of positive value.* In the light of the term's breadth of meaning and usage, its differentia may best

[6] This is in line with the treatment of harmony found, for example, in Santayana's *Life of Reason* (New York, 1905), or R. B. Perry's *General Theory of Value* (New York, 1926).

[7] G. E. Moore, *Principia Ethica* (Cambridge, 1903), p. 182.

be regarded as a pattern of the elements that have emerged. An ideal is, then, a valued proposed state of existence which stirs a man so that he is moved to work towards its achievement. It remains for a time within or near the center of his ethical stage. It is not easy to achieve but need not be inherently unachievable; at least it can be approximated. Because it is a relatively stable source of attraction over a considerable period, it is either abstract in the sense of general, or difficult and requiring an extensive marshalling of resources. It is not a rank and file value, but one which, while a value itself, often acts as a basis of organization and discrimination within the mass of values. And in any individual's scale of values his ideals are to be found near the top.

No doubt a stricter definition of 'ideal' could be offered arbitrarily, but it is doubtful whether it would serve the purpose of analyzing that element in ethical theories in which we are here interested. It is possible, of course, that for the construction of an improved ethical theory greater refinement of definition would be required. Such refinement would best follow, not precede, the fuller study of the source and role of ideals in human life.

WHY DO MEN HAVE IDEALS?

The question why men have ideals asks in part for the role that ideals play in human life, in part for a wider causal or explanatory picture. In both respects the question falls into the domain of what we have called, in Part Four, 'context inquiries.' Now, since we have suggested that ethical theories in their underlying existential perspectives—that is, their view of man and his world, human nature, the human predicament [8]—embody different answers to causal-explanatory questions, we may expect that interpretations of the significance of ideals will go in different directions. Comparative investigation shows that this is indeed the case. On the whole, the types of interpretation may be classified into two broad groups—theological and idealist on the one hand, and materialist and naturalist on the other. Cutting

[8] See above, pp. 22ff. and 214ff.

across these are emphases on different phases of man and nature, such as the biological, the psychological, the social and historical.[9] A causal-explanatory treatment of ideals such as the present, which is not going to reckon with all the existential perspectives in detail, can have only a limited aim: to call attention to facets of the problem often neglected, to sift out common elements in the different interpretations and especially those that raise scientific issues capable in principle of some solution, to pinpoint differences, and in general to fasten attention on properties of ideals that may be helpful in describing a particular ideal more adequately in preparation for its evaluation.

Theological and idealist approaches to ideals. In theological and idealist accounts of ideals, the phenomenon of having or pursuing an ideal is ultimately in some form or other given a cognitive status. Ideals provide a revelation of the special spiritual character or structure of the world. Sometimes this is regarded as a metaphysical or ontological structure (e.g., God's nature), sometimes as a specifically axiological structure of eternal values.

The note of the eternal runs through the whole range of idealist analyses. For Plato, human ideals of justice or beauty or truth all represent the striving of the imprisoned soul led on by the glimmer of the real or the eternal to which it belongs. And in spite of its dynamism, the Hegelian outlook is ultimately bent on catching—to use Bosanquet's phrase—"the heart-beat of the Absolute in our actual world." [10] Bosanquet strongly attacks tying ideals to purpose and striving within a temporal context; purpose represents merely the incompleteness of the finite self. "The great enemy of all sane idealism is the notion that the ideal belongs to the future. The ideal is what we can see in the light of the whole, and the way in which it shapes the future for us is only an incident—and never the most important incident—

---

[9] For a fuller outline of the different types of existential perspectives and criteria for their evaluation, see my *Science and the Structure of Ethics,* Ch. II.

[10] Bernard Bosanquet, *The Principle of Individuality and Value* (London, 1912), p. 20. Cf. Royce's frank assertion: "I am in quest of the Eternal" (*The Philosophy of Loyalty* [New York, 1911], p. 10).

of our reading of past, present, and future in their unity." [11] Similarly, a contemporary realistic idealism such as Hartmann's demands an eternal realm of self-subsistent values.

In none of these approaches, however, is the stress on purely contemplative appreciation of the ideal. Plato recognizes a bringing to birth in beauty and insists that really to see the good is to strive towards it. Bosanquet is not interested in the abstract as such; a growing self-consciousness works its way into the pattern of life and striving. And Hartmann, although his basic stress is on discernment of values by man's value-sense, nevertheless calls for ideals that are "forward-looking," "practically feasible," "ethically significant," and criticizes "an exalted but impracticable and chimerical ideal." [12] But ultimately, all these existential or temporal processes have a largely instrumental role. In essence, man through his ideals outgrows or transcends himself, and revelation of the real in one form or another is the ultimate role of human ideals.

Materialist and naturalist approaches to ideals. In materialist analyses, and in naturalistic theory which is generally materialistic on its ethical side, ideals are given a place in the matrix of time and change. All forms specify some existential conditions or matrix of human needs or problems within which ideals arise and function as projected solutions. The qualities that arise in consciousness in these processes need not be denied or deprecated either in their reality or their value, but they are not isolated from their association and roles with respect to underlying processes.

Sometimes the stage is set in physico-biological terms. In Santayana, for example, in spite of an exalted Platonic element, it is "the friction of material forces" that is turned into "the light of ideal goods." [13] Where biological impulses meet with obstructions or else require cooperation, ideals are generated to provide solutions and mobilize energy—ideals of love, the family, economic systems, and other social institutions and group sentiments. By contrast, Santayana in one context points to the failure

11 Bosanquet, *ibid.*, p. 136.
12 *Op. cit.*, II, 323.
13 *Reason in Society* (New York, 1905), p. 9.

of breathing to generate a host of ideal systems. The plentiful presence of air, the individual character of the process of its appropriation, the absence of conflicts about it,[14] all make it a background activity of little stimulation in the production of ideals.

Sometimes the stage for ideals is set in the light of psychological concepts. Especially in recent treatments, the influence of psychoanalytic schools has raised questions of the point in the development of the self at which ideals may arise, what types of functions they serve and what dynamic processes they represent, and so forth.[15]

Occasionally, the stage has been set for ideals in the context of social and historical conceptions. Thus Spencer is specific about the shift in ideals from a military to an industrial society, and Marx assigns ideals a different meaning not merely in different epochs, but, in their content, in different classes. He analyzes universal ideals in the same way, their universality expressing common or recurrent features of hitherto existing societies. (Justice, for example, reflects the cry against exploitation in all prior class societies.)

Some properties of a particular ideal. A number of specific properties of ideals will be found helpful in preparing an ideal for evaluation.

Every ideal that is found in human life has some type of relation or attachment to people who hold or pursue it. The materialist and naturalist outlooks may say that the very being or existence of an ideal lies in its being held or pursued. The idealist or eternalist outlooks may stress the independence of the ideal from the contingent fact that it is appreciated by particular human beings; Hartmann, for example, assumes ideals are eternally self-subsistent and only the act of discernment is local and temporal. In either case, it is possible to focus attention on the

---

[14] Except, a contemporary psychology would add, where breathing in the child becomes crossed with other demands in the parental relation, and psychological disturbances arise; or where, the sociologist would point out, industrial factors produce smog and other impurities, generating social ideals of a pure atmosphere or romantic back-to-the-country longings.

[15] See the suggestions below, in the discussion of "genuineness" as a criterion in evaluating ideals.

succession of people in time and space who have had this attachment to a given ideal. Let us speak then of the *location of an
ideal* as the set of individuals or groups for whom it has functioned as an ideal during the period it has so functioned.

Again, whether one philosophical outlook will prefer to speak
of ideals themselves as changing, and another of ideals as eternal
but men's relation to them changing, there is in both cases a
phenomenon of change which it is possible to describe once we
have the location of the particular ideal. In this sense, we may
think of the history of an ideal and speak of the succession of
qualities and relations it has during its history as its *career*. In
this respect, change is a normal feature of ideals and the career
of an ideal is to be found on the face of history as events. Thus
an ideal may have a coming-into-being and even a passing-away.
There is no inconsistency in the notion of the death of an ideal.
In fact, we may even speak of the natural death of an ideal. The
natural death of a successful ideal is to pass from feelings to
human institutions and, when so embedded, to be taken for
granted to such an extent that intensity due to tension disappears, so that only a madman would act contrary to it. This does
not mean that the values it embodies will have died, nor is it
our aim to kill all ideals. But we cannot be alarmed by such
questions as Bosanquet's "Are fruition or perfection really the
death of value?" [16] In the case of some ideals at least—peace on
earth, for example—natural death through achievement in the
sense described is overdue.

We may next introduce the conception of the *base* or *foundations of an ideal*. This is constituted by the needs in the individual or group expressed by the ideal, or on which the ideal rests.
That every ideal has a base in this sense follows in part from the
definition of an ideal. Since it is set at some distance, there will
be intermediary goals; since it acts in a capacity of organizing and
discriminating within the mass of values, it in some sense gives
them form. But fundamentally the thesis that every ideal has
foundations is an empirical lesson of those human sciences which
study ideals in terms of their social and psychological functioning. This concept has obvious applicability to the materialist
and naturalist outlooks illustrated above. But it is also applicable

16 *Op. cit.*, p. 137.

to idealist and theological outlooks, since these generally embody some conception of the self and its needs in its striving toward the ideal.

The concepts of the location and the base of an ideal enable us to pinpoint two common fallacies in dealing with ideals, which we may combine under the single title of *the fallacy of the misplaced base*. By vagueness of reference, a given ideal may be wrongfully located. We may, for example, speak of religious freedom as if it were the rights of one Christian sect against another Christian sect not to be shut out from the field of missionary work. If so, our location is people of the seventeenth century; a present-day ideal of religious freedom rests on the demands of all people, non-Christian as well as Christian, non-religious as well as religious. Or again, if rightly located, an ideal may be referred to only a part of the base, that is, only some of the needs on which it rests. Thus the ideal of educational opportunity is often discussed as if it were primarily the expression of the desires of more intelligent youth to utilize their capacities by entering the professions. This neglects the needs of the community for expansion of its professional service. It is almost as if the ideal of a good medical education were discussed solely from the point of view of enhancing the position of doctors without reference to the need of the community as patients.

Where the needs in a base are in conflict—as they may be even in the individual, and often are in the group—the fallacy of the misplaced base can produce considerable distortion. Thus the whole Machiavellian cynicism toward political ideals comes largely from seeing them as simply the propagandist weapons of those in power. That is, the ideals are referred only to their base in the ruling group. A more realistic view would see liberty, for example, as an ideal expressing the effort of the mass of men struggling to lighten their burdens. Hence, the Machiavellian-type theory by its very analysis places itself at the side of the ruling class in its most cynical phase, and its neglect of the aims of the subjects simply reflects an acceptance of their position. It is not surprising that this whole approach to ideals had great vogue in the thirties during the rise of fascism. It was the shadow of fascist values hanging over the political theory of liberal democratic countries. A good example of such analysis of ideals is Burnham's treatment of "freedom from want" during World War II. When men were starving in a great part of the globe, when public pressure in Britain and America was growing for expanded social security, when international instruments were being proposed for industrialization of undeveloped areas, all Burnham could offer to estimate the ideal was to call it meaningless in terms of real politics since "men are wanting beings; they are freed from want only by death." [17] Thus he placed the base in the physical phenomenon of tissue needs rather than the social and historical needs of men.

An analysis of the basis of a given ideal, plus an understanding of its causality, enables one to judge the degree to which its occurrence is unavoidable, partially controllable, or wholly subject to control. Let us call these the *controllability* of an ideal.

A general ideal is unavoidable if it arises almost invariably from pervasive features of human life or is almost dictated by universal needs. For example, since doing has an obvious bearing on satisfying needs we may expect that achievement as such has an ideal quality; perhaps this is so, although it is not always explicitly noted. Similarly, the pressure of numerous needs demanding satisfaction may be the background which renders unavoidable some such ideal as happiness. Its unavoidability may be judged from the fact that even ethical systems rejecting it often add that their values (virtue, for instance) constitute "true" happiness.

A particular ideal is relatively unavoidable if it appears invariably under special psychological and cultural conditions. Thus the ideals of success and progress are probably unavoidable in the present stage of our culture. The establishment of the precise conditions underlying them is by no means a simple task.

The molding of the character of youth has often given rise to conceptions of greater control over the formation of ideals. From the ancient contrast of Sparta and Athens to the modern rapid transformations witnessed in Nazi Germany and in Russia, the notion of greater self-consciousness and greater control of the development of men has had a wide appeal—although the possi-

[17] James Burnham, *The Machiavellians* (New York, 1943), p. 26. Cf. p. 177.

bility of concentrated power implicit in such a conception has an ominous potential. Yet the problem itself is unavoidable, and one of the major educational lessons of democratic experience in the twentieth century has been that children do not automatically grow up democratically-minded if simply let alone, but that the character they develop depends upon the structure of their personal and institutional surroundings.

In addition to the properties of ideals we have considered, further properties—such as distance, dynamism, intensity, etc.,—will be identified in determining criteria of evaluation below.

EVALUATION OF IDEAL AS AN ETHICAL CATEGORY

Evaluation of the specific category of ideal is simpler than evaluation of the generic category of goal or end which we considered in the previous chapter. The reason is perhaps that we are more familiar with people who lack ideals than with people who are without goals. There is, for example, the opportunist who never allows himself to be committed to any goal distant enough to assume ideal proportions. His aim is a kind of immediate satisfaction, or drifting in the present with goals within easy reach. He does not deprecate others having ideals, but thinks they are too much bother. Another possibility is the cynic, who thinks having ideals is a kind of self-deceit. In general, not merely in terms of isolated individuals, a society might formulate its ethical ideas so as to omit this ethical category. The causal bases of such a situation is an empirical question. A priori, a number of hypotheses suggest themselves. The society might be on such a low material level that neither time nor energy might be available for projecting ideals. Under such conditions, ideals might appear serving a compensatory function, but it is equally possible that imagination would people the world with fear objects rather than ideal surrogates. Or again, a high state of abundance is conceivable in which goals were so readily achieved that no ideals developed. It seems more probable, however, that in the circumstances of this globe and its history, some very definite and strong ideals would be necessary in achieving and maintaining such an abundance. Hence, ideals might be required as girders in the ethico-social structure.

Nietzsche's attack on the category. While Nietzsche sometimes seems to be criticizing only a particular set of ideals, instead of ideals as such, in other contexts he directs his attack upon the whole category. There is, for example, his assertion that ideals are dangerous because they lower realities, but they are occasionally indispensable as cures. Sometimes he attacks ideals as arising from weakness: "The 'ideal' is at the same time the penalty man pays for the enormous expenditure which he has to defray in all real and pressing duties. Should reality cease to prevail, there follow dreams, fatigue, weakness: an 'ideal' might even be regarded as a form of dream, fatigue, or weakness." [18] Yet even in such contexts one cannot be sure that it is not specific ideals he is objecting to. For he adds: " 'Innocence' to them is idealized stultification; 'blessedness' is idealized idleness; 'love,' the ideal state of the gregarious animal that will no longer have an enemy. And thus everything that lowers and belittles man is elevated to an *ideal*." In any case, therefore, unless one employs the specific will to power stage-setting Nietzsche offers, in which all striving expresses a will to dominate or master, it is better to see his criticisms as attempts to distinguish between spurious ideals expressing weakness, and genuine ideals issuing from strength.

Functional values of the category. There are many grounds upon which the role of ideals is to be positively evaluated. These will become clearer in the discussion of criteria for evaluation of specific ideals. In general, there are both positive and instrumental values involved. Among the former is heightened consciousness, a more intense plane of living. Among the latter is the degree of progress made possible by the organizing role of ideals, and the way in which they support the social structure. In addition, there are, no doubt, considerable costs in individual psychological economy, as well as in exercise of social controls. Dominant agreement could doubtless be secured on the general desirability of having ideals, with most dissent transferred to issues involving selection of specific ideals, or else reduced to a

18 *The Will to Power*, tr. Ludovici (New York, 1924), I, 270. Cf. his eloquent description in *The Genealogy of Morals*, tr. Samuel (London, 1923), pp. 47-49, of the way in which the "workshops where ideals are manufactured" specialize in turning weakness into merit, impotence into goodness, misery into blessedness.

wish that life on the globe were less complex than it actually has turned out to be.[19]

CRITERIA FOR EVALUATION OF SPECIFIC IDEALS

Since ideals are ends or goals of positive value, differentiated by a configuration of several elements,[20] it follows that the criteria suggested in the previous chapter for evaluation of ends will have some application to the evaluation of ideals.[21] But, of course, the differentiating features of ideals may prevent this application from being immediate and direct. The criteria have to be reconsidered in the specific contexts. For example, the attractiveness of ideals may not be the same in type as the attractiveness of ends, because ideals are usually more remote, and the question of attainability may take a different form for the same reason. Again, because ideals act as a basis of organization and discrimination within the mass of values, it is likely that something more complex than the criterion of constructiveness or destructiveness is required. Moreover, at the present stage of ethical theory the theory of ends is not yet systematically developed, so that we are not in the position of making deductions for a particular area from fundamental principles about the general field. The identification of criteria and the formation of standards tend to be mere piecemeal inductive pursuits, attempting to classify and systematize criteria found operative in human life. Finally, as we saw in dealing with ends and values, we must be conscious of the value assumptions that go into accepting a given point of appraisal as a criterion.

In what follows, we therefore suggest seven *points of reference* in looking at an ideal and attempting to decide whether it merits strengthening or supplanting. With respect to these points of reference, criteria can be fashioned by the combination of shared values with established knowledge.

---

[19] The prototype of such a view is the readiness with which Plato in the *Republic* abandons his first simple bucolic ideal state for the more complex regimented structure. Socially, the objection to ideals involving organization may often be a wish for the simplicity of the past.

[20] See above, pp. 326f.

[21] See above, pp. 309f.

Strength of foundations. Ideals may be compared on the basis of the needs which serve as their foundations. There is no ground for a priori delimitation of the types of needs here involved. They may be biological (food and sex), psychological (affection), social (group bases of patriotism), and usually draw on many elements. In the foundations, often no sharp distinction is drawn between needs and goals and values; complex ideals may arise in the attempt to actualize other goals and values as well as to express more primary needs.

From this point of view, we may note that no ideal is well-founded if it rests upon trivial or transient needs, or, from a social point of view, upon the needs of a very few. Hence, duration of needs, numbers affected, importance of the needs among other needs, interconnectedness of needs forming a solid base, all become relevant even though they themselves require greater precision or allow of only rough qualitative judgment. Thus the strength of political ideals comes from the primary needs of the masses. The strength of the ideal of truth is tremendous, since its foundation is the whole range of uncertainty and insecurity in human life, both in regard to nature and the relations of men.

Whether strength of foundations as so described becomes a criterion of the worth of ideals depends upon the values embedded in the framework of judgment. Its strength may be held against an ideal by one who disdains the common, rejects the lasting or the substantial in favor of the fleeting, or aims at one-sidedness rather than many-sidedness in the expression of man's nature. Such antitheses are more often found in judgments of aesthetic value than in ethical judgments. By and large, and certainly from a social point of view, strength rather than weakness of foundations is a merit in an ideal, as in a building.

Intensity. Intensity in the judgment of ideals corresponds to attractiveness in the evaluation of goals, attention falling more on the subject's reaction because of the far-off character of the ideal. Intensity is commonly regarded as a mark of degree of value. Bentham included it among the measures of a pleasure's worth. Perry defines it with precision in his *General Theory of Value* as the degree of an interest's arousal (since value is taken to be the object of interest); that is, "the degree in which it has acquired command of the body as a whole; or, the extent to which the several parts of the body are determined, whether in their functioning or in their inhibition, by the requirements of the interest." [22] This states in behavioral fashion the same point that Plato makes of the ideal, that it grips the whole soul and draws it onward.

A certain degree of intensity is required to constitute a value as an ideal. The lower limit is the merely wishful, the upper the urgent. No exact measure is possible, nor is it needed, since intensity is probably the feature which most intimately reveals to us that certain envisaged content has become an ideal. The location of the upper limit is clearly itself a question of value rather than definition. Sometimes there comes a point at which absolute devotion to the ideal is felt as a kind of selling of the self into slavery. Perhaps the limit would be judged at different points for different fields of content or different strength of foundations. The same intensity that in the fight for national liberation is a mark of high ideals would be deemed fanaticism in the clash of political parties in a well-functioning democracy. The judgment of fanaticism is not, however, to be equated with one hundred per cent intensity. It probably indicates a qualitative distinction in the way in which the ideal is held, and may indicate fresh emotional elements in the foundations.

For the most part, below the upper limit, the more intensely held ideal is reckoned of greater worth. But this is itself a separate valuation resting on the fact that the quality of high intensity is itself desired. This is clear from the contrasting attitudes towards ecstasy in different societies. In some, ecstasy is valued and standardized as an objective; in others, it is felt as excessive departure from moderation of feeling. The use of an intensity scale in the evaluation of ideals is thus itself a function of social valuation. This does not, however, preclude the possibility of the establishment of invariant psychological elements of desirability.

Motor-power or dynamism. Because of the importance of action in pursuit of the ideal, we do not stop short with the mere fact of intensity, but ask the further question: what specific form does the intense reaction take? Ideals may thus be estimated by the extent to which they spur to action, merely satisfy in contemplation providing a warm glow of feeling, or even inhibit

22 P. 629.

action. In setting these effects in this order, we intend an estimation of worth. It is important again to recognize this at the outset as valuational in character. The implied assumption is that an ideal should lead men to act toward some resolution of the needs and problems on which it rests. It must be admitted that an opposing valuation is possible, namely, that an ideal has no other function than that of intensification of consciousness. We all know people to whom holding an ideal is merely an emotional response, and for whom the needs on which the ideal rests are merely grounds for feeling sorrow. One wishes their souls would seethe a little less with sorrow, however sincere, and that they would *do* a little more. William James somewhere tells the story of the grand lady who weeps for the world's woes before the fireside, while her coachman stands freezing outside waiting for her. Dewey points out that setting up ideals without reference to existing social conditions or the means to achieve them commonly results "in an esthetic disgust with the present which seeks refuge in what is aloof and which through refusal to face existing conditions actually operates to perpetuate them." [23] Similarly Hartmann calls for ideals that are forward-looking and criticizes retrospective ideals such as "paradise" and the "golden age" because "the mood which corresponds to them is that of a downward course, the vain mourning for a vanished splendor." [24] Prospective ideals, on the other hand, throw the weight of responsibility on man.

In the light of such critiques, the negative valuation of motorpower need not be accepted at its face value. The disparagement of the dynamic role of an ideal probably represents a retreat through a sense of difficulty rather than a contrary valuation.[25] All that is increasingly being learned about psychological developmental processes and the inhibition of expression and action would seem to bear out such an approach.

[23] Dewey and Tufts, *op. cit.,* p. 382.

[24] Hartmann, *op. cit.,* II, 326.

[25] It is possible that this may apply only to ethical ideals, not esthetic ones. In contrast, Socrates recognized (in the *Symposium*) that the apprehension of beauty is at the same time a desire for birth in beauty. It is also important to note that the dynamic character is asserted as desirable in ethical and social *ideals,* not necessarily in all *values.*

The motor-power of an ideal refers to the way in which it is held by an individual. A high motor-power does not as such imply that action leads in fact to the resolution of the needs underlying the ideal. The efficacy of the action has to be separately evaluated.

Genuineness. The problem of the genuine and the spurious is not a simple one in the case of ideals, but it is sharper in its outlines than in the case of goals. Sometimes it refers to the psychological relations of the ideal in the person holding it; sometimes it refers to the types of consequences that would flow from the achievement of the ideal. Each of these may be considered separately.

The criterion of genuineness in the psychological accounts has by no means been standardized. For example, Fenichel, referring to Fromm's account in *Escape from Freedom,* says:

> Freud was criticized for not having differentiated between 'real' ideals which are wholeheartedly accepted by the total personality and 'ungenuine' ideals which one believes one has to follow because an external or introjected authority demands it. But even the most genuine ideals have been created by introjection. The difference lies in the commensurability or incommensurability of introject and subject, that is, in the previous history of the relationship to the objects whose introjections formed the ideal.[26]

But of course, the similarity of causal processes need not preclude phenomenal differences in the ideals, in terms of which a judgment of genuineness may be defined. For example, Karen Horney writes:

> In contrast to authentic ideals, the idealized image has a static quality. It is not a goal toward whose attainment he strives but a fixed idea which he worships. Ideals have a dynamic quality; they arouse an incentive to approximate them; they are an indispensable and invaluable force for growth and development. The idealized image is a decided hindrance to growth because it either denies shortcomings or merely condemns them. Genuine ideals make for humility, the idealized image for arrogance.[27]

[26] Otto Fenichel, *The Psychoanalytic Theory of Neurosis* (New York, 1945), p. 106.

[27] Karen Horney, *Our Inner Conflicts* (New York, 1945), p. 98. Cf. William James' point that in the case of some ideals we actually experience relief in

One way of regarding such psychological distinctions is to say that they are not concerned with differentiating genuine and spurious, but with detecting the fallacy of the misplaced base. A given individual holds as an ideal a particular line of achievement, thinking he holds it out of a deep interest in the subject; the psychologist suspects it is but a desire to please parent surrogates. Or men make an ideal of asceticism; Nietzsche unmasks the base as weakness.[28] There is, however, no objection to using the degree of insight the holder of the ideal has, as part criterion of genuineness, if in addition the qualities of the ideal and its holding are correlated with definite patterns in the picture of the person's psychological economy and dynamics.

In the second sense, referring to consequences that would flow from achieving the ideal, the test is a much simpler one. But perhaps this is only because it posits initially a correct analysis of the base. The reference would then be simply to whether the ideal, if actually achieved, would meet the needs which it represents or on which it rests. If it would, it is genuine, whether it is attainable or not, whether it is worth striving for or not. If it would not meet the underlying needs, the ideal is spurious. A spurious ideal is like a quack remedy. Many political ideals which have won great devotion—high tariffs or social credit or free silver or technocracy—have proved spurious. The cosmic pessimist, taking man's basic need to be the stilling of desire, would no doubt find all ideals spurious.

It should be noted that the judgment of genuineness is made within a context of the needs upon which the ideal rests. It is quite possible that a given ideal may be spurious in one such context and genuine in another, just as a medical remedy might be effective for one illness and actually dangerous for another. Investigation into the genuineness of an ideal has this incidental advantage, that it makes us probe for the bases of the ideal. Sometimes we discover that we are holding the ideal on quite an unexpected basis.

Genuineness as so defined is a necessary condition of worth in

giving them up, exhibiting thereby their pretentious character. (*Principles of Psychology* [New York, 1890], I, 311.)

28 See above, p. 335. Cf. Nietzsche's comment that man will wish *Nothingness* rather than not wish *at all*. (*Genealogy of Morals*, p. 211.)

any ideal. It is the most obvious point at which ideals must submit to scientific scrutiny, strength of feeling or attraction being no guarantee of authenticity. It is conceivable, however, that in some ethical systems genuineness should be given a very minor role as a criterion of ideals. Some theories, for example, that place a high value on intense striving irrespective of objective, may fear the dissolving effect of rational scrutiny of objectives. But the pressure of primary needs works in the long run against the acceptance of such an ethics.

Attainability. Perry rejects attainability as a criterion of comparative value on the ground that this would give supreme value to the reduction of life to its primitive appetites and because the greatest values are most remote, uncertain, and precarious.[29] This argument is decisive against a simple direct correlation, but the criterion requires more careful consideration in connection with ideals.

'Attainable' has several different meanings, deriving from the different meanings of 'possible.' In the sense of logical possibility of attainment, certainly an ideal to be of worth must contain no inherent contradiction. The dove was posing an impossible ideal when she, as Kant describes it, "cleaving the air in her free flight, and feeling its resistance, might imagine that its flight would be still easier in empty space." [30] Nor can we retrospectively commend pursuit of squaring the circle as a tenable ideal, after impossibility is revealed. Some may be inclined to see considerable value in the pursuit of the unattainable. But we may doubt whether the unattainable is here construed as the logically impossible. And if it is, it would seem likely that the value elements come from the generic fact of pursuing an ideal.

A second sense of 'possibility' is compatibility with existent scientific knowledge. Possibility of attainment in this sense seems a reasonable criterion of an ideal's worth if the knowledge on which it rests is well established. Thus the ideal of a reliable system of astrology is, on the basis of well-established knowledge, an unachievable one and therefore not worth striving for. But we must be careful in the exercise of such judgments; for ex-

[29] R. B. Perry, *op. cit.*, pp. 610-11.

[30] *Critique of Pure Reason*, tr. Kemp Smith, p. 47. Kant is here criticizing the Platonic view that reason would do better freed from experience.

ample, dominant political theory from Plato at least to Hobbes took fully democratic government to be an impossible ideal because of an "established" psychology of the mass of men.

In a third sense 'attainable' refers to probability of ready achievement, including such tests as availability of resources and probable duration of effort. In this case, it does seem a very dangerous criterion for the worth of an ideal. In individual life, it might mean a too ready acceptance of limitations imposed by the status quo. In general, it might contract men's vision and the range of their striving, thus hindering increasing actualization of the ideal of progress. The ideal of progress is thus one of the valuational bases for a low estimate of attainability (in this sense) as a criterion of ideals. The question of character values is also involved in this estimation. In his essay on "Eastern and Western Ideals of Happiness," Bertrand Russell contrasts the Eastern approach of setting up ideals that are achievable and sticking to them with the western approach of setting up ideals that are out of reach and then resorting to a double standard with a bifurcation of praise and practice. Others, however, have taken the remoteness of our ideals and the tension set up thereby to be an essential element in our drive toward expansion and higher levels of progress. There are many unanswered questions in the relation of ideal types, character structures, and social institutions and movements. The determination of the role of attainability (in the third sense) as a criterion of the worth of ideals thus requires additional psychological study.

Part of such inquiry would include some conception of happiness and the relation of elements of restless drive and contentment within it. Flugel suggests that "in our present civilization, with the value it attaches to progress and achievement, ideals that are pitched too far below capacities do not in the majority of cases bring contentment, but rather, in the long run, boredom or dissatisfaction. It is therefore the task of mental hygiene to discover the optimum ideal that is neither too far above nor too far below the level of capacity." [31] Another factor involved would be the estimation of suffering in the pattern of a desirable life and the degree to which it would be seen (as Hartmann, for example, sees it) as a stimulant to the sense of value,

[31] J. C. Flugel, *Man, Morals, and Society* (New York, 1945), p. 51.

or minimized on principle in every way. In general, the whole question of the "distance" of an ideal—infinite (Melancthon's "God demands the impossible," or the striving for absolute purity), indefinite (on and on forever), moderate ("a man's reach should exceed his grasp"), or finite ("a peaceful old age")—requires systematic study in terms of the effect on the hand that grasps and the spirit that guides it. These complexities are raised not to suggest an impossible task, but to indicate how judgments concerning criteria of ideals themselves may embody other ideals.

Effectiveness. Effectiveness is different from genuineness and from motor-power. Genuineness refers simply to the ideal in a kind of abstraction (except for its relation to the identified base), hypothetically achieved, and notes that it would in fact resolve the underlying needs or problems. Motor-power concerns the state of the person who holds the ideal. Effectiveness, however, includes a reference to the whole causal milieu in which action is carried on. Two ideals, both genuine and of equal motor-power, may be quite different in the degree to which action upon them resolves the common needs upon which both rest. The judgment of such degree in the case of an ideal may be said to estimate its effectiveness.[32] Such judgment refers in the first place to a particular historical context, although it is possible that universal judgments may hold for some ideals where the relevant context remains broadly identical.

In practice, judgments of effectiveness are often difficult to make since they involve explicit recognition of the ideal and the needs upon which it rests, distinction of ideal from means, and causal judgments of the outcome of given types of action. But, in spite of this complexity, effectiveness of even highly abstract ideals may be estimated, given sufficient historical scope. Take as an example the ideal of pacifism.

---

[32] Kant appears to have had such a criterion in mind when he said of the view that it is nature's plan to bring about a state in which all the capacities implanted by her in mankind can be fully developed, "We see by it that philosophy may also have its millenial view, but in this case, the Chiliasm is of such a nature that the very idea of it—although only in a far-off way—may help to further its realization; and such a prospect is, therefore, anything but visionary." ("The Natural Principle of the Political Order, Considered in Connection with the Idea of a Universal Cosmo-Political History," in *Kant's Principles of Politics,* tr. W. Hastie [Edinburgh, 1891], p. 21.)

The ideal of pacifism may in the first place be that of peace on earth or a situation in which no one kills anyone else. The needs on which it rests are obvious; they stem from the devastation, material and psychological, of recurrent warfare, as well as intra-societal conflict and brutality. We are not dealing just with a specific need to avoid killing, but with a whole host of positive human needs that killing thwarts and the human values which it violates. The pacifist rule of absolute avoidance of killing by a given individual would thus express an intended means toward achieving the ideal. Jawaharlal Nehru, for example, thus conceived pacifism in India; it is clear from his autobiography (*Towards Freedom*) that he regarded nonviolence as the best means for freeing India in the light of her traditions and lack of power and organization. Tolstoi, whose book, *The Kingdom of God is Within You*, exercised a crucial influence in the development of Gandhi's outlook, also stressed the view that pacifism is an effective means. He thought that violence simply invites counterviolence, but nonresistance startles, hence provokes reflection and stirs conscience. He expected a rising tide of nonresistance to overwhelm all governments resting on violence, all wars, and all coercive institutions. In thus posing the question, he was offering a prediction which history has not fulfilled. Instead, there came more complete ruthlessness, the concentration camp, and mass slaughter. Instrumental pacifism in the modern world thus embodied what have appeared to be erroneous judgments of means (its role in the liberation of India being a partial exception, depending on the analysis of the historical phenomenon). But its ideal—a world of nonkilling—need not lose its effectiveness if the means be altered. For the ideal alone does not dictate this means and better means might be sought instead, for example as some have hoped, in realistic world organization backed by force.

Pacifism which is unwilling to reckon with historical lessons about means is quite different in type. Here the question becomes pertinent whether its ideal is in fact peace on earth. Even if it held as an ideal that *everyone* hold to the principle of nonviolence it would be bound to concern itself with the best means of securing such universal conformity. Instead we find, in such absolute pacifism as Gandhi's seemed at times to be, not simply the assumption of the ultimate availability of every soul for the appeal of the soul-force expressed in an active nonviolence, but an unreadiness to reckon with consequences in any form. Such an approach may come to hold that strict adherence to principle somehow expresses the true welfare of the soul and that the worldly consequences of adherence—life or death to others or to oneself—are of no consequence. Human welfare is thus reduced to the cleanliness of the soul, and every man's task is to look out for his own. The ideal of such absolute pacifism is not therefore peace on earth but a personal state of spiritual cleanliness.[33]

The needs underlying this ideal are not as immediately obvious as those of peace on earth. They are more personal in character. Whatever their technical analysis may be in terms of contemporary psychological theory, we can discern at least the desire for internal peace and security, the mistrust of the external world, and, to use Kant's phrase, a contempt for the "serpentine windings of Utilitarianism" in the reckoning of probabilities.

In the light of such an analysis, the ideal of absolute pacifism has proved today to have a negative effectiveness, in spite of its high motor-power. Even in personal terms, limiting it to its narrower ideal, it does not seem to bring to those who hold it the internal peace and security they desire. On the contrary, in refusing to make judgments of responsibility and degrees of guilt of conflicting parties in war, they are sometimes compelled to obliterate the distinctions between brutal torture and killing in defense, and thus to blunt their own moral sensitivity.

Necessity. Necessity hardly seems like a criterion of worth in an ideal. In fact, a priori, one might expect it to contribute a negative element. But in the special case of ideals, once a possible

---

[33] The distinction here drawn sharply between instrumental and absolute pacifism is not always clear in a given individual. He may affirm his belief on instrumental grounds, and it might even be true that *if* he were convinced of the erroneous nature of his judgment of means, his pacifism would disappear as an absolute principle of conduct. But it may be equally true that his attitude to the judgment of means may be so colored that as a matter of fact no historical or scientific investigation would convince him, or, even more, he would resist inquiry. We have therefore a transitional stage from one type of pacifism to the other; the individual is theoretically an instrumental pacifist, in conduct and attitude an absolute pacifist. If the ideals of the two are different, we have in him actually a transition of ideals.

state of affairs has assumed an ideal quality, necessity may enhance rather than detract from its worth.

An ideal whose achievement is indispensable to the fulfillment of a mass of accepted values, or, sometimes, to the very possibility of striving for them, will be said to possess *ethical necessity*. The mass of values are to be found in the matrix of existent interests and strivings of the person or group or area of existence to which the ideal is attached, that is, the subjects discovered in locating the ideal. Supplementary criteria are usually involved so that we may speak about the subject as a whole, not some relative part. Such necessity is not mere hypothetical necessity (do X if you want Y). Thus the ideal of wealth does not have ethical necessity to any man just because it would satisfy some of his aims, but only to a man the very core of whose striving requires wealth as a necessary condition—for example, the man whose whole being is bound up with lavish aims of a "worldly" type, or one who aspires to the kind of generosity Aristotle pictures in the liberal or magnanimous man. It is this reference to the *whole* subject or its *dominant* element which prompts our description of it as "ethical" necessity.

The method of judging when the ideal is relevant to the whole or a dominant part of the subject varies, of course, with the type of subject. In a person, ethical necessity may be identified as a quality of the experience of the ideal; its necessity looms, as it were, in the field of his conscious striving. Of course, this felt quality may not adequately represent the facts of existence. To determine whether it does involves a scientific scrutiny of the context of the ideal. Its genuineness, motor-power, and effectiveness must be assessed. The degree of its strength of foundations in the person concerned is probably the key to its reference to the whole or dominant part of the subject. And possible alternatives to this ideal must be considered in estimating indispensability.

When, instead of an individual, we are concerned with a people or a country there will be implicit additional criteria for making simple assertions about the whole unit rather than relative assertions about groups within it. In the light of existing knowledge, assumptions are made about the existing pattern of major or common interests or needs of the country as a whole.

Thus in World War II, in some countries occupied by the Nazis, national liberation was an ethically necessary ideal, since without its achievement nothing but slavery and extermination faced the people, and the dominant interests of most people became incapable of fulfillment.

A judgment of what is ethically necessary for mankind is similar in type to that about a country, and is based on the needs and alternatives facing people in all or most lands.[34] Thus there might be wide agreement today on the assertion that, in the sense defined, peace is ethically necessary to mankind. Such judgments are to be distinguished from the claims of some idealist theories that there is a kind of inherent necessity in the ethical ideal in and by itself. The assertion we are considering is the outcome of, not prior to, the scientific mapping of existent needs and values and the reckoning of alternatives and instrumentalities.[35]

If an ideal has the property of ethical necessity, its worth is definitely increased to those for whom it is an ideal. For there is added to its value the fact that other values will be achieved by its own actualization. The fact that an ideal is ethically necessary does not as such, however, guarantee its achievement. Many a life has been profoundly disappointed and many a country has perished. And in the case of mankind, major ideals of the vast mass of the people have gone unfulfilled. But there have been times in which some ethically necessary ideals appeared to have irresistible driving forces enlisted on their side and so to be certain of

[34] Mankind is usually the subject of reference in an unqualified judgment of ethical necessity. Sometimes, however, an ideal may be considered ethically necessary without apparent reference to any subject. Probably a universal reference is intended, and the ideal is considered important to the achievement of all or most other values under any conditions. Such claims are sometimes made, in effect, for reason or loyalty or honesty. Thus Santayana, in his *Life of Reason*, treats reason as a principle of order for integrating and expressing impulse. Royce, in his *Philosophy of Loyalty*, makes loyalty the value of attachment to any value. Cabot, in his *Honesty*, regards honesty not merely as essential in every field and trait, but eventually as the mark of growth of the soul.

[35] I have developed this conception to a considerably greater extent, as the theory of the valuational base, in *Ethical Judgment: The Use of Science in Ethics*, Ch. IX.

fulfillment. When this happens, and the reference is to mankind, we may speak of *historical necessity* as a property of the ideal.

Such historical necessity first appears as a quality of the career of an ideal. Some ideals climb the ladder of success, as people often do, by a kind of attractiveness and a knack of fitting into every opportunity which comes their way. This adaptability involves an occasional skewing of the ideal here and there. Other ideals remain in abeyance until the world comes their way. They are prophetically announced centuries ahead of time, as visions rather than programs. As the world ripens for their coming, they assume more practical form. Their motor-power becomes greater and their effectiveness increases. Attempts are made in their name to alter the lives of men. Hosts assemble under their banner. They are elaborated into systems of life. When conditions finally are matured the ideal triumphs with overwhelming power. It does not so much conquer men as spring up within all phases of their thought and action as what they have been looking for. Philosophers and litterateurs then describe its advance in terms of their favorite metaphors—a river overflowing its banks, a "wave of the future," a universal growth from widely scattered seeds, or the systematic swelling of consciousness.

Such is the phenomenon of historical necessity seen as a property of an ideal's career. It appears also in the quality of consciousness of an individual holding to the ideal. Such quality is, however, markedly affected by the temperament and philosophic outlook of the individual. A whole phenomenology of the historically necessary ideal would be required to distinguish different components—the sense of destiny or of community with the forward surge of mankind, the feeling of floating with the stream or of fashioning the channels along which it will flow, the particular shade of the feeling of responsibility, and so forth.

From the point of view of scientific judgment, the historical necessity of an ideal is, as we suggested, a special case of ethical necessity in which the reference is to the whole or major part of mankind, and in which it is assumed that the probability of achievement is very high. This probability is estimated on the basis of the extent of the underlying needs and values, the nonexistence of feasible alternatives, and the extent to which the energies and interests of the vast majority of men become increasingly directed toward the ideal. It involves, in short, a summation of the trend of forces on a world-wide scale.

Three possible misunderstandings are to be avoided:

(1) It would be incorrect to see the historical necessity of an ideal as simply the possession of sufficient power by its propounders to put it over. This conception, congenial chiefly to the cynical view of ideals (which treats political ideals, for example, as propagandist slogans in the struggle for power), embraces every historical basis—even patterns of men's values and striving—indiscriminately within the notion of power. It thus misses all the distinguishing features of the process.

(2) It is a mistake, in the second place, to argue that on such a conception any ideal—even a spurious one—that for a time achieves a dominating place is therefore historically necessary. Certainly it may be felt in the consciousness of many individuals to have this quality, but this consciousness need not, as we saw in the case of ethical necessity, adequately represent the facts of existence. The ideals of fascism, for example, had already shown their spurious character to the people of Spain, Czechoslovakia, and even Italy, while Nazi power was spreading over Europe and reaction everywhere spoke of the wave of the future. Even world conquest would not have demonstrated historical necessity of these ideals since for the greater part of mankind then in servitude they would not then have possessed even the quality of being ideals.

(3) In the third place, this conception of some human ideals having historical necessity at certain periods must not be construed as an attempt to generate the normative out of the merely existential. For there is no attempt to derive values from bare facts. We are dealing with values throughout, starting with the needs and ideals of men and ascertaining which of them fall into the special patterns of ethical and historical relationships we have designated as historical necessity. Of course, a given individual may not share the ideal in question. He would rather regard this historically necessary ideal as a bandwagon on which others have jumped, and he may instead reject the tendencies of history and suffer the consequences. No individual can be forced to value

what he is confronted with, unless there are values or needs within him to provide a foothold. Judgments of historical necessity among ideals refer to the existent pattern of needs and values and the historical role that a given ideal comes to play among them, not to the coercion of a given individual. It is to the mass of men who will be better off by its achievement that the ideal is enhanced in worth by its historical necessity. For there are added the values of probable actualization, of wide scope and therefore fellowship, as well as the further values which, as was suggested above, a phenomenological analysis of the historically necessary ideal may reveal.

Historical necessity as a possible quality of ideals means, therefore, neither the idealization of all that prevails nor the claim that the ethical because it is ethical will therefore prevail. It does offer, however, an insight into the role that ideals may come to play under certain conditions.

On combining the criteria. Our examination of these seven points of reference constitutes only a first step in the logic of the evaluation of ideals. There remain two types of questions. One concerns the method of combining the criteria into a coherent pattern, if this is feasible, for application in human life. The second concerns the general justification for the selection of these as against other possible points of reference, hence other possible criteria.

The first problem in more complicated than it seems. We cannot simply say that an ideal is of greater worth according to the degree in which it satisfies more of our criteria, although in a rough sense this is undoubtedly true. Perhaps the usual formulation of the problem is at fault. There is no simple or abstract scale on which all ideals may be ranged irrespective of type of task or field of application. One type is that of the individual who seeks to bring his ideals into some hierarchy or at least systematic order as a guide to conduct. His individual ethos, his personality viewed in the light of his temperament and abilities would be crucial in providing additional considerations and even in weighting our criteria. Another type is that of the legislator who would be led by his work to emphasize strength of foundations and necessity. The educator seeking to mold a unity of character would probably assign a greater role to intensity and motor-power. Again, the stage of life is relevant to the weighting of criteria; if philosophers sometimes impatiently brand certain ideals as childish, they imply at least that one sort of ideals is appropriate to a child, another to an adult. And in addition to such types of problems, shifts in the process of evaluation may be required by sharp changes in social conditions.[36]

Why this set of criteria? The justification of our criteria against other possible sets is likewise a multiple problem. There are perhaps criteria, such as compatibility and inclusiveness, which might have been added. But in part these are wide criteria for all values, not specifically ideals, and in part they are contained indirectly under strength of foundations and ethical necessity. As against other complete alternative sets, the following issues would be involved in choice of criteria:

(a) There may be logical grounds for preferring one set, if it is more refined and includes as subelements many of the criteria of rival sets. In that case, it is more systematic in the logical sense of the term.

(b) A set of criteria usually rests also on some underlying conception of the job that ideals are to do in human life. This is based in turn on a psychological conception of man. Here the naturalistic theory of mind and human nature is our basis, and its truth is the justification ultimately sought for our analysis. To this extent justification has a factual or scientific component.

(c) Probably most important, however, is the valuational or ethical basis. We noted above that the seven points of reference became criteria of evaluation only on the assumption of certain values. Some of these were values of a higher order of generality, such as intensity of feeling, or achievement as against mere feeling or contemplation. Some were the values of logic and scientific method, such as consistency and truth of judgments involved in ideals. Some were broad instrumentalities, such as the "distance" of ideals in the problem of attainability and the kind of character it yielded. Some, again, as in strength of foundations and historical necessity, meant placing ourselves on the side of the needs of mankind as against the desires of an isolated individual or a narrow group. In any case, the use of the proposed points of

[36] Cf. my *Ethical Judgment*, pp. 318-30.

reference as criteria involves a valuational act. Hence, it follows that criteria for the estimation of ideals are themselves not purely measures of "more" in some neutral or generalized quantitative sense. Rather they involve the interplay of ideal with ideal or ideal with values. Criteria of ideals are thus values that in virtue of their generality, their pervasiveness, and their broad instrumentality, have become principles or standards or guides for more concrete, more specialized values. They issue from a fundamental value point of view, allegiance, or acceptance, which need not be historically or psychologically prior to the whole brood of values which men hold, but which emerges in their lives and conduct as a systematic basis and support. Thus if we look back on the values embodied in the seven criteria listed above, they seem to express in rough outline the ideal of a *maximum achievement, in rich experience, of the aims of the mass of the people of the globe.* As a commitment, this must be recognized as only one of a number which in the history of ethics have been urged as fundamental. The existence of historical alternatives does not, however, make this one ethically arbitrary. It might be less confusing if 'ethically arbitrary,' instead of being equated with 'ultimate' or 'contingent,' were defined within the ethical field in terms of a difference of degree so as to distinguish between mere difference of taste and issues as crucial as life versus death.

POSTSCRIPT

A few final comments may be offered on the general picture of an ethical-theory methodology with four operative standpoints—analytic, descriptive, causal-explanatory, and evaluative. One clear central lesson was that there is no need for hypostatization of entities to correspond to the methods. We do not need a separate material for each of them, as if we had to postulate four separate coordinate realms—for example, concepts or ideas for analysis, experience for description, nature for causation, value for evaluation. Nor was there any need to multiply faculties correlated with each of the domains, to account for their apprehension. The central matrix is the world, with its processes and qualities and human activities. Analyzing is part of thinking about them—a sharpening of the apparatus in reflecting about the phenomena. Describing is a controlled activity of symbolic representation. Causation refers to modes of relation, production, and alteration among phenomena. Evaluation is an activity of men in orienting themselves to their world and to one another. When we focus wholly on each as a method, its scope is unrestricted. And because each is an enterprise, not a territory, and because each functions in intimate relation to the others, they constitute as a whole a systematic conceptual apparatus for advancing ethical theory.

This conclusion involves a number of cautions. The first is that a different methodological systematization might be possible. There is a pie to be cut, but there is no injunction about the number and size of the slices. Only remember that if some are larger and the number is kept the same, others will be smaller. It is quite possible to limit description, for example, in such a way as to minimize interpretive elements, and at the same time, by limiting analysis strictly, to make a fresh method out of interpretation. Again, if analysis is regarded as solely retrospective ("How can you analyze what hasn't been said?") then speculative analysis becomes a separate method.[1] The way in which the pie is

1 See above, p. 103.

cut seems to me to reflect largely the lessons of the existent state of logic and the sciences that deal with the phenomena of man's thinking. Particular justification for the methods here presented lies retrospectively in the arguments in their exploration and prospectively in the role that we may find their schematic distinction to play in advancing ethical theory and solving its problems.

A second caution concerns the unity of the methods. There is no one way, as philosophers are well aware from the problems of monism and pluralism, in which the investigation of unity may be approached. Their unity may lie, as suggested above, in the field of their operation—human life and its activities and objects. Or it may lie in some specific structural properties of human life; it is tempting to say that human life always involves some reflection, some confrontation, some control, some reckoning. Or a developmental unity may be discoverable; there may be an early time in the growth of the individual when wanting, being aware of, and grasping are undifferentiated, and the differentiation may turn out to proceed in a lawlike manner. Or there may be an evolutionary unity in which the relevant differentiation takes place in the rising scale first of life, and then of society. In short, the unity of the methods is to be found in scientific scrutiny of origins and functioning.

A third caution is about metaphysics. Methodology has fundamental relations to basic philosophical outlooks. But of course, methodological decisions are also involved in how metaphysics is itself to be carried on. Let us not plunge here into these troubled waters or try to specify the nature of metaphysics in an afterthought. I would simply caution against setting up a one-to-one relation between the methodology here offered for ethical theory and any one basic philosophical outlook. Some of its features may prove more congenial to one rather than another metaphysics. For example, the broad resistance to a sharp separation of fields as distinct from enterprises is reminiscent of the older objective idealisms or the modern materialisms and naturalisms. In construction, indeed, I will work within a naturalist perspective. But the hypothesis guiding this methodological study has been a wider one. It is, rather, that what in the old-fashioned language was called the "real" forces itself through all our philosophical constructions when they are seen in their full context in human life. Some constructions may, however, be partial "symptoms," others clearer representations. This lesson can be stated in any philosophical language, if one cultivates the tolerant art of philosophical translation. Thus, if a given ethical theory uses narrow concepts, the concepts will be worked harder, perhaps become blurred in application, and they may not do the whole job. And inquiry into the way the theory works in the full context of human life will show what job is not being done, what is done obliquely, what is denied to be part of the job, and so forth. A comparative procedure thus stands the best chance of discerning the structure of the total field, and finding the common or basic elements (components, tasks, problems, categories), whether they lie in what a particular theory delimits as its field or not. But it is a difficult procedure, for it foregoes the privilege of laying down the law, or calling other views nonsense, or any of the other techniques by which a provincialism succeeds only in flaunting itself.

A fourth and final caution. I should like to repeat that I have not here—except by suggestion in some of the case studies—offered an ethical theory. Nor have I, except in a preliminary way in working out coordinates of criticism and in fashioning the third descriptive level, even mapped in detail the structure of an ethical theory. Accordingly, if any reader on finishing the book should have gained a false impression and wondered why he has not been given a theory of the good, or a solution to the problem of the meaning of obligation, or the like, I can only ask his patience and refer him to later work which I hope will be forthcoming.

INDEXES

NAME INDEX

SUBJECT INDEX

Abundance, relation to ethical theory, Ch. XII; specific effects, 289-93

Aesthetic judgments, 187

Agent ethics, 233ff. *See also* Onlooker, Spectator ethics

Aims, of analysis, 103ff.

Ambivalence, 39

Analysis, Ch. IV; context provoking analysis, 88f.; how initial questions formulated, 89ff.; how proposed answer dealt with, 91f.; data leading to turning-point, 93-99; decision-process, 100-3; aims, 103-6; underlying theory, 106-9; criteria of correctness, 109f.

Appraisal, 59, 190

Ascription, 149f.

Aspiration, 177. *See also* Ideals, Moral phenomena

Attainability, 309, 342ff.

Attractiveness, 309, 314

Autonomy effect, 120, 176

Base, of an ideal, 331f.

Bad, 15, 128

Behavioral description, 167ff.

Behaviorism, 167f.

Better, 41, 225; as basic ethical concept, 262-67

Biological interpretations of value. *See* Value

British analytical school, 225, 252

Care, as virtue, 291

Category-mistake, 245

Causality concept, 242; causal standpoint, Ch. X

Christianity, 34

Cognitivism, *vs.* practicalism, 77-81

Common law, 108

Comparative value. *See* Value

Compromise, 203f.

Conduct, description of, 201ff.

Conflict-potential, of ends, 309

Consequences, in relation to ends, 306

Consequential *vs.* essential, 90

Constructiveness, of ends, 309

Content of an idea: distinguished from context, 243f.; content extension, 258-67

Context of an idea, distinguished from content, 27f., 243f.

Context relations to content, 244-59; causal origins of ideas, 244; control possibilities, 244f.; functions of ideas, 245; in phenomenological approach, 246ff.; in materialist approach, 248ff.; in pragmatic approach, 250; in logical-linguistic approaches, 251-57; conclusions from comparison of approaches, 257-59

Contextual implication, 95

Contextual meaning, 256

Controllability, of an ideal, 333f.

Coordinates of criticism in ethical theory, Ch. II; logical, 15-21; scientific, 21-27; historical, 27-32; valuational, 32-48

Coordinating definitions, 18

Correctness: among conflicting theories, 63; in analysis, 109

Consistency, 39f.

Data of ethics, 176-84

Decalogue, 204f., 212f.

Decision-base, of the philosopher, 277f.

Decision-methods, 214

Decision-processes, 100ff.

Defeasible concepts, 149

Definition, 125-28; in ethics, Ch. V; analytical, 112; contextual, 130; genetic, 133; implicit, 130; operational, 128; synonymous, 128; theoretical, 129, 136f.; unscheduled modes, 126, 131-37